WHAT CAN THIS BOOK DO FOR YOU?

Within a few years, your high school experience will lead you into the work world of adults. This book is designed to give you guidance, ideas, and answers about the many options life offers and the steps you will need to take for each.

WHAT FIRST?

Take a few minutes to claim ownership of this book. Write your name in it. In pencil, lay out your career and life goals as you see them today. Consider the obstacles you may have to overcome in order to achieve your goals. If you don't have a formal plan, that's ok. Answering these questions will spark your imagination and help you make one. The first steps might not be easy, but there are no right or wrong answers. As you continue working through this book, refer to these goals and feel free to fill in any blanks you left or to change your ideas.

WHAT NEXT?

Your needs, goals, ideas, and talents are unique to you. What is right for you may not be right for others. But the steps in the process of choosing a career direction (and understanding what education you might need to get there) are the same whether you aspire to repair car engines or design the next generation of space shuttles.

THINK OF THIS BOOK AS A ROAD MAP

Knowing where you want to go and what roads will lead you there is the first step in the process. You can always change your destination and chart a new course. We're providing the map. The rest is up to you.

GETTING A JUMP ON THE ROAD TO SUCCESS

S0-AZO-652

Name_____

Age_____

Grade_____

Date Started_____

My current goal after I graduate from high school is to:

_____

_____

At school, to reach my goal I'll need:

Curriculum planning:

_____

_____

Clubs, teams, associations:

_____

_____

Career research:

_____

_____

Outside of school, to reach my goal I'll need:

Volunteer work:

_____

Shadowing/mentor program:

_____

_____

Job experience:

_____

_____

Extracurricular activities:

_____

Challenges my goal presents:

_____

_____

Ideas to overcome these challenges:

About The Thomson Corporation and Peterson's

The Thomson Corporation, with 2002 revenues of US$7.8 billion, is a global leader in providing integrated information solutions to business and professional customers. The Corporation's common shares are listed on the Toronto and New York stock exchanges (TSX: TOC; NYSE: TOC). Its learning businesses and brands serve the needs of individuals, learning institutions, corporations, and government agencies with products and services for both traditional and distributed learning. Peterson's (www.petersons.com) is a leading provider of education information and advice, with books and online resources focusing on education search, test preparation, and financial aid. Its Web site offers searchable databases and interactive tools for contacting educational institutions, online practice tests and instruction, and planning tools for securing financial aid. Peterson's serves 110 million education consumers annually.

For more information, contact Peterson's, 2000 Lenox Drive, Lawrenceville, NJ 08648;

800-338-3282; or find us on the World Wide Web at www.petersons.com/about.

ACKNOWLEDGEMENTS: Peterson's would like to acknowledge the following authors for their contribution to this publication: Kenneth Edwards, Michele Kornegay, Emily Law, Brenna McBride, Charlotte Thomas, Nathaniel Thomas, and Amy Tomcavage.

For permission to use material from this text or product, contact us by

Phone: 800-730-2214

Fax: 800-730-2215

Web: www.thomsonrights.com

ISBN: 0-7689-1425-6 (Middle Atlantic)   0-7689-1426-4 (Midwest)

0-7689-1430-2 (New England)   0-7689-1429-9 (South)

0-7689-1428-0 (Texas)   0-7689-1427-2 (West)

Printed in the United States of America

10 9 8 7 6 5 4 3 2 1   06 05 04

6th Edition

Dear Student:

Whether graduation seems light-years away or alarmingly close, it's never too early—or too late—to think about what comes after high school. Do you know what your next step will be?

Get a Jump! can help you figure that out. This book is designed to help you launch your career, whether this means going on for more education or directly entering the workforce. You have a multitude of options and some crucial choices to make. In the pages that follow, we have tried to give you a jumpstart on planning the future that's right for you.

The book is arranged in five parts. Part 1 has all the guidance you'll need to make the transition to high school. Part 2 provides general introductory information about your options after high school and how to use your high school education to plan for the next phase of your life. Part 3 offers more detailed information about postsecondary education, whether you choose a two-year, four-year, vocational/career college, or the military. Part 4 provides useful information about the workplace and how to handle stress, peer pressure, conflict, and other obstacles you may encounter. Finally, Part 5 contains appendices for each state in your geographic region of the United States, including valuable information on two- and four-year colleges and universities in your area and your state's high school graduation requirements, internships, scholarship and financial aid programs, summer opportunities, and vocational /career colleges.

We hope you find this publication helpful as you begin thinking about the rest of your life. If you have questions or feedback on *Get a Jump!*, please contact us at:
Editor-Get A Jump!
Peterson's, part of The Thomson Corporation
2000 Lenox Drive
Lawrenceville, NJ 08648

Sincerely,

Peterson's Editorial Staff

Contents

Contents

YOU'RE GOING TO BE A FRESHMAN...

YOU KNOW WHAT IT'S SUPPOSED TO BE LIKE—being a freshman in high school should be COOL. But what will it REALLY be like? Will you be able to figure it all out? Of course you will . . . especially since you are reading this! Your high school years will be like nothing else you have experienced and you are going to have questions about everything. Luckily, it's right here that you will be able to get answers. Whether you are wondering about how to keep your "stuff" organized, choosing your classes, or how important is a GPA, we are here to help! So, come on, jump in-you're going to be a FRESHMAN!

To Students, Parents, and Counselors:

It was my pleasure to experiment with using **Get a Jump!** in selected high schools and elementary schools in Chicago. While the logistics of how high school students are scheduled and how they move from class to class made the job of getting the material to them and guiding them through it very challenging, the material was well received by the high schools, and those students who were exposed to the book were excited by all of the information provided in this publication.

Conversely, the elementary school students, which in Chicago means K-8, especially sixth-eighth graders, are a captive audience and, with assistance from a teacher, were much easier to get together in a group for presentation on a grade by grade and class by class basis. These students were so attentive and curious about high school and what happens there, and I was more than surprised that the students at both the high schools and elementary schools lacked knowledge about such things as: What is a transcript? What is a GPA? What are class ranks? What are honors classes and AP classes?

When I relayed these "discoveries" back to Peterson's, the idea of adding a special chapter on just these types of questions and issues facing the middle school student getting ready to make the transition to high school was a natural evolution. "The Big Step Up from Middle School to High School" gives parents, guidance counselors, and, most importantly, students the information they need to successfully make that transition—answering not only the questions about transcripts, GPAs, class ranks, and honors and AP classes but also giving advice on participation in extracurricular activities, how to deal with the differences between middle school and high school, setting goals, staying organized, and how to study. And this advice comes not just from Peterson's, but also from guidance counselors, parents, and students all over the country!

Finally, as a college administrator who has worked with high schools, elementary schools, and junior high schools for more than thirty years, I find **Get a Jump!** to be a book that has been long overdue. It is an excellent vehicle for young people who seek guidance in planning their educational futures! Best of luck to all of you!

Nathaniel Thomas, Ph.D.

THE BIG JUMP FROM MIDDLE SCHOOL TO HIGH SCHOOL

Even if you've never said anything to anyone else, chances are the thought of your first year of high school is totally scary, especially with all these questions whirling around in your head:

Who will I sit with at lunch **What if my best friends don't have lunch when I do** WHERE IS THE VENDING MACHINE How will I find my way around the halls What will I do when I have only four minutes to get to my next class What happens if I get lost *Will I remember my locker combination* WHAT HAPPENS IF I CAN'T OPEN MY LOCKER **What happens if there aren't any lockers** How will I carry all those books around in my backpack What if my best friend isn't in the same classes as me What if I don't know anyone in my classes *What if I don't know where the bathroom is* WHAT HAPPENS IF I FORGET WHERE TO GO FOR MY CLASS WHAT IF, WHAT IF, WHAT IF THE SENIORS ARE MEAN TO ME AND TREAT ME LIKE DIRT??????????

IN MIDDLE SCHOOL, you knew where everything was. You knew exactly who would be sitting next to you at lunch. You knew all the teachers. All the teachers knew you. You were at the top of the heap.

Now you're starting all over again

First of all, take a deep breath, sit back, and realize that it's okay to have the ups and downs, the doubts, and the feelings that zip back and forth between "I can't wait to get into high school" to "I'm hiding under my bed and never coming out." The first few weeks of high school, you're surrounded by a lot of kids who are bigger, who seem to know an awful lot more than you do, and who know exactly where to go. You'll wonder what it will be like, trying out for sports teams or shows and activities with the tenth, eleventh, and twelfth graders.

ADVICE FROM A COUNSELOR

"Freshmen are afraid the upper class students will pick on them, but honestly, that's not true. Upper class students are not the least bit interested in freshmen."

Helen Erbe
Guidance Counselor
Jackson Memorial High School
Jackson, New Jersey

Second, the friend of a friend's brother who told you he hated ninth grade isn't you. Everyone adjusts to high school in different ways and at different speeds. For some kids, the transition from middle school to high school takes a short time, like days or weeks. For others, the adjustment takes longer, especially if they're not admitting to themselves and others what their feelings are and letting others help them get over their insecurities.

ADVICE FROM A SENIOR

Sometimes freshmen give older students too much power. My advice is don't be afraid to be yourself.

Kristen Seghers, Senior,
West Windsor-Plainsboro High School South,
Princeton Junction, New Jersey

Third, you are not alone. All those big kids ahead of you have gone through the same fears and have had the same feelings, too. They made it through, and you will too. It's most likely that the sophomores, juniors, and seniors are too busy dealing with the problems of being sophomores, juniors, and seniors to be concerned if you forgot your locker combination and have to go slinking off to the school office to find out what it is.

ADVICE FROM A PARENT

"Stephen was nervous about starting ninth grade. It took him only about two to three days to catch on."

Sharon Blumenthal
Parent to Stephen, who is going into the tenth grade.

THE DIFFERENCES: MIDDLE SCHOOL VS. HIGH SCHOOL

There's no getting around it. High school is a different ball game. It's like you're used to playing soccer and all of a sudden in order to score, you're expected to throw the ball, not kick it. Some of the major differences between middle school and high school are:

YOU ARE MORE INDEPENDENT. In middle school, you were part of a group. You did the same things together—ate lunch, took the same classes, goofed off. Same teachers, same schedule. It's a big adjustment to realize that you will have your own schedule of classes that could be very different from your best friend's. You will be in classes with people you don't know because there are different levels of classes. You could be in the middle level of a math class and your friend in the upper level class.

ADVICE FROM A JUNIOR

When I was a freshman, I got into band camp and got to know kids in the band. Then when I was walking through the halls I knew more people other than just the freshmen. If you know people around you then you'll feel comfortable. If you feel comfortable then you'll be more willing to do new things. My high school is a huge high school. The idea is to make as many friends as you can. So talk to everybody.

*Matt Wolf, Junior,
Doherty High School,
Colorado Springs, Colorado*

YOU HAVE TO TAKE MORE RESPONSIBILITY. In middle school you probably had fewer choices about which classes you could take. In high school, there are many more choices about your education, especially as you go into your sophomore year. You'll get to choose some classes, or electives as they're called. As a freshman, the choices you have of electives are limited. Most freshmen can choose only one elective. Sophomores only two. At the junior and senior levels, you'll have more and more choices to make, depending on your goals and interests.

THE WAY YOU ARE GRADED IS DIFFERENT IN HIGH SCHOOL. Your teachers in middle school were probably a lot more lenient when it came to late homework. They were more likely to look at your past record and give you a little leeway. Teachers in high school aren't as likely to accept excuses. "I forgot" won't work. In high school your grades are based on numbers. Two points off if you didn't get your homework done and turned in on time.

YOU HAVE TO SPEAK UP FOR YOURSELF. In middle school, your parents probably helped you if you got into a tough situation, say with a teacher. They were the ones making the phone call or visiting the teacher. In high school, there will be times when you will have to deal with situations on your own, such as speaking with a teacher about homework, or getting your voice heard in clubs and activities even though you're the youngest one there. In high school, you have to develop the ability to get advice from your parents and counselors, figure out how to solve the problem, and then take action.

ADVICE FROM A SENIOR

"Speak up if you have a good idea. In sports or clubs, sometimes younger people have good ideas or strategies and ways to help out, but they don't want to say anything."

Kristen Seghers, Senior, West Windsor-Plainsboro High School South, Princeton Junction, New Jersey

THERE'S SO MUCH TO DO!

Your freshman year is a time for you to explore your interests—what's it like being a crime scene investigator, a computer graphics designer, a veterinarian, etc.

Explore your interests via elective classes. One of the main purposes of high school electives is to allow you to investigate career interests. Though you will be required to take a variety of basic classes like math, English, history, and science, your choice of electives can point you in the direction of a future college major. It could very well be that something you enjoy doing as a freshman could end up being the start of a career.

You can take electives in areas like computers, art, accounting, or music. Say you think you'd like to be in business some day, sitting in an office overlooking the city. You can begin to realize that dream by taking accounting as an elective. You may find out you really like working with numbers. Or, you may find out you'd rather be building high rises instead of sitting in them.

Explore your interests via clubs and activities. In addition to sports, high school offers many clubs and activities outside of what you'll learn in the classroom.

You may think these activities are there just so you can have some fun. While that's true, they also give you the opportunity to find out what your interests are. Extracurricular activities can help you find what goals you want to set and then how to reach them.

ADVICE FROM A JUNIOR

I would have definitely joined more clubs and done more activities in my freshman year. Say if you join a drama club as a freshman, you can be at the top when you get to be a junior or senior. If you wait to join when you're a junior, you'll be at the bottom end. Colleges want you to be a leader so you have to start going for the top of activities when you're a freshman.

Matt Wolf, Junior,
Doherty High School,
Colorado Springs, Colorado

Here's a sample list of clubs and activities in which you can participate. Every school is different, so you'll have to find out what your high school offers, but this list will give you an idea of what you can expect.

- ☑ Auto club
- ☑ Band
- ☑ Bowling club
- ☑ Cheerleading
- ☑ Choir
- ☑ Forensic club
- ☑ Math club
- ☑ Mock Trial
- ☑ Newspaper
- ☑ Science club

Explore your interests via volunteer work. High schools often offer opportunities for you to do volunteer work. Are you interested in working with younger kids? In being a lawyer? In helping those who are sick? You can volunteer to help out in a hospital or law office, for instance. By volunteering and working alongside people who are doing the things you may like to do, you can quickly judge if you really do like hospitals or law offices.

TO HONOR OR NOT TO HONOR: CHOOSING CLASSES

One of the most critical decisions you're going to have to make in your first year of high school is whether to take classes on a regular level or on an honors level. You may have heard about AP classes, or Advanced Placement classes. You can't take those until your junior or senior year, but the time to start planning for this high academic level is actually in your freshman year. If your goal is to take college courses in high school (that's what AP classes are), you should start demonstrating a high level of performance in the ninth grade by taking honors classes. AP classes are very competitive with little wiggle room for poor grades or performance as you move from freshman, to sophomore, to junior.

But first you need to know the difference between "regular," honors, and AP classes.

Classes at the "regular" level

Different high schools may have different labels for this level, but basically, if you're in a "regular" level class, you're getting what you need in that subject area to meet the requirements to graduate from high school in four years and go on to college. Do the work expected of you, turn in all your homework, do well on the tests, and you'll get that piece of paper in four years that says you've completed the necessary subjects to become a high school graduate.

Classes at the honors level

Honors level classes require more from you. You'll do more reading and writing that demands more in-depth understanding of the subject matter. Classes at this level develop critical thinking skills by asking you to interpret situations and events. Honors classes are designed to provide you with an in-depth investigation into a subject.

Teachers will expect you to participate in class discussions. You will learn to feel comfortable with a subject so you'll be able to talk about it. For instance, when studying the civil war in an honors class, you'll delve deeper into the conditions that brought the war about, in addition to dates, geographic locations, and famous names. Then you'll look at how the war affected history and learn something about the social and political issues that followed.

Classes at the AP (Advanced Placement) level

In AP classes, you're actually learning at the college level. You are expected to do the assignments and perform on the tests as you would if you were in college. No wonder you can't take AP classes until your junior and senior year. In order to even get into an AP class, you must be a high achiever.

While the hurdles to getting into an AP class are high, the advantages for those who do well in AP classes are huge. The AP exams are given to students across the whole U.S.A. in May and are scored on a level from 1–5, with 5 being tops. If you get a 3, 4, or 5 in the exam of a particular class, you may be able to waive the introductory level of that class in college. Some colleges may even award you college credit!

Not only will this save you time and money, but you'll also impress college admissions offices with the fact that you're taking AP classes. Colleges look favorably on students who worked hard in high school

and did well in difficult subjects. During the college admission process, some colleges "weight" the different levels of classes you take. For instance, they'll give you more points for an A in an honors class than they would for an A in a "regular class." An A in a class at a regular level may count as a 4, while an A in an honors level class would count as a 5 and a B in an honors level would count as a 4.

Some things to consider before taking the honors plunge

Many students do well in honors classes. Others struggle, whereas they may have done very well starting off in a "regular" level class. Once they've become familiar with the different way classes are taught and what's expected academically of high school students, they will be able to handle an honors class with ease.

You must be honest with yourself and with your parents. Sometimes parents see their kids through rosy glasses and think their sons and daughters are geniuses. Meanwhile, the son or daughter is struggling to cope with the whole change from middle school to high school, and falls behind. Your mindset has a lot to do with how well you'll do in high school, so it's much better to begin high school at a level that fits you.

If you are terrible at writing, but love science, that's your clue about which honors classes to take and in which sequence. You may take a science honors class your first semester. See how you do. Then you can add an English honors course the second semester.

If you're not confident about you study habits or organizational skills, the first semester of high school is a time to slowly dip your tootsies in the honors pool. Feel the temperature of the water by doing well in a "regular "class, flex your mind muscles, and then dive into honors. The goal is to excel in what you do well and then take the classes that challenge you.

The WORST mistake you can make is to select an honors class because your best friend decided to take it. How well you do in high school determines if many of the doors to your future plans will be open. If you do poorly, you begin to close doors even in your freshman year.

What if you want to be a chef and your parents are determined for you to go to Harvard?

That's a tough situation and the above example is a little on the exaggerated side, but as a freshman, now is the time to address a difference of opinion about your future plans with your parents. So, say you do want to be a chef. You know that honors classes demand a lot more studying and time and that to get into culinary schools or other vocational tracks, you don't need to get A's in honors classes. However, your parents know you could get A's without too much effort. High school counselors will probably encourage you to take the honors classes. Why not leave your options open? As a freshman, your plans can change a lot before you graduate. If you start out with the plan to be a chef set in concrete and leave no room for change, you could get to your junior year and decide that you hate the smell of burning food. You would rather get a degree in business from a top college. If you'd taken honors classes, you'd be in a good position to go to the university of your choice.

ADVICE FROM A SENIOR

"When you're a freshman, it's hard to see the big picture of your future. I couldn't see it and probably could have done better than I did if I'd talked to some older people or taken a peek at college stuff and seen how important things are."

Kristen Seghers, Senior,
West Windsor-Plainsboro High School South,
Princeton Junction, New Jersey

Advice for your parents

Make sure your child can do well in the honors or AP classes before you start pushing for all A's at that level. Each child has different skills. Let's imagine your child takes honors classes in everything that's offered that first year. The child works extremely hard and comes home with a C in science. You're devastated. Your child is devastated. You've never seen a C on a report card. To help your child make the right decisions about honors and AP classes, talk with your child and your child's guidance counselor.

WHAT IN THE WORLD IS A GPA AND WHAT THE HECK IS A TRANSCRIPT?

Your GPA (Grade Point Average). If you haven't already heard about the GPA, those three letters—G, P, and A—are going to mean a lot as you move from freshman to senior. There's no getting around that the GPA is important to your future: what college you can attend, what kind of upper level high school classes you can take (such as those AP classes), what academic and athletic scholarships you may get, or for what special programs you may qualify.

In short, the GPA is the average of all your grades starting from your freshman year. A little planning in your freshman year can go a long way toward a high GPA when you graduate. If you know the impact a GPA can have, you may do things a little differently in your freshman year.

It's good to know how your GPA is computed. Different schools have their own ways to total up a GPA, but this will give you the basic idea.

In general, schools score letter grades as follows:

A = 4 points

B = 3 points

C = 2 points

D = 1 point

F = 0 points

Some schools give higher points for grades earned in honors courses. That's something you would need to check out in the school office. So, let's take a hypothetical student's grades for one semester:

English	A	4 points
History	B	3 points
Music	A	4 points
Math	C	2 points
Spanish	B	3 points
Physical Education	A	4 points

The points total 20 points. Divide that by the number of classes, which is 6, and you get a GPA of 3.33 for one semester.

Let's take the next semester and see how our student did.

English	A	4 points
History	A	4 points
Music	A	4 points
Math	B	3 points
Spanish	C	2 points
Physical Education	A	4 points

That totals 21 points divided by 6, which equals 3.5 GPA. Now, add the total number of points over these last two semesters, which is 41 and divide by the number of classes and you get 3.42 GPA.

This is a simplified version of how schools score GPAs because some high schools give different points to each class level. For instance, an A in English is worth more points than an A in physical education.

Your transcript. A transcript goes with you through high school and shows the final grade you received on each of your courses. Your transcript is a history of the classes you took and what grade you achieved in that class. It's what colleges ask for to assess what kind of a student you are.

As a freshman, you need to lay a good foundation academically. Competitive colleges that attract thousands of applications look carefully at your transcript. They're not only looking at your final GPA.

They're also looking at how you challenged yourself during your high school years. Did you take courses that stretched you academically, like honors and AP classes, or did you take only those classes you were required to take?

Some important things to know about transcripts

Transcripts differ from school to school. You need to find out what your school records on your transcript. For example, say you got good grades but missed a lot of classes because you just didn't feel like showing up. If your transcript shows the number of times you were not in class, and you're going for a top college or university, your good grades (and high GPA) won't look so good.

- Some schools show how many absences you had for each class.
- Some schools are on the trimester system, which means you'll have three sets of grades for each year.
- Some schools show plus and minus grades, such as a B+ or an A−, and some don't.
- Some schools don't count the freshman year when adding up your GPA.
- Some schools don't show your rank in your class, such as 168 out of 388, but instead use a quartile system, such as ranking you in the top 25% of your class.
- Some schools show your GPA as "weighted," which means that you get an extra credit point for an honors or AP class.
- Some schools show your "citizenship" record in classes. Did you contribute to the class or were you disruptive?
- Some schools will send a profile of your school with your transcript to colleges showing the community in which the school is located, the student population, how many honors and AP classes are offered, the number of periods in a day that classes are offered, etc.

KEY TO TRANSCRIPT EXPLANATION

What's What on Your Transcript

A. Your personal information:

Name

Address

Social Security Number or Student ID number (if you don't have a social security number)

Date of Birth

Ethnic Code

NOTE: Parents can request that your social security number, date of birth, and ethnic code be deleted from the transcript when it is sent to various colleges.

B. Abbreviations of the classes you've taken.

C. **Term GPA** is the number of grade points you earn each semester. In the transcript example on the following page, each letter grade is given a number of points, with honors classes getting an extra point:

English 1 Honors (with an extra point for honors)	B	= 4 points
Freehand Drawing 1	A	= 4 points
Spanish 1	B	= 3 points
Algebra 1	B	= 3 points
PE 9	B	= 3 points
Intro to Science 1	C	= 2 points
Government/Law 1	B	= 3 points

Add the points up and you get 22 points. Then divide that total (22) by the number of classes this student took, which is 7. Carry that out to 4 decimal points and you get 3.1429 grade points.

Cumulative GPA is taking the number of grade points from all your previous semesters and adding them up and then dividing them by the number of semesters. Let's look again at this student's transcript for the second semester:

Computer Apps	B	= 3 points
English 2 Honors (with an extra point for honors)	C	= 3 points
Freehand Drawing 1	A	= 4 points
Spanish 1	B	= 3 points
Algebra 1	B	= 3 points
Intro to Science 1	A	= 4 points
Government/Law 1	B	= 3 points

Add the points up and you get 23 points. Then divide that total (23) by 7 (the number of classes) and carry that figure out 4 decimals to get 3.2857 points. Add the two semesters' points (3.1429 and 3.2857) together and divide by the number of semesters, which is 2, and you get the cumulative GPA of 3.2143.

D. Letter grade you earned in each class.

E. Number of absences in each class.

F. Number of credits you earned in each class—you get one credit per class and you need 44 to graduate at this high school. Every school district has a different number of classes you need to graduate or, in some states, every district might be the same.

G. In this transcript, the letter G instead of an A, B, C, D, or F indicates that this course is not taken into account when figuring out your GPA. An "H" would indicate that you dropped the class without a penalty, like an "F". This student didn't drop any classes.

H. **Unofficial Transcript** means that it hasn't been signed or stamped with an official stamp. Transcripts are mailed directly to the school or colleges of your choice. Sometimes they can be transported by the student in a sealed envelope.

I. The date you entered the high school.

J. The date you left the high school.

K. Overall weighted—if your school gives extra points for honors or AP classes when figuring out your GPA, it will be noted here.

L. Your final cumulative GPA.

M. The total amount of credits you attempted.

N. Your class standing and the number of students who were in your senior class when you graduated. This student was 168 out of 388 students in the senior class.

O. Total Credits Earned in High School.

P. Notes about the clubs, sports, and committees in which you participated can be added here with verification from the person responsible for that extracurricular activity.

Q. Signature—the transcript must be signed and have an official seal in order to be accepted as an official transcript.

Colorado Springs Dist 11 (H)
Unofficial Transcript

Doherty High School   719-328-6400
4515 Barnes Rd
Colorado Springs, CO 80917

Entry Date	Counselor	Graduation Date
07/01/1999 (I)		05/20/2003
Exit Date	Exit Reason	Diploma Type
06/06/2003 (J)	W19-Graduated	High School Diploma

GPA Type	GPA	Crdt Atmpt	Class Rank
Overall Weighted	3.0476	42.0000	168 of 388
(K)	(L)	(M)	(N)

Total Credits Earned   44.0000 (O)

Issued To (A)	Print Date
	09/08/2003
	1 of 1

Subject Cd Course	Mrk1	Abs	Credits
Doherty High School Grd 09 Semester 1 02/00			
EN English 1, Honors	B	3	1.0000
HU Frhand Drwng1	A	5	1.0000
HU Spanish 1	B	4	1.0000
MA Algebra 1	B	5	1.0000
PE PE 9	B	7	1.0000
SC Intro to Science 1	C	6	1.0000
SS Gov/Law 1	B	5	1.0000
TERM: GPA 3.1429 CREDITS 7.0000			
CUMULATIVE: GPA 3.1429 CREDITS 7.0000			
Doherty High School Grd 09 Semester 2 06/00			
CM Computer Apps	B	1	1.0000
EN English 2, Honors	C	1	1.0000
HU Frhand Drwng2	A	2	1.0000
HU Spanish 2	B	4	1.0000
MA Algebra 2	B	1	1.0000
SC Intro to Science 2	A	1	1.0000
SS Gov/Law 2	B	3	1.0000
TERM: GPA 3.2857 CREDITS 7.0000			
CUMULATIVE: GPA 3.2143 CREDITS 14.0000			
Doherty High School Grd 10 Semester 1 01/01			
E3 English 3	B	3	1.0000
HL Health	C	1	1.0000
HU Spanish 3	B	1	1.0000
MA Geometry 1	B	2	1.0000
PA Todays Foods	B		1.0000
SC Biology 1	B	3	1.0000
SS World & US History 3	C	2	1.0000
TERM: GPA 2.7143 CREDITS 7.0000			
CUMULATIVE: GPA 3.0476 CREDITS 21.0000			
Doherty High School Grd 10 Semester 2 06/01			
E4 English 4	B	11	1.0000
HU Frhand Drwng3	A	6	1.0000
HU Spanish 4	B	6	1.0000
MA Geometry 2	C	3	1.0000
PE PE 10	B	7	1.0000
SC Biology 2	B	7	1.0000
SS World & US History 4	C	6	1.0000
TERM: GPA 2.8571 CREDITS 7.0000			
CUMULATIVE: GPA 3.0000 CREDITS 28.0000			

Subject Cd Course	Mrk1	Abs	Credits
Doherty High School Grd 11 Semester 1 01/02			
A1 Hist: US & World 5	C	9	1.0000
E5 English 5	B	9	1.0000
HU Psychology	B	13	1.0000
MA Algebra 3	B	10	1.0000
PA Automotive Tech 1	A	5	1.0000
TERM: GPA 3.0000 CREDITS 5.0000			
CUMULATIVE: GPA 3.0000 CREDITS 33.0000			
Doherty High School Grd 11 Semester 2 05/02			
A2 Hist: US & World 6	B	17	1.0000
E6 English 6	B	21	1.0000
EL Student Tutor	G	14	1.0000
HU Psychology, Advanced	A	19	1.0000
MA Algebra 4	B	14	1.0000
TERM: GPA 3.2500 CREDITS 5.0000			
CUMULATIVE: GPA 3.0270 CREDITS 38.0000			
Doherty High School Grd 12 Semester 1 12/02			
CE Cons Econ	B	13	1.0000
EN Creative Writing	A	15	1.0000
EN Senior Speed Reading 1	B	17	1.0000
PE PE A		9	1.0000
PE Physical Ed	G		1.0000
SC College Prep Chem 1	C	19	1.0000
TERM: GPA 3.2000 CREDITS 6.0000			
CUMULATIVE: GPA 3.0476 CREDITS 44.0000			

Mrk 1: Course Grade

Student Notes (P)	

(Q) _____
School Official's Signature

TIPS FOR A SMOOTH START

Write down a list of things you want to accomplish. If you have a rough idea of where you're headed, you'll have an easier time getting there. You've already set goals for yourself. Maybe it was to score more points on a video game than the kid down the street. Maybe it was to ride a bike faster or do more maneuvers on a skateboard. When you get into high school, it's important to set goals for yourself from the start. Obviously, the goals will change over time, but having a list of goals—like I want to make the football team; I want to take some honors classes; I want to run for class president; I want to be the editor of the school year book—will help you stay motivated and give you something to work toward.

Make your goals specific. For example:

A vague goal is:

I want to be a better student than I was in middle school.

A specific goal is:

The reason I wasn't a good student in middle school is because I didn't turn in my homework. Starting off in high school, I'm going to turn in all my homework on time.

ADVICE FROM A SENIOR

"When I was a freshman, I was intimidated by the older kids' appearance of greatness and their accomplishments. I thought, 'Wow, I can't get to their level.' But don't give up because you think there's too much competition, especially if it's something you really want to do."

Kristen Seghers, Senior,
West Windsor-Plainsboro High School South,
Princeton Junction, New Jersey

Get involved in clubs and activities immediately. We've already talked about how clubs and activities help narrow your interests and focus you on what you want to do in the future. But extracurricular activities serve another very important purpose for high school freshmen. You'll find friends who like the same things you do. You'll be with older kids so you'll get to know some juniors and seniors. You'll gain confidence in yourself as you work together with other kids. You'll become comfortable with being in high school a lot quicker than if you hang around on the fringes looking in instead of being in the middle of the action, whether it's on a soccer team, chess club, or—whatever!

ADVICE FROM A PARENT

"Every Friday afternoon before leaving school, Jessica gets her locker organized. It's easy for it to get out of control because kids are stuffing things in there all week. Then they can't find something when they need it and the time between classes is so short."

Jodi Domsky
Parent of Jessica, who just started ninth grade and was very organized in middle school.

Get organized. In high school, being organized does not mean showing up in class on time with your teeth brushed. Being organized is brought to a whole different level in high school. Some kids are naturally this way. In middle school, they knew what homework had to be done, when it was due, and what was required.

In high school, the list of things to organize gets longer. You still have to show up on time and whether your teeth are brushed is up to you, but you do have to have all the supplies you need with you.

That sparkly pink pen in your hand won't do to take the test the teacher just handed you. Your teacher specifically told you to bring a blue or black ballpoint. Now where is it? I thought I put it in my backpack. Oh no, here's the sandwich I forgot to eat yesterday on top of my history homework. Your room may be a disaster, but your notebooks, binders, and calendar need to be in tiptop shape.

You're organizing for more classes and carrying around a lot more books and papers than you ever did in middle school. You're going to be involved in sports and clubs. Unless you're organized, you're going to spend more time dealing with chaos and confusion

ADVICE FROM A TEACHER

Typically, middle school students get one big binder with four to five dividers. All their classes' materials are in one binder. It doesn't work that way for high school. They have too much. They can't put homework, notes, handouts and other pieces of paper in one section of the binder. When the binder system fails by mid-October, then they take everything that was in the binder and stuff it in a backpack. Now it's a 15-minute ordeal to find something in the backpack.

Heidi Pimentel

Spanish teacher

Pioneer High School

San Jose, California

and moldy sandwiches than getting your homework done and having all the fun there is to have in high school. Each week in high school goes by at blazing speed and things can get out of control very quickly.

This is what organized students know:

- What was assigned in each class
- When the homework is due
- When the next test is scheduled
- What I need to bring to each class
- Where the supplies I need are located

Organization skills will stay with you the rest of your life. Now's a great time to learn how easy your life will be when you're organized.

ADVICE FROM A JUNIOR

I wasn't very organized and should have been. In middle school, you don't have as many classes as in high school. It's harder to plan for seven classes instead of three or four a day.

Matt Wolf, Junior, Doherty High School, Colorado Springs, Colorado

The way to get organized is to set up a system. It can be someone else's system or your own. The important thing is to have some way to keep track of when assignments are due, when tests are coming, and what nights are taken up with practices or meetings. Each week, go through and set up a new schedule for the coming week. It sounds like a lot of work, but when Thursday hits and your head is spinning, you'll be glad you have a schedule to hang on to. You could have three tests on the same day. Wouldn't it be helpful to know that way ahead of time instead of remembering the day of the tests?

Manage your time. Time management is a term that you've probably heard and put into the "I'll deal with that when I get older" category. Guess what, you're older! You have to take your time and manage it, which means figuring out what you have to do and how much time you have to do it.

It's going to be easy to say, "I'll do my homework after dinner," but you have to take into account that basketball practice doesn't end until 8 p.m., and when you get home you'll want something to eat. So, in reality, you're doing homework until 10 or 11 o'clock, and you have to get up at 6 o'clock.

In high school, your workload increases as you move into the upper classes. If you don't learn how to manage your time, you will only have to struggle that much harder. Plus you have all those other activities eating away at the 24 hours in each day.

Ask questions. You've heard the saying, "No question is a stupid question." Well, kids going into ninth grade seem to forget the "NO" part of that sentence and instead replace it with "All my questions are stupid." No matter if you went down the wrong hall and can't find your classroom. No matter if you need help in signing up for a club you really want to join. No matter if you didn't understand what the teacher was saying. The guidance counselors and teachers are there to help you get adjusted and pointed in the right direction.

Take advantage of the help the guidance counselors can give you. You'd be amazed at the number of things you can find in the guidance office—advice on good study habits, advice on planning for college, advice about what to do with that class in which you're having a problem. Use it, because it's there for you.

ADVICE FROM A COUNSELOR

"As students transition to high school, it is important to develop self-advocacy skills. If you need or want something, you will have to seek out the resources to get the help or support that you desire. If you are struggling academically in a particular subject, you need to seek out your teacher for extra help. Your school counselor is an excellent resource to help you develop your self-advocacy skills and to help problem-solve other situations. Once you are in college, your parents will not be there, so start early so you will feel comfortable approaching the resources available."

Leslie Fisher
Lead Counselor
West Windsor-Plainsboro High School South
Princeton Junction, New Jersey

BEWARE OF THE BLACK HOLE OF THE BACK PACK

It looks like an ordinary backpack (or whatever it is you use to carry your books and school papers), but don't be fooled by its innocent appearance. Somewhere between the time you get out of middle school and into high school, it turns into a black hole—casually destroying finished homework, cheerfully ripping through notes you saved for a test, cunningly hiding the special pen you like.

You may have been organized in middle school, but once you get into high school, the backpack can turn into an endless pit into which you stuff everything; however, whatever it is you need to find in its endless depths cannot be found without a major search and rescue.

The reason for this dilemma that will suddenly appear in your life is that in high school, you've got a lot more papers to organize. Homework is given in most classes. You're getting handouts that have to be saved for a test that will come up in three weeks, along with that list of notes of supplies you're supposed to bring to science class and the day planner you bought.

You must ramp up the way you keep things organized to keep up with high school. One suggestion is to get a three-subject spiral notebook for each class. Section one is for taking notes in class. Section two is for homework. Section three is for tearing out sheets of paper. You now have everything you need for one subject in one notebook. The pages can't come out unless you tear them out and it's chronological, so you can look back at past notes and tell what was discussed when.

With this system, or any other that suits you best, your backpack will turn into an ordinary useful bag, and when your history teacher asks you to pull out the notes from last week's class, you will know exactly where to find them.

Top 10 Mistakes

Everyone makes mistakes, but if you can avoid these TOP TEN as you begin your freshman year, you'll be in much better shape. Drum roll, please. We'll start with the worst.

1. My freshman year doesn't count. My senior year is far away. If I mess up, I can always get back on track in the tenth grade. While it's true you can make up for bad choices and slip-ups, your freshman year is the foundation upon which the rest of your high school years, and then college, rest. Freshman year isn't practice or a trial period—it's the real thing!

2. I'm picking this class because my friend is taking it. Your friend picked the class in beginning biology because she's always liked squiggly green bugs. You don't like looking in microscopes. You won't find out what a mistake you've made until you're way behind on homework and have failed several tests, when you could have been getting A's in that writing class you wanted to take but didn't.

3. I'll just skip this class. One day won't make a difference. Not so. In high school, attendance counts. Many schools have policies that cause you to lose credits if you miss class a certain number of times. Even the best of students will miss classes because of illness or other unforeseen events. But remember, much of the teaching in high school is cumulative, meaning that each day is built on what happened in the class the day before. If you get out of the loop, it's really hard to get back in.

4. I don't need to write down that assignment. I'll remember it. Most likely, you'll only remember the assignment until you leave the classroom, then it's history. By the time you get home, you have a vague recollection of what the teacher said you had to do. Then you have to call someone in the class to ask about the assignment and that person isn't home, so you miss doing the homework.

5. I spilled soda on my homework and now I'll be late turning it in if I do it over, so I'll just forget about it. You should talk to your teacher about making up lost or forgotten homework. Even though the teacher will probably take off some points, you guarantee getting no points if you don't turn it in at all! So, while the assignment may be late, at least it will be counted. Don't be afraid to ask your teacher about turning in late assignments—better late than never!

6. Sorry, I can't join that club, I have to study all the time. In your freshman year, it's especially important to become part of the school community. Not only will you get to know other kids who like the same things you do, but you'll also explore what you like to do.

7. Everyone else in this class understood what the teacher just said except me, so I won't ask him to explain it. You will be surprised to know that if you didn't understand or need more explanation, probably everyone else feels the same way too. Be brave. Ask the question and have everyone else in your class silently thanking you. Plus, most importantly, you'll understand what the teacher was saying.

8. I don't want to talk to the teacher about the problems I'm having with her class. Teachers aren't mind-readers. They have no clue that you're struggling until they see your work. If you're having problems, it's okay to say, "I just don't get fractions." Teachers love to teach and part of teaching is helping their students understand things.

9. There's a situation at school that's making me uncomfortable. I'll just tell my friend about it and not go to the counselor's office. Big or small, serious or not, whatever problems you're having or whatever situations are bothering you, your high school counselors are there to help you, protect you, guide you, comfort you. Your best friend may be able to sympathize with your problem, but chances are your friend can't solve the issue as effectively as a counselor or teacher can.

10. I really don't need all that much sleep. That may have been true during the summer when you could sleep late. Now you're up and out with the sunrise. Trouble is, when you go to bed late, you find yourself nodding off in first period. All that brain power to adjust to high school takes energy. Energy comes from a good night's sleep.

MAKE SURE YOUR PARENTS READ THIS!

Some of you have been through the process of transitioning your son or daughter from middle school to high school. For some of you, it's your first time. Helen Erbe, a guidance counselor at Jackson Memorial High School in Jackson, New Jersey, has been a guidance counselor in middle school, elementary school, and now in high school. She says that having been at all levels, the transitions from elementary to middle and middle to high school are the most traumatic for your kids. The range of emotions swings from fearful to happy and back again. The transition brings out all your child's insecurities. But the cumulative wisdom of other parents and guidance counselors can help you help your children. Here are some tried and tested tips.

- Find out what tryouts for high school clubs, activities, and sports take place in the summer and see if your child may be interested in joining.

- While your child is still in middle school, take her to the high school on casual trips such as to the library, to the swimming pool, to a play, so she will already be familiar with the building and things to do before ninth grade starts.

- Before high school starts, take your child on a test run to walk the halls and meet teachers who are there early to set up their classrooms. Then let him come back by himself for another test run.

- Encourage involvement in school activities other than just sports. In general, the students who are involved in extracurriculars enjoy school and have greater academic success. Advise your child to start gradually in the freshman year with a few activities and then add more as he moves toward his senior year.

- Help your child set up a system to organize homework assignments, test dates, and other activities.

- Give your child space to try things on her own. Get her to advocate for her interests and needs on her own. School administrators and teachers love parent involvement but it's important to let kids deal with some of the issues alone.

- Set realistic goals for your child. It's good for children to be challenged but if the goals are too ambitious, children give up reaching any goals.

Part 2

JUMP-START YOUR FUTURE

COME ON, ADMIT IT. You know that big question—what will I do when I graduate from high school?—is right around the corner. Some of your classmates know what they want to do, but you're freaking out about all of the decisions you still have to make.

You've got a lot of possibilities from which to choose. Maybe you'll attend a two-year or four-year college or vocational/career college. Or you'll join the armed services. Or perhaps you'll go right into the workplace with a full-time job. But before you march across that stage to get your diploma, *Get a Jump!* will help you to begin thinking about your options and to open up doors you never knew existed.

A LOOK AT YOURSELF

Deciding what to do with your life is a lot like flying. Just look at the many ways you can fly and the many directions your life can take.

A TEACHER ONCE asked her students to bring something to class that flies. Students brought kites, balloons, and models of airplanes, blimps, hot-air balloons, helicopters, spaceships, gliders, and seaplanes. But when class began, the teacher explained that the lesson was about career planning, not flying.

She was making the point that your plans for life after high school can take many forms. How you will make the journey is an individual matter. That's why it's important to know who you are and what you want before taking off.

You may not choose your life's career by reading *Get a Jump!* (GAJ), but you'll learn how to become part of the decision-making process and find resources that can help you plan your future.

Ready to Fly?

Just having a high school diploma is not enough for many occupations. But, surprise, surprise, neither is a college degree. Different kinds of work require different kinds of training. Knowing how to operate a particular type of equipment, for instance, takes special skills and work experience that you might not learn in college. Employers always want to hire the best-qualified people available, but this does not mean that they always choose those applicants who have the most education. The *type* of education and training you have is just as important as *how much*. Right now, you're at the point in your life where you can choose how much and what kind of education and training you want to get.

If you have a definite career goal in mind, like being a doctor, you probably already know what it will take in terms of education. You're looking at about four years of college, then four years of medical school, and, in most states, one year of residency. Cosmetologists, on the other hand, complete a state-approved training program that ranges from eight to eighteen months.

But for most of you, deciding what to do after high school is not so easy. Perhaps you haven't chosen a field of work yet. You might just know for certain that you want a job that will give you status and a big paycheck. Or maybe you know what you want to do, but you're not sure what kind of education you'll need. For instance, you may love fixing cars, and the idea of being an auto mechanic sounds great. But you need to decide whether to learn on the job, attend a vocational school, seek an apprenticeship, or pursue a combination of these options.

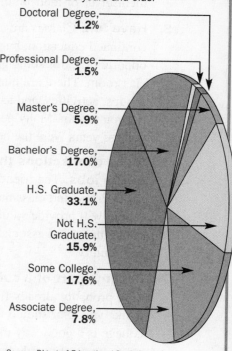

EDUCATIONAL ATTAINMENT
Highest level of education attained by persons 25 years and older

Doctoral Degree, **1.2%**
Professional Degree, **1.5%**
Master's Degree, **5.9%**
Bachelor's Degree, **17.0%**
H.S. Graduate, **33.1%**
Not H.S. Graduate, **15.9%**
Some College, **17.6%**
Associate Degree, **7.8%**

Source: Digest of Educational Statistics, U.S. Department of Commerce, Bureau of the Census, Current Population Survey

THE TOP 10 REASONS TO CONTINUE YOUR EDUCATION

Continuing your education after high school is one choice that can give you a good start no matter what your final career decision is. There are many good reasons to do so. If you think college is not for you at all, take a look at this list. It just might change your mind.

10. **Fulfill a dream—or begin one.** Some people hope to become teachers or scientists. For many, continuing their education provides the opportunity to make that wish a reality for themselves or their family.

9. **Have fun.** Classes are an important part of continued education, but there are plenty of opportunities for some great times outside the classroom. There are hundreds of sports, clubs, groups, activities, and associations just waiting for you to join. Many people say that their college years were the best years of their lives.

8. **Make connections that can link you to future jobs.** The friends, professors, supervisors, and classmates you meet after high school will provide valuable ties for future jobs, committees, and associations within the community.

7. **Become part of a cultural stew.** As you have probably already figured out, not everyone is like you. Nor should they be. Being in college is a good way to expose yourself to many types of people from various backgrounds and geographic locations, with different viewpoints and opinions. You may discover that you like people and things you never knew existed.

6. **Meet new people.** By furthering your education, you will widen your circle of friends and, chances are, form meaningful lifelong relationships.

5. **Do what you love doing and get paid for it.** Have you ever taken a test during which everything clicked or played a video game and caught on immediately? This is what happens when you combine education and training with the right job. Work becomes more like play, which is far more satisfying and rewarding than just going through the motions.

4. **Exercise your mind.** Just as physical exercise keeps your body in shape, mental exercise keeps your mind free of cobwebs. No matter what your area of interest, education holds the key to the most interesting and challenging information you can imagine. Explore your outer limits and become a lifelong learner.

3. **Earn a higher income.** Although money isn't everything, it is necessary for survival. A good education prepares you to become a solid member of society. (See the chart below, "Increase Your Earning Power.")

2. **Learn critical-thinking and analytical skills.** More than any other skill, education teaches you to think. Furthering your learning will help you to think critically, organize and analyze information, and write clearly.

1. **You won't get left behind.** In the twenty-first century, you will need to be prepared to change jobs and continually learn new skills in order to keep up with changes in industry, communications, and technology. Education and training will give you that preparation.

INCREASE YOUR EARNING POWER

People with more education tend to earn more money. Look at the average yearly earnings of workers over the age of 25 by education level.

Professional Degree	$80,230
Doctoral Degree	$70,476
Master's Degree	$55,302
Bachelor's Degree	$46,276
Associate Degree	$35,389
Some College	$32,400
High School Diploma	$28,807
Less Than High School Diploma	$21,391

Source: Bureau of the Census; Bureau of Labor Statistics

Breaking Down the Barriers to Continuing Your Education

Some of you may say, "Forget the reasons why I *should* continue my education. I *can't* because (fill in the blank)." Let's see if your objections stand up.

You say:

Nobody in my family has ever gone to college.

GAJ says:

You can be the first! It's a little scary and not always easy, but just think how great you'll feel being the first person in your family to receive a degree, diploma, or certificate.

You say:

My grades are not good enough.

GAJ says:

Don't let less-than-perfect grades stand in your way. Different institutions have different requirements, including what grades they accept. Schools also evaluate you for admission as a whole person, including your participation in extracurricular activities; your talents, such as academics and athletics; and your employment and volunteer history. There are also classes that you can take to improve your skills in various subject areas. Get a tutor now or form a study group to improve your grades as much as possible. Talk to your guidance counselor about what the appropriate curriculum for you is so you'll have more options when making decisions about continuing your education.

You say:

I can't afford it.

GAJ says:

Many families cannot afford to pay education costs completely out of pocket. That's why there are so many opportunities for financial aid, scholarships, grants, and work-study programs. Federal, state, school-sponsored, private, and career-specific financial aid resources are available to students who take the time to look. Talk to a guidance counselor, go to the library, and look on the Internet. Read the "Financial Aid Dollars and Sense" chapter of GAJ for more information about how to finance your continued education. Be creative and persistent. It can happen for you.

You say:

I don't know how to apply or where I want to go.

GAJ says:

Fortunately, there are resources to help you decide which institution to select. Talk to friends, family members, neighbors, your guidance counselor, pastor, coach, or librarian. Take a look at the Appendix at the back of GAJ for a guide to two-year and four-year colleges, as well as vocational/career colleges in your state.

You say:

I think it may be too difficult for me.

GAJ says:

Think back to something you have done in your life that seemed too difficult in the beginning. Didn't you find that once you began, put your mind to it, and stuck with it that you succeeded? You can do almost anything if you set your mind to it and are willing to work for it.

You say:

I'm not sure I'll fit in.

GAJ says:

One of the best things about furthering your education is the chance to meet new people and be part of new experiences in new surroundings. Colleges and other continuing education options attract a wide variety of students from many different backgrounds. Chances are you won't have any problem finding someone else with interests that are similar to yours. Because schools differ in size, location, student body, and lifestyle, you'll surely find one that meets your needs. Advance visits and interviews can help you determine which school is right for you.

FASTEST-GROWING OCCUPATIONS

Want to have a career that's going places? Check out this chart to see which occupations are expected to grow the fastest by the year 2010 and what type of training you'll need to get the job.

Occupation	Expected Openings	Required Education
Computer Software Engineers, applications	760,000	Bachelor's degree
Computer Support Specialists	996,000	Associate degree
Computer Software Engineers, systems software	601,000	Bachelor's degree
Network and Computer Systems Administrators	416,000	Bachelor's degree
Network Systems and Data Communications Analysts	211,000	Bachelor's degree
Desktop Publishers	63,000	Postsecondary Vocational Training
Database Administrators	176,000	Bachelor's degree
Personal and Home Care Aides	672,000	On-the-job training
Computer Systems Analysts	689,000	Bachelor's degree
Medical Assistants	516,000	On-the-job-training
Social and Human Service Assistants	418,000	On-the-job training
Physician Assistants	89,000	Bachelor's degree
Medical Records and Health Information Technicians	202,000	Associate degree
Computer and Information Systems Managers	463,000	Master's degree
Home Health Aides	907,000	On-the-job training
Physical Therapist Aides	53,000	On-the-job training
Occupational Therapist Aides	12,000	On-the-job training
Physical Therapist Assistants	64,000	Associate degree
Audiologists	19,000	Master's degree
Fitness Trainers and Aerobics Instructors	222,000	Postsecondary Vocational Training
Computer and Information Scientists	39,000	Doctoral degree
Veterinary Assistants and Lab Animal Caretakers	77,000	On-the-job training
Occupational Therapist Assistants	23,000	Associate degree
Veterinary Technologists and Technicians	69,000	Associate degree
Speech-language Pathologists	122,000	Master's degree
Mental Health and Substance Abuse Social Workers	116,000	Master's degree
Dental Assistants	339,000	On-the-job training
Dental Hygienists	201,000	Associate degree
Special Education Teachers, grades Pre-K to 6	320,000	Bachelor's degree
Pharmacy Technicians	259,000	On-the-job training

Source: Bureau of Labor Statistics, Occupational Outlook Handbook

You say:

I don't even know what I want to do with my life.

GAJ says:

Many students don't know this about themselves until they get to experience some of the possibilities. Take the Self-Assessment Inventory on page 26 to help you determine what your interests and talents are. Read "Choosing Your Major" on page 97 for a listing of the most popular college majors and their related careers.

You say:

There is no way I can pursue my education full-time.

GAJ says:

Part-time students are becoming the norm. In fact, a recent study determined that 43 percent of undergraduate students attend school part-time. Most schools offer evening and weekend classes, and many offer work-study opportunities to help students pay for their education. Also, some employers will pay or reimburse you if you are working and want to further your education. If you are enrolled part-time, it does take longer to graduate. But if full-time enrollment is not an option for you, don't give up the opportunity to continue your education. There are many nontraditional ways to achieve your goals.

CHOOSING A CAREER YOU'LL BE HAPPY WITH

Did you know that of the estimated 15 million people searching for employment in the American job market, approximately 12 million are looking for a new occupation or a different employer? That's an awful lot of people who aren't happy with their jobs. Hopefully, you won't be one of them if you take some time to consider what it is you really want to do now, while you're still in school. Is there a particular type of job you've always dreamed of doing? Or perhaps you're one of the many high school students who say:

"I Kind of Know What I Want, But I'm Not Really Sure."

A good way to gather information about potential occupations is by talking with people who have achieved goals that are similar to yours. Talk to teachers, neighbors, and adult friends about their work experiences. The formal name for that activity is an "informational interview." You're interviewing them about the work they do—not to get a job from them but to gather information about their jobs.

If you don't have any contacts in a field that sparks your interest, do some poking around in the workplace. For instance, if you're interested in a career in nursing, you could visit a hospital, doctor's office, or nursing home. Most people love to talk about themselves, so don't be afraid to ask if they'll chat with you about their profession. Offering to volunteer your services can be the best way to know whether you'll be happy doing that type of work.

"I Don't Have a Clue about What I Want to Do."

If you're completely unsure about what kind of work you'd like to do, contact a career counselor who can help you explore your options and possibly administer some interest and aptitude tests. You also might think about contacting a college career planning and placement office, a vocational school placement office, the counseling services of community agencies, or a private counseling service, which may charge you a fee. Many high schools offer job-shadowing programs, where students actually shadow someone in a particular occupation for an entire day or more. Don't forget that as a high school student, your best resource is your high school guidance counselor. Take a look at the list of the Fastest-Growing Occupations on page 24 to get a sampling of the careers with the largest projected job growth in the coming years.

ON THE HUNT FOR INFORMATION

Regardless of how unsure you may be about what you want to do after high school, here's a list of things you can do to get the information you need to head in the right direction. Many people start off thinking they want one career and end up doing something completely different. But this is a good place to begin:

- Investigate careers both in and out of school. Participate in mentoring, job shadowing, and career day opportunities whenever possible.

- Get some on-the-job experience in a field that interests you.

- Research two-year and four-year colleges, vocational/career colleges, and apprenticeship programs.

- Participate in school and state career development activities.

- Prepare for and take aptitude and college entrance tests.

Here are a few Web sites where you can receive valuable direction by completing a career interest questionnaire or by reading about various occupations:

Peterson's

www.petersons.com

On Peterson's Web site, you can read helpful articles about the workplace and search for undergraduate academic and career-oriented degree and certificate programs.

Occupational Outlook Handbook

www.bls.gov/oco

The Bureau of Labor Statistics, an agency within the U.S. Department of Labor, produces this Web site, which offers more information than you'll ever need about specific careers.

SELF-ASSESSMENT INVENTORY

In addition to looking to outside sources for information, there's another rich source of data: yourself. Knowing what you want to do begins with knowing yourself—the real you. The better you understand your own wants and needs, the better you will be able to make decisions about your career goals and dreams. This self-assessment inventory can help.

Who do you admire most, and why?

What is your greatest strength?

What is your greatest talent?

What skills do you already have?

DESCRIBE HOW YOU CURRENTLY USE THESE SKILLS IN YOUR LIFE:

Athletic ability

Mechanical ability

Ability to work with numbers

Leadership skills

Teaching skills

Artistic skills

Analytical skills

CHECK THE AREAS THAT MOST INTEREST YOU.

☐ Providing a practical service for people

☐ Self-expression in music, art, literature, or nature

☐ Organizing and record keeping

☐ Meeting people and supervising others

☐ Helping others in need, either mentally, spiritually, or physically

☐ Solving practical problems

☐ Working in forestry, farming, or fishing

☐ Working with machines and tools

☐ Taking care of animals

☐ Physical work outdoors

☐ Protecting the public via law enforcement or fire fighting

☐ Medical, scientific, or mathematical work

☐ Selling, advertising, or promoting

WHAT GIVES YOU SATISFACTION?

Answer the following questions True (T) or False (F).

T F I get satisfaction not from personal accomplishment, but from helping others.

T F I'd like to have a job in which I can use my imagination and be inventive.

T F In my life, money will be placed ahead of job security and personal interests.

T F It is my ambition to have a direct impact on other people's lives.

T F I am not a risk-taker and would prefer a career that offers little risk.

T F I enjoy working with people rather than by myself.

T F I would not be happy doing the same thing all the time.

WHAT MATTERS THE MOST TO YOU?

Rate the items on the list below from 1 to 10, with 10 being extremely important and 1 being not at all important.

___ Good health	___ Seeing the world
___ Justice	___ Love
___ Marriage/family	___ Fun
___ Faith	___ Power
___ Fame	___ Individualism
___ Beauty	___ Charity
___ Safety	___ Honor
___ Friendship	___ Intelligence
___ Respect	___ Wealth
___ Accomplishment	

Mapping Your Future

www.mapping-your-future.org

On this site, you can find out how to choose a career and how to reach your career goals. You can also pick up useful tips on job hunting, resume writing, and job interviewing techniques. This site also provides a ten-step plan for determining and achieving your career goals.

University of Waterloo Career Development Manual

www.cdm.uwaterloo.ca/

This site provides a thorough online career interest survey, and strategies you can use to get the job that's right for you.

Motivational Appraisal of Personal Potential

www.assessment.com

Features a free 71-question career assessment that analyzes your motivation and points you to the ten best careers for you.

HotJobs.com

www.hotjobs.com

Includes information about thousands of job and career fairs, advice on resumes, and much more.

WHAT WOULD YOU DO IF YOU WERE IN A BLIZZARD SURVIVAL SITUATION?

Check the one that would be your most likely role.

- ☐ The leader
- ☐ The one who explains the situation to the others
- ☐ The one who keeps morale up
- ☐ The one who invents a way to keep warm and melt snow for water
- ☐ The one who listens to instructions and keeps the supplies organized
- ☐ The one who positions sticks and rocks to signal SOS

LOOKING AHEAD AND LOOKING BACK

What are your goals for the next five years?

Where would you like to be in ten years?

What has been your favorite course, and why?

What was your least favorite course, and why?

Who was your favorite teacher, and why?

What are your hobbies?

What are your extracurricular activities?

What jobs have you held?

What volunteer work, if any, have you performed?

Have you ever shadowed a professional for a day? If so, what did you learn?

Do you have a mentor? If so, who? What have you learned from this person?

Do you want to stay close to home, or would you prefer to travel to another city after high school?

WHAT ARE YOUR CAREER GOALS?

The interests, skills, and knowledge supporting my career goals are:

To fulfill my career goals, I will need additional skills and knowledge in:

I will obtain the additional skills and knowledge by taking part in the following educational activities:

I will need a degree, certification, and/or specialized training in:

When I look in the classified ads of the newspaper, the following job descriptions sound attractive to me:

WHAT ARE YOUR IMMEDIATE PLANS AFTER HIGH SCHOOL?

After high school, I plan to:

- ☐ work full-time
- ☐ work part-time and attend school
- ☐ attend college full-time
- ☐ attend technical college
- ☐ enter the military

WHAT WILL YOU NEED TO GET WHERE YOU'RE GOING?

The information I have given indicates that I will be selecting courses that are primarily:

- ☐ College path (Four-year or two-year education that offers liberal arts courses combined with courses in your area of interest.)
- ☐ Vocational path (One or more years of education that includes hands-on training for a specific job.)
- ☐ Combination of the two

MY PERFECT JOB WOULD BE ...

Let your imagination run wild You can have any job you want. What's it like? Start by describing to yourself the following job conditions:

Work conditions What hours are you willing to work? Do you feel most satisfied in an environment that is indoors/outdoors, varied/regular, noisy/quiet, or casual/traditional?

Duties What duties do you feel comfortable carrying out? Do you want to be a leader, or do you perform best as a team player?

People Do you want to work with other people or more independently? How much people contact do you want/need?

Education How much special training or education is required? How much education are you willing to seek? Can you build upon the education or experience you have to date? Will you need to gain new education or experience?

Benefits What salary and benefits do you expect? Are you willing to travel?

Disadvantages There are disadvantages with almost any job. Can you imagine what the disadvantages may be? Can you confirm or disprove these beliefs by talking to someone or researching the industry or job further? If these disadvantages really exist, can you live with them?

Personal qualities What qualities do you want in the employer you ultimately choose? What are the most important qualities that you want in a supervisor? In your coworkers?

Look over your responses to this assessment. Do you see recurring themes in your answers that start to show you what kind of career you might like? If not, there are many more places to get information to decide where your interests lie. You can go to your guidance counselor for advice. You can take the Campbell ™ Interest and Skills Inventory, the Strong Interest Inventory, the Self-Directed Search, or other assessment tests that your guidance counselor recommends.

Chapter 3

THE FIRST STEPS TO A CAREER

Don't be too surprised when your summer job turns into your career.

THE WORD "CAREER" has a scary sound to it when you're still in high school. Careers are for college graduates or those who have been in the workplace for years. But unless you grew up knowing for sure that you wanted to fly airplanes or be a botanist, what will you do? You'll be happy to know that interests you have now can very possibly lead to a college major or into a career. A job at a clothing store, for instance, could lead to a career designing clothes. Perhaps those hours you spend chasing Laura Croft, Tomb Raider, will lead to a career creating video games! Maybe you baby-sit and love being around kids, so teaching becomes an obvious choice. Perhaps cars fascinate you, and you find out you want to fix them for a living.

This chapter will show you how you can begin exploring your interests—sort of like getting into a swimming pool starting with your big toe, rather than plunging in. Vocational/career and tech-prep programs, summer jobs, and volunteering are all ways you can test various career paths to decide if you like them.

THE VOCATIONAL/CAREER EDUCATION PATH

If you're looking for a more real-world education, add yourself to the nearly 11 million youths and adults who are getting a taste of the workplace through vocational and career education programs offered in high schools across the nation. These programs are designed to help you develop competency in the skills you'll need in the workplace as well as in school.

What makes this kind of program different is that you learn in the classroom and in the "real world" of the workplace. Not only do you learn the academics in school, but you also get hands-on training by job shadowing, working under a mentor, and actually performing a job outside of school. Your interests and talents are usually taken into consideration, and you can choose from a variety of traditional, high-tech, and service industry training programs. Take a look at the following categories and see what piques your interest.

STUDENT COUNSEL

Q: What do you like about vocational training?

A: I jumped into the tech center my first year when I was a junior because I thought it was a good way to get out of school. But as the year went on, I said, "Hey, this is a good place to be because it's giving me job experience, and I'm learning how to dress and present myself like I was at a real job." I go during the first 3 or last 3 hours out of the school day. When we're in class, we get to do real jobs for people who ask our instructor for help. Then our teacher lets our creative minds go. We just designed a CD cover. One guy here designed a motorcycle and built it, and now he has three people asking him to come and work for them.

Trisha Younk
Tuscola County Tech Center
Reese High School
Reese, Michigan

Agricultural education. These programs prepare students for careers in agricultural production, animal production and care, agribusiness, agricultural and industrial mechanics, environmental management, farming, horticulture and landscaping, food processing, and natural resource management.

Business education. Students prepare for careers in accounting and finance and computer and data processing as well as administrative/secretarial and management/supervisory positions in professional environments (banking, insurance, law, public service).

Family and consumer sciences. These programs prepare students for careers in child care, food management and production, clothing and interiors, and hospitality and facility care. Core elements include personal development, family life and planning, resource management, and nutrition and wellness.

Trade and industrial and health occupations. Students prepare for careers in auto mechanics, the construction trades, cosmetology, electronics, graphics, public safety, and welding. Health occupation programs offer vocational training for careers in dental and medical assisting, practical nursing, home health care, and medical office assisting.

Marketing education. These programs prepare students for careers in sales, retail, advertising, food and restaurant marketing, and hotel management.

There are many vocational/career education programs available; the kinds listed above represent only a few of the possibilities. To find a program that suits your interests and that is located near you, refer to the college and university listings in the Appendix of this book. Or, you can get more information about vocational education programs by calling 202-205-5451 or e-mailing the U.S. Department of Education, Office of Vocational and Adult Education via its Web site, www.ed.gov/offices/OVAE.

FROM THE GUIDANCE OFFICE

Q: What if going to college is not for me?

A: When adults ask kids what they want to do as a career, kids feel pressured. They think adults want them to identify with one single career. But there are more than 40,000 job titles a person can hold. We tell kids to pick a path first. When you exit high school, there are three paths you can take. One is to the workplace. One leads to the military as a career or as a stepping stone. The third leads to more education—a professional degree, a four-year degree, or a two-year degree. They have to determine which path they'll take.

One of the main selling points about getting career education in high school is that nearly every employer wants you to have some experience before you are hired. In career tech, students are in a workplace environment and can list their time as work experience, and they'll have previous employers who can vouch for them.

Lenore Lemanski
Counselor, Technology Center
Tuscola ISD
Caro, Michigan

THE TECH-PREP PATH

An even more advanced preparation for the workplace and/or an associate degree from a college is called tech-prep. It's an educational path that combines college-prep and vocational/technical courses of study.

During the sequence of courses, the focus is on blending academic and vocational/technical competencies. When you graduate from high school, you'll be able to jump right into the workforce or get an associate degree. But if you want to follow this path, you've got to plan for it starting in the ninth grade. Ask your guidance counselor for more information.

USING THE SUMMER TO YOUR ADVANTAGE

When you're sitting in class, a summer with nothing to do might seem appealing. But after you've listened to all of your CDs, aced all of your video games, hung out at the same old mall, and talked to your friends on the phone about being bored, what's left? How about windsurfing on a cool, clear New England lake? Horseback riding along breathtaking mountain trails? Parlez en français in Paris? Trekking through spectacular canyon lands or living with a family in Costa Rica, Spain, Switzerland, or Japan? Exploring college majors or possible careers? Helping out on an archeological dig or community-service project? Along the way, you'll meet some wonderful people and maybe even make a couple of lifelong friends.

Interested? Get ready to pack your bags and join the 1 million kids and teens who will be having the summer of a lifetime at thousands of terrific camps, academic programs, sports clinics, arts workshops, internships, volunteer opportunities, and travel adventures throughout North America and abroad.

Oh, you don't have the money, you say? Not to worry. There are programs to meet every budget, from $50 workshops to $4,500 world treks and sessions that vary in length from just a couple of hours to a couple of months.

For a list of summer opportunities, take a look at the Appendix in this book. You can also find out about summer opportunities by visiting www.petersons. com.

FROM THE GUIDANCE OFFICE

Q: What options are open to students who take high school career/technology classes and who feel they can't go to college?

A: Students have the opportunity to develop many skills through classes, student organizations, and career/technology classes during high school. These skills form an essential core that they can use to continue on to college, enter the job market, or participate in additional training after graduation. When students can identify those skills and make the connection by applying and expanding their skills as lifelong learners, then the possibilities are endless.

Linda S. Sanchez
Career and Technology Counselor
South San Antonio I.S.D.
Career Education Center
San Antonio, Texas

FLIP BURGERS AND LEARN ABOUT LIFE

A lot of teenagers who are anxious to earn extra cash spend their summers in retail or food service since those jobs are plentiful. If you're flipping burgers or helping customers find a special outfit, you might think the only thing you're getting out of the job is a paycheck. Think again. You will be amazed to discover that you have gained far more.

Being employed in these fields will teach you how to get along with demanding (and sometimes downright unpleasant) customers, how to work on a team, and how to handle money and order supplies. Not only do summer jobs teach you life skills, but they also offer ways to explore potential careers. What's more, when you apply to college or for a full-time job after high school graduation, the experience will look good on your application.

Sometimes, summer jobs become the very thing you want to do later in life. Before committing to a college major, summer jobs give you the opportunity to try out many directions. Students who think they want to be engineers, lawyers, or doctors might spend the summer shadowing an engineer, being a gofer in a legal firm, or volunteering in a hospital.

However, rather than grab the first job that comes along, find out where your interests are and build on what is natural for you. Activities you take for granted provide clues to what you are good at. What about that bookcase you built? Or those kids you love to baby-sit? Same thing with that big party you arranged. The environments you prefer provide other hints, too. Perhaps you feel best in the middle of a cluttered garage or surrounded by people. That suggests certain types of jobs.

Getting a summer job while in high school is the first step in a long line of work experiences to come. And the more experience you have, the better you'll be at getting jobs all your life. To search for summer jobs on the Internet, visit www.petersons.com, and click on the Summer Opportunities button.

TRY YOUR HAND AT AN INTERNSHIP

Each year, thousands of interns work in a wide variety of places, including corporations, law firms, government agencies, media organizations, interest groups, clinics, labs, museums, and historical sites. How popular are internships? Consider the recent trends. In the early 1980s, only 1 in 36 students completed an internship or other experiential learning program. Compare this to 2000, where one study found that 86 percent of college students had completed internships, with 69 percent reporting having had two or more. And an increasing number of high school students are signing up for internships now, too.

The Employer's Perspective

Employers consider internships a good option in both healthy and ailing economies. In healthy economies, managers often struggle to fill their positions with eager workers who can adapt to changing technologies. Internships offer a low-cost way to get good workers into "the pipeline" without offering them a full-time position up front. In struggling economies, on the other hand, downsizing often requires employers to lay off workers without thinking about who will cover their responsibilities. Internships offer an inexpensive way to offset position losses resulting from these disruptive layoffs.

The Intern's Perspective

If you are looking to begin a career or supplement your education with practical training, internships are a good bet for several reasons.

1. **Internships offer a relatively quick way to gain work experience and develop job skills.** Try this exercise. Scan the Sunday want ads of your newspaper. Choose a range of interesting advertisements for professional positions that you would consider taking. List the desired or required job skills and work experiences specified in the ads. How many of these skills and experiences do you have?

Chances are, if you are still in school or a recent graduate, you don't have most of the skills and experience that employers require of their new hires. What do you do?

The growing reality is that many entry-level positions require skills and experiences that schools and part-time jobs don't provide. Sure, you know your way around a computer. You have some customer service experience. You may even have edited your school's newspaper or organized your junior prom. But you still lack the relevant skills and on-the-job experiences that many hiring managers require. A well-chosen internship can offer a way out of this common dilemma by providing you job training in an actual career field. Internships help you take your existing knowledge and skills and apply them in ways that will help you compete for good jobs.

2. **Internships offer a relatively risk-free way to explore a possible career path.** Believe it or not, the best internship may tell you what you *don't* want to do for the next ten or twenty years. Think about it. If you put all your eggs in one basket, what happens if your dream job turns out to be the exact opposite of what you want or who you are? Internships offer a relatively low-cost opportunity to "try out" a career field to see if it's right for *you*.

3. **Internships offer real opportunities to do career networking and can significantly increase your chances of landing a good full-time position.** Have you heard the saying: "It's not what you know, but who you know"? The reality is that who you know (or who knows you) can make a big difference in your job search. Studies show fewer than 20 percent of job placements occur through traditional application methods, including newspaper and trade journal advertisements, employment agencies, and career fairs. Instead, 60 to 90 percent of jobs are found through personal contacts and direct application.

Career "networking" is the exchange of information with others for mutual benefit. Your career network can tell you where the jobs are and help you compete for them. Isn't it better to develop your networking skills now, when the stakes aren't as high, than later when you are competing with everyone else for full-time jobs? The internship hiring process and the weeks you actually spend on the job provide excellent opportunities to talk with various people about careers, your skills, and ways to succeed.

VOLUNTEERING IN YOUR COMMUNITY

You've probably heard the saying that money isn't everything. Well, it's true, especially when it comes to volunteering and community service. There are a number of benefits you'll get that don't add up in dollars and cents but do add up to open doors in your future.

Community service looks good on a college application. Admissions staff members look for applicants who have volunteered and done community service in addition to grades. You could have gotten top grades, but if that's all that's on your application, you won't come across as a well-rounded person.

Community service lets you try out careers. How will you know you'll like a certain type of work if you haven't experienced it? For instance, you might think you want to work in the health-care field. Volunteering in a hospital will let you know if this is really what you want to do.

Community service is an American tradition. You'll be able to meet some of your own community's needs and join with all of the people who have contributed their talents to our country. No matter what your talents, there are unlimited ways for you to serve your community. Take a look at your interests, and then see how they can be applied to help others.

Here are some ideas to get you started:

❑ **Do you like kids?** Volunteer at your local parks and recreation department, for a Little League team, or as a big brother or sister.

❑ **Planning a career in health care?** Volunteer at a blood bank, clinic, hospital, retirement home, or hospice. There are also several organizations that raise money for disease research.

❑ **Interested in the environment?** Volunteer to assist in a recycling program. Create a beautification program for your school or community. Plant trees and flowers or design a community garden.

❑ **Just say no.** Help others stay off drugs and alcohol by volunteering at a crisis center, hotline, or prevention program. Help educate younger kids about the dangers of drug abuse.

❑ **Lend a hand.** Collect money, food, or clothing for the homeless. Food banks, homeless shelters, and charitable organizations need your help.

❑ **Is art your talent?** Share your knowledge and skills with youngsters, the elderly, or local arts organizations that depend on volunteers to help present their plays, recitals, and exhibitions.

❑ **Help fight crime.** Form a neighborhood watch or organize a group to clean up graffiti.

❑ **Your church or synagogue may have projects that need youth volunteers.** The United Way, your local politician's office, civic groups, and special interest organizations also provide exceptional opportunities to serve your community. Ask your principal, teachers, or counselors for additional ideas.

For more information on joining in the spirit of youth volunteerism, write to the Federal Consumer Information Center, Dept. 501G, Pueblo, Colorado 81009, and request the *Catch the Spirit* booklet. Also check out the FCIC's Web site at www.pueblo.gsa.gov.

Part 3

THE ROAD TO MORE EADUCATION

SOME PEOPLE WAKE up at age three and announce that they want to be doctors, teachers, or marine biologists—and they do it.

They're the exceptions. Many high school students don't have a clue about what they want to be. They dread the question, "So, what are you doing after graduating from high school?" Unfortunately, some of those same people also end up in careers that don't satisfy them.

You don't have to plan the rest of your life down to the last detail, but you can start to take some general steps toward your future and lay the groundwork. Then, when you do decide what you want to do, you'll be able to seize hold of your dream and go with it.

PLANNING YOUR EDUCATION IN HIGH SCHOOL

Some people are planners. They make a plan, and they follow it. Then there are the non-planners.

Non-planners see the words "plan" and "future" and say, "Yeah, yeah, I know." Meanwhile, they're running out the door for an appointment they were supposed to be at 5 minutes ago.

Unfortunately, when it comes time to really do something about those goals and future hopes, the non-planners often discover that much of what should have been done wasn't done—which is not good when they're planning their future after high school. What about those classes they should have taken? What about those jobs they should have volunteered for? What about that scholarship they could have had if only they'd found out about it sooner?

But there is hope for poor planners. Now that you've thought about yourself and the direction you might want to go after graduating, you can use this chapter to help you plan what you should be doing while still in high school and when you should be doing it.

Regardless of what type of education you're pursuing on after high school, here's a plan to help you get there.

YOUR EDUCATION TIMELINE

Use this timeline to help you make sure you're accomplishing everything you need to accomplish on time.

Ninth Grade

- As soon as you can, meet with your counselor to begin talking about colleges and careers.

- Make sure you are enrolled in the appropriate college-preparatory or tech-prep courses.

- Get off to a good start with your grades. The grades you earn in ninth grade will be included in your final high school GPA and class rank.

- College might seem a long way off now, but grades really do count toward college admission and scholarships.

- Explore your interests and possible careers. Take advantage of Career Day opportunities.

- Get involved in extracurricular activities (both school and non-school-sponsored).

- Talk to your parents about planning for college expenses. Continue or begin a savings plan for college.

- Look at the college information available in your counselor's office and school and public libraries. Use the Internet to check out college Web sites. Visit Peterson's at www.petersons.com to start a list of colleges that might interest you.

- Tour a nearby college, if possible. Visit relatives or friends who live on or near a college campus. Check out the dorms, go to the library or student center, and get a feel for college life.

⏰ Investigate summer enrichment programs. Visit www.petersons.com for some neat ideas about summer opportunities.

Tenth Grade

Fall

⏰ In October, take the Preliminary SAT/National Merit Scholarship Qualifying Test (PSAT/NMSQT) for practice. When you fill out your test sheet, check the box that releases your name to colleges so you can start receiving brochures from them.

⏰ Ask your guidance counselor about the American College Testing program's PLAN (Pre-ACT) assessment program, which helps determine your study habits and academic progress and interests. This test will prepare you for the ACT Assessment next year.

⏰ Take geometry if you have not already done so. Take biology and a second year of a foreign language.

⏰ Become familiar with general college entrance requirements.

⏰ Participate in your school's or state's career development activities.

PARENT PERSPECTIVE

Q: **When should parents and their children start thinking about preparing for college?**

A: **The discussion needs to start in middle school. If parents don't expose their children to these concepts at that time, then it can be too late in the game. Children need to take the right courses in high school. Many kids here end up going to junior colleges because they don't meet the minimum requirements when they graduate. Many universities and private colleges don't count some of the classes kids take in high school. You can't wait until the child is 18 and then say, "Maybe we should do something about getting into college."**

Kevin Carr
Parent
Oak Park, California

⏰ Visit Petersons.com for advice on test taking and general college entrance requirements.

Winter

⏰ Discuss your PSAT score with your counselor.

⏰ The people who read college applications aren't looking just for grades. Get involved in activities outside the classroom. Work toward leadership positions in the activities that you like best. Become involved in community service and other volunteer activities.

⏰ Read, read, read. Read as many books as possible from a comprehensive reading list, like the one on pages 42 and 43.

⏰ Read the newspaper every day to learn about current affairs.

⏰ Work on your writing skills—you'll need them no matter what you do.

⏰ Find a teacher or another adult who will advise and encourage you to write well.

Spring

⏰ Keep your grades up so you can have the highest GPA and class rank possible.

⏰ Ask your counselor about postsecondary enrollment options and Advanced Placement (AP) courses.

⏰ Continue to explore your interests and careers that you think you might like.

⏰ Begin zeroing in on the type of college you would prefer (two-year or four-year, small or large, rural or urban). To get an idea of what's available, take a look at college profiles on Petersons.com.

⏰ If you are interested in attending a military academy such as West Point or Annapolis, now is the time to start planning and getting information.

⏰ Write to colleges and ask for their academic requirements for admission.

- Visit a few more college campuses. Read all of the mail you receive from colleges. You may see something you like.

- Attend college fairs.

- Keep putting money away for college. Get a summer job.

- Consider taking SAT II Subject Tests in the courses you took this year while the material is still fresh in your mind. These tests are offered in May and June.

Eleventh Grade

Fall

- Meet with your counselor to review the courses you've taken, and see what you still need to take.

- Check your class rank. Even if your grades haven't been that good so far, it's never too late to improve. Colleges like to see an upward trend.

- If you didn't do so in tenth grade, sign up for and take the PSAT/NMSQT. In addition to National Merit Scholarships, this is the qualifying test for the National Scholarship Service and Fund for Negro Students and the National Hispanic Recognition Program.

- Make sure that you have a social security number.

- Take a long, hard look at why you want to continue your education after high school so you will be able to choose the best college or university for your needs.

- Make a list of colleges that meet your most important criteria (size, location, distance from home, majors, academic rigor, housing, and cost). Weigh each of the factors according to their importance to you.

- Continue visiting college fairs. You may be able to narrow your choices or add a college to your list.

PARENT PERSPECTIVE

Q: How involved should parents get in the selection of a college for their children?

A: Parents are getting more involved than ever before in supporting their children in the college process. This phenomenon is due to two factors:

(1) This generation of parents has been much more involved with their children in dealing with the outside world than were their parents.

(2) The investment made by today's parents is much more than that made by parents 20 or 30 years ago. As parents focus on the cost of this big-ticket item, there's interest to be more involved, to get the proper return.

Parents certainly should be involved in the college selection and application process. Studies clearly indicate that parental support in this process and throughout the college years can make a big difference in the success of a student. But this process also should be a learning opportunity in decision making for students. In that regard, parents shouldn't direct the student but provide input and the framework to assist their students.

Parents should not feel uncomfortable making suggestions to help their children through the thought and selection process—especially when it comes to identifying schools that their pocketbooks can accommodate. However, the child must be comfortable with the final decision and must have ultimate responsibility for the selection of the school. When students have made the final decision, it can help in their level of commitment because they've invested in it. They have a responsibility to do well and complete their academics at that location.

Richard Flaherty
President, College Parents of America

- Speak to college representatives who visit your high school.

- If you want to participate in Division I or Division II sports in college, start the certification process. Check with your counselor to make sure you are taking a core curriculum that meets NCAA requirements.

- If you are interested in one of the military academies, talk to your guidance counselor about starting the application process now.

SIX STUDY SKILLS THAT LEAD TO SUCCESS

1. **SET A REGULAR STUDY SCHEDULE. No one at college is going to hound you to do your homework. Develop the study patterns in high school that will lead to success in college. Anyone who has ever pulled an all-nighter knows how much you remember when you are on the downside of your fifth cup of coffee and no sleep—not much! Nothing beats steady and consistent study habits.**

2. **SAVE EVERYTHING. To make sure your history notes don't end up in your math notebook and your English papers don't get thrown at the bottom of your friend's locker, develop an organized system for storing your papers. Stay on top of your materials, and be sure to save quizzes and tests. It is amazing how questions from a test you took in March can miraculously reappear on your final exam.**

3. **LISTEN. Teachers give away what will be on the test by repeating themselves. If you pay attention to what the teacher is saying, you will probably notice what is being emphasized. If what the teacher says in class repeats itself in your notes and in review sessions, chances are that material will be on the test. So really listen.**

4. **TAKE NOTES. If the teacher has taken the time to prepare a lecture, then what he or she says is important enough for you to write down. Develop a system for reviewing your notes. After each class, rewrite them, review them, or reread them. Try highlighting the important points or making notes in the margins to jar your memory.**

5. **USE TEXTBOOKS WISELY. What can you do with a textbook besides lose it? Use it to back up or clarify information that you don't understand from your class notes. Reading every word may be more effort than it is worth, so look at the book intelligently. What is in boxes or highlighted areas? What content is emphasized? What do the questions ask about in the review sections?**

6. **FORM A STUDY GROUP. Establish a group that will stay on task and ask one another the questions you think the teacher will ask. Compare notes to see if you have all the important facts. And discuss your thoughts. Talking ideas out can help when you have to respond to an essay question.**

Winter

- Collect information about college application procedures, entrance requirements, tuition and fees, room and board costs, student activities, course offerings, faculty composition, accreditation, and financial aid. The Internet is a good way to visit colleges and obtain this information. Begin comparing the schools by the factors that you consider to be most important.

- Discuss your PSAT score with your counselor.

- Begin narrowing down your college choices. Find out if the colleges you are interested in require the SAT I, ACT Assessment, or SAT II Subject Tests for admission.

- Register for the SAT I and additional SAT II Subject Tests, which are offered several times during the winter and spring of your junior year (see the "Tackling the Tests" chapter for a schedule). You can take them again in the fall of your senior year if you are unhappy with your scores.

- Register for the ACT Assessment, which is usually taken in April or June. You can take it again late in your junior year or in the fall of your senior year, if necessary.

- Begin preparing for the tests you've decided to take.

- Have a discussion with your parents about the colleges in which you are interested. Examine financial resources, and gather information about financial aid. Check out the "Financial Aid Dollars and Sense" chapter for a step-by-step explanation of the financial aid process.

- Set up a filing system with individual folders for each college's correspondence and printed materials.

Spring

- Meet with your counselor to review senior-year course selection and graduation requirements.

- Discuss ACT Assessment/SAT I scores with your counselor. Register to take the ACT Assessment and/or SAT I again if you'd like to try to improve your score.

- Discuss the college essay with your guidance counselor or English teacher.

- Stay involved with your extracurricular activities. Colleges look for consistency and depth in activities.

- Consider whom you will ask to write your recommendations. Think about asking teachers who know you well and who will write positive letters about you. Letters from a coach, activity leader, or an adult who knows you well outside of school (e.g., volunteer work contact) are also valuable.

- Inquire about personal interviews at your favorite colleges. Call or write for early summer appointments. Make necessary travel arrangements.

- See your counselor to apply for on-campus summer programs for high school students. Apply for a summer job or internship. Be prepared to pay for college applications and testing fees in the fall.

- Request applications from schools you're interested in by mail or via the Internet.

Summer

- Visit the campuses of your top-five college choices.

- After each college interview, send a thank-you letter to the interviewer.

- Talk to people you know who have attended the colleges in which you are interested.

- Continue to read books, magazines, and newspapers.

- Practice filling out college applications, and then complete the final application forms or apply on line through the Web sites of the colleges in which you're interested.

- Volunteer in your community.

- Compose rough drafts of your college essays. Have a teacher read and discuss them with you. Polish them, and prepare final drafts. Proofread your final essays at least three times.

- Develop a financial aid application plan, including a list of the aid sources, requirements for each application, and a timetable for meeting the filing deadlines.

ADMISSIONS ADVICE

Q: Other than grades and test scores, what are the most important qualities that you look for in students?

A: We consider the types of classes students have taken. A grade of a B in an honors class is competitive to an A in a regular course. We seek not only academically talented students but those who are well rounded. They need to submit their interests and activities, letters of recommendation, and writing samples in addition to their test scores. We look for someone that's involved in his or her community and high school, someone that holds leadership positions and has a balance of activities outside of academics. This gives us a look at that person as a whole.

Cheyenna Smith
Admission Counselor
University of Houston
Houston, Texas

Twelfth Grade

Fall

- Continue to take a full course load of college-prep courses.

- Keep working on your grades. Make sure you have taken the courses necessary to graduate in the spring.

- Continue to participate in extracurricular and volunteer activities. Demonstrate initiative, creativity, commitment, and leadership in each.

- To male students: you must register for selective service on your eighteenth birthday to be eligible for federal and state financial aid.

- Talk to counselors, teachers, and parents about your final college choices.

- Make a calendar showing application deadlines for admission, financial aid, and scholarships.

- Check resource books, computer programs, and your guidance office for information on scholarships and grants. Ask colleges about scholarships for which you may qualify.

Check out Petersons.com for information on scholarships.

⏰ Give recommendation forms to the teachers you have chosen, along with stamped, self-addressed envelopes so your teachers can send them directly to the colleges. Be sure to fill out your name, address, and school name on the top of the form. Talk to your recommendation writers about your goals and ambitions.

⏰ Give School Report forms to your high school's guidance office. Fill in your name, address, and any other required information. Verify with your guidance counselor the schools to which transcripts, test scores, and letters are to be sent. Give your counselor any necessary forms at least two weeks before they are due or whenever your counselor's deadline is, whichever is earlier.

⏰ Register for and take the ACT Assessment, SAT I, or SAT II Subject Tests, as necessary.

⏰ Be sure you have requested (either by mail or on line) that your test scores be sent to the colleges of your choice.

⏰ Mail or send electronically any college applications for early decision admission by November 1.

⏰ If possible, visit colleges while classes are in session.

⏰ If you plan to apply for an ROTC scholarship, remember that your application is due by December 1.

⏰ Print extra copies or make photocopies of every application you send.

Winter

⏰ Attend whatever college-preparatory nights are held at your school or by local organizations.

⏰ Send midyear grade reports to colleges. Continue to focus on your schoolwork!

⏰ Fill out the Free Application for Federal Student Aid (FAFSA) and, if necessary, the Profile®. These forms can be obtained from your guidance counselor or at www.fafsa.ed.gov/ to download the forms or to file electronically. These forms may not be processed before January 1, so don't send them before then.

⏰ Mail or send electronically any remaining applications and financial aid forms before winter break. Make sure you apply to at least one college that you know you can afford and where you know you will be accepted.

⏰ Follow up to make sure that the colleges have received all application information, including recommendations and test scores.

⏰ Meet with your counselor to verify that all forms are in order and have been sent out to colleges.

Spring

⏰ Watch your mail between March 1 and April 1 for acceptance notifications from colleges.

⏰ Watch your mail for notification of financial aid awards between April 1 and May 1.

⏰ Compare the financial aid packages from the colleges and universities that have accepted you.

⏰ Make your final choice, and notify all schools of your intent by May 1. If possible, do not decide without making at least one campus visit. Send your nonrefundable deposit to your chosen school by May 1 as well. Request that your guidance counselor send a final transcript to the college in June.

⏰ Be sure that you have received a FAFSA acknowledgment.

⏰ If you applied for a Pell Grant (on the FAFSA), you will receive a Student Aid Report (SAR) statement. Review this notice, and forward it to the college you plan to attend. Make a copy for your records.

⏰ Complete follow-up paperwork for the college of your choice (scheduling, orientation session, housing arrangements, and other necessary forms).

Summer

⏰ If applicable, apply for a Stafford Loan through a lender. Allow eight weeks for processing.

⏰ Receive the orientation schedule from your college.

⏰ Get residence hall assignment from your college.

⏰ Obtain course scheduling and cost information from your college.

⏰ Congratulations! You are about to begin the greatest adventure of your life. Good luck.

CLASSES TO TAKE IF YOU'RE GOING TO COLLEGE

Did you know that classes you take as early as the ninth grade will help you get into college? Make sure you take at least the minimum high school curriculum requirements necessary for college admission. Even if you don't plan to enter college immediately, take the most demanding courses you can handle.

Review the list of Suggested Courses on this page. Some courses, categories, and names vary from state to state, but this list may be used as a guideline. Talk with your guidance counselor to select the curriculum that best meets your needs and skills.

Of course, learning also occurs outside of school. While outside activities will not make up for poor academic performance, skills learned from jobs, extracurricular activities, and volunteer opportunities will help you become a well-rounded student and will strengthen your college or job application.

Getting a Head Start on College Courses

You can take college courses while still in high school so that when you're in college, you'll be ahead of everyone else. The formal name is postsecondary

---

SUGGESTED COURSES

College-Preparatory Curriculum

ENGLISH. Four units, with emphasis on composition (English 9, 10, 11, 12)

MATHEMATICS. Three units (algebra I, algebra II, geometry) are essential: trigonometry, precalculus, calculus, and computer science are recommended for some fields of study

SOCIAL SCIENCE. Three units (American history, world history, government/economics)

SCIENCE. Four units (earth science, biology, chemistry, physics)

FOREIGN LANGUAGE. Three units (at least 2 years in the same language)

FINE ARTS. One to 2 units

OTHER. Keyboarding, computer applications, computer science I, computer science II, physical education, health

College-Preparatory Curriculum Combined with a Career Education or Vocational Program

ENGLISH. Four units

MATHEMATICS. Three units (algebra I, algebra II, geometry)

SOCIAL SCIENCE. Three units (American history, world history, government/economics)

SCIENCE. Two units (earth science, biology)

FOREIGN LANGUAGE. Three units (at least 2 years in the same language)

FINE ARTS. One to 2 units

OTHER. Keyboarding, computer applications, physical education, and health and half-days at the Career Center during junior and senior years

---

enrollment. (In Texas, the formal names are dual credit—academic credit and articulated credit—career and technology credit.) What it means is that some students can take college courses and receive both high school and college credit for the courses taken. It's like a two-for-one deal!

Postsecondary enrollment is designed to provide an opportunity for qualified high school students to experience more advanced academic work. Participation in a postsecondary enrollment program is not intended to replace courses available in high school but rather to enhance the educational opportunities available to students while in high school. There are two options for postsecondary enrollment:

Option A: Qualified high school juniors and seniors take courses for college credit. Students enrolled under Option A must pay for all books, supplies, tuition, and associated fees.

Option B: Qualified high school juniors and seniors take courses for high school and college credit. For students enrolled under this option, the local school district covers the related costs, provided that the student completes the selected courses. Otherwise, the student and parent will be assessed the costs.

Certain preestablished conditions must be met for enrollment, so check with your high school counselor for more information.

SUGGESTED READING LIST FOR GRADES 9 THROUGH 12

Instead of flipping on the TV or putting on those headphones, how about picking up a book instead? Reading not only will take you to wonderful, unexplored worlds in your imagination, but there are practical reasons as well. Reading gives you a more well-rounded background. College admissions and future employers pick up on that. And you'll be able to answer the questions, "Did you read that book? What did you think of it?" How many of the books on this list have you read?

Adams, Richard
Watership Down

Aesop
Fables

Agee, James
A Death in the Family

Anderson, Sherwood
Winesburg, Ohio

Anonymous
Go Ask Alice

Asimov, Isaac
Short Stories

Austen, Jane
Emma
Northanger Abbey
Pride and Prejudice
Sense and Sensibility

Baldwin, James
Go Tell It on the Mountain

Balzac, Honore de
Pere Goriot

Beckett, Samuel
Waiting for Godot

Bolt, Robert
A Man for All Seasons

Brontë, Charlotte
Jane Eyre

Brontë, Emily
Wuthering Heights

Brooks, Gwendolyn
In the Mecca
Riot

Browning, Robert
Poems

Buck, Pearl
The Good Earth

Butler, Samuel
The Way of All Flesh

Camus, Albert
The Plague
The Stranger

Cather, Willa
Death Comes for the Archbishop
My Antonia

Cervantes, Miguel
Don Quixote

Chaucer, Geoffrey
The Canterbury Tales

Chekhov, Anton
The Cherry Orchard

Chopin, Kate
The Awakening

Collins, Wilkie
The Moonstone

Conrad, Joseph
Heart of Darkness
Lord Jim
The Secret Sharer
Victory

Crane, Stephen
The Red Badge of Courage

Dante
The Divine Comedy

Defoe, Daniel
Moll Flanders

Dickens, Charles
Bleak House
David Copperfield
Great Expectations
Hard Times
Oliver Twist
A Tale of Two Cities

Dickinson, Emily
Poems

Dinesen, Isak
Out of Africa

Dostoevski, Fyodor
The Brothers Karamazov
Crime and Punishment

Douglas, Frederick
The Life of Frederick Douglas

Dreiser, Theodore
An American Tragedy
Sister Carrie

Early, Gerald
Tuxedo Junction

Eliot, George
Adam Bede
Middlemarch
The Mill on the Floss
Silas Marner

Eliot, T. S.
Murder in the Cathedral

Ellison, Ralph
Invisible Man

Emerson, Ralph Waldo
Essays

Faulkner, William
Absalom, Absalom!
As I Lay Dying
Intruder in the Dust
Light in August
The Sound and the Fury

Fielding, Henry
Joseph Andrews
Tom Jones

Fitzgerald, F. Scott
The Great Gatsby
Tender Is the Night

Flaubert, Gustave
Madame Bovary

Forster, E. M.
A Passage to India
A Room with a View

Franklin, Benjamin
The Autobiography of Benjamin Franklin

Galsworthy, John
The Forsyte Saga

Golding, William
Lord of the Flies

Goldsmith, Oliver
She Stoops to Conquer

Graves, Robert
I, Claudius

Greene, Graham
The Heart of the Matter
The Power and the Glory

Hamilton, Edith
Mythology

Hardy, Thomas
Far from the Madding Crowd
Jude the Obscure
The Mayor of Casterbridge
The Return of the Native
Tess of the D'Urbervilles

Hawthorne, Nathaniel
The House of the Seven Gables
The Scarlet Letter

Hemingway, Ernest
A Farewell to Arms
For Whom the Bell Tolls
The Sun Also Rises

Henry, O.
Stories

Hersey, John
A Single Pebble

Hesse, Hermann
Demian
Siddhartha
Steppenwolf

Homer
The Iliad
The Odyssey

Hughes, Langston
Poems
The Big Sea

Hugo, Victor
Les Misérables

Huxley, Aldous
Brave New World

Ibsen, Henrik
A Doll's House
An Enemy of the People
Ghosts
Hedda Gabler
The Master Builder
The Wild Duck

James, Henry
The American
Daisy Miller
Portrait of a Lady
The Turn of the Screw

Joyce, James
Dubliners
A Portrait of the Artist as a Young Man

Kafka, Franz
The Castle
The Metamorphosis
The Trial

Keats, John
Poems

Kerouac, Jack
On the Road

Koestler, Arthur
Darkness at Noon

Lawrence, Jerome, and Robert E. Lee
Inherit the Wind

Lewis, Sinclair
Arrowsmith
Babbitt
Main Street

Llewellyn, Richard
How Green Was My Valley

Machiavelli
The Prince

MacLeish, Archibald
J.B.

Mann, Thomas
Buddenbrooks
The Magic Mountain

Marlowe, Christopher
Dr. Faustus

Maugham, Somerset
Of Human Bondage

McCullers, Carson
The Heart Is a Lonely Hunter

Melville, Herman
Billy Budd
Moby-Dick
Typee

Miller, Arthur
The Crucible
Death of a Salesman

Monsarrat, Nicholas
The Cruel Sea

Naylor, Gloria
Bailey's Cafe
The Women of Brewster Place

O'Neill, Eugene
The Emperor Jones
Long Day's Journey Into Night
Mourning Becomes Electra

Orwell, George
Animal Farm
1984

Pasternak, Boris
Doctor Zhivago

Poe, Edgar Allan
Short Stories

Remarque, Erich
All Quiet on the Western Front

Rolvaag, O. E.
Giants in the Earth

Rostand, Edmond
Cyrano de Bergerac

Salinger, J. D.
The Catcher in the Rye

Sandburg, Carl
Abraham Lincoln: The Prairie Years
Abraham Lincoln: The War Years

Saroyan, William
The Human Comedy

Sayers, Dorothy
The Nine Tailors

Shakespeare, William
Plays and Sonnets

Shaw, George Bernard
Arms and the Man
Major Barbara
Pygmalion
Saint Joan

Sheridan, Richard B.
The School for Scandal

Shute, Nevil
On the Beach

Sinclair, Upton
The Jungle

Sophocles
Antigone
Oedipus Rex

Steinbeck, John
East of Eden
The Grapes of Wrath
Of Mice and Men

Stowe, Harriet Beecher
Uncle Tom's Cabin

Swift, Jonathan
Gulliver's Travels

Thackeray, William M.
Vanity Fair

Thoreau, Henry David
Walden

Tolstoy, Leo
Anna Karenina
War and Peace

Trollope, Anthony
Barchester Towers

Turgenev, Ivan
Fathers and Sons

Twain, Mark
Pudd'nhead Wilson

Updike, John
Rabbit, Run

Vergil
The Aeneid

Voltaire
Candide

Walker, Alice
The Color Purple
Meridian

Warren, Robert Penn
All the King's Men

Waugh, Evelyn
Brideshead Revisited
A Handful of Dust

Wharton, Edith
The Age of Innocence

White, T. H.
The Once and Future King
The Sword in the Stone

Wilde, Oscar
The Importance of Being Earnest
The Picture of Dorian Gray

Wilder, Thornton
Our Town

Williams, Tennessee
The Glass Menagerie
A Streetcar Named Desire

Wolfe, Thomas
Look Homeward, Angel

Woolf, Virginia
Mrs. Dalloway
To the Lighthouse

Wouk, Herman
The Caine Mutiny

Wright, Richard
Black Boy
Native Sun

Source: The National Endowment for the Humanities.

For more book recommendations, see what college professors suggest in Arco's **Reading Lists for College-Bound Students,** *available at your local bookstore.*

5 Chapter

TACKLING THE TESTS

Unless you've been on another planet for the last two or three years, you've probably heard older high school students buzzing about the alphabet soup list of college entrance exams—SAT, ACT Assessment, and PSAT.

OME OF THE STUDENTS who are getting ready to take one of these tests look like they're in various states of hysteria. Others have been studying for months on end, so when they open their mouths, out pops the definition for "meretricious" or the answer to "What is the ratio of 3 pounds to 6 ounces?" Well, the talk that you've heard about the tests is partly true. They are a big deal and can be crucial to your academic plans. On the other hand, you don't have to walk in cold. Remember that word "planning"? It's a whole lot nicer than the word "panic." Preparing for the tests takes a lot of planning and time, but if you're reading this chapter, you're already ahead of the game.

A FEW FACTS ABOUT THE MAJOR TESTS

The major standardized tests students take in high school are the PSAT, SAT I, and ACT Assessment. Colleges across the country use them to get a sense of a student's readiness to enter their ivy-covered halls. These tests, or "boards" as they are sometimes called, have become notorious because of how important they can be. There is a mystique that surrounds them. People talk about the "magic number" that will get you into the school of your dreams.

Beware! There is a lot of misinformation out there. First and foremost, these are not intelligence tests; they are reasoning tests designed to evaluate the way you think. These tests assess the basic knowledge and skills you have gained through your classes in school, and they also gauge the knowledge you have gained through outside experience. The material on these tests is not curriculum-based, but the tests do emphasize those academic experiences that educational institutions feel are good indicators of your probable success in college.

THE ACT ASSESSMENT

The ACT Assessment is a standardized college entrance examination that measures knowledge and skills in English, mathematics, reading, and science reasoning and the application of these skills to future academic tasks. The ACT Assessment consists of four multiple-choice tests.

Test 1: English

- 75 questions, 45 minutes
- Punctuation
- Grammar and usage
- Sentence structure
- Strategy
- Organization
- Style

Test 2: Mathematics

- 60 questions, 60 minutes
- Pre-algebra
- Elementary algebra
- Intermediate algebra

- Coordinate geometry
- Plane geometry
- Trigonometry

Test 3: Reading

- 40 questions, 35 minutes
- Prose fiction
- Humanities
- Social studies
- Natural sciences

Test 4: Science Reasoning

- 40 questions, 35 minutes
- Biology
- Physical science
- Chemistry
- Physics

Each section is scored from 1 to 36 and is scaled for slight variations in difficulty. Students are not penalized for incorrect responses. The composite score is the average of the four scaled scores. Beginning in the 2004–05 school year, there will be an optional writing component added to the ACT Assessment.

To prepare for the ACT Assessment, ask your guidance counselor for a free guidebook called *Preparing for the ACT Assessment*. Besides providing general test-preparation information and additional test-taking strategies, this guidebook describes the content and format of the four ACT Assessment subject area tests, summarizes test administration procedures followed at ACT Assessment test centers, and includes a practice test.

THE SAT I

The SAT I measures developed verbal and mathematical reasoning abilities as they relate to successful performance in college. It is intended to supplement the secondary school record and other information about the student in assessing readiness for college. There is one unscored, experimental

section on the exam, which is used for equating and/or pretesting purposes and can cover either the mathematics or verbal subject area.

Verbal Reasoning

- 78 questions, 75 minutes
- Analogies
- Sentence completions
- Critical reading passages

Mathematical Reasoning

- 60 questions, 75 minutes
- Student-produced responses
- Quantitative comparisons
- Regular math

Experimental Section

- 30 minutes

Students receive one point for each correct response and lose a fraction of a point for each incorrect response (except for student-produced responses). These points are totaled to produce the raw scores, which are then scaled to equalize the scores for slight variations in difficulty for various editions of the test. Both the verbal scaled score range and the math scaled

THE NEW SAT I

You've probably heard a rumor that the SAT I is changing. The rumor's true, but don't worry: Nothing will happen until 2005. In case you're not planning on taking the exam until then, here's what you have to look forward to:

- **The dreaded Analogy questions in the Verbal section will disappear. Taking their place will be more Reading Comprehension passages.**

- **The Verbal section will get a new name: "Critical Reading."**

- **A third section, Writing, will be added. It will be similar to the SAT II Writing Test, with multiple-choice grammar usage questions and a 25-minute essay. Your essay will be read and scored, and then it will be posted on a Web site for college admissions officials to read when they review your college application package.**

- **Quantitative Comparisons will disappear from the Math section, replaced by multiple-choice math questions from Algebra II.**

- **The current test takes 3 hours to complete; the new SAT I will take 3½ hours.**

- **Instead of a top score of 1600 points, the new SAT I will have a top score of 2400 points.**

score range are from 200 to 800. The total scaled score range is from 400 to 1600.

To prepare for the SAT I, you should carefully review the pamphlet, *Taking the SAT I: Reasoning Test*, which you should be able to get from your guidance counselor. Also, most libraries and bookstores stock a large selection of material about the SAT I and other standardized tests.

RECOMMENDED TEST-TAKING DATES

Sophomore Year

| October | PSAT/NMSQT and PLAN (for practice, planning, and preparation) |
| May–June | SAT II Subject Tests (if necessary) |

Junior Year

| October | PSAT/NMSQT (for the National Merit Scholarship Program and practice) |
| January–June | ACT Assessment and/or SAT I, SAT II Subject Tests (if necessary—for college admission) |

Senior Year

| October–December | ACT Assessment and/or SAT I, SAT II Subject Tests (if necessary—for college admission) |

Which Should I Take? The ACT Assessment vs. the SAT I

It's not a bad idea to take both. This assures that you will have the test scores required for admission to all schools, because some colleges accept the results of one test and not the other. Some institutions use test results for proper placement of students in English and math courses.

You should take the ACT Assessment and SAT I during the spring of your junior year, if not earlier. This enables you to retake the test in the fall of your senior year if you're not satisfied with your scores. Also, this makes it possible for institutions to receive all test scores before the end of January. Institutions generally consider the better score when determining admission and placement. Because most scholarship applications are processed between December and April of the senior year, your best score results can then be included in the application.

THE PSAT/NMSQT

The Preliminary SAT/National Merit Scholarship Qualifying Test, better known as the PSAT/NMSQT, is a practice test for the SAT I. Many students take the PSAT more than once because scores tend to increase with repetition and because it allows students to become more comfortable with taking standardized tests. During the junior year, the PSAT is also used as a qualifying test for the National Merit Scholarship Program and the National Scholarship Service and Fund for Negro Students. It is also used in designating students for the National Hispanic Scholar Recognition Program. The PSAT includes a writing skills section, which consists entirely of multiple-choice questions. This section does *not* appear on the SAT I.

Verbal Reasoning

- Approximately 50 questions, two 25-minute sections

- Analogies

- Sentence completion

- Critical reading passages

Mathematical Reasoning

- 40 questions, two 25-minute sections
- Student-produced responses
- Quantitative comparisons
- Regular math

Writing Skills

- 39 questions, one 30-minute section
- Identifying sentence errors
- Improving sentences
- Improving paragraphs

Students receive a score in each content area (verbal, math, and writing). Each score ranges from 20 to 80 and is totaled with the others for the combined score. The total score ranges from 60 to 240.

WHAT DOES IT TAKE TO GET IN?

College Admission Policy	Class Rank	Average ACT Assessment Range (1–36)	Average SAT I Range (400–1600)
Highly Selective	Top 10% of class, very strong academic record	27–31	1220–1380
Selective	Top 25% of class, strong academic record	22–27	1150–1230
Traditional	Top 50% of class, good academic record	20–23	950–1070
Liberal	Many accepted from lower half of class	18–21	870–990
Open	All accepted to limit of capacity	17–20	830–950

ADMISSIONS ADVICE

Q: What can students who don't have the best grades do to improve their chances of getting into the college of their choice?

A: We encourage students to take the SAT I or ACT Assessment more than once and see how they do. There are options for students who may not meet the academic requirements because they've had to work or are gifted in other areas, such as art or athletics, or who perhaps have been through something tragic. We ask them to submit letters or recommendations, a personal statement, and any other documentation that might help support their cases. What were the factors that affected their grades? What else can they offer the university?

We often encourage students who still may not meet the requirements to start at a community college and then transfer. We'll look at their college credit vs. their high school credit. They can prove to us that they can handle a college curriculum.

Cheyenna Smith
Admission Counselor
University of Houston

Selection Index (used for National Merit Scholarship purposes)

- Verbal + Math + Writing
- Score Range: 60 to 240
- Mean Junior Score: 147

National Merit Scholarship Program

- Semifinalist Status: Selection Index of 201 to 222
- Commended Student: Selection Index of 199

SAT II SUBJECT TESTS

Subject Tests are required by some institutions for admission and/or placement in freshman-level courses. Each Subject Test measures one's knowledge of a specific subject and the ability to apply that knowledge. Students should check with each institution for its specific requirements. In general, students are required to take three Subject Tests (one English, one mathematics, and one of their choice).

Subject Tests are given in the following areas: biology, chemistry, Chinese, English language proficiency, French, German, Italian, Japanese, Korean, Latin, literature, mathematics, modern

Hebrew, physics, Spanish, U.S. history, world history, and writing. These tests are 1 hour long and are primarily multiple-choice tests. Three Subject Tests may be taken on one test date.

Scored like the SAT I, students gain a point for each correct answer and lose a fraction of a point for each incorrect answer. The raw scores are then converted to scaled scores that range from 200 to 800.

THE TOEFL TEST

The Test of English as a Foreign Language (TOEFL) is designed to help assess a student's grasp of English if it is not the student's first language. Performance on the TOEFL test may help interpret scores on the verbal section of the SAT I. The test consists of four sections: listening, structure, reading, and a writing section. The computer-based test and the paper-based test are given at more than 1,260 centers in 180 countries and are administered by Educational Testing Service (ETS). For further information, visit www.toefl.org.

WHAT OTHER TESTS SHOULD I KNOW ABOUT?

The AP Program

This program allows high school students to try college-level work and build valuable skills and study habits in the process. Subject matter is explored in more depth in AP courses than in other high school classes. A qualifying score on an AP test—which varies from school to school—can earn you college credit or advanced placement. Getting qualifying grades on enough exams can even earn you a full year's credit and sophomore standing at more than 1,400 higher-education institutions. There are currently thirty-four AP courses in nineteen different subject areas, including art, biology, and computer science. Speak to your guidance counselor for information about your school's offerings.

College-Level Examination Program (CLEP)

The CLEP enables students to earn college credit for what they already know, whether it was learned in school, through independent study, or through other experiences outside of the classroom. Approximately 2,900 colleges and universities now award credit for qualifying scores on one or more of the 34 CLEP exams. The exams, which are 90 minutes in length and are primarily multiple choice, are administered at participating colleges and universities. For more information, check out the Web site at www.collegeboard.com/clep.

Armed Services Vocational Aptitude Battery (ASVAB)

ASVAB is a career exploration program consisting of a multi-aptitude test battery that helps students explore their interests, abilities, and personal preferences. A career exploration workbook gives students information about the workplace, and a career information resource book helps students match their personal characteristics to the working world. Finally, an occupational outlook handbook describes in detail approximately 250 civilian and military occupations. Students can use ASVAB scores for military enlistment up to two years after they take the test. A student can take the ASVAB as a sophomore, junior, or senior, but students cannot use their sophomore scores to enter the armed forces. Ask your guidance counselor or your local recruiting office for more information. Also, see Chapter 11, "The Military Option."

General Educational Development (GED) Test

If you have not completed your high school education, you may earn an equivalence by taking the GED test, sponsored by your state Department of Education. However, taking the GED test is not a legitimate reason for dropping out of school. In fact, it is more difficult to get into the armed services with only a GED, and some employees have difficulty getting promoted without a high school diploma.

You're eligible to take the GED if you are not enrolled in high school, have not yet graduated from high school, are at least 16 years old, and meet your local requirements regarding age, residency, and length of time since leaving school.

There are five sections to the GED test, covering writing skills, social studies, science, interpreting literature and the arts, and mathematics. Part II of the Writing Skills Test requires writing an essay. The GED costs an average of $35 but can vary from state to state, and the application fee may be waived under certain circumstances. You should contact your local GED office to arrange to take the exam. Call 800-62-MYGED to find your local GED office and for more information.

WHAT CAN I DO TO PREPARE FOR THESE TESTS?

Know what to expect. Get familiar with how the tests are structured, how much time is allowed, and the directions for each type of question. Get plenty of rest the night before the test and eat breakfast that morning.

There are a variety of products, from books to software to videos, available to help you prepare for most standardized tests. Find the learning style that suits you best. As for which products to buy, there are two major categories—those created by the test makers and those created by private companies. The best approach is to talk to someone who has been through the process and find out which product or products he or she recommends.

Some students report significant increases in scores after participating in coaching programs. Longer-term programs (40 hours) seem to raise scores more than short-term programs (20 hours), but beyond 40 hours, score gains are minor. Math scores appear to benefit more from coaching than verbal scores.

Preparation Resources

There are a variety of ways to prepare for standardized tests—find a method that fits your schedule and your budget. But you should definitely prepare. Far too many students walk into these tests cold, either because they find standardized tests frightening or annoying or they just haven't found the time to study. The key is that these exams are standardized. That means these tests are largely the same from administration to administration; they always test the same concepts. They have to, or else you couldn't compare the scores of people who took the tests on different dates. The numbers or words may change, but the underlying content doesn't.

So how do you prepare? At the very least, you should review relevant material, such as math formulas and commonly tested vocabulary words, and know the directions for each question type or test section. You should take at least one practice test and review your mistakes so you don't make them again on test day. Beyond that, you know best how much preparation you need. You'll also find lots of material in libraries or bookstores to help you: books and software from the test makers and from other publishers (including Peterson's) or live courses that range from national test-preparation companies to teachers at your high school who offer classes. Peterson's new interactive and personalized SAT Online Course at www.petersonstestprep.com is another resource you'll want to check out.

THE TOP 10 WAYS *NOT* TO TAKE THE TEST

10. **Cramming the night before the test.**
9. **Not becoming familiar with the directions before you take the test.**
8. **Not becoming familiar with the format of the test before you take it.**
7. **Not knowing how the test is graded.**
6. **Spending too much time on any one question.**
5. **Not checking spelling, grammar, and sentence structure in essays.**
4. **Second-guessing yourself.**
3. **Forgetting to take a deep breath to keep from—**
2. **Losing It!**
1. **Writing a one-paragraph essay.**

THE COLLEGE SEARCH

Now that you have examined your interests, talents, wants, and needs in great detail, it's time to start investigating colleges.

THE BEST RESOURCES

There are thousands of colleges and universities in the United States, so before you start filling out applications, you need to narrow down your search. There are a number of sources that will help you do this.

WELCOME TO *CollegesWantYou!*

Is the traditional process of searching for colleges getting old—fast? Well stop looking for colleges and let them find you with *CollegesWantYou*ˢᴹ, the new-school approach to the search and selection process.

Unlike other college search and selection tools, *CollegesWantYou*ˢᴹ doesn't expect you to sort through page after page of generic college listings. Instead, enter information on your preferences, test scores, and extracurricular activites into the online form, and before you know it, colleges that meet your specifications will be in touch with you. And the best part is, you only need to enter your personal information once to connect with hundreds of colleges.

Save time. Keep your sanity. Get the information you need directly from colleges and universities across the country and take the next step in college search and selection. You can get to *CollegesWantYou*ˢᴹ by going to www.collegeswantyou.com.

Your Guidance Counselor

Your guidance counselor is your greatest asset in the college search process. He or she has access to a vast repository of information, from college bulletins and catalogs to financial aid applications. He or she knows how well graduates from your high school have performed at colleges across the country, and has probably even visited many of the colleges to get some first-hand knowledge about the places she has sent her students to. The more your guidance counselor sees you and learns about you, the easier it is for her to help you. So make sure you stop by her office often, whether it's to talk about your progress or just to say "hi."

Your Teachers

Use your teachers as resources, too. Many of them have had twenty to thirty years of experience in their field. They have taught thousands of students and watched them go off to college and careers. Teachers often stay in contact with graduates and know about their experiences in college and may be familiar with the schools you are interested in attending. Ask your teachers how they feel about the match between you and your choice schools and if they think you will be able to succeed in that environment.

Your Family

Your family needs to be an integral part of the college selection process, whether they are financing your education or not. They have opinions and valuable advice. Listen to them carefully. Try to take in all their information and see if it applies to you. Does it fit with who you are and what you want? What works and what doesn't work for you? Is some of what they say dated? How long ago were their experiences, and how relevant are they today? Take in the information, thank them for their concern, compare what they have said with the information you are gathering, and discard what doesn't fit.

Colleges and Universities

Don't forget to go to college fairs. Usually held in large cities in the evening, they are free and sponsored by your local guidance counselors' association and the National Association of College Admissions Counselors (NACAC). The admissions counselors of hundreds of colleges, vocational/career colleges, and universities attend college fairs each year. Whether your questions are as general as what the overall cost of education is at a particular institution or as specific as how many biology majors had works published last year, the admissions office works to assist you in locating the people who can answer your questions. Bring a shopping bag for all the information you will get.

Admissions officers also visit high schools. Don't forget to attend these meetings during your junior and senior years. In general, college admissions counselors come to a school to get a general sense of the high school and the caliber and personality of the student body. Although it is difficult to make an individual impression at these group sessions, the college counselors do take names on cards for later contact, and you will occasionally see them making notes on the cards when they are struck by an astute questioner. It is helpful to attend these sessions because consistent contact between a student and a college is tracked by colleges and universities. An admissions decision may come down to examining the size of your admissions folder and the number of interactions you have had with the school over time.

College and university brochures and catalogs are a good place to look, too. After reading a few, you will discover that some offer more objective information than others. You will also start to learn what information colleges think is essential to present. That's important. If a college's brochure does not present the same information as most of the other college brochures, you have to ask yourself why. What might this say about the college's academic offerings, athletic or extracurricular programs, or campus life? What does the campus look like? How is the campus environment presented in the brochure? The brochures should present clues to what schools feel are their important majors, what their mission is, and which departments they are spending their budgets on. Take the time to do these informational resources

PARENT PERSPECTIVE

Q: Now that you've been through the process of getting three of your children into college, what's your best advice for parents and teens?

A: Apply early and meet deadlines. Both of our older sons were sitting there after high school graduation wondering why they were on college waiting lists: "I have good grades. I can't figure it out." At eighteen, they don't see tomorrow, much less way down the line, but do you want to deal with their heartbreak at not getting into the college where they want to be? It's their future. It's hard because they're in their senior year and you want it to be fun for them. However, you see the reality out there that they will be facing for the rest of their lives. They don't want to look at it, but you have to keep bringing them back to it—not in a preachy way. If they start earlier than their senior year, it won't be as much of a shock when they become seniors.

Jeanette and Amedee Richard
San Antonio, Texas

justice. They have a great deal to say to the careful reader.

A college's Web site can give you a glimpse of campus life that does not appear in the college's brochure and catalog. It is true that the virtual tour will show you the shots that the college marketing department wants you to see, showing the campus in the best light, but you can use the home page to see other things, too. Read the student newspaper. Visit college-sponsored chat rooms. Go to the department in the major you are investigating. Look at the Course Bulletin to see what courses are required.

ONLINE HELP

To help you find two-year and four-year colleges or universities in your specific region, take a look at the Appendix in the back of this book for a listing of schools in each state of your region. Then check out the following online resources for additional information on college selection, scholarships, student information, and much more.

Peterson's Undergraduate Channel. Petersons.com provides information and tools that will help you prepare, search, and pay for college. You can search

CRITERIA TO CONSIDER

Depending on your personal interests, the following characteristics should play a role in helping you narrow down the field of colleges you are considering.

AFFILIATION
Public
Private, independent
Private, church affiliated
Proprietary

SIZE
Very small (fewer than 1,000 students)
Small (1,000–3,999 students)
Medium (4,000–8,999 students)
Large (9,000–19,999 students)
Very large (more than 20,000 students)

COMMUNITY
Rural
Small town
Suburban
Urban

LOCATION
In your hometown
Less than 3 hours from home
More than 3 hours from home

HOUSING
Dorm
Off-campus apartment
Home
Facilities and services for students with disabilities

STUDENT BODY
All male
All female
Coed
Minority representation
Primarily one religious denomination
Primarily full-time students
Primarily part-time students

Primarily commuter students
Primarily residential students

ACADEMIC ENVIRONMENT
Majors offered
Student-faculty ratio
Faculty teaching reputation
Instruction by professors versus teaching assistants
Facilities (such as classrooms and labs)
Libraries
Independent study available
International study available
Internships available

FINANCIAL AID
Scholarships
Grants
Loans
Work-study program
Part-time or full-time jobs

SUPPORT SERVICES
Academic counseling
Career/placement counseling
Personal counseling
Student health facilities

ACTIVITIES/SOCIAL CLUBS
Clubs, organizations
Greek life
Athletics, intramurals

ATHLETICS
Division I, II, or III
Sports offered
Scholarships available

SPECIALIZED PROGRAMS
Honors programs
Services for students with disabilities or special needs

for a school by name or location. In addition to college search and selection tools, the undergraduate channel on Petersons.com also offers tips on financial aid, test preparation, and online applications.

The National Association for College Admission Counseling. This home page offers information for professionals, students, and parents. The Internet address is www.nacac.com.

U.S. Department of Education. This federal agency's National Center for Education Statistics produces reports on every level of education, from elementary to postgraduate. Dozens are available for downloading. You can hook up with these and other links at www.ed.gov/index.jsp.

CAMPUS VISITS

You've heard the old saying, "A picture is worth a thousand words." Well, a campus visit is worth a thousand brochures. Nothing beats walking around a campus to get a feel for it. Some students report that all they needed to know that they loved or hated a campus was to drive through it. Then there is the true story of the guy who applied to a school because it had a prestigious name. Got accepted. Didn't visit, and when he arrived to move into the dorms, discovered to his horror it was an all-male school. A visit would have taken care of that problem.

The best time to experience the college environment is during the spring of your junior year or the fall of your senior year. Although you may have more time to visit colleges during your summer off, your observations will be more accurate when you can see the campus in full swing. Open houses are a good idea and provide you with opportunities to talk to students, faculty members, and administrators. Write or call in advance to take student-conducted campus tours. If possible, stay overnight in a dorm to see what living at the college is really like.

Bring your transcript so that you are prepared to interview with admission officers. Take this opportunity to ask questions about financial aid and other services that are available to students. You can get a good snapshot of campus life by reading a copy of the student newspaper. The final goal of the campus visit is to study the school's personality and decide if it matches yours. Your parents should be involved with the campus visits so that you can share your impressions. Here are some additional campus visit tips:

- Read campus literature prior to the visit.
- Ask for directions, and allow ample travel time.
- Make a list of questions before the visit.
- Dress in neat, clean, and casual clothes and shoes.
- Ask to meet one-on-one with a current student.

- ☑ Ask to meet personally with a professor in your area of interest.
- ☑ Ask to meet a coach or athlete in your area of interest.
- ☑ Offer a firm handshake.
- ☑ Use good posture.
- ☑ Listen, and take notes.
- ☑ Speak clearly, and maintain eye contact with people you meet.
- ☑ Don't interrupt.
- ☑ Be honest, direct, and polite.
- ☑ Be aware of factual information so that you can ask questions of comparison and evaluation.
- ☑ Be prepared to answer questions about yourself. Practice a mock interview with someone.
- ☑ Don't be shy about explaining your background and why you are interested in the school.
- ☑ Ask questions about the background and experiences of the people you meet.
- ☑ Convey your interest in getting involved in campus life.
- ☑ Be positive and energetic.
- ☑ Don't feel as though you have to talk the whole time or carry the conversation yourself.
- ☑ Relax, and enjoy yourself.
- ☑ Thank those you meet, and send thank-you notes when appropriate.

After you have made your college visits, use the "College Comparison Worksheet" on page 56 to rank the schools in which you're interested. This will help you decide not only which ones to apply to, but also which one to attend once you receive your acceptance letters.

THE COLLEGE INTERVIEW

Not all schools require or offer an interview. However, if you are offered an interview, use this one-on-one time to evaluate the college in detail and to sell yourself to the admission officer. The following list of questions can help you collect the information you may need to know.

WRITING TO A COLLEGE FOR INFORMATION

If neither you nor your guidance counselor has an application for a college that you are interested in, write a brief letter to the college admissions office to request an application.

Date

Your Name
Street Address
City, State, Zip

Office of Admission
Name of College
Street Address
City, State, Zip

To Whom It May Concern:

I am a (freshman, sophomore, junior, senior) at (name of your school) and plan to graduate in (month) (year).

Please send me the following information about your college: a general information brochure, program descriptions, an admission application, financial aid information, and any other information that might be helpful. I am considering _____ as my major field of study (optional, if you know your preferred field of study).

I am interested in visiting your campus, taking a campus tour, and meeting with an admission counselor and a financial aid officer. I would also like to meet with an adviser or professor in the (your preferred field of study) department, if possible. I will contact you in a week to set up a time that is convenient.

If you would like to contact me directly, I can be reached at (your phone number with area code and e-mail address). Thank you.

Sincerely,

(Signature)
Your Name

- ☑ How many students apply each year? How many are accepted?
- ☑ What are the average GPA and average ACT Assessment or SAT I score(s) for those accepted?
- ☑ How many students in last year's freshman class returned for their sophomore year?
- ☑ What is the school's procedure for credit for Advanced Placement high school courses?

(Continued on page 56)

THE MATCHING GAME Read each question and respond by circling Y (Yes), N (No), or C (Combination). Complete all the questions and return to the top. Highlight each action that coordinates with your answer, and then read it. Where you chose C, read both actions. Is there a pattern? Do the questions seem to lead to a certain type of college or university? Certain size? Certain location? Read the suggestions at the end of "The Matching Game" for more ideas.

Question	Yes/No/Combination	Action
1. Do I have a goal in life?	Y N C	**Y:** State it._____. **N:** Don't worry, many students start college without knowing what they want to do. Look into colleges that specialize in the arts and sciences.
2. Do I know what I want to achieve with a college diploma?	Y N C	**Y:** List specifically what your goals are. _____ **N:** Think about what college can offer you.
3. Do I want to broaden my knowledge?	Y N C	**Y:** Consider a liberal arts college. **N:** You might need to consider other options or educational opportunities.
4. Do I want specific training?	Y N C	**Y:** Investigate technical colleges or professional training programs in universities. **N:** You don't know what you want to study. Only 20 percent of seniors who apply to college are sure.
5. Am I looking for a balanced workload?	Y N C	**Y:** When you are visiting colleges, ask students about how they handle the work load. **N:** Check the work load carefully. If no one is on campus on a sunny day, it may not be the school for you
6. Am I self-directed enough to finish a four-year college program?	Y N C	**Y:** Consider only four-year colleges and universities. **N:** Maybe a two-year junior or community college is a better way to begin your college experience. Also consider a vocational/career college.
7. Do I know what I do well?	Y N C	**Y:** Identify majors related to your abilities. _____ **N:** Spend a little more time asking yourself questions about your interests. Speak to your counselor and do an interest inventory.
8. Do I like to spend time learning any one subject more than others?	Y N C	**Y:** List majors related to that area. _____ _____ **N:** Look at your high school courses. Which ones do you like better than others? _____
9. Do I know what matters to me and what my values are?	Y N C	**Y:** Look for the schools that talk about the values on their campus. Do the values confirm or conflict with your values? **N:** Values are less important to you, so places that really expound their values may seem confining to you.
10. Do I need to be in affluent surroundings?	Y N C	**Y:** Look at the schools that deliver that package. Check the small, private liberal arts colleges. **N:** How strong is your reaction against this setting? If it is strong, check larger, more diverse settings, like an urban school.
11. Am I going to college for the financial gains?	Y N C	**Y:** What majors are going to give you the payback you want? Look at business colleges and professional programs, like premed. **N:** If a big financial payback does not interest you, look at social service majors, like counseling, teaching, and social work.
12. Am I focused?	Y N C	**Y:** Search out the programs that will offer you the best options. **N:** Avoid those schools whose programs are not strong in your focused area.
13. Am I conservative in my views and behavior?	Y N C	**Y:** The political policies of schools are important. Look into them carefully. You might look at the schools in the Midwest or the South. **N:** If you're a liberal, look closely at the political climate. Check the schools in the Northeast and on the West Coast.

14. Do I need to be around people who are similar to me?

Y N C

Y: If you are African American, check the historically black colleges. If socioeconomic level or a certain look is important to you, study the student populations carefully during campus visits. If it is religious orientation you are interested in, look into religiously sponsored colleges and universities.
N: Look at large, midsize, and small universities in urban settings.

15. Are the name and prestige of the school important to me?

Y N C

Y: Look into the Ivies and the competitive schools to see if you are eligible and what they offer you. Broaden your search to include other colleges and compare their offerings to your specific needs and interests.
N: Don't exclude the well-known institutions if they fit in every other way.

16. Do I like sports?

Y N C

Y: Large universities with Division I teams will give you all the sports you need—as a competitor or a fan. If you do not want to compete at that level, check schools in other divisions. Look at the liberal arts colleges for athletes.
N: Look into smaller universities and liberal arts colleges with good teams.

17. Am I a techie?

Y N C

Y: Check for computer engineering courses at technical universities and large universities near research centers and major computer business areas. Ask about hardwiring, e-mail, and computer packages before you enroll.
N: It still helps to know what computer services are available where you enroll.

18. Do I need to live in or be near a city?

Y N C

Y: How close to a city do you need to be? In the city or an hour away? Do you still want a campus feel? Consider these questions as you visit campuses.
N: Do you need space, natural beauty, and peaceful surroundings to think? Look into small liberal arts schools in rural and suburban settings. Explore universities in the Midwest and South.

19. Will I need counseling for support?

Y N C

Y: Investigate the quality of student services and the mechanism for accessing them. Smaller schools often pride themselves on their services. Look at liberal arts colleges. Universities connected to medical centers often provide extensive services.
N: It is still good to know what is offered.

20. Do I need an environment in which questioning is important?

Y N C

Y: Liberal arts colleges, honors colleges, and smaller universities place an emphasis on academic inquiry.
N: You like to hear others discuss issues, gather as much information and opinions as you can, and think it over by yourself. Try the university setting.

Suggestions

Here are some ideas for you to consider based on the way you answered the questions.

1. If you answered *no* to numbers 2 and 3, why not investigate apprenticeships, vocational/career colleges, armed services options, and certification or two-year college programs?

2. If you answered *yes* to numbers 4, 11, and 17, technical or professional colleges and universities with hands-on training may give you the education you want.

3. If you answered *yes* to numbers 9, 10, and 20, you are leaning toward a liberal arts setting.

4. If you answered *yes* to numbers 5 and 6, examine the competitive and Ivy League colleges.

5. If you answered *no* to numbers 9, 10, 14, and 20 and yes to 16, 17, and 18, larger universities may offer you the best options.

Once you have completed your self-evaluation, made a decision whether college is for you, have some ideas about your personality and likes and dislikes, and can relate them to the different personalities of colleges, it is time to gather information. It needs to be quality information from the right sources. The quality of information you put into your search now will determine whether your list of colleges will represent a good or a bad match.

As a freshman, will I be taught by professors or teaching assistants?

How many students are there per teacher?

When is it necessary to declare a major?

Is it possible to have a double major or to declare a major and a minor?

What are the requirements for the major in which I am interested?

How does the advising system work?

Does this college offer study abroad, cooperative programs, or academic honors programs?

What is the likelihood, due to overcrowding, of getting closed out of the courses I need?

What technology is available, and what are any associated fees?

How well equipped are the libraries and laboratories?

Are internships available?

How effective is the job placement service of the school?

What is the average class size in my area of interest?

Have any professors in my area of interest recently won any honors or awards?

What teaching methods are used in my area of interest (lecture, group discussion, fieldwork)?

How many students graduate in four years in my area of interest?

What are the special requirements for graduation in my area of interest?

What is the student body like? Age? Sex? Race? Geographic origin?

What percentage of students live in dormitories? Off-campus housing?

What percentage of students go home for the weekend?

COLLEGE COMPARISON WORKSHEET

Fill in your top five selection criteria and any others that may be of importance to you. Once you narrow your search of colleges to five, fill in the colleges across the top row. Using a scale of 1 to 5, where 1 is poor and 5 is excellent, rate each college by your criteria. Total each column to see which college rates the highest based upon your criteria.

SELECTION CRITERIA	COLLEGE 1	COLLEGE 2	COLLEGE 3	COLLEGE 4	COLLEGE 5
1.					
2.					
3.					
4.					
5.					
OTHER CRITERIA					
6.					
7.					
8.					
9.					
10.					
TOTAL					

Sample criteria (Use this list as a starting point—there may be other criteria important to you not listed here.): Arts facilities, athletic facilities, audiovisual center, campus setting, class size, classrooms/lecture halls, computer labs, dining hall, dorms, financial aid, fraternity/sorority houses, majors offered, religious facilities, professor profiles, student-faculty ratio, student profile, student union, surrounding community.

- What are some of the regulations that apply to living in a dormitory?
- What are the security precautions taken on campus and in the dorms?
- Is the surrounding community safe?
- Are there problems with drug and alcohol abuse on campus?
- Do faculty members and students mix on an informal basis?
- How important are the arts to student life?
- What facilities are available for cultural events?
- How important are sports to student life?
- What facilities are available for sporting events?
- What percentage of the student body belongs to a sorority/fraternity?
- What is the relationship between those who belong to the Greek system and those who don't?
- Are students involved in the decision-making process at the college? Do they sit on major committees?
- In what other activities can students get involved?
- What percentage of students receive financial aid based on need?
- What percentage of students receive scholarships based on academic ability?
- What percentage of a typical financial aid offer is in the form of a loan?
- If my family demonstrates financial need on the FAFSA (and PROFILE®, if applicable), what percentage of the established need is generally awarded?
- How much did the college increase the cost of room, board, tuition, and fees from last year?
- Do opportunities for financial aid, scholarships, or work-study increase each year?
- When is the admission application deadline?
- When is the financial aid application deadline?
- When will I be notified of the admission decision?
- If there is a deposit required, is it refundable?

Keep in mind that you don't need to ask all these questions—in fact, some of them may have already been answered for you in the catalog, on the Web site, or in the interview. Ask only the questions for which you still need answers.

SHOULD YOU HEAD FOR THE IVY LEAGUES?

Determining whether to apply to one of the eight Ivy League schools is something you should think long and hard about. Sure, it can't hurt to toss your application into the ring if you can afford the application fee and the time you'll spend writing the essays. But if you want to figure out if you'd be a legitimate candidate for acceptance at one of these top-tier schools, you should understand the type of student that they look for and how you compare, says John Machulsky, a guidance counselor at Lawrence High School in New Jersey. Take a look at these statistics:

- Only 30 percent or fewer applicants are accepted at these highly competitive colleges each year.
- Most Ivy League students have placed in the top 10 percent of their class and have SAT I scores in the 700 levels for math and verbal each or ACT Assessment scores of 29 or higher.

- Because Ivy League schools are so selective, they want a diverse student population. That means they want students that represent not only the fifty states but also a wide selection of other countries.

Lirio Jimenez, a guidance counselor at New Brunswick High School in New Jersey, says that being accepted by an Ivy League school is a process that starts early in the ninth grade. You should select demanding courses and maintain good grades in those courses throughout all four years of high school. Get involved in extracurricular activities as well, and, of course, do well on your standardized tests. When it comes time to apply for college, select at least three schools: one ideal, one possible, and one shoe-in. Your ideal can be an Ivy League if you wish.

Get A Jump! certainly doesn't want to discourage you from applying to one of these prestigious schools. We're in your corner and want to see you get the best education possible. However, students are sometimes more concerned about getting accepted than with taking a hard look at what a school has to offer them. Often, a university or college that is less competitive than an Ivy League may have exactly what you need to succeed in the future. Keep that in mind as you select the colleges that will offer you what you need.

STUDENT COUNSEL

Q: **What made you choose to apply to an Ivy League school?**

A: **My mother recommended that I apply to Princeton. She said, "Why not just try? What do you have to lose? All they can tell you is no." I was afraid of being rejected. I wasn't a straight-A student, and I thought they weren't going to want me—they get thousands of applications. Through the whole college process I had a whole lot of self-doubt. Looking back, I realize that you won't know if you don't try. Take the chance and fill out the application. If you don't get in, it doesn't mean you're less intelligent. It just wasn't the correct fit.**

Zoelene Hill
Princeton University

MINORITY STUDENTS GO TO COLLEGE

African-American, Hispanic, Asian-American, and Native-American high school students have a lot of doors into higher education opening for them. In fact, most colleges want to respond to the social and economic disadvantages of certain groups of Americans. They want to reflect the globalization of our economy. They want their student populations to look like the rest of America, which means people from many different backgrounds and ethnic groups. This isn't just talk either. You'll find that most colleges have at least one member of the admissions staff who specializes in recruiting minorities.

One of the reasons college admissions staff are recruiting minorities and want to accommodate their needs is because there are more minorities thinking of attending college—and graduating. Let's put some numbers to these statements. According to the Department of Education, in 1976, 16 percent of college students were minorities, compared to 27 percent in 1997. Much of the change can be attributed to rising numbers of Hispanic and Asian students. The proportion of Asian and Pacific Islander students rose from 2 percent to 6 percent, and the Hispanic proportion rose from 4 percent to 9 percent during that same time period. The proportion of African-American students fluctuated during most of the early part of the period before rising slightly to 11 percent in 1997, the last year for which data was collected on this subject.

Get a Jump! has a lot of information in this section to help you make decisions about college and paying for college. Perhaps the most important information we can give you is that if you want to go to college, you can. There are a lot of organizations ready to assist you. So go for it. See the list of organizations in this section and check with the colleges in which you're interested to connect with the minority affairs office.

Academic Resources for Minority Students

In addition to churches, sororities and fraternities, and college minority affairs offices, minority students can

SHOULD YOU ATTEND A HISTORICALLY BLACK COLLEGE OR UNIVERSITY?

Choosing which college to attend is usually a difficult decision for anyone to make, but when an African-American student is considering attending a historically black college or university (HBCU), a whole other set of family and cultural issues are raised.

There are many valid reasons that favor one or the other. Some are obvious differences. Parents and their children have to be honest with themselves and take a long, hard look at the needs of the student and how the campus environment can fulfill them. To help you decide, here are some questions to ask:

DO I KNOW WHAT'S REALLY IMPORTANT TO ME?

Look at the reasons why you want a degree and what you want to achieve with it. Is the choice to attend an HBCU yours or your family's? Do you have a particular field of study you want to pursue? Sometimes students can get so caught up in applying to a particular institution, they don't realize it doesn't even offer their major.

HOW WILL THIS CAMPUS FIT MY PLANS FOR THE FUTURE?

There's no substitute for doing your homework about the campuses you're seriously considering. Know the reputation of those campuses in the community and among employers and the general population. Find out about student retention, graduation, and placement rates.

DOES THIS CAMPUS HAVE THE FACILITIES AND LIVING CONDITIONS THAT SUIT MY COMFORT LEVEL?

Finding a campus where you're comfortable is a big factor in choosing a college. What do you want in campus facilities and living conditions? For instance, if you currently attend a small private high school in a suburban setting, perhaps you wouldn't like living on a large urban campus with peers who don't mirror your kind of background.

WHAT LEVEL OF SUPPORT WILL I GET ON CAMPUS?

Students considering institutions where few people are like them should look at the available support systems and organizations that will be available to them. Parents need to feel comfortable with the contact person on campus.

When all the factors that determine the choice of a college are laid out, the bottom line is which institution best meets your needs. For some African-American students, an HBCU is the best choice. For others, it's not. African-American students reflect many backgrounds, and there is no single decision that will be right for everyone.

receive information and assistance from the following organizations:

ASPIRA

ASPIRA's mission is to empower the Puerto Rican and Latino community through advocacy and the education and leadership development of its youth.

1444 Eye Street, NW, Suite 800
Washington, D.C. 20005
202-835-3600
www.aspira.org

INROADS

A national career-development organization that places and develops talented minority youth (African American, Hispanic American, and Native American) in business and industry.

10 South Broadway, Suite 700
St. Louis, Missouri 63102
314-241-7488
www.inroads.org

National Action Council for Minorities in Engineering (NACME)

An organization that aims to provide leadership and support for the national effort to increase the representation of successful African-American, American Indian, and Latino women and men in engineering and technology, math- and science-based careers.

350 Fifth Avenue, Suite 2212
New York, New York 10118-2299
212-279-2626
www.nacme.org

National Association for the Advancement of Colored People (NAACP)

The purpose of the NAACP is to improve the political, educational, social, and economic status of minority groups; to eliminate racial prejudice; to keep the public aware of the adverse effects of racial discrimination; and to take lawful action to secure its elimination, consistent with the efforts of the national organization.

4805 Mt. Hope Drive
Baltimore, Maryland 21215
877-NAACP-98 (toll-free)
www.naacp.org

STUDENT COUNSEL

Q: How did you make the decision to attend a historically black college or university?

A: Selecting a college was one of the hardest decisions I've ever had to make. As a recipient of the National Achievement Scholarship and a National History Day winner, I was offered scholarships to a number of colleges across the country, including many HCBUs. I tried to figure out which institution would be able to give me the most help in achieving my goals. I finally decided on Florida A&M University (FAMU) in my hometown of Tallahassee.

There are many pluses to attending college in my hometown. By living on campus, I have the freedom to make my own decisions and live as a young adult while being close to the loving support of my parents. Also, FAMU will help me succeed in my objective of obtaining a bachelor's degree in broadcast journalism. As I look back, I am glad that I, unlike some of my other high school peers, did not rush to judgment during the process of choosing a college. I am very happy with my decision.

Larry Rivers
Florida A&M University

The National Urban League

The Campaign for African-American Achievement of the National Urban League provides services for African Americans and economically disadvantaged people. These services include basic academic development, GED test preparation for youths and adults, after-school tutoring for children, parent training classes, scholarships, an annual tour of historically black colleges and universities, and summer employment for youths.

> 120 Wall Street
> New York, New York 10005
> 212-558-5300
> www.nul.org

United Negro College Fund (UNCF)

The UNCF serves to enhance the quality of education by raising operating funds for its 39 member colleges and universities, providing financial assistance to deserving students, and increasing access to technology for students and faculty at historically black colleges and universities.

> 8260 Willow Oaks Corporate Drive
> Fairfax, Virginia 22031-8044
> 800-331-2244 (toll-free)
> www.uncf.org

The American Indian Higher Education Consortium (AIHEC)

AIHEC's mission is to support the work of tribal colleges and the national movement for tribal self-determination through four objectives: maintain commonly held standards of quality in American Indian education; support the development of new tribally controlled colleges; promote and assist in the development of legislation to support American Indian higher education; and encourage greater participation by American Indians in the development of higher education policy.

> 121 Oronoco Street
> Alexandria, Virginia 22314
> 703-838-0400
> www.aihec.org

The Gates Millennium Scholars (GMS)

The Gates Millennium Scholars, funded by a grant from the Bill & Melinda Gates Foundation, was established in 1999 to provide outstanding African-American, American-Indian/Alaska Natives, Asian-Pacific Islander Americans, and Hispanic-American students with an opportunity to complete an undergraduate college education in all discipline areas and a graduate education for those students pursuing studies in mathematics, science, engineering, education, or library science. The goal of GMS is to promote academic excellence and to provide an opportunity for thousands of outstanding students with significant financial need to reach their fullest potential.

> P.O. Box 10500
> Fairfax, Virginia 22031-8044
> 877-690-4677 (toll-free)
> www.gmsp.org/flash.htm

Hispanic Association of Colleges and Universities (HACU)

The Hispanic Association of Colleges and Universities is a national association representing the accredited colleges and universities in the United

States where Hispanic students constitute at least 25 percent of the total student enrollment. HACU's goal is to bring together colleges and universities, corporations, government agencies, and individuals to establish partnerships for promoting the developing Hispanic-serving colleges and universities; improving access to and the quality of postsecondary educational for Hispanic students; and meeting the needs of business, industry, and government through the development and sharing of resources, information, and expertise.

4204 Gardendale Street, Suite 216
San Antonio, Texas 78229
512- 692-3805
www.buscapique.com/latinusa/buscafile/sud/hacu.htm

Hispanic Scholarship Fund (HSF)

The Hispanic Scholarship Fund is the nation's leading organization supporting Hispanic higher education. HSF was founded in 1975 with a vision to strengthen the country by advancing college education among Hispanic Americans. In support of its mission, HSF provides the Latino community with college scholarships and educational outreach support.

55 Second Street, Suite 1500
San Francisco, California
877-473-463 (toll-free)
www.hsf.net/about/index.htm

STUDENTS WITH DISABILITIES GO TO COLLEGE

The Americans with Disabilities Act (ADA) requires educational institutions at all levels, public and private, to provide equal access to programs, services, and facilities. Schools must be accessible to students, as well as to employees and the public, regardless of any disability. To ensure such accessibility, they must follow specific requirements for new construction, alterations or renovations, academic programs, and institutional policies, practices, and procedures. Students with specific disabilities have the right to request and expect accommodations, including auxiliary aids and services that enable them to participate in and benefit from all programs and activities offered by or related to a school.

TIPS FOR STUDENTS WITH DISABILITIES

- Document your disability with letters from your physician(s), therapist, case manager, school psychologist, and other service providers.
- Get letters of support from teachers, family, friends, and service providers that detail how you have succeeded despite your disability.
- Learn the federal laws that apply to students with disabilities.
- Research support groups for peer information and advocacy.
- Visit several campuses.
- Look into the services available, the pace of campus life, and the college's programs for students with disabilities.
- Ask about orientation programs, including specialized introductions for or about students with disabilities.
- Ask about flexible, individualized study plans.
- Ask if the school offers technology such as voice synthesizers, voice recognition, and/or visual learning equipment to its students.
- Ask about adapted intramural/social activities.
- Ask to talk with students who have similar disabilities to hear about their experiences on campus.
- Once you select a college, get a map of the campus and learn the entire layout.
- If you have a physical disability, make sure the buildings you need to be in are accessible to you. Some, even though they comply with the ADA, aren't as accessible as others.
- Be realistic. If you use a wheelchair, for example, a school with an exceptionally hilly campus may not be your best choice, no matter what other accommodations it has.

To comply with ADA requirements, many high schools and universities offer programs and information to answer questions for students with disabilities and to assist them both in selecting appropriate colleges and in attaining full inclusion once they enter college. And most colleges and universities have disabilities services offices to help students negotiate the system. When it comes time to apply to colleges, write to the ones that you're interested in to find out what kinds of programs they have in place. When it comes time to narrow down your choices, make a request for a visit.

What Is Considered a Disability?

A person is considered to have a disability if he or she meets at least one of three conditions. The individual must:

1. have a documented physical or mental impairment that substantially limits one or more major life activities, such as personal self-care, walking, seeing, hearing, speaking, breathing, learning, working, or performing manual tasks;

2. have a record of such an impairment; or

3. be perceived as having such an impairment.

Physical disabilities include impairments of speech, vision, hearing, and mobility. Other disabilities, while less obvious, are similarly limiting; they include diabetes, asthma, multiple sclerosis, heart disease, cancer, mental illness, mental retardation, cerebral palsy, and learning disabilities.

Learning disabilities refer to an array of biological conditions that impede a person's ability to process and disseminate information. A learning disability is commonly recognized as a significant deficiency in one or more of the following areas: oral expression, listening comprehension, written expression, basic reading skills, reading comprehension, mathematical calculation, or problem solving. Individuals with learning disabilities also may have difficulty with sustained attention, time management, or social skills.

If you have a disability, you will take the same steps to choose and apply to a college as other students, but you should also evaluate each college based on your special need(s). Get organized, and meet with campus specialists to discuss your specific requirements. Then, explore whether the programs, policies, procedures, and facilities meet your specific situation.

It is usually best to describe your disability in a letter attached to the application so the proper fit can be made between you and the school. You will probably need to have your psychoeducational evaluation and testing record sent to the school. Some colleges help with schedules and offer transition courses, reduced course loads, extra access to professors, and special study areas to help address your needs.

Remember, admission to college is a realistic goal for any motivated student. If you invest the time and effort, you can make it happen.

STUDENT COUNSEL

The following quotes are from students who attend a college that offers services for learning disabled students.

"I have delayed development. I need help getting things done, and I need extra time for tests. As long as I'm able to go up to teachers and ask questions, I do well on tests."

—Anita

"I have dyslexia. I thought the term 'disabilities services' was for people with visual and hearing impairments. But when I got here, I found it covered a variety of disabilities. It was like Christmas. You got everything you wanted and more."

—Debra

"I am hard of hearing. I was always afraid I wouldn't be able to hear what [teachers] said. It's hard to read lips and listen at the same time. With note takers, I still get what I need even if the teacher moves around. They want you to make it through."

—Jeannette

DIRECTORY FOR STUDENTS WITH DISABILITIES

The following resources can help students, families, and schools with the legal requirements for accommodating disabilities. They can also link you with other groups and individuals that are knowledgeable in students' rights and the process of transition into postsecondary education.

Also, there are special interest, education, support, and advocacy organizations for persons with particular disabilities. Check with your counselor or contact one of the following organizations for information:

ACT Assessment Administration

Special Testing
2255 North Aubuque Road
P.O. Box 4028
Iowa City, Iowa 52243
319-337-1332
www.act.org

Association on Higher Education and Disability (AHEAD)

AHEAD
P.O. Box 540666
Waltham, Massachusetts 02454
781-788-0003
www.ahead.org

Attention Deficit Disorder Association (ADDA)

1788 Second Street, Suite 200
Highland Park, Illinois 60035
847-432-ADDA
www.add.org

Children and Adults with Attention-Deficit/ Hyperactivity Disorders (CHADD)

8181 Professional Place,
Suite 150
Landover, Maryland 20785
800-233-4050 (toll-free)
www.chadd.org

ERIC Clearing House on Disabilities and Gifted Education

1110 North Glebe Road
Arlington, Virginia 22201-5704
800-328-0272 (toll-free)
www.ericec.org

Council for Learning Disabilities

CLD
P.O. Box 4014
Leesburg, Virginia 20177
www.cldinternational.org

HEATH Resource Center National Clearinghouse on Postsecondary Education for Individuals with Disabilities

HEATH
The George Washington University
HEATH Resource Center
2121 K Street, NW, Suite 220
Washington, D.C. 20037
800-544-3284 (toll-free)
www.heath.gwu.edu

International Dyslexia Association

The Chester Building
8600 LaSalle Road
Baltimore, Maryland 21286-2044
800-222-3123 (toll-free)
www.interdys.org

Learning Disabilities Association of America (LDA)

4156 Library Road
Pittsburgh, Pennsylvania 15234
412-341-1515
www.ldanatl.org

National Center for Learning Disabilities (NCLD)

381 Park Avenue South,
Suite 1401
New York, New York 10016
888-575-7373 (toll-free)
www.ncld.org

National Information Center for Children and Youth with Disabilities

P.O. Box 1492
Washington, D.C. 20013
800-695-0285 (toll-free)
www.nichcy.org

Recording for the Blind & Dyslexic

20 Roszel Road
Princeton, New Jersey 08540
866-RFBD-585
www.rfbd.org

SAT Services for Students with Disabilities

The College Board Services for Students with Disabilities
P.O. Box 6226
Princeton, New Jersey 08541-6226
609-771-7137
www.collegeboard.com

7 Chapter

APPLYING TO COLLEGE

The big moment has arrived. It's time to make some decisions about where you want to apply.

ONCE YOUR LIST IS FINALIZED, the worst part is filling out all the forms accurately and getting them in by the deadlines. Because requirements differ, you should check with all the colleges that you are interested in attending to find out what documentation is needed and when it is due.

WHAT SCHOOLS LOOK FOR IN PROSPECTIVE STUDENTS

As if you were sizing up the other team to plan your game strategy, you'll need to understand what admissions committees want from you as you assemble all the pieces of your application.

Academic record: Admission representatives look at the breadth (how many), diversity (which ones), and difficulty (how challenging) of the courses on your transcript.

Grades: You should show consistency in your ability to work to your potential. If your grades are not initially good, colleges look to see that significant improvement has been made. Some colleges have minimum grade point averages that they are willing to accept.

Class rank: Colleges may consider the academic standing of a student in relation to the other members of his or her class. Are you in the top 25 percent of your class? Top half? Ask your counselor for your class rank.

Standardized test scores: Colleges look at test scores in terms of ranges. If your scores aren't high but you did well academically in high school, you shouldn't be discouraged. There is no set formula for admission. Even at the most competitive schools, some students' test scores are lower than you would think.

Extracurricular activities: Colleges look for depth of involvement (variety and how long you participated), initiative (leadership), and creativity demonstrated in activities, service, or work.

Recommendations: Most colleges require a recommendation from your high school guidance counselor. Some ask for references from teachers or other adults. If your counselor or teachers don't know you well, you should put together a student resume, or brag sheet, that outlines what you have done during

PARENT PERSPECTIVE

Q: How did you help your daughter get into college?

A: The key is to start early, like in the junior year. We didn't do that. At this point in the fall of our daughter's senior year, deadlines are coming up, and we haven't really looked at any colleges yet or gone on visits. It's kind of like choosing a house to buy without going to the house. The parent's role is to ask a lot of questions to get your child to figure out exactly what it is he or she wants to do. It's a big decision.

We hired a financial aid consultant who is helping us look at different colleges. The biggest worry is the FAFSA form. If you get it wrong, and they send it back to you—you have to start all over again. In the meantime, you're behind and others are getting grants. The whole process is very confusing, and there's no one to walk you through it. We've looked at different colleges on the Internet, and college fairs are a good resource. Plus, our daughter has done a lot on her own.

Doug and Judy Ames
Colorado Springs, Colorado

your four years of high school. In this chapter, you'll find a worksheet that will help you put together your resume.

College interview: Required by most colleges with highly selective procedures. For further information, see "The College Interview" in the previous chapter.

ADMISSION PROCEDURES

Your first task in applying is to get application forms. That's easy. You can get them from your high school's guidance department, at college fairs, or by calling or writing to colleges and requesting applications. (See "Writing to a College for Information" in the previous chapter.) The trend, however, is leaning toward online applications, which you can do at the school's Web site. Admission information can also be gathered from college representatives, catalogs, Web sites, and directories; alumni or students attending the college; and campus visits. Take a look at "Do's and Don'ts for Filling out Your Applications" on page 70 for some guidelines.

Which Admissions Option Is Best for You?

One of the first questions you will be asked on applications for four-year colleges and universities is which admission option you want. What they're talking about is whether you want to apply early action, early decision, deferred admission, etc.

Four-year institutions generally offer the following admissions options:

Early admission: A student of superior ability is admitted into college courses and programs before completing high school.

Early decision: A student declares a first-choice college, requests that the college decide on acceptance early (between November and January), and agrees to enroll if accepted. Students with a strong high school record who are sure they want to attend a certain school should consider early decision admission. (See "More on Early Decision," on the next page.)

PARENT PERSPECTIVE

Q: What can parents do to help their children make decisions about colleges?

A: Parents and teens should visit college campuses early and trust their gut feelings about whether the campus feels right. Above all, don't be blinded by name-brand colleges and the strong peer pressure that seems to steer your teen in the direction of prestigious colleges. Just as in shopping for clothing: Would you rather have a name brand or something that fits you well and makes you feel comfortable?

Ask your teen some questions. Do you really want to live in a pressure-cooker for the next four years? Some students thrive in a highly competitive environment, but many do not—even if they are excellent students. Before making a final decision, a teen should spend three or four days at the two colleges that interest him or her the most.

Senior year in high school is a time when teens go through many changes and experiment with many different roles. This can be bewildering to parents. Be patient. Realize that the time is equally bewildering to your son or daughter. Parents can be supportive and understanding, even though their teen may seem to be pushing them away. Offer guidance about choosing the right college, even though your teen might seem to be rejecting it. Teens hear everything, though they might not show it.

Marilyn Wedge, Ph.D.
Parent, family therapist, and educational consultant
Agoura Hills, California

Early action: Similar to early decision, but if a student is accepted, he or she has until the regular admission deadline to decide whether or not to attend.

Early evaluation: A student can apply under early evaluation to find out if the chance of acceptance is good, fair, or poor. Applications are due before the regular admission deadline, and the student is given an opinion between January and March.

Regular admission: This is the most common option offered to students. A deadline is set when all applications must be received, and all notifications are sent out at the same time.

Rolling admission: The college accepts students who meet the academic requirements on a first-come, first-served basis until it fills its freshman class. No strict application deadline is specified. Applications are reviewed and decisions are made immediately (usually within two to three weeks). This method is commonly used at large state universities, so students should apply early for the best chance of acceptance.

Open admission: Virtually all high school graduates are admitted, regardless of academic qualifications.

Deferred admission: An accepted student is allowed to postpone enrollment for a year.

If you're going to a two-year college, these options apply to you. Two-year colleges usually have an "open-door" admission policy, which means that high school graduates may enroll as long as space is available. Sometimes vocational/career colleges are somewhat selective, and competition for admission may be fairly intense for programs that are highly specialized.

More on Early Decision

Early decision is a legally binding agreement between you and the college. If the college accepts you, you pay a deposit within a short period of time and sign an agreement stating that you will not apply to other colleges. To keep students from backing out, some colleges mandate that applicants' high school counselors cannot send transcripts to other institutions.

STUDENT COUNSEL

Q: **What made you want to apply to college early decision?**

A: I visited lots of schools in Pennsylvania, but the minute I walked on the campus at Gettysburg, I knew I wanted to come here. I liked the way the campus was set up. It was small, and everything was together. The student-teacher ratio was low, and it had a good political science program. It had everything that I wanted.

But if you want to go early decision, you have to visit the schools to be able to compare and contrast the different campuses. Many of the schools will have the same things, like small class size, but the way you feel about the campus is the largest factor because that's where you will be living. I visited Gettysburg four times, so when I went early decision, I was confident about it. I realized it was a huge step and knew I had to be sure. But after visiting here so many times, I knew I'd be unhappy anywhere else.

Kelly Keegan
Gettysburg College

In many ways, early decision is a win-win for both students and colleges. Students can relax and enjoy their senior year of high school without waiting to see if other colleges have accepted them. And colleges know early in the year who is enrolled and can start planning the coming year.

When Is Early Decision the Right Decision?

For good and bad reasons, early decision is a growing trend, so why not just do it? Early decision is an excellent idea that comes with a warning. It's not a good idea unless you have done a thorough college search and know without a shred of doubt that this is the college for you. Don't go for early decision unless you've spent time on the campus, in classes and dorms, and you have a true sense of the academic and social climate of that college.

Early decision can get sticky if you change your mind. Parents of students who have signed agreements and then want to apply elsewhere get angry at high school counselors, saying they've taken away their rights to choose among colleges. They try to force them to send out transcripts even though their children have committed to one college. To guard against this scenario, some colleges ask parents and students to sign a statement signifying their understanding that early decision is a binding plan. Even some high schools now have their own form for students and parents to sign acknowledging that they completely realize the nature of an early decision agreement.

The Financial Reason Against Early Decision

Another common argument against early decision is that if an institution has you locked in, there's no incentive to offer applicants the best financial packages. The consensus seems to be that if you're looking to play the financial game, don't apply for early decision.

However, some folks argue that the best financial aid offers are usually made to attractive applicants. In general, if a student receives an early decision offer, they fall into that category and so would get "the sweetest" financial aid anyway. That doesn't mean that there aren't colleges out there using financial incentives to get students to enroll. A strong candidate who applies to six or eight schools and gets admitted to them all will look at how much money the colleges throw his or her way before making a decision.

Before You Decide...

If you're thinking about applying for early decision at a college, ask yourself these questions first. You'll be glad you did.

- Why am I applying early decision?
- Have I thoroughly researched several colleges and know what my options are?
- Do I know why I'm going to college and what I want to accomplish there?
- Have I visited several schools, spent time in classes, stayed overnight, and talked to professors?
- Do the courses that the college offers match my goals?
- Am I absolutely convinced that one college clearly stands out above all others?

MORE MUMBO JUMBO

Besides confusing terms like deferred admission, early decision, and early evaluation, just discussed, you'll most likely stumble upon some additional terms that might bamboozle you. Here, we explain a few more:

Academic Calendar

Traditional semesters: Two equal periods of time during a school year.

Early semester: Two equal periods of time during a school year. The first semester is completed before Christmas.

Trimester: Calendar year divided into three equal periods of time. The third trimester replaces summer school.

Quarter: Four equal periods of time during a school year.

4-1-4: Two equal terms of about four months separated by a one-month term.

Accreditation

Accreditation is recognition of a college or university by a regional or national organization, which indicates that the institution has met its objectives and is maintaining prescribed educational standards. Colleges may be accredited by one of six regional associations of schools and colleges and by any one of many national specialized accrediting bodies.

Specialized accreditation of individual programs is granted by national professional organizations. This is intended to ensure that specific programs meet or exceed minimum requirements established by the professional organization. States may require that students in some professions that grant licenses graduate from an accredited program as one qualification for licensure.

Accreditation is somewhat like receiving a pass/fail grade. It doesn't differentiate colleges and universities that excel from those that meet minimum requirements. Accreditation applies to all programs within an institution, but it does not mean that all programs are of equal quality within an institution. Accreditation does not guarantee transfer recognition by other colleges. Transfer decisions are made by individual institutions.

Affiliation

Not-for-profit colleges are classified into one of the following categories: state-assisted, private/independent, or private/church-supported. The institution's affiliation does not guarantee the quality or nature of the institution, and it may or may not have an effect on the religious life of students.

State-assisted colleges and universities and private/independent colleges do not have requirements related to the religious activity of their students. The influence of religion varies among private/church-supported colleges. At some, religious services or study are encouraged or required; at others, religious affiliation is less apparent.

Articulation Agreement

Articulation agreements facilitate the transfer of students and credits among state-assisted institutions of higher education by establishing transfer procedures and equitable treatment of all students in the system.

One type of articulation agreement links two or more colleges so that students can continue to make progress toward their degree, even if they must attend different schools at different times. For example, some states' community colleges have agreements with their universities that permit graduates of college parallel programs to transfer with junior standing.

A second type of articulation agreement links secondary (high school) and postsecondary institutions to allow students to gain college credit for relevant vocational courses. This type of agreement saves students time and tuition in the pursuit of higher learning.

Because articulation agreements vary from school to school and from program to program, it is recommended that students check with their home institution and the institution they are interested in attending in order to fully understand the options available to them and each institution's specific requirements.

Cross-Registration

Cross-registration is a cooperative arrangement offered by many colleges and universities for the purpose of increasing the number and types of courses offered at any one institution. This arrangement allows students to cross-register for one or more courses at any participating host institution. While specific cross-registration program requirements may vary, typically a student can cross-register without having to pay the host institution additional tuition.

If your college participates in cross-registration, check with your home institution concerning any additional tuition costs and request a cross-registration

form. Check with your adviser and registrar at your home institution to make sure that the course you plan to take is approved, and then contact the host institution for cross-registration instructions. Make sure that there is space available in the course you want to take at the host institution, as some host institutions give their own students registration priority.

To participate in cross-registration, you may need to be a full-time student (some programs allow part-time student participation) in good academic and financial standing at your home institution. Check with both colleges well in advance for all of the specific requirements.

THE COMPLETE APPLICATION PACKAGE

Freshman applications can be filed any time after you have completed your junior year of high school. Colleges strongly recommend that students apply by April (at the latest) of their senior year in order to be considered for acceptance, scholarships, financial aid, and housing. College requirements may vary, so always read and comply with specific requirements. In general, admission officers are interested in the following basic materials:

- A completed and signed application and any required application fee.

- An official copy of your high school transcript, including your class ranking and grade point average. The transcript must include all work completed as of the date the application is submitted. Check with your guidance counselor for questions about these items. If you apply on line, you must inform your guidance counselor and request that he or she send your transcript to the schools to which you are applying. Your application will not be processed without a transcript.

- An official record of your ACT Assessment or SAT I scores.

- Other items that may be required include letters of recommendation, an essay, the

(Continued on page 70)

COLLEGE APPLICATION CHECKLIST Keep track of your applications by inserting a check mark or the completion date in the appropriate column and row.

	College 1	College 2	College 3	College 4
Campus visit				
Campus interview				
Letters of recommendation				
NAME:				
Date requested				
Follow-up				
NAME:				
Date requested				
Follow-up				
NAME:				
Date requested				
Follow-up				
Counselor recommendation form to counselor				
Secondary school report form to counselor				
Test scores requested				
Transcripts sent				
Application completed				
Essay completed				
All signatures collected				
Financial aid forms enclosed				
Application fee enclosed				
Copies made of all forms and documentation enclosed in application packet				
Postage affixed/return address on envelope				
Letters of acceptance/denial/wait list received				
Colleges notified of intent				
Tuition deposit sent				
Housing and other forms submitted to chosen college				
Orientation scheduled				

secondary school report form and midyear school report (sent in by your guidance counselor after you fill out a portion of the form), and any financial aid forms required by the college.

Use the "College Application Checklist" on the previous page to make sure you have everything you need before you send off that application.

Filling out the Forms

Filling out college applications can seem like a daunting task, but there are six easy steps to follow for the successful completion of this part of your college selection process.

Step 1: Practice Copies

Make a photocopy of each college's application to which you plan to apply. Since the presentation of your application may be considered an important aspect in the weighting for admission, you don't want to erase, cross out, or use white-out on your final application. Make all your mistakes on your copies. When you think you have it right, then transfer the information to your final original copy or go on line to enter it on the college's electronic application. If you are mailing in your applications, try to use a word processor, and make the effort to line up your responses in those tiny spaces. Remember, at the larger universities, the application packet may be the only part of you they see.

Step 2: Decide on Your Approach

What is it about your application that will grab the admission counselor's attention so that it will be pulled out of the sea of applications on his or her desk for consideration? Be animated and interesting in what you say. Be memorable in your approach to your application, but don't overdo it. You want the admissions counselor to remember you, not your Spanish castle made of popsicle sticks. Most importantly, be honest and don't exaggerate your academics and extracurricular activities. Approach

DO'S AND DON'TS FOR FILLING OUT YOUR APPLICATIONS

One of the most intimidating steps of applying for admission to college is filling out all the forms. This list of do's and don'ts will help you put your best foot forward on your college applications.

DO

- ☑ Read applications and directions carefully.
- ☑ Make sure that everything that is supposed to be included is enclosed.
- ☑ Fill out your own applications. Type the information yourself to avoid crucial mistakes.
- ☑ Start with the simple applications and then progress to the more complex ones.
- ☑ Make copies of applications, and practice filling one out before you complete the original.
- ☑ Type or neatly print your answers, and then proofread the applications and essays several times for accuracy. Also ask someone else to proofread them for you.
- ☑ If asked, describe how you can make a contribution to the schools to which you apply.
- ☑ Be truthful, and do not exaggerate your accomplishments.
- ☑ Keep a copy of all forms you submit to colleges.
- ☑ Be thorough and on time.

DON'T

- ☑ Use correction fluid. If you type your application, use a correctable typewriter or the liftoff strips to correct mistakes. Better yet, fill out your application on line.
- ☑ Write in script. If you don't have access to a computer or typewriter, print neatly.
- ☑ Leave blank spaces. Missing information may cause your application to be sent back or delayed while admission officers wait for complete information.
- ☑ Be unclear. If the question calls for a specific answer, don't try to dodge it by being vague.
- ☑ Put it off!

this process with integrity every step of the way. First of all, it is the best way to end up in a college that is the right match for you. Second, if you are less than truthful, the college will eventually learn about it. How will they know? You have to supply support materials to accompany your application, things like transcripts and recommendations. If you tell one story and they tell another, the admissions office will notice the disparity—another red flag!

Step 3: Check the Deadlines

In September of your senior year, organize your applications in chronological order. Place the due dates for your final list of schools next to their names on your stretch, target, and safety list and on your "College Application Checklist." Work on the earliest due date first.

Step 4: Check the Data on You

You need to make sure that the information you will be sending to support your applications is correct. The first thing to double-check is your transcript. This is an important piece because you must send a transcript with each application you send to colleges. Take a trip to the guidance office and ask for a "Transcript Request Form." Fill out the request for a formal transcript indicating that you are requesting a copy for yourself and that you will pick it up. Pay the fee if there is one.

When you get your transcript, look it over carefully. It will be several pages long and will include everything from the titles of all the courses that you have taken since the ninth grade along with the final grade for each course to the community service hours you have logged each year. Check the information carefully. It is understandable that with this much data, it is easy to make an input error. Because this information is vital to you and you are the best judge of accuracy, it is up to you to check it. Take any corrections or questions you have back to your guidance counselor to make the corrections. If it is a questionable grade, your counselor will help you find out what grade should have been posted on your

transcript. Do whatever needs to be done to make sure your transcript has been corrected no later than October 1 of your senior year.

Step 5: List Your Activities

When you flip through your applications, you will find a section on extracurricular activities. It is time to hit your word processor again to prioritize your list of extracurricular activities and determine the best approach for presenting them to your colleges. Some students will prepare a resume and include this in every application they send. Other students will choose to develop an "Extracurricular, Academic, and Work Experience Addendum" and mark those specific sections of their application, "See attached Addendum."

If you are a powerhouse student with a great deal to say in this area, it will take time to prioritize your involvement in activities and word it succinctly yet interestingly. Your "Brag Sheet" will help (see "The Brag Sheet" on page 72). Put those activities that will have the strongest impact, show the most consistent involvement, and demonstrate your leadership abilities at the top of the list. This will take time, so plan accordingly. If you feel you have left out important information because the form limits you, include either an addendum or your resume as a back-up.

Step 6: Organize Your Other Data

What other information can you organize in advance of sitting down to fill out your applications?

The Personal Data Section

Most of this section is standard personal information that you will not have any difficulty responding to, but some items you will need to think about. For example, you may find a question that asks, "What special college or division are you applying to?" Do you have a specific school in mind, like the College of Engineering? If you are not sure about your major, ask yourself what interests you the most and then enter that college. Once you are in college and have a better sense of what you want to do, you can always change your major later.

(Continued on page 73)

THE BRAG SHEET

At the beginning of this chapter, we described how a student resume can help your guidance counselors and teachers write their letters of recommendation for you. Putting together a list of your accomplishments will also help you organize all of the information you will need to include when you fill out your college applications.

ACADEMICS

GPA (Grade Point Average) _____

THE HONORS COURSES I HAVE TAKEN ARE:

English _____

History _____

Math _____

Science _____

Language _____

Electives _____

THE AP COURSES I HAVE TAKEN ARE:

English _____

History _____

Math _____

Science _____

Language _____

Electives _____

STANDARDIZED TEST SCORES

PSAT _____

1st SAT I _____

2nd SAT I _____

ACT Assessment _____

SAT II SUBJECT TESTS

Test 1 _____ Score _____

Test 2 _____ Score _____

Test 3 _____ Score _____

SPECIAL TALENTS

I have received the following academic awards:

_____

_____

_____

I have performed in these various theatrical productions: _____

_____

I am lettered in the following sports: _____

I have played on the following traveling teams: _____

_____

I am a member of the following musical groups: _____

_____

EXTRACURRICULAR ACTIVITIES

I participate on a regular basis in the following extracurricular activities: _____

_____

I have held the following offices: _____

_____

I have established the following extracurricular organizations:

_____

I have held the following after-school and summer jobs: _____

_____

GOALS

I plan to major in the following area in college: _____

_____

The application will provide an optional space to declare ethnicity. If you feel you would like to declare an area and that it would work to your advantage for admission, consider completing this section of the application.

You are also going to need your high school's College Entrance Examination Board (CEEB) number. That is the number you needed when you filled out your test packets. It is stamped on the front of your SAT and ACT Assessment packets, or, if you go to the guidance department, they'll tell you what it is.

The Standardized Testing Section

Applications ask you for your test dates and scores. Get them together accurately. All your College Board scores should be recorded with the latest test results you received. Your latest ACT Assessment record will only have the current scores unless you asked for all your past test results. If you have lost this information, call these organizations or go to your guidance department. Your counselor should have copies. Be sure the testing organizations are sending your official score reports to the schools to which you're applying. If you are planning to take one of these tests in the future, the colleges will want those dates, too; they will wait for those scores before making a decision. If you change your plans, write the admissions office a note with the new dates or the reason for canceling.

The Senior Course Load Section

Colleges will request that you list your present senior schedule by semester. Set this information up in this order: List any AP or honors-level full-year courses first; these will have the most impact. Then list other required full-year courses and then required semester courses, followed by electives. Make sure you list first-semester and second-semester courses appropriately. Do not forget to include physical education if you are taking it this year.

Your Recommendation Writers

Most schools will require you to submit two or three letters of recommendation from adults who know you well.

Guidance Counselor Recommendations

Nearly all colleges require a letter of recommendation from the applicant's high school guidance counselor. Some counselors will give students an essay question that they feel will give them the background they need in order to structure a recommendation. Other counselors will canvass a wide array of individuals who know a student in order to gather a broader picture of the student in various settings. No one approach is better than the other. Find out which approach is used at your school. You will probably get this information as a handout at one of those evening guidance programs or in a classroom presentation by your school's guidance department. If you are still not sure you know what is expected of you or if the dog has eaten those papers, ask your guidance counselor what is due and by what date. Make sure that you complete the materials on time and that you set aside enough of your time to do them justice.

Teacher Recommendations

In addition to the recommendation from your counselor, colleges may request additional recommendations from your teachers. Known as formal recommendations, these are sent directly to the colleges by your subject teachers. Most colleges require at least one formal recommendation in addition to the counselor's recommendation. However, many competitive institutions require at least two, if not three, academic recommendations. Follow a school's directions regarding the exact number. A good rule-of-thumb is to have recommendations from teachers in two subject areas (e.g., English and math).

Approach your recommendation writers personally to request that they write for you. If they agree, provide them with a copy of your Brag Sheet. On the other hand, you may be met with a polite refusal on the order of "I'm sorry, but I'm unable to write for you. I've been approached by so many seniors already that it would be difficult for me to accomplish your recommendation by your due dates." This teacher may really be overburdened with requests for recommendations, especially if this is a senior English teacher, or the teacher may be giving you a signal that someone else may be able to write a stronger piece for you. Either way, accept the refusal politely, and seek another recommendation writer.

How do you decide whom to ask? Here are some questions to help you select your writers:

- How well does the teacher know you?
- Has the teacher taught you for more than one course? (A teacher who taught you over a two- to three-year period has seen your talents and skills develop.)
- Has the teacher sponsored an extracurricular activity in which you made a contribution?
- Do you get along with the teacher?
- Does the college/university indicate that a recommendation is required or recommended from a particular subject-area instructor?
- If you declare an intended major, can you obtain a recommendation from a teacher in that subject area?

Other Recommendation Writers

Consider getting recommendations from your employer, your rabbi or pastor, the director of the

summer camp where you worked for the last two summers, and so on—but only if these additional letters are going to reveal information about you that will have a profound impact on the way a college will view your candidacy. Otherwise, you run the risk of overloading your application with too much paper.

Writing the Application Essay

Application essays show how you think and how you write. They also reveal additional information about you that is not in your other application material. Not all colleges require essays, and those that do often have a preferred topic. Make sure you write about the topic that is specified and keep to the length of pages or words. If the essay asks for 300 words, don't submit 50 or 500. Some examples of essay topics include:

Tell us about yourself. Describe your personality and a special accomplishment. Illustrate the unique aspects of who you are, what you do, and what you want out of life. Share an experience that made an impact on you, or write about something you have learned from your parents.

Tell us about an academic or extracurricular interest or idea. Show how a book, experience, quotation, or idea reflects or shapes your outlook and aspirations.

Tell us why you want to come to our college. Explain why your goals and interests match the programs and offerings of that particular school. This question requires some research about the school. Be specific.

Show us an imaginative side of your personality. This question demands originality but is a great opportunity to show off your skills as a writer. Start writing down your thoughts and impressions well before the essay is due. Think about how you have changed over the years so that if and when it comes time to write about yourself, you will have plenty of information. Write about something that means a lot to you, and support your thoughts with reasons and examples. Then explain why you care about your topic.

The essay should not be a summary of your high school career. Describe yourself as others see you, and

FROM THE GUIDANCE OFFICE

Q: Why are essays so important to the college application?

A: Students focus more on grades than anything else. They think grades are the be-all and end-all and that an SAT score will get them in. For most selective schools, that's just one piece of the pie. Many of the schools in the upper 20 percent of competitive schools consider the essay more heavily. Essays show whether the student is a thinker, creative, and analytical. They're looking for the type of personality that can shine rather than one that simply can spit out names and dates. When everyone has high SATs in a pool of applicants, the essay is what makes one student stand out over another.

Patsy Lovelady
Counselor
MacArthur High School
San Antonio, Texas

use a natural, conversational style. Use an experience to set the scene in which you will illustrate something about yourself. For example, you might discuss how having a disabled relative helped you to appreciate life's simple pleasures. Or you may use your athletic experiences to tell how you learned the value of teamwork. The essay is your chance to tell something positive or enriching about yourself, so highlight an experience that will make the reader interested in you.

Outline in the essay what you have to offer the college. Explain why you want to attend the institution and how your abilities and goals match the strengths and offerings at the university. Write, rewrite, and edit. Do not try to dash off an essay in one sitting. The essay will improve with time and thought. Proofread and concentrate on spelling, punctuation, and content. Have someone else take a look at your essay. Make copies and save them after mailing the original.

Admission officers look for the person inside the essay. They seek students with a breadth of knowledge and experiences, someone with depth and perspective. Inner strength and commitment are admired, too. Not everyone is a winner all the time. The essay is a tool you can use to develop your competitive edge. Your essay should explain why you should be admitted over other applicants.

As a final word, write the essay from the heart. It should have life and not be contrived or one-dimensional. Avoid telling them what they want to hear; instead, be yourself.

SPECIAL INFORMATION FOR ATHLETES

If you weren't a planner before, but you want to play sports while in college or go to college on an athletic scholarship, you'd better become a planner now. There are many regulations and conditions you need to know ahead of time so that you don't miss out on possible opportunities.

First, think about whether or not you have what it takes to play college sports. It's a tough question to ask, but it's a necessary one. In general, playing college sports requires the basic skills and natural

SAMPLE APPLICATION ESSAY

Here is one student's college application essay. She answered the question, "Indicate a person who has had a significant influence on you, and describe that influence."

Mrs. Morrone did not become my guidance counselor until my sophomore year of high school. During my first meeting with her, I sat across from her in an uncomfortable vinyl chair and refused to meet her eyes as I told her about my long and painful shyness, how I detested oral reports, and how I feared raising my hand in class or being called on to answer a question—all because I didn't want to be the center of attention.

She did not offer me advice right away. Instead, she asked me more about myself—my family, my friends, what kinds of music, books, and movies I liked. We talked easily, like old friends, and it was not long before I began to look forward to our weekly meetings. Her office was one of the few places where I felt like I could be myself and let my personality shine through, where I knew that I was accepted and liked unconditionally.

In November of that year, the drama club announced auditions for the spring play, The Glass Menagerie. I had studied it in English class and it was one of my favorites; not surprisingly, I identified strongly with the timid Laura. I talked with Mrs. Morrone about the play and how much I liked theater. At one point I sighed, "I'd love to play Laura."

"Why don't you try out for the show?" Mrs. Morrone suggested.

The very idea of performing, onstage, in a spotlight, in front of dozens of people frightened me. She did not press the matter, but at the end of the session she encouraged me to bring a copy of the play to our next few meetings and read some of the character's lines, "just for fun." I did, and found myself gradually transforming into Laura as I recited her lines with increasing intensity.

After a couple of these amateur performances, she told me that I was genuinely good as Laura, and she would love to see me at least audition for the part. "I would never force you to do it," she said, "but I would hate to see you waste your potential." I insisted that I was too frightened, but she promised that she would come and watch my audition. She told me to pretend she was the only person in the audience.

A week later, I did read for the part of Laura. Mrs. Morrone beamed with pride in the back of the auditorium. I discovered that I truly enjoyed acting; slipping into another character cracked the shell that I had built around myself. I did not get the part, but I had found a passion that enriched my life in immeasurable ways. I owe Mrs. Morrone so much for putting me on the path to becoming a professional actress and for helping me to finally conquer my shyness. Without her quiet support and strength, none of this would have come to pass.

FROM THE GUIDANCE OFFICE

Q: What's a big mistake high school athletes make when thinking about college?

A: Some athletes think that their athletic ability alone will get them a scholarship and do not believe that their academics must be acceptable. The Division I or II schools cannot offer scholarships if the student has not met the academic standards required by the school for admission. Our counselors start reminding students in the freshman year and every year after that the courses they take do make a difference in how colleges view their transcripts. Students can't start preparing in their senior year of high school.

Sue Bradshaw
Guidance Counselor
Sterling High School
Baytown, Texas

ability, a solid knowledge of the sport, overall body strength, speed, and sound academics. Today's athletes are stronger and faster because of improved methods of training and conditioning. They are coached in skills and techniques, and they begin training in their sport at an early age. Remember, your talents will be compared with those from across the U.S. and around the world.

Second, know the background. Most college athletic programs are regulated by the National Collegiate Athletic Association (NCAA), an organization that has established rules on eligibility, recruiting, and financial aid. The NCAA has three membership divisions: Division I, Division II, and Division III. Institutions are members of one or another division according to the size and scope of their athletic programs and whether they provide athletic scholarships.

If you are planning to enroll in college as a freshman and you wish to participate in Division I or Division II athletics, you must be certified by the NCAA Initial-Eligibility Clearinghouse (www.ncaaclearinghouse.net). The Clearinghouse was established as a separate organization by the NCAA member institutions to ensure consistent interpretation of NCAA initial-eligibility requirements for all prospective student athletes at all member institutions.

You should start the certification process when you are a junior in high school. Check with your counselor to make sure you are taking a core

curriculum that meets NCAA requirements. Also, register to take the ACT Assessment or SAT I as a junior. Submit your Student Release Form (available in your guidance counseling office) to the Clearinghouse by the beginning of your senior year.

Initial Eligibility of Freshman Athletes for Division I and II

Students who plan to participate in NCAA Division I or II college sports must obtain the Student Release Form from their high school, complete it, and send it to the NCAA Clearinghouse. This form authorizes high schools to release student transcripts, including test scores, proof of grades, and other academic information, to the Clearinghouse. It also authorizes the Clearinghouse to release this information to the colleges that request it. The form and corresponding fee must be received before any documents will be processed. (Fee waivers are available for economically disadvantaged students. Check with your counselor for fee waiver information.)

Students must also make sure that the Clearinghouse receives ACT Assessment and/or SAT I score reports. Students can have score reports sent directly to the Clearinghouse by entering a specific code (9999) printed in the ACT Assessment and SAT I registration packets.

Once a year, high schools will send an updated list of approved core courses (formerly 48H), which lists each course offering that meets NCAA core course requirements. The Clearinghouse personnel will validate the form. Thereafter, the Clearinghouse will determine each student's initial eligibility. Collegiate institutions will request information from the Clearinghouse on the initial eligibility of prospective student-athletes. The Clearinghouse will make a certification decision and report it directly to the institution.

Three types of eligibility are possible:

1. Certification of eligibility for expense-paid campus visits.

2. Preliminary certification of eligibility to participate in college sports (appears likely to meet all NCAA requirements but not yet graduated).

ATHLETIC RESUME

Name _____

Address _____

_____

High school address and phone number

_____

_____

_____

Coach's name _____

Height/weight _____

Foot speed (by specific event) _____

Position played _____

Weight classification _____

GPA _____

Class rank _____

ACT Assessment or SAT I scores (or when you plan to take them)_____

_____

Athletic records held_____

_____

All-state teams _____

Special awards _____

Off-season accomplishments _____

Weightlifting exercises _____

Vertical jumps _____

Push-ups _____

Bench jumps _____

Shuttle run _____

Leadership characteristics _____

Former successful athletes from your high school

_____

Outstanding capabilities_____

Citizenship _____

Alumni parents/relatives _____

Include the following with your resume:

- **Team schedule with dates and times**
- **Videotape with jersey number identified**
- **Newspaper clippings about you and/or your team**

3. Final certification granted when proof of graduation is received.

Additional information about the Clearinghouse can be found in the *Guide for the College-Bound Student-Athlete*, published by the NCAA. To get a copy of this guide, call 800-638-3731 (toll-free). You can also visit the NCAA Web site at www.ncaa.org.

National Association of Intercollegiate Athletics (NAIA) Regulations

The National Association of Intercollegiate Athletics (NAIA) has different eligibility requirements for student-athletes. To be eligible to participate in intercollegiate athletics as an incoming freshman, two of the following three requirements must be met:

1. Have a 2.0 (C) or higher cumulative final grade point average in high school.

2. Have a composite score of 18 or higher on the ACT Assessment or an 860 total score or higher on the SAT I on a single test administered on a national test date.

3. Have a top-half final class rank in his or her high school graduating class.

Student-athletes must also have on file at the college an official ACT Assessment or SAT I score report from the appropriate national testing center. Results reported on the student's high school transcript are not acceptable. Students must request that their test scores be forwarded to the college's admission office.

If you have additional questions about NAIA eligibility, contact them at:

NAIA
23500 W. 105 Street
P.O. Box 1325
Olathe, Kansas 66051-1325
Telephone: 913-791-0044
Web: www.naia.org

AUDITIONS AND PORTFOLIOS

If you decide to study the arts, such as theater, music, or fine arts, you may be required to audition or show your portfolio to admissions personnel. The following tips will help you showcase your talents and skills when preparing for an audition or portfolio review.

Music Auditions

High school students who wish to pursue a degree in music, whether it is vocal or instrumental, typically must audition. If you're a singer, prepare at least two pieces in contrasting styles. One should be in a foreign language, if possible. Choose from operatic, show music, or art song repertories, and make sure you memorize each piece. If you're an instrumentalist or pianist, be prepared to play scales and arpeggios, at least one etude or technical study, and a solo work. Instrumental audition pieces need not be memorized. In either field, you may be required to do sight-reading.

When performing music that is sight-read, you should take time to look over the piece and make certain of the key and time signatures before proceeding with the audition. If you're a singer, you should bring a familiar accompanist to the audition.

"My advice is to ask for help from teachers, try to acquire audition information up front, and know more than is required for the audition," says one student. "It is also a good idea to select your audition time and date early."

"Try to perform your solo in front of as many people as you can as many times as possible," says another student. "You may also want to try to get involved in a high school performance."

Programs differ, so students are encouraged to call the college and ask for audition information. In general, music departments seek students who demonstrate technical competence and performance achievement.

Admission to music programs varies in degree of competitiveness, so you should audition at a minimum of three colleges and a maximum of five to amplify your opportunity. The degree of competitiveness varies also by instrument, especially if a renowned musician teaches a certain instrument. Some colleges offer a second audition if you feel you did not audition to your potential. Ideally, you will be accepted into the music program of your choice, but keep in mind that it's possible to not be accepted. You must then make the decision to either pursue a music program at another college or consider another major at that college.

Dance Auditions

At many four-year colleges, an open class is held the day before auditions. A performance piece that combines improvisation, ballet, modern, and rhythm is taught and then students are expected to perform the piece at auditions. Professors look for coordination, technique, rhythm, degree of movement, and body structure. The dance faculty members also assess your ability to learn and your potential to complete the curriculum. Dance programs vary, so check with the college of your choice for specific information.

Art Portfolios

A portfolio is simply a collection of your best pieces of artwork. The pieces you select to put in your portfolio should demonstrate your interest and aptitude for a serious education in the arts. A well-developed portfolio can help you gain acceptance into a prestigious art college and increase your chances of being awarded a scholarship in national portfolio competitions. The pieces you select should show diversity in technique and variety in subject matter. You may show work in any medium (oils, photography, watercolors, pastels, etc.) and in either black-and-white or color. Your portfolio can include classroom assignments as well as independent projects. You can also include your sketchbook.

Specialized art colleges request that you submit an average of ten pieces of art, but remember that quality is more important than quantity. The admission office staff will review your artwork and transcripts to assess your skill and potential for success. Usually, you will present your portfolio in person; however, some schools allow students to mail slides if distance is an issue. There is no simple formula for success other than hard work. In addition, there is no such thing as a "perfect portfolio," nor any specific style or direction to achieve one.

Tips for Pulling Your Portfolio Together:

- ☞ Try to make your portfolio as clean and organized as possible.

- ☞ It is important to protect your work, but make sure the package you select is easy to handle and does not interfere with the viewing of the artwork.

- ☞ Drawings that have been rolled up are difficult for the jurors to handle and view. You may shrink-wrap the pieces, but it is not required.

- ☞ Avoid loose sheets of paper between pieces.

- ☞ If you choose to mount or mat your work (not required), use only neutral gray tones, black, or white.

- ☞ Never include framed pieces or three smudge.

- ☞ A slide portfolio should be presented in a standard 8 × 11 plastic slide sleeve, which can be purchased at any photo or camera supply store.

- ☞ Be sure paintings are completely dry before you place them in your portfolio.

- ☞ Label each piece with your name, address, and high school.

Theater Auditions

Most liberal arts colleges do not require that students who audition be accepted into the theater department unless the college offers a Bachelor of Fine Arts (B.F.A.) degree in theater. You should apply to the college of your choice prior to scheduling an audition.

You should also consider spending a full day on campus so that you may talk with theater faculty members and students, attend classes, meet with your admission counselor, and tour the facilities.

Although each college and university has different requirements, you should prepare two contrasting monologues taken from plays of your choice if you're auditioning for a B.F.A. acting program. Musical theater requirements generally consist of one up-tempo musical selection and one ballad, as well as one monologue from a play or musical of your choice. The total of all your pieces should not exceed 5 minutes. Music for the accompanist, a resume of your theater experience, and a photo are also required.

Tips to Get You Successfully through an Audition:

- ☞ Choose material suitable for your age.

- ☞ If you choose your monologue from a book of monologues, you should read the entire play and be familiar with the context of your selection.

- ☞ Select a monologue that allows you to speak directly to another person; you should play only one character.

- ☞ Memorize your selection.

- ☞ Avoid using characterization or style, as they tend to trap you rather than tapping deeper into inner resources.

FINANCIAL AID DOLLARS AND SENSE

Getting financial aid can be intimidating—but don't let that stop you.

I T'S COMPLICATED, and there are a lot of pieces to this puzzle. Leave a few out or put too many in, and the puzzle doesn't come out right. However, if you look at each piece separately rather than trying to understand the whole process all at once, it will be much easier to absorb. The trick is to start early, be organized, and plan ahead.

Finding the money you need to attend a two- or four-year institution or vocational/career college is a challenge, but you can do it if you devise a strategy well before you actually start applying to college. Financial aid comes from a lot of different sources. But this is where GAJ comes in. You'll find lots of help here to locate those sources and find out where to get advice. Financial aid is available to help meet both direct educational costs (tuition, fees, books) and personal living expenses (food, housing, transportation).

PROJECTED COLLEGE EXPENSES

The following chart estimates the cost of one year of college education, including tuition, room, and board. Estimates are based on a 6 percent annual increase.

School Year	Public 4-Year	Private 4-Year
2003–2004	$13,500	$28,900
2007–2008	17,000	36,500
2010–2011	20,250	43,500
2014–2015	25,600	54,900

Source: The College Entrance Examination Board

Times have changed to favor the student in the financial aid process. Because the pool of potential traditional college students has diminished, colleges and universities are competing to attract the top students to their school. In fact, some colleges and universities no longer use financial aid primarily as a method to help students fund their college education but rather as a marketing and recruitment tool. This puts students and families at an advantage, one that should be recognized and used for bargaining power.

It used to be that colleges and universities offered need-based and merit-based financial aid to only needy and/or academically exceptional students. Now some schools offer what might be called incentive or discount aid to encourage students to choose them over another college. This aid, which is not necessarily based on need or merit, is aimed at students who meet the standards of the college but who wouldn't necessarily qualify for traditional kinds of aid.

A BIRD'S-EYE VIEW OF FINANCIAL AID

You and your family should be assertive in negotiating financial aid packages. It used to be that there was no room for such negotiation, but in today's environment, it is wise to be a comparison shopper. Families should wait until they've received all of their financial offers and then talk to their first-choice college to see if the college can match the better offers from other colleges.

To be eligible to receive federal/state financial aid, you must maintain satisfactory academic progress toward a degree or certificate. This criterion is

FINANCIAL AID GLOSSARY

ASSETS. The amount a family has in savings and investments. This includes savings and checking accounts, a business, a farm or other real estate, and stocks, bonds, and trust funds. Cars are not considered assets, nor are such possessions as stamp collections or jewelry. The net value of the principal home is counted as an asset by some colleges in determining their own awards but is not included in the calculation for eligibility for federal funds.

CITIZENSHIP/ELIGIBILITY FOR AID. To be eligible to receive federally funded college aid, a student must be one of the following:

1. A United States citizen;

2. A non-citizen national;

3. A permanent resident with an I-151 or I-551 without conditions;

4. A participant in a suspension of deportation case pending before Congress; or

5. A holder of an I-94 showing one of the following designations: "Refugee," "Asylum Granted," "Indefinite Parole" and/or "Humanitarian Parole," "Cuban/Haitian Entrant, Status Pending," or "Conditional Entrant" (valid if issued before April 1, 1980).

Individuals in the U.S. on an F1 or F2 visa or on a J1 or J2 exchange visa cannot get federal aid.

COOPERATIVE EDUCATION. A program offered by many colleges in which students alternate periods of enrollment with periods of employment, usually paid, and that can lengthen the usual baccalaureate program to five years.

EXPECTED FAMILY CONTRIBUTION (EFC) OR PARENTAL CONTRIBUTION. A figure determined by a congressionally mandated formula that indicates how much of a family's resources should be considered "available" for college expenses. Factors such as taxable and nontaxable income and the value of family assets are taken into account to determine a family's financial strength. Allowances for maintaining a family and future financial needs are then taken into consideration before determining how much a family should be able to put toward the cost of college.

INDEPENDENT STUDENT. A student who reports only his or her own income (and that of a spouse, if relevant) when applying for federal financial aid. Students who will be 24 or older by December 31, 2002, will automatically be considered "independent" for 2003–2004. Students who are under 24 will be considered independent if they are:

• married as of the date of filing the FAFSA.

• the supporter of a legal dependent other than a spouse.

• a veteran of the U.S. Armed Forces.

• an orphan or ward of the court.

• classified as independent by a college's financial aid administrator because of other unusual circumstances.

• a graduate or professional student.

MERIT-BASED AID. Any form of financial aid awarded on the basis of personal achievement or individual characteristics without reference to financial need.

SUBSIDIZED LOAN. While enrolled at least half-time, this loan does not accure interest. For Subsidized Federal Stafford and/or Direct Loans, the government pays interest to the lender on behalf of the borrower while the student is in college and during approved grace periods.

established by each college or university. You'll also need a valid social security number, and all male students must register for selective service on their eighteenth birthday.

You apply for financial aid during your senior year. Every school requires the Free Application for Federal Student Aid (FAFSA), which cannot be filed until after January 1 of your senior year. Your application will be processed in about 4 weeks if you use the paper application or about one week if you apply on line at www.fafsa.ed.gov. You'll then receive a Student Aid Report (SAR), which will report the information from the FAFSA and show your calculated Expected Family Contribution (EFC—the number used in determining your eligibility for federal student aid). Each school you listed on the application, as well as your state of legal residence, will also receive your FAFSA information. If you are

COLLEGE FUNDS AVAILABLE

Use this chart to estimate your family's resources that will be available for college expenses. Check your progress at the end of your sophomore and junior years to see if your plans for seeking financial aid need to be revised.

YOUR RESOURCES	Estimated amount available	Actual amount: 11 grade	Actual amount: 12th grade
Savings and other assets			
Summer earnings			
Part-time work during school year			
Miscellaneous			
PARENTS' RESOURCES			
From their current income			
From college savings			
Miscellaneous (insurance, annuities, stocks, trusts, home equity, property assets)			
TOTAL			

Source: American College Testing Program

to attract students from all income levels, offer significant amounts of financial aid. Public-supported institutions tend to offer less financial aid because the lower tuition acts as a form of assistance (see "Projected College Expenses"). In addition, students attending school in their home state often have more aid possibilities than if they attend an out-of-state college. Use the "College Funds Available" chart to determine how much you and your family can contribute to your education and the "College Cost Comparison" table to figure out which schools best suit you financially.

TYPES OF FINANCIAL AID

Be sure that you understand the differences between the types of financial aid so you are fully prepared to apply for each. One or more of these financial resources may make it possible to pursue the education you want.

Grants: Grants are usually given to students with financial need. But the term is also used for athletics (Division I only), academics, demographics, and special talents. Grants do not have to be repaid.

Scholarships: Scholarships, also called "merit aid," are awarded for academic excellence. Repayment is not required.

Loans: Student loans, which have very favorable terms and conditions, are sponsored by the federal government, state governments, and through commercial lending institutions. The Financial Aid Office is the best source of information on student loans. These must be repaid, generally after you graduate or leave school.

College Work-Study: College Work-Study is a federally sponsored program that enables colleges to hire students for employment. If eligible, students work a limited number of hours throughout the school year. Many colleges use their own funds to hire students to work in the many departments and offices

applying to higher cost colleges or some scholarship programs, you also may have to file the PROFILE application. This should be completed in September or October of your senior year. More information on the PROFILE is available from your high school guidance office or on the Web at www.collegeboard.org. There is a fee charged with the PROFILE®.

You must reapply for federal aid every year. Also, if you change schools, your aid doesn't necessarily go with you. Check with your new school to find out what steps you must take to continue receiving aid.

Once you've decided to which schools you want to apply, talk to the financial aid officers of those schools. There is no substitute for getting information from the source when it comes to understanding your financial aid options. That personal contact can lead you to substantial amounts of financial aid.

If you qualify for admission, don't let the sticker price of the college or program scare you away, because you may get enough financial assistance to pay for the education you want. Don't rule out a private institution until you have received the financial aid package from the school. Private colleges, in order on campus. If you do not receive a federal work-study grant, you should contact the Student Employment Office or the Financial Aid Office to help locate nonfederal work-study positions that may be available.

FINANCIAL AID PROGRAMS

A number of sources of financial aid are available to students from the federal government, state governments, private lenders, foundations and private agencies, and the colleges and universities themselves. In addition, as discussed earlier, there are four different forms of aid: grants, scholarships, loans, and work-study.

The federal government is the single largest source of financial aid for students, making more than an estimated $60 billion available in loans, grants, and other aid to millions of students. Following are listings of federal financial aid programs available to you.

FEDERAL GRANTS

The federal government offers a number of educational grants, which are outlined below:

Federal Pell Grant

The Federal Pell Grant is the largest grant program in the nation; about 4 million students receive awards annually. This grant is intended to be the base or starting point of assistance for lower-income families. Eligibility for a Federal Pell Grant depends on the EFC, or Expected Family Contribution. (See the "Financial Aid Glossary" for a description of commonly used terms.) The actual Pell Grant award amounts depend on how much funds are appropriated by Congress each year. The maximum for the 2003–2004 school year is $4,050. How much you will receive depends not only on your EFC, but also on your cost of attendance and whether you're a full-time or part-time student.

Federal Supplemental Educational Opportunity Grant (FSEOG)

As its name implies, the Federal Supplemental Educational Opportunity Grant (FSEOG) provides

COLLEGE COST COMPARISON WORKSHEET

Chart your course to see which college or university best fits your financial resources. Your totals in expenses and funds available should be the same amount. If not, you have a funding gap, meaning that you have more expenses than funds available and will need to take out a loan (most likely), or vice versa (less likely).

EXPENSES	College 1	College 2	College 3	College 4
Tuition and fees	$	$	$	$
Books and supplies	$	$	$	$
Room and board	$	$	$	$
Transportation	$	$	$	$
Miscellaneous	$	$	$	$
TOTAL	$	$	$	$
FUNDS AVAILABLE				
Student and parent contributions	$	$	$	$
Grants	$	$	$	$
Scholarships	$	$	$	$
Work-study	$	$	$	$
TOTAL	$	$	$	$
Funding gap	$	$	$	$

additional need-based federal grant money to supplement the Federal Pell Grant. Each participating college is given funds to award to especially needy students. The maximum award is $4,000 per year, but the amount a student receives depends on the college's policy, the availability of FSEOG funds, the total cost of education, and the amount of other aid awarded.

FEDERAL SCHOLARSHIPS

The following comprise the scholarships available through the federal government:

ROTC Scholarships

The Armed Forces (Army, Air Force, Navy, Marines) may offer up to a four-year scholarship that pays full college tuition plus a monthly allowance; however, these scholarships are very competitive and based upon GPA, class rank, ACT Assessment or SAT scores, and physical qualifications. Apply as soon as possible before December 1 of your senior year. Contact the headquarters of each of the armed forces for more information: Army, 800-USA-ROTC; Air Force, 800-423-USAF; Navy, 800-USA-NAVY; Marines, 800-MARINES (all numbers are toll-free).

Scholarships from Federal Agencies

Federal agencies, such as the CIA, NASA, Department of Agriculture, and Office of Naval Research, offer an annual stipend as well as a scholarship. In return, the student must work for the agency for a certain number of years or else repay all the financial support. See your counselor for more information.

FINANCIAL AID ADVICE

Q: **What do you wish students and their parents knew about financial aid?**

A: **They don't know they should get their financial application filed early enough, so if we run into snags, it can be corrected. They make mistakes, such as not answering the question about the amount of taxes paid the previous year. A lot of parents think that if they didn't send in a check to the IRS, they didn't pay taxes. Something as simple as that causes a lot of problems. If their financial information is recorded incorrectly, it can really mess them up. They should read all the information on the financial aid form, and if they have questions, they should ask someone. Speaking from my experience, if you can't get in touch with the college you're child is thinking of attending, then call a local college. Any time an application doesn't go through the system smoothly, it can cause major problems.**

Now that you can apply over the Internet, the applications are much simpler and worded in layman's terms. If applicants miss filling in some information, that will trigger a warning that they omitted something. I realize that not all students have access to the Internet, but they can go to the public library and look into getting onto the Internet there.

Trudy Masters, Financial Aid Officer

Lee College

Baytown, Texas

Robert C. Byrd Honors Scholarship

To qualify for this scholarship, you must demonstrate outstanding academic achievement and excellence in high school as indicated by class rank, high school grades, test scores, and leadership activities. Award amounts of $1,500 are renewable for four years. Contact your high school counselor for application information. Deadlines may vary per state, so also contact your state's Department of Education.

FEDERAL LOANS

Following are methods through which you may borrow money from the federal government:

Federal Perkins Loan

This loan provides low-interest (5 percent) aid for students with exceptional financial need (students with the lowest Expected Family Contribution). The Federal Perkins Loans are made through the college's Financial Aid Office—that is, the college is the lender. For undergraduate study, you may borrow a maximum of $4,000 per year for up to five years of undergraduate study and may take up to ten years to repay the loan, beginning nine months after you graduate, leave school, or drop below half-time status. No interest accrues while you are in school and, under certain conditions (e.g., if you teach in a low-income area, work in law enforcement, are a full-time nurse or medical technician, or serve as a Peace Corps or VISTA volunteer), some or all of your loans may be either partially paid or cancelled in full. Payments also can be deferred under certain conditions, such as unemployment.

FFEL Stafford Student Loan

An FFEL Stafford Student Loan may be borrowed from a participating commercial lender, such as a bank, credit union, or savings and loan association. This is a variable rate loan, capped at a maximum of 8.25 percent. If you qualify for a need-based subsidized FFEL Stafford Student Loan, the interest is paid by the federal government while you are enrolled in school. There is also an unsubsidized FFEL Stafford Student Loan that is not based on need and for which you are eligible, regardless of your family income.

The maximum amount you may borrow as a dependent student is $2,625 for freshman, $3,500 for sophomores, and $5,500 for juniors and seniors, with a maximum of $23,000 for your undergraduate program. The maximum amount for independent students is $6,625 for freshman, $7,500 for sophomores, and $10,500 for juniors and seniors, with a maximum of $46,000 for your undergraduate program. (The subsidized amount for independent students is the same as for dependent students, based on financial need.) There may be up-front origination fees charged for these loans that are deducted from the loan proceeds.

To apply for an FFEL Stafford Student Loan, you must first complete a FAFSA to determine eligibility for the subsidized amount of your loan. You should contact your school's Financial Aid Office to determine the most efficient method of selecting a lender, since many schools have established a preferred lender list. If your school does not have a preferred lender list, contact any local financial institution in your area or your state's Department of Higher Education for assistance. The lender will help you through the process, including a one-time signing of a promissory note. The proceeds of the loan, less any fees, will be sent to your college to be credited to your account.

If you qualify for a subsidized Stafford Loan, you don't have to pay interest while in school. For an unsubsidized FFEL Loan, you will be responsible for paying the interest from the time the loan is disbursed. However, most FFEL lenders will permit you to delay making payments and will add the interest to your loan. Once the repayment period "…starts, you should contact the lender and/or your school's Financial Aid Office to discuss repayment options. For many students, it is wise to consider consolidating all of your student loans into one loan program."

William D. Ford Federal Direct Stafford Loans

The Federal Direct Loan program is very similar to the FFEL Stafford Loan program except that the school serves as the lender. There is no need to contact a private financial institution for your student loans. About 30 percent of all U.S. colleges participate in the Direct Loan program. The terms and conditions of the

THINKING AHEAD TO PAYING BACK YOUR STUDENT LOAN

More than ever before, loans have become an important part of financial assistance. The majority of students find that they must borrow money to finance their education. If you accept a loan, you are incurring a financial obligation. You will have to repay the loan in full, along with all of the interest and any additional fees (collection, legal, etc.). Since you will be making loan payments to satisfy the loan obligation, carefully consider the burden your loan amount will impose on you after you leave college. Defaulting on a student loan can jeopardize your financial future. Borrow intelligently.

SOME REPAYMENT OPTIONS

A number of repayment options are available to borrowers of federally guaranteed student loans.

The Standard Repayment Plan requires fixed monthly payments (at least $50) over a fixed period of time (up to ten years). The length of the repayment period depends on the loan amount. This plan usually results in the lowest total interest paid because the repayment period is shorter than under the other plans.

The Extended Repayment Plan allows loan repayment to be extended over a period from generally twelve to thirty years, depending on the total amount borrowed. Borrowers still pay a fixed amount each month (at least $50), but usually monthly payments will be less than under the Standard Repayment Plan. This plan may make repayment more manageable; however, borrowers usually will pay more interest because the repayment period is longer.

The Graduated Repayment Plan allows payments to start out low and increase every two years. This plan may be helpful to borrowers whose incomes are low initially but will increase steadily. A borrower's monthly payments must be at least half but may not be more than one-and-a-half times what he or she would pay under Standard Repayment. As in the Extended Repayment Plan, the repayment period will usually vary from twelve to thirty years, depending on the total amount borrowed. Again, monthly payments may be more manageable at first because they are lower, but borrowers will pay more interest because the repayment period is longer.

The Income Contingent Repayment Plan bases monthly payments on adjusted gross income (AGI) and the total amount borrowed. This is currently only available to students who participate in Direct Loans; however, some FFEL lenders and guaranty agencies provide income-sensitive repayment plans. As income rises or falls each year, monthly payments will be adjusted accordingly. The required monthly payment will not exceed 20 percent of the borrower's discretionary income as calculated under a published formula. Borrowers have up to twenty-five years to repay; after that time, any unpaid amount will be discharged, and borrowers must pay taxes on the amount discharged. In other words, if the federal government forgives the balance of a loan, the amount is considered to be part of the borrower's income for that year.

two loan programs are essentially the same. There are many repayment plans available to meet your needs, and these will be explained to you during your "exit interview" during your final term of school.

Parent Loans for Undergraduate Students (PLUS)

The PLUS loans are for parents of dependent students and are designed to help families with cash-flow problems. There is no needs test to qualify, and the loans are made by FFEL lenders or directly by the Department of Education. The loan has a variable interest rate that cannot exceed 9 percent, and there is no specific yearly limit; your parents can borrow up to the cost of your education, less other financial aid received. Repayment begins sixty days after the money is advanced. There may be an origination fee of up to 4 percent charged for these loans. Parent borrowers must generally have a good credit record to qualify for PLUS loans.

The PLUS loan will be processed under either the Direct or the FFEL system, depending on the type of loan program for which the college has contracted.

Nursing Student Loan Program

These loans are awarded to nursing students with demonstrated financial need. This loan has a 5 percent interest rate, repayable after completion of studies. Repayment is to be completed within ten years. Contact your college's Financial Aid Office for deadline and other information, including maximum borrowing amounts.

OTHER FEDERAL PROGRAMS

The following programs offer alternative ways to earn money for college:

Federal Work-Study (FWS)

The Federal Work Study program provides both on- and off-campus jobs to students who have financial need. Funding for this program is from federal grants to the institutions, plus a partial match from the employer. Students work on an hourly basis and are paid at least the minimum wage. Students are allowed to work up to the amount of the grant authorized by the college. Contact the Financial Aid Office for more information.

AmeriCorps

AmeriCorps is a national service program for a limited number of students. Participants work in a public or private nonprofit agency that provides service to the community in one of four priority areas: education, human services, the environment, and public safety. In exchange, they earn a stipend for living expenses and up to $4,725 for up to two years to apply toward college expenses. Students can work either before, during, or after they go to college and can use the funds to either pay current educational expenses or repay federal student loans. If you successfully complete one full-time term of service (at least 1,700 hours over one year or less), you will be eligible for an award of $4,725. If you successfully complete one part-time term of service (at least 900 hours over two years or less), you will be eligible for an award of $2,362.50. You should speak to your college's Financial Aid Office for more details about this program and any other new initiatives available to students.

FAMILIES' GUIDE TO TAX CUTS FOR EDUCATION

Many new tax benefits for adults who want to return to school and for parents who are sending or planning to send their children to college will be available due to the balanced budget that was signed into law in 1997. These tax cuts effectively make the first two years of college universally available, and they give many more working Americans the financial means to go back to school if they want to choose a new career or upgrade their skills. Millions of families are eligible for the Hope and Lifetime Learning tax credits each year, as well as the newer taxable income deduction allowed for tuition and fees.

HOPE Scholarship Tax Credit

The HOPE Scholarship tax credit helps make the first two years of college or career school universally available. Students receive a 100 percent tax credit for the first $1,000 of tuition and required fees and a 50 percent credit on the second $1,000. This credit is available for tuition and required fees minus grants, scholarships, and other tax-free educational assistance and became available for payments made after December 31, 1997, for college enrollment after that date.

The credit is gradually reduced for families with Adjusted Gross Incomes between $41,000 and $51,000 if single, or between $82,000 and $102,000 if married. These limits are adjusted for inflation every year. The credit can be claimed in two years for students who are in their first two years of college or career school and who are enrolled on at least a half-time basis in a degree or certificate program for any portion of the year. The taxpayer can claim a credit for his own tuition expense or for the expenses of his or her spouse or dependent children.

The Lifetime Learning Tax Credit

This tax credit is targeted at adults who want to go back to school, change careers, or take a course or two to upgrade their skills and to college juniors, seniors, graduate, and professional degree students. A family will receive a 20 percent tax credit for the first $5,000 of tuition and required fees paid each year through 2002 and for the first $10,000 thereafter. Just like the HOPE Scholarship tax credit, the Lifetime Learning tax credit is available for tuition and required fees minus grants, scholarships, and other tax-free educational assistance; families may claim the credit for amounts paid on or after July 1, 1998, for college or career school enrollment beginning on or after July 1, 1998. The maximum credit is determined on a per-taxpayer (family) basis, regardless of the number of postsecondary students in the family, and is phased out at the same income levels as the HOPE Scholarship tax credit. Families will be able to claim the Lifetime Learning tax credit for some members of their family and the HOPE Scholarship tax credit for others who qualify in the same year.

Tuition and Fees Tax Deduction

The Tuition and Fees Tax Deduction can reduce the amount of your taxable income by as much as $3,000 per year. This deduction is subtracted from your income, which means you can claim this deduction even if you do not itemize your deductions on Schedule A of Form 1040. This deduction may benefit you if you do not qualify for the Hope or Lifetime Learning Tax Credits because your income is too high. This program is available for four years, 2002 through 2005. You cannot claim this tax deduction in tax year 2002 if your Adjusted Gross Income (AGI) for 2002 is more than $64,000 for a single tax payer, or more than $130,000 for married taxpayers. Participating in the Hope and/or Lifetime Tax credits does not preclude participation in this program, as long as the same student is not used as the basis for each deduction, credit or exclusion and the family does not exceed the Lifetime Learning maximum per family. Check with the IRS or your accountant for more information.

APPLYING FOR FINANCIAL AID

Applying for financial aid is a process that can be made easier when you take it step by step.

1. You must complete the Free Application for Federal Student Aid (FAFSA) to be considered for federal financial aid. Pick up the FAFSA from your high school guidance counselor or college financial aid office or download it from the Department of Education's Web site at www.fafsa.ed.gov. The FAFSA is due any time after January 1 of the year you will be attending school. Submit the form as soon as possible but never before the first of the year. If you need to estimate income tax information, it is easily amended later in the year.

2. Apply for any state grants. Most states use the FASFA for determining state aid, but be sure to check out the specific requirements with your state Higher Education Assistance agency. Your high school guidance office can answer most questions about state aid programs.

3. Some schools (usually higher cost private colleges) require an additional form know as the PROFILE®. This application is needed for institutional grants and scholarships controlled by the school. Check to see if the schools you are applying to require the PROFILE® form. Additional information is available from your high school guidance office or online through the College Board at www.collegeboard.com. There is a fee associated with this form. Some schools may require an institutional aid application. This is usually found with the admission application. Contact each college you are considering to be sure you have filed the required forms.

4. Complete individual colleges' required financial aid application forms on time. These deadlines are usually before March 15, but check to be sure.

5. Make sure your family completes the required forms during your senior year of high school.

6. Always apply for grants and scholarships before applying for student loans. Grants and scholarships are essentially free money. Loans must be repaid with interest.

Use the "Checklist for Seniors" on the following page to keep track of the financial aid application process.

NATIONAL, STATEWIDE, AND LOCAL SCHOLARSHIPS

Without a doubt, the best source for up-to-date information on private scholarships is available on the Internet. There are a variety of excellent Web sites to explore, including www.petersons.com and www.scholarships.com among others. The most important thing to be careful about is scholarship scams, where you are asked either to pay for a scholarship search by an independent organization or pay a "processing fee" to a particular organization to receive their scholarship. We have more detailed information on this issue later in this chapter.

State and Local Scholarships

It is not possible within the scope of this book to list all of the sources of state and local scholarship dollars. The following are excellent resources for seeking financial assistance:

- Your guidance counselor
- A high school teacher or coach
- Your high school and elementary school PTA (yes, many elementary school PTAs award scholarships to alumni)
- The local librarian
- College admissions office
- Your parents' alma mater
- Your employer
- Your parents' employer
- Professional and social organizations in your community
- The local Financial Aid office of a college in your area
- Your state Higher Education Assistance Agency

CHECKLIST FOR SENIORS

Applying for financial aid can become confusing if you don't record what you've done and when. Use this chart to keep track of important information. Remember to keep copies of all applications and related information.

COLLEGE APPLICATIONS	COLLEGE 1	COLLEGE 2	COLLEGE 3	COLLEGE 4
Application deadline				
Date sent				
Official transcript sent				
Letters of recommendation sent				
SAT/ACT Assessment scores sent				
Acceptance received				

INDIVIDUAL COLLEGE FINANCIAL AID AND SCHOLARSHIP APPLICATIONS

	COLLEGE 1	COLLEGE 2	COLLEGE 3	COLLEGE 4
Application deadline				
Date sent				
Acceptance received				

FREE APPLICATION FOR FEDERAL STUDENT AID (FAFSA), FINANCIAL AID FORM (FAF), AND/OR PROFILE

	COLLEGE 1	COLLEGE 2	COLLEGE 3	COLLEGE 4
Form required				
Date sent				
School's priority deadline				

PROFILE® ACKNOWLEDGMENT (if filed)

	COLLEGE 1	COLLEGE 2	COLLEGE 3	COLLEGE 4
Date received				
Correct (Y/N)				
Date changes made, if needed				
Date changes were submitted				

STUDENT AID REPORT

	COLLEGE 1	COLLEGE 2	COLLEGE 3	COLLEGE 4
Date received				
Correct (Y/N)				
Date changes made, if needed				
Date changes were submitted				
Date sent to colleges				

FINANCIAL AWARD LETTERS

	COLLEGE 1	COLLEGE 2	COLLEGE 3	COLLEGE 4
Date received				
Accepted (Y/N)				

Source: The Dayton-Montgomery County Scholarship Program

SCHOLARSHIPS FOR MINORITY STUDENTS

The following is just a sample of the many scholarships available to minority students.

Blackfeet Nation Higher Education Grants

Available to members of the Blackfeet Tribe. Up to $3,500 in awards.
P.O. Box 850
Browning, Montana 59417
406-338-7539
www.blackfeetnation.com

Bureau of Indian Affairs Higher Education Grant Programs

Available to undergraduates in a federally recognized tribe. Award amounts vary.
1849 C Street, NW, MS 3512-MIB
Washington, D.C. 20240
202-208-3478
www.oiep.bia.edu

Hispanic Scholarship Fund College Scholarship Program

Limited to Hispanic students enrolled at a two- or four-year institution. Up to $3,000 in awards.
Hispanic Scholarship Fund
55 Second Street, Suite 1500
San Francisco, California 94105
415-808-2300
www.hsf.net

National Achievement Scholarship Program

Limited to African-American high school students who have taken the PSAT/NMSQT. Up to $2,500 in awards.
Achievement Scholarship Program
1560 Sherman Avenue, Suite 200
Evanston, Illinois 60201-4897
847-866-5100
www.nationalmerit.org/achieve.htm

National Association of Minority Engineering Program Administrators National Scholarship Fund

Limited to African-American, Hispanic, and Native-American/Eskimo students with interest and potential for an undergraduate degree in engineering. Up to $5,000.
NAMEPA National Scholarship Foundation
1133 West Morse Boulevard, Suite 201
Winter Park, Florida 32789
407-647-8839
www.namepa.org

Jackie Robinson Foundation Scholarship

For minority students accepted to a four-year college and with demonstrated academic achievement and financial need. Award up to $6,000.
3 West 35th Street, 11th Floor
New York, New York 10001-2204
212-290-8600
www.jackierobinson.org

APPLYING FOR SCHOLARSHIPS

Here are some tips to help make a success of your scholarship hunt.

1. **Start early.** Your freshman year is not too early to plan for scholarships academically, choose extracurricular activities that will highlight your strengths, and get involved in your church and community—all things that are important to those who make scholarship decisions.

2. **Search for scholarships.** The best source of scholarships can be found on the Internet. There are many great Web sites that are free, including www.petersons.com .For more information, you should also check www.finaid.org and http://www.ed.gov/ studentaid/student.html. Scholarship information is also available at your local library.

3. **Apply, apply, apply.** One student applied for nearly sixty scholarships and was fortunate enough to win seven. "Imagine if I'd applied for five and only gotten one," she says.

4. **Plan ahead.** It takes time to get transcripts and letters of recommendation. Letters from people who know you well are more effective than letters from prestigious names who know you only vaguely.

5. **Be organized.** In the homes of scholarship winners, you can often find a file box where all relevant information is stored. This method allows you to review deadlines and requirements every so often. Computerizing the information, if possible, allows you to change and update information quickly.

6. **Follow directions.** Make sure that you don't disqualify yourself by filling the forms out incorrectly, missing the deadline, or failing to supply important information. Type your applications, if possible, and have someone proofread them.

WHAT YOU NEED TO KNOW ABOUT ATHLETIC SCHOLARSHIPS

Whether you're male or female or interested in baseball, basketball, crew, cross-country, fencing, field hockey, football, golf, gymnastics, lacrosse, sailing, skiing, soccer, softball, swimming and diving, tennis, track and field, volleyball, or wrestling, there may be scholarship dollars available for you. But, here's that word again—planning. You must plan ahead if you want to get your tuition paid for in return for your competitive abilities.

At the beginning of your junior year, ask your guidance counselor to help you make sure that you take the required number and mix of academic courses and to inform you of the SAT I and ACT Assessment

TYPES OF ATHLETIC SCHOLARSHIPS

Colleges and universities offer two basic types of athletic scholarships: the institutional grant, which is an agreement between the athlete and the college, and the conference grant, which also binds the college to the athlete. The difference is that the athlete who signs an institutional grant can change his or her mind and sign with another team. The athlete who signs a conference contract cannot renegotiate another contract with a school that honors conference grants. Here are the various ways that a scholarship may be offered:

Full four-year. Also known as full ride, these scholarships pay for room, board, tuition, and books. Due to the high cost of awarding scholarships, this type of grant is being discouraged by conferences around the country in favor of the one-year renewable contract or the partial scholarship.

Full one-year renewable contract. This type of scholarship, which has basically replaced the four-year grant, is automatically renewed at the end of each school year for four years if the conditions of the contract are met. The recruiter will probably tell you in good faith that the intent is to offer a four-year scholarship, but he is legally only allowed to offer you a one-year grant. You must ask the recruiter as well as other players what the record has been of renewing scholarships for athletes who comply athletically, academically, and socially. Remember—no athlete can receive more than a full scholarship.

One-year trial grant (full or partial). A verbal agreement between you and the institution that at the end of the year, your renewal will be dependent upon your academic and athletic performance.

Partial scholarship. The partial grant is any part of the total cost of college. You may be offered room and board but not tuition and books, or you may be offered just tuition. The possibility exists for you to negotiate to a full scholarship after you complete your freshman year.

Waiver of out-of-state fees. This award is for out-of-state students to attend the college or university at the same fee as an in-state student.

score minimums that must be met to play college sports. Also ask your counselor about academic requirements, because you must be certified by the NCAA Initial-Eligibility Clearinghouse, and this process must be started by the end of your junior year.

But before you do all that, think. Do you want and need an athletic scholarship? Certainly, it is prestigious to receive an athletic scholarship, but some athletes compare having an athletic scholarship to having a job at which you are expected to perform. Meetings, training sessions, practices, games, and (don't forget!) studying take away from social and leisure time. Also, with very few full-ride scholarships available, you will most likely receive a partial scholarship or a one-year renewable contract. If your scholarship is not renewed, you may be left scrambling for financial aid. So ask yourself if you are ready for the demands and roles associated with accepting an athletic scholarship.

If you decide that you want an athletic scholarship, you need to market yourself to beat the stiff competition. Think of yourself as a newly designed sports car, and you're selling the speed, look, and all those other goodies to a waiting public. The point is that you're going to have to sell, or market, your abilities to college recruiters. You're the product, and the college recruiter is the buyer. What makes you stand out from the rest?

College recruiters look for a combination of the following attributes when awarding athletic scholarships: academic excellence, a desire to win, self-motivation, ability to perform as a team player, willingness to help others, cooperation with coaching staff, attitude in practice, attitude in games/matches, toughness, strength, optimal height and weight, and excellence.

In order to successfully sell your skills to a college or university, you'll need to take three main steps: 1) locate the colleges and universities that offer scholarships in your sport, 2) contact the institution in a formal manner, and 3) follow up each lead.

Finding and Getting Athletic Scholarships

Ask your coach or assistant coaches for recommendations; learn about the conference or institution from newspaper or television coverage; ask your guidance counselor; review guidebooks, reference books, and the Internet; ask alumni; or attend a tryout or campus visit. You can also call the NCAA to request a recruiting guide for your sport. The following steps can help you snag that scholarship:

1. **Contact the school formally.** Once you make a list of schools in which you are interested, get the names of the head coaches as and write letters to the top twenty schools on your list. Then compile a factual resume of your athletic and academic accomplishments. Put together 10 to 15 minutes of video highlights of your athletic performance (with your jersey number noted), get letters of recommendation from your high school coach and your off-season coach, and include a season schedule.

2. **Ace the interview.** When you meet a recruiter or coach, exhibit self-confidence with a firm handshake, by maintaining eye contact, and by making sure that you are well groomed. According to recruiters, the most effective attitude is quiet confidence, respect, sincerity, and enthusiasm.

3. **Ask good questions.** Don't be afraid to probe the recruiter by getting answers to the following questions: Do I qualify athletically and academically? If I am recruited, what would the parameters of the scholarship be? For what position am I being considered? It's okay to ask the recruiter to declare what level of interest he or she has in you.

4. **Follow up.** Persistence pays off when it comes to seeking an athletic scholarship, and timing can be everything. There are four good times when a follow-up letter from your coach or a personal letter from you is extremely effective: prior to your senior season, during or just after the senior season, just prior to or after announced conference-affiliated signing dates or national association signing dates, and late summer, in case others scholarship offers have been withdrawn or declined.

To sum up, you know yourself better than anyone, so you must look at your skills—both athletic and academic—objectively. Evaluate the skills you need to improve, and keep the desire to improve alive in your heart. Develop your leadership skills, and keep striving for excellence with your individual achievements. Keep your mind open as to what school you want to attend, and keep plugging away, even when you are tired, sore, and unsure. After all, athletes are trained to be winners!

MYTHS AND MISCONCEPTIONS ABOUT SCHOLARSHIPS AND FINANCIAL AID

The scholarship and financial aid game is highly misunderstood by many high school students. And high school guidance counselors, overburdened with paperwork and complaints, often lack the time to fully investigate scholarship opportunities and to inform students about them. The myths and misconceptions persist while the truth about scholarships remains hidden, the glittering prizes and benefits unknown to many teenagers.

Myth 1: Scholarships are rare, elusive awards won only by valedictorians, geniuses, and whiz kids.

The truth is that with proper advice and strategies, private scholarships are very much within the grasp of high school students who possess talent and ability in almost any given field. Thousands of high school students like you compete and win.

Myth 2: My chances of being admitted to a college are reduced if I apply for financial aid.

The truth is that most colleges have a policy of "need-blind" admissions, which means that a student's financial need is not taken into account in the admission decision. However, there are a few colleges that do consider ability to pay before deciding whether or not to admit a student. There are a few more that look at ability to pay of those whom they placed on a waiting list to get in or those students who applied late. Some colleges will mention this in their literature, others may not. In making decisions about the college application and financing process, however, families should apply for financial aid if the student needs the aid to attend college.

Myth 3: All merit scholarships are based on a student's academic record.

The truth is that many of the best opportunities are in such areas as writing, public speaking, leadership, science, community service, music and the arts, foreign languages, and vocational-technical skills. So that means you don't always have to have a 3.99 GPA to win if you excel in a certain area.

Myth 4: You have to be a member of a minority group to get a scholarship.

The truth is that there are indeed some scholarships that are targeted toward women and minority students. There are also scholarships for which you must be a member of a specific national club or student organization (such as 4-H and the National Honor Society), which makes these scholarships just as exclusive. But most scholarship opportunities are not exclusive to any one segment of the population.

Myth 5: If you have need for and receive financial aid, it's useless to win a scholarship from some outside organization because the college will just take away the aid that the organization offered.

It's true that if you receive need-based aid, you can't receive more than the total cost of attendance (including room and board, books, and other expenses, not just tuition). If the financial aid that you've been awarded meets the total cost and you win an outside scholarship, colleges have to reduce something. But usually, they reduce the loan or work-study portion of your financial aid award before touching the grant portion that they've awarded you. This means that you won't have to borrow or earn as much. Also, most colleges don't meet your full financial need when you qualify for need-based financial aid. So, if you do win an outside scholarship, chances are that your other aid will not be taken away or reduced.

SCHOLARSHIP SCAMS

Unfortunately for prospective scholarship seekers, the private aid sector exists virtually without patterns or rules. Regrettably, the combination of the urgency to locate money, limited time, and a complex and bewildering system has created opportunities for fraud. Although most scholarship sponsors and most scholarship search services are legitimate, schemes that pose as either legitimate scholarship search services or scholarship sponsors have cheated thousands of families.

These fraudulent businesses advertise in campus newspapers, distribute flyers, mail letters and postcards, provide toll-free phone numbers, and even have sites on the Web. The most obvious frauds operate as scholarship search services or scholarship clearinghouses. Another quieter segment sets up as a scholarship sponsor, pockets the money from the fees and charges that are paid by thousands of hopeful scholarship seekers, and returns little, if anything, in proportion to the amount it collects. A few of these frauds inflict great harm by gaining access to individuals' credit or checking accounts with the intent to extort funds.

The Federal Trade Commission (FTC), in Washington, D.C., has a campaign called Project $cholar$cam to confront this type of fraudulent activity. There are legitimate services. However, a scholarship search service cannot truthfully guarantee that a student will receive a scholarship, and students almost always will fare as well or better by doing their own homework using a reliable scholarship information source, such as Peterson's *Scholarships, Grants & Prizes* or *www.petersons.com*, than by wasting money and time with a search service that promises a scholarship.

The FTC warns you to be alert for these six warning signs of a scam:

1. **"This scholarship is guaranteed or your money back."** No service can guarantee that it will get you a grant or scholarship. Refund guarantees often have impossible conditions attached. Review a service's refund policies in writing before you pay a fee.

2. **"The scholarship service will do all the work."** Unfortunately, nobody else can fill out the personal information forms, write the essays, and supply the references that many scholarships may require.

3. **"The scholarship will cost some money."** Be wary of any charges related to scholarship information services or individual scholarship applications, especially in significant amounts. Before you send money to apply for a scholarship, investigate the sponsor.

4. **"You can't get this information anywhere else."** In addition to Peterson's, scholarship directories from other publishers are available in any large bookstore, public library, or high school guidance office.

5. **"You are a finalist"** or **"You have been selected by a national foundation to receive a scholarship."** Most legitimate scholarship programs almost never seek out particular applicants. Most scholarship sponsors will contact you only in response to an inquiry because they generally lack the budget to do anything more than this. Should you think that there is any real possibility that you may have been selected to receive a scholarship, before you send any money, investigate first to be sure that the sponsor or program is legitimate.

6. **"The scholarship service needs your credit card or checking account number in advance."** Never provide your credit card or bank account number on the telephone to the representative of an organization that you do not know. Get information in writing first. An unscrupulous operation does not need your signature on a check. It will scheme to set up

situations that will allow it to drain a victim's account with unauthorized withdrawals.

In addition to the FTC's six signs, here are some other points to keep in mind when considering a scholarship program:

- Fraudulent scholarship operations often use official-sounding names, containing words such as *federal, national, administration, division, federation,* and *foundation.* Their names are often a slight variant of the name of a legitimate government or private organization. Do not be fooled by a name that seems reputable or official, an official-looking seal, or a Washington, D.C., address.

- If you win a scholarship, you will receive written official notification by mail, not by telephone. If the sponsor calls to inform you, it will follow up with a letter in the mail. If a request for money is made by phone, the operation is probably fraudulent.

- Be wary if an organization's address is a box number or a residential address. If a bona fide scholarship program uses a post office box number, it usually will include a street address and telephone number on its stationery.

- Beware of telephone numbers with a 900-area code. These may charge you a fee of several dollars a minute for a call that could be a long recording that provides only a list of addresses or names.

- Watch for scholarships that ask you to "act now." A dishonest operation may put pressure on an applicant by saying that awards are on a "first-come, first-serve" basis. Some scholarship programs will give preference to the earlier qualified applications. However, if you are told, especially on the telephone, that you must respond quickly but that you will not hear about the results for several months, there may be a problem.

- Be wary of endorsements. Fraudulent operations will claim endorsements by groups with names similar to well-known private or government organizations. The Better Business Bureau (BBB) and government agencies do not endorse businesses.

Don't pay money for a scholarship to an organization that you've never heard of before or whose legitimacy you can't verify. If you have already paid money to such an organization and find reason to doubt its authenticity, call your bank to stop payment on your check, if possible, or call your credit card company and tell it that you think you were the victim of consumer fraud.

To find out how to recognize, report, and stop a scholarship scam, you may write to the Federal Trade Commission's Consumer Response Center at 600 Pennsylvania Avenue NW, Washington, D.C. 20580. On the Web, go to www.ftc.gov, or call 877-FTC-HELP (toll-free). You can also check with the Better Business Bureau (BBB), which is an organization that maintains files of businesses about which it has received complaints. You should call both your local BBB office and the BBB office in the area of the organization in question; each local BBB has different records. Call 703-276-0100 to get the telephone number of your local BBB, or look at www.bbb.org for a directory of local BBBs and downloadable BBB complaint forms.

FINANCIAL AID ON THE WEB

A number of good financial aid resources exist on the Web. It is quick and simple to access general financial aid information, links to relevant Web sites, loan information, employment and career information, advice, scholarship search services, interactive worksheets, forms, and free expected family contribution (EFC) calculators.

Also visit the Web sites of individual colleges to find more school-specific financial aid information.

FAFSA Online

The Free Application for Federal Student Aid (FAFSA) can be filed on the Web at www.fafsa.ed.gov. You can download a worksheet from this Web site, since the questions are formatted differently from the paper application. FAFSA on the Web is a much quicker process and helps eliminate errors. To file electronically, the student and one parent will need an electronic signature pin number. To get a PIN, go to www.pin.ed.gov. The pin number will be sent to you within 24 hours.

The Education Resource Institute (TERI)

TERI is a private, not-for-profit organization that was founded to help middle-income Americans afford a college education. This site contains a database describing more than 150 programs that aim to increase college attendance from underrepresented groups. (The target population includes students from low-income families and those who are the first in their family to pursue postsecondary education.) Visit TERI's Web site at www.teri.org.

FinAid

This Web site offers numerous links to valuable financial aid information, including scholarship search engines. You can find the site at www.finaid.org.

Mapping Your Future

This site is sponsored by a group of guaranty agencies that participate in the Federal Family Education Loan Program (FFELP). They are committed to providing information about higher education and career opportunities. Information is available to help parents of middle school students plan for college and for adults returning to higher education to learn new skills. You can find this site at www.mapping-your-future.org.

Student Financial Assistance Information, U.S. Department of Education

This page takes you to some of the major publications on student aid, including the latest edition of the Student Guide. Visit www.ed.gov/finaid.html.

Petersons.com

Get advice on finding sources to pay for college and search for scholarships at www.petersons.com/finaid/.

FIND MONEY FOR COLLEGE

Don't have enough money to pay for college? Afraid your family makes too much and you can't get financial aid? Regardless of your financial situation, BestCollegeDeals® helps you quickly and easily identify each college's unique financial aid packages—student loans, grants, discounts, scholarships—and little-known financial deals you've probably never even heard of.

How does it work? It's simple!

1. Provide financial information about your family in a safe, secure environment that ensures your privacy.

2. Calculate, with help from BestCollegeDeals®, your Estimated Expected Family Contribution (EFC), the amount of money you may be expected to pay toward your college education.

3. Choose location, enrollment size, and whether you're interested in a public, private, all-women's, or all-men's college or university.

4. Get a list of colleges, and information about their financial aid offerings, that match your preferences.

5. Discover great need- and merit-based (merit awards include scholarships, grants, and prizes that are given for academic achievement) financial deals that you can't find anywhere else!

No matter what your level of income, BestCollegeDeals® gives your family personalized support. BestCollegeDeals® helps you and your family better understand the financial aid process. Go to www.bestcollegedeals to learn more!

AESmentor.com

American Education Services works with nearly 4 million students through its guaranty, servicing, and financial aid processing system. Its Web site provides information on paying and saving for college as well as an application process for securing student loans.

FINANCIAL AID DIRECTORY

You can use these numbers for direct access to federal and state agencies and processing services.

FEDERAL STUDENT AID INFORMATION CENTER

Provides duplicate student aid reports and aid applications to students. Also answers questions on student aid, mails Department of Education publications, makes corrections to applications, and verifies college federal aid participation. Write to the Federal Student Aid Information Center, P.O. Box 84, Washington, D.C. 20044-0084, call 800-4-Fed-Aid (toll-free), or visit their Web site at www.studentaid.ed.gov

VETERANS BENEFITS ADMINISTRATION

Provides dependent education assistance for children of disabled veterans. College-bound students should call the VBRO to determine whether or not they qualify for assistance, what the benefits are, and if a parent's disability qualifies them for benefits. Call 800-827-1000 (toll-free) or visit their Web site at www.gibill.va.gov.

ACT FINANCIAL AID NEED ESTIMATOR (FANE)

Mails financial tabloids to students, provides information on filling out financial aid forms, and estimates financial aid amounts. Also mails financial need estimator forms. Forms are also accessible on line. Go to www.ACT.org or write to P.O. Box 168, 2201 N. Dodge Street, Iowa City, Iowa 52243-0168, or call 319-337-1615.

COLLEGE SCHOLARSHIP SERVICE (PROFILE)

Provides free applications and registration forms for federal student aid. Helps students fill out applications. Call 800-239-5888 (toll-free) or visit www.profileonline.collegeboard.com/index.jsp.

COLLEGE FOR TEXANS

Here is everything a Texan needs to know about preparing for, applying for and paying for college or technical school. And it's all in one up-to-date, easy-to-navigate site as big as the state itself. And remember $2 billion is available every year to help Texans attend college. Go to www.collegefortexans.com for more information.

WHAT TO EXPECT IN COLLEGE

If you were going on a long trip, wouldn't you want to know what to expect once you reached your destination? The same should hold true for college.

GET A JUMP! CAN'T FILL IN all the details of what you'll find once you begin college. However, we can give you information about some of the bigger questions you might have, such as how to choose your classes or major and how you can make the most of your life outside the classroom.

CHOOSING YOUR CLASSES

College is designed to give you freedom, but at the same time, it teaches you responsibility. You will probably have more free time than in high school, but you will also have more class material to master. Your parents may entrust you with more money, but it is up to you to make sure there's enough money in your bank account when school fees are due. The same principle applies to your class schedule: You will have more decision-making power than ever, but you also need to know and meet the requirements for graduation.

To guide you through the maze of requirements, all students are given an adviser. This person, typically a faculty member, will help you select classes that meet your interests and graduation requirements. During your first year or two at college, you and your adviser will choose classes that meet general education requirements and select electives, or non-required classes, that pique your interests. Early on, it is a good idea to take a lot of general education classes. They are meant to expose you to new ideas and help you explore possible majors. Once you have selected a major, you will be given an adviser for that particular area of study. This person will help you understand and meet the requirements for that major.

In addition to talking to your adviser, talk to other students who have already taken a class you're interested in and who really enjoyed how a professor taught the class. Then try to get into that professor's class when registering. Remember, a dynamic professor can make a dry subject engaging. A boring professor can make an engaging subject dry.

As you move through college, you will notice that focusing on the professor is more important than focusing on the course title. Class titles can be cleverly crafted. They can sound captivating. However, the advice above still holds true: "Pop Culture and Icons" could turn out to be awful, and "Beowulf and Old English" could be a blast.

When you plan your schedule, watch how many heavy reading classes you take in one semester. You don't want to live in the library or the dorm study lounge. In general, the humanities, such as history, English, philosophy, and theology, involve a lot of reading. Math and science classes involve less reading; they focus more on solving problems.

Finally, don't be afraid to schedule a fun class. Even the most intense program of study will let you take a few electives. So take a deep breath, dig in, and explore!

CHOOSING YOUR MAJOR

You can choose from hundreds of majors—from accounting to zoology—but which is right for you? Should you choose something traditional or select a major from an emerging area? Perhaps you already know what career you want, so you can work backward to decide which major will best help you achieve your goals.

If you know what you want to do early in life, you will have more time to plan your high school curriculum, extracurricular activities, jobs, and community service to coincide with your college major. Your college selection process may also focus upon the schools that provide strong academic programs in a certain major.

Where Do I Begin?

Choosing a major usually starts with an assessment of your career interests. Once you have taken the self-assessment test in Part 1, you should have a clearer understanding of your interests, talents, values, and goals. Then review possible majors, and try several on for size. Picture yourself taking classes, writing papers, making presentations, conducting research, or working in a related field. Talk to people you know who work in your fields of interest and see if you like what you hear. Also, try reading the classified ads in your local newspaper. What jobs sound interesting to you? Which ones pay the salary that you'd like to make? What level of education is required in the ads you find interesting? Select a few jobs that you think you'd like and then consult the following list of majors to see which major(s) coincide. If your area of interest does not appear here, talk to your counselor or teacher about where to find information on that particular subject.

Majors and Related Careers

Agriculture

Many agriculture majors apply their knowledge directly on farms and ranches. Others work in industry (food, farm equipment, and agricultural supply companies), federal agencies (primarily in the Departments of Agriculture and the Interior), and state and local farm and agricultural agencies. Jobs might be in research and lab work, marketing and sales, advertising and public relations, or journalism and radio/TV (for farm communications media). Agriculture majors also pursue further training in biological sciences, animal health, veterinary medicine, agribusiness management, vocational agriculture education, nutrition and dietetics, and rural sociology.

Architecture

Architecture and related design fields focus on the built environment as distinct from the natural environment of the agriculturist or the conservationist. Career possibilities include drafting, design, and project administration in architectural, engineering, landscape design, interior design, industrial design, planning, real estate, and construction firms; government agencies involved in construction, housing, highways, and parks and recreation; and government and nonprofit organizations interested in historic or architectural preservation.

Area/Ethnic Studies

The research, writing, analysis, critical thinking, and cultural awareness skills acquired by area/ethnic studies majors, combined with the expertise gained in a particular area, make this group of majors valuable in a number of professions. Majors find positions in administration, education, public relations, and communications in such organizations as cultural, government, international, and (ethnic) community agencies; international trade (import-export); social service agencies; and the communications industry (journalism, radio, and TV). These studies also provide a good background for further training in law, business management, public administration, education, social work, museum and library work, and international relations.

Arts

Art majors most often use their training to become practicing artists, though the settings in which they work vary. Aside from the most obvious art-related career—that of the self-employed artist or craftsperson—many fields require the skills of a visual artist. These include advertising; public relations; publishing; journalism; museum work; television, movies, and theater; community and social service agencies concerned with education, recreation, and entertainment; and teaching. A background in art is also useful if a student wishes to pursue art therapy, arts or museum administration, or library work.

Biological Sciences

The biological sciences include the study of living organisms from the level of molecules to that of populations. Majors find jobs in industry; government agencies; technical writing, editing, or illustrating; science reporting; secondary school teaching (which usually requires education courses); and research and laboratory analysis and testing. Biological sciences are also a sound foundation for further study in medicine, psychology, health and hospital administration, and biologically oriented engineering.

Business

Business majors comprise all the basic business disciplines. At the undergraduate level, students can major in a general business administration program or specialize in a particular area, such as marketing or accounting. These studies lead not only to positions in business and industry but also to management positions in other sectors. Management-related studies include the general management areas (accounting, finance, marketing, and management) as well as special studies related to a particular type of organization or industry. Management-related majors may be offered in a business school or in a department dealing with the area in which the management skills are to be applied. Careers can be found throughout the business world.

Communication

Jobs in communication range from reporting (news and special features), copywriting, technical writing, copyediting, and programming to advertising, public relations, media sales, and market research. Such positions can be found at newspapers, radio and TV stations, publishing houses (book and magazine), advertising agencies, corporate communications departments, government agencies, universities, and firms that specialize in educational and training materials.

Computer, Information, and Library Sciences

Computer and information science and systems majors stress the theoretical aspects of the computer and emphasize mathematical and scientific disciplines. Data processing, programming, and computer technology programs tend to be more practical; they are more oriented toward business than to scientific applications and to working directly with the computer or with peripheral equipment. Career possibilities for computer and information sciences include data processing, programming, and systems development or maintenance in almost any setting: business and industry, banking and finance, government, colleges and universities, libraries, software firms, service bureaus, computer manufacturers, publishing, and communications.

STUDENT COUNSEL

Q: Why did you choose a seven-year premed program instead of a traditional four-year college program?

A: I'm one of those people who knew what I wanted to do since I was very little, so that made choosing easier. If I was not 100 percent sure that I wanted to go into medicine, I would not be in this seven-year program. For students who are interested but not really sure that they want to go into medicine, they should pick a school they will enjoy, get a good education, and then worry about medical school. That way, if they decide in their junior year that medicine is not for them, they have options.

Elliot Servais
Premed
Boston University

STUDENT COUNSEL

Q: What advice do you have for high school students who are considering going into engineering?

A: In high school, take AP courses in a lot of different areas. That gives you an idea of what those subjects will be like in college. I knew I was good at science and math but didn't know which direction would really interest me. I took an AP English course and didn't do so well. Then I took a chemistry course and knew I could see myself digging deeper. An AP course will give you an idea if this subject is something you want to pursue as a major.

Most engineering majors don't have to decide on what engineering discipline they want until their sophomore year. As a freshman, you can take courses and not really know what type of engineering you want. I took an introduction to engineering course, and it convinced me that this is what I want to do. Your freshman year will give you a flavor for different engineering majors so you don't end up in your junior year and realize you don't like that major. The first semester here is totally an adjustment period.

Michael Romano
Chemical Engineering
Cornell University

Library science gives preprofessional background in library work and provides valuable knowledge of research sources, indexing, abstracting, computer technology, and media technology, which is useful for further study in any professional field. In most cases, a master's degree in library science is necessary to obtain a job as a librarian. Library science majors find positions in public, school, college, corporate, and government libraries and research centers; book publishing (especially reference books); database and information retrieval services; and communications (especially audiovisual media).

Education

Positions as teachers in public elementary and secondary schools, private day and boarding schools, religious and parochial schools, vocational schools, and proprietary schools are the jobs most often filled by education majors. However, teaching positions also exist in noneducational institutions, such as museums, historical societies, prisons, hospitals, and nursing homes, as well as jobs as educators and

trainers in government and industry. Administrative (nonteaching) positions in employee relations and personnel, public relations, marketing and sales, educational publishing, TV and film media, test development firms, and government and community social service agencies also tap the skills and interests of education majors.

Engineering and Engineering Technologies

Engineering and science technology majors prepare students for practical design and production work rather than for jobs that require more theoretical, scientific, and mathematical knowledge. Engineers work in a variety of fields, including aeronautics, bioengineering, geology, nuclear engineering, and quality control and safety. Industry, research labs, and government agencies where technology plays a key role, such as in manufacturing, electronics, construction communications, transportation, and utilities, hire engineering as well as engineering technology and science technology graduates regularly. Work may be in technical activities (research, development, design, production, testing, scientific programming, or systems analysis) or in nontechnical areas where a technical degree is needed, such as marketing, sales, or administration.

Foreign Language and Literature

Knowledge of foreign languages and cultures is becoming increasingly recognized as important in today's international world. Language majors possess a skill that is used in organizations with international dealings as well as in career fields and geographical areas where languages other than English are prominent. Career possibilities include positions with business firms with international subsidiaries; import-export firms; international banking; travel agencies; airlines; tourist services; government and international agencies dealing with international affairs, foreign trade, diplomacy, customs, or immigration; secondary school foreign language teaching and bilingual education (which usually require education courses); freelance translating and

(Continued on page 103)

MAKING THAT MAJOR DECISION: REAL-LIFE ADVICE FROM COLLEGE SENIORS

Somewhere between her junior and senior year in high school, Karen Gliebe got the psychology bug. When choosing a major in college, she knew just what she wanted. Justin Bintrim, on the other hand, did a complete 180. He thought he'd study physics, then veered toward philosophy. It wasn't until he took survey courses in literature that he found where his heart really lay, and now he's graduating with a degree in English.

You might find yourself at either end of this spectrum when choosing a major. Either you'll know just what you want or you'll try on a number of different hats before finally settling on one. To give you a taste of what it could be like for you, meet four college seniors who have been through the trials and errors of choosing their majors. Hopefully you'll pick up some pointers from them or at least find out that you don't have to worry so much about what your major will be.

From Grove City College, a liberal arts school in Pennsylvania, meet Karen Gliebe, who will graduate with a degree in psychology, and English major Justin Bintrim. From Michigan State University, meet computer engineering major Seth Mosier and Kim Trouten, who is finishing up a zoology degree. Here's what they had to say:

HOW THEY CHOSE THEIR MAJORS

Karen: During high school, I volunteered at a retirement center, and my supervisor gave me a lot of exposure to applied psychology. After my freshman year in college, I talked to people who were using a psychology degree. You put in a lot of work for a degree and can wonder if it's worth all the work. It helps to talk to someone who has gone through it so you can see if that's what you want to be doing when you graduate.

Justin: I wasn't sure about what my major would be. One professor told me to take survey courses to see if I was interested in the subject. I took English literature, math, psychology, and philosophy. I liked English the best and did well in it. The next semester, I took two English courses and decided to switch my major. My professors told me not to worry about choosing a major. They said to get my feet wet and we'll talk about your major in two years. I decided that if they're not worried about a major, I wouldn't be either, but I still had it on my mind. I was around older students who were thinking about their careers, so I talked to them about the jobs they had lined up.

Seth: I liked computers in high school. In college, I started out in computer science but got sick of coding. My interest in computers made me pick computer science right off the bat. I didn't know about computer engineering until I got to college.

Kim: I wanted to be a veterinarian but after two years decided that I didn't want to go to school for that long. I was still interested in animals and had two options. One was in animal science, which is working more with farm animals, or going into zoology. I decided to concentrate on zoo and aquarium science. Besides being a vet, the closest interaction with animals would be being a zookeeper.

THE ELECTIVES THEY TOOK AND WHY

Karen: My adviser told me to take different classes, so I took philosophy, art, religion, and extra psychology classes that weren't required.

Justin: I was planning to do a double major, but my professors said to take what interested me. English majors have lots of freedom to take different courses, unlike science majors.

Seth: Because I'm in computer engineering, I don't get to take a lot of electives. I am taking a swimming class right now and took a critical incident analysis class where we looked at major accidents. I wanted something that wasn't computer engineering-related but extremely technical.

Kim: I took some kinesiology classes, which was pretty much an aerobics class. I needed to work out and figured I could get credit for it. I also took sign language because I'm interested in it.

WHAT THEY'RE GOING TO DO WITH THEIR DEGREES

Karen: I want to go to graduate school and hopefully get some experience working with kids.

Justin: I'm applying to graduate school in English literature and cultural studies. I want to do research and become a college professor.

Seth: I'm going to work for the defense department. It's not the highest offer I've gotten, but it will be the most fun, which is more important to me than the money.

Kim: My goals have changed again. I don't plan on using my degree. I just got married a year ago, and my husband and I want to go into full-time ministry. I'll work for a while, and then we'll go overseas.

THE CHANGES THEY WOULD MAKE IN THE CLASSES THEY TOOK IF THEY COULD

Karen: There are classes I wouldn't necessarily take again. But even though I didn't learn as much as I wanted to, it was worth it. I learned how to work and how to organize my efforts.

Justin: I should have worried less about choosing a major when I first started college. I didn't have the perspective as to how much time I had to choose.

Seth: I have friends who would change the order in which they took their humanities classes. I was lucky enough to think ahead and spread those classes out over the entire time. Most [engineering] students take them their freshman year to get them all out of the way. Later on, they're locked in the engineering building all day. Because I didn't, it was nice for me to get my mind off engineering.

Kim: Something I can't change are the labs. They require a lot of work, and you only get one credit for 3 hours. Some labs take a lot of work outside of class hours. I had a comparative anatomy lab, which kept me busy over entire weekends. I suggest you don't take a lot of classes that require labs all at once.

THEIR ADVICE FOR YOU

Karen: You don't have to know what you want to do with the rest of your life when you get to college. Most people don't even stay with the major they first choose. Colleges recognize that you will see things you may have not considered at first. Some high school students say they won't go to college unless they know what they want to do.

Justin: If it's possible, take a little of this and a little of that. If you're an engineering student, you'll have it all planned out [for you], but if you're a liberal arts major and are not sure, you probably can take something from each department.

Seth: If possible, take AP exams in high school. You'll be able to make a decision about a major. Freshmen who think they want to do engineering suffer through math and physics classes. Then by their sophomore or junior year, they realize they don't want to be engineers. If they'd taken AP classes, they'd know by their freshman year.

Kim: When I changed my major, I was worried that I might have spent a year in classes that wouldn't count toward my new major. But you shouldn't be scared to change majors because if you stick with something you don't like, you'll have to go back and take other classes anyway.

Though these four seniors arrived at a decision about which major they wanted in different ways, they had similar things to say:

- It's okay to change your mind about what you want out of college.

- To find out which major you might want, start with what you like to do.

- Talk to professionals who have jobs in the fields that interest you.

- Ask your professors about what kinds of jobs you could get with the degree you're considering.

- Talk to seniors who will be graduating with a degree in the major you're considering.

- Take electives in areas that interest you, even though they may have nothing to do with your major.

- College is a time to explore many different options, so take advantage of the opportunity.

interpreting (high level of skill necessary); foreign language publishing; and computer programming (especially for linguistics majors).

Health Sciences

Health professions majors, while having a scientific core, are more focused on applying the results of scientific investigation than on the scientific disciplines themselves. Allied health majors prepare graduates to assist health professionals in providing diagnostics, therapeutics, and rehabilitation. Medical science majors, such as optometry, pharmacy, and the premedical profession sequences, are, for the most part, preprofessional studies that compose the scientific disciplines necessary for admission to graduate or professional school in the health or medical fields. Health service and technology majors prepare students for positions in the health fields that primarily involve services to patients or working with complex machinery and materials. Medical technologies cover a wide range of fields, such as cytotechnology, biomedical technologies, and operating room technology.

Administrative, professional, or research assistant positions in health agencies, hospitals, occupational health units in industry, community and school health departments, government agencies (public health, environmental protection), and international health organizations are available to majors in health fields, as are jobs in marketing and sales of health-related products and services, health education (with education courses), advertising and public relations, journalism and publishing, and technical writing.

Home Economics and Social Services

Home economics encompasses many different fields—basic studies in foods and textiles as well as consumer economics and leisure studies—that overlap with aspects of agriculture, social science, and education. Jobs can be found in government and community agencies (especially those in education, health, housing, or human services), nursing homes, child-care centers, journalism, radio/TV, educational media, and publishing. Types of work also include marketing, sales, and customer service in consumer-related industries, such as food processing and packaging, appliance manufacturing, utilities, textiles, and secondary school home economics teaching (which usually requires education courses).

Majors in social services find administrative positions in government and community health, welfare, and social service agencies, such as hospitals, clinics, YMCAs and YWCAs, recreation commissions, welfare agencies, and employment services. See the "Law and Legal Studies" section for information on more law-related social services.

Humanities (Miscellaneous)

The majors that constitute the humanities (sometimes called "letters") are the most general and widely applicable and the least vocationally oriented of the liberal arts. They are essentially studies of the ideas and concerns of human kind. These include classics, history of philosophy, history of science, linguistics, and medieval studies. Career possibilities for humanities majors can be found in business firms, government and community agencies, advertising and public relations, marketing and sales, publishing, journalism and radio/TV, secondary school teaching in English and literature (which usually requires education courses), freelance writing and editing, and computer programming (especially for those with a background in logic or linguistics).

Law and Legal Studies

Students of legal studies can use their knowledge of law and government in fields involving the making, breaking, and enforcement of laws; the crimes, trials, and punishment of law breakers; and the running of all branches of government at local, state, and federal levels. Graduates find positions of all types in law firms, legal departments of other organizations, the court or prison system, government agencies (such as law enforcement agencies or offices of state and federal attorneys general), and police departments.

Mathematics and Physical Sciences

Mathematics is the science of numbers and the abstract formulation of their operations. Physical sciences involve the study of the laws and structures of physical matter. The quantitative skills acquired through the study of science and mathematics are especially useful for computer-related careers. Career possibilities include positions in industry (manufacturing and processing companies, electronics firms, defense contractors, consulting firms); government agencies (defense, environmental protection, law enforcement); scientific/technical writing, editing, or illustrating; journalism (science reporting); secondary school teaching (usually requiring education courses); research and laboratory analysis and testing; statistical analysis; computer programming; systems analysis; surveying and mapping; weather forecasting; and technical sales.

Natural Resources

A major in the natural resources field prepares students for work in areas as generalized as environmental conservation and as specialized as groundwater contamination. Jobs are available in industry (food, energy, natural resources, and pulp and paper companies), consulting firms, state and federal government agencies (primarily the Departments of Agriculture and the Interior), and public and private conservation agencies. See the "Agriculture" and "Biological Sciences" sections for more information on natural resources-related fields.

Psychology

Psychology majors involve the study of behavior and can range from the biological to the sociological. Students can study individual behavior, usually that of humans, or the behavior of crowds. Students of psychology do not always go into the more obvious clinical fields, the fields in which psychologists work with patients. Certain areas of psychology, such as industrial/organizational, experimental, and social, are not clinically oriented. Psychology and counseling careers can be in government (such as mental health

agencies), schools, hospitals, clinics, private practice, industry, test development firms, social work, and personnel. The careers listed in the "Social Sciences" section are also pursued by psychology and counseling majors.

Religion

Religion majors are usually seen as preprofessional studies for those who are interested in entering the ministry. Career possibilities for religion also include casework, youth counseling, administration in community and social service organizations, teaching in religious educational institutions, and writing for religious and lay publications. Religious studies also prepare students for the kinds of jobs other humanities majors often pursue.

Social Sciences

Social sciences majors study people in relation to their society. Thus, social science majors can apply their education to a wide range of occupations that deal with social issues and activities. Career opportunities are varied. People with degrees in the social sciences find careers in government, business, community agencies (serving children, youth, senior citizens), advertising and public relations, marketing and sales, secondary school social studies teaching (with education courses), casework, law enforcement, parks and recreation, museum work (especially for anthropology, archaeology, geography, and history majors), preservation (especially for anthropology, archaeology, geography, and history majors), banking and finance (especially for economics majors), market and survey research, statistical analysis, publishing, fundraising and development, and political campaigning.

Technologies

Technology majors, along with trade fields, are most often offered as two-year programs. Majors in technology fields prepare students directly for jobs; however, positions are in practical design and production work rather than in areas that require more theoretical, scientific, and mathematical knowledge.

Engineering technologies prepare students with the basic training in specific fields (e.g., electronics, mechanics, or chemistry) that are necessary to become technicians on the support staffs of engineers. Other technology majors center more on maintenance and repair. Work may be in technical activities, such as production or testing, or in nontechnical areas where a technical degree is needed, such as marketing, sales, or administration. Industries, research labs, and government agencies in which technology plays a key role—such as in manufacturing, electronics, construction, communications, transportation, and utilities—hire technology graduates regularly.

Still Unsure?

Relax! You don't have to know your major before you enroll in college. More than half of all freshmen are undecided when they start school and prefer to get a feel for what's available at college before making a decision. Most four-year colleges don't require students to formally declare a major until the end of their sophomore year or beginning of their junior year. Part of the experience of college is being exposed to new subjects and new ideas. Chances are your high school never offered anthropology. Or marine biology. Or applied mathematics. So take these classes and follow your interests. While you're fulfilling your general course requirements, you might stumble upon a major that appeals to you, or maybe you'll discover a new interest while you're volunteering or involved with other extracurricular activities. Talking to other students might lead to new options you'll want to explore.

Can I Change My Major If I Change My Mind?

Choosing a major does not set your future in stone, nor does it necessarily disrupt your life if you need to change your major. However, there are advantages to choosing a major sooner rather than later. If you wait too long to choose, you may have to take additional classes to satisfy the requirements, which may cost you additional time and money.

THE OTHER SIDE OF COLLEGE: HAVING FUN!

There is more to college than writing papers, reading books, and sitting through lectures. Your social life plays an integral part in your college experience.

Meeting New People

The easiest time to meet new people is at the beginning of something new. New situations shake people up and make them feel just uncomfortable enough to take the risk of extending their hand in friendship. Fortunately for you, college is filled with new experiences. There are the first weeks of being the newest students. This can be quickly followed by being a new member of a club or activity. And with each passing semester, you will be in new classes with new teachers and new faces. College should be a time of constantly challenging and expanding yourself, so never feel that it is too late to meet new people.

But just how do you take that first step in forming a relationship? It's surprisingly easy. The first few weeks of school will require you to stand in many lines. Some will be to buy books; others will be to get meals. One will be to get a student I.D. card. Another will be to register for classes. While standing in line, turn around and introduce yourself to the person behind you. Focus on what you have in common and try to downplay the differences. Soon you will find the two of you have plenty to talk about. When it is time to leave the line, arrange to have coffee later or to see a movie. This will help you form relationships with the people you meet.

Be open to the opportunities of meeting new people and having new experiences. Join clubs and activities. Investigate rock-climbing. Try ballet. Write for the school paper. But most of all, get involved.

Campus Activities

College life will place a lot of demands on you. Your classes will be challenging. Your professors will expect more from you. You will have to budget and manage your own money. But there is a plus side you probably haven't thought of yet: college students do have free time.

The average student spends about three hours a day in class. Add to this the time you will need to spend studying, eating, and socializing, and you will still have time to spare. One of the best ways to use this time is to participate in campus activities.

Intramural Sports

Intramurals are sports played for competition between members of the same campus community. They provide competition and a sense of belonging without the same level of intensity in practice schedules. Anyone can join an intramural sport. Often there are teams formed by dormitories, sororities, or fraternities that play team sports such as soccer, volleyball, basketball, flag-football, baseball, and softball. There are also individual intramural sports such as swimming, golf, wrestling, and diving. If you want to get involved, just stop by the intramural office. Usually it is located near the student government office.

Student Government

Student government will be set up in a way that is probably similar to your high school. Students form committees and run for office. However, student government in college has more power than in high school. The officers address all of their class's concerns directly to the President of the college or university and the Board of Trustees. Most student governments have a branch responsible for student activities that brings in big name entertainers and controversial speakers. You may want to get involved to see how such contacts are made and such appearances negotiated.

Community Service

Another aspect of student life is volunteering, commonly called community service. Many colleges offer a range of opportunities. Some allow you to simply commit an afternoon to a cause, such as passing out food at a food bank. Others require an ongoing commitment. For example, you might decide to help an adult learn to read every Thursday at 4 p.m. for three months. Some colleges will link a service commitment with class credit. This will enhance your learning, giving you some real-world experience. Be sure to stop by your community service office and see what is available.

Clubs

There are a variety of clubs on most college campuses spanning just about every topic you can imagine. Amnesty International regularly meets on most campuses to write letters to help free prisoners in foreign lands. Most college majors band together in a club to discuss their common interests and career potential. There are also clubs that are based on the use of certain computer software or that engage in outdoor activities like sailing or downhill skiing. The list is endless. If you cannot find a club for your interest, consider starting one of your own. Stop by the student government office to see what rules you will need to follow. You will also need to find a location to hold meetings and post signs to advertise your club. When you hold your first meeting, you will probably be surprised at how many people are willing to take a chance and try a new club.

Greek Life

A major misconception of Greek life is that it revolves around wild parties and alcohol. In fact, the vast majority of fraternities and sororities focus on instilling values of scholarship, friendship, leadership, and service in their members. From this point forward, we will refer to both fraternities and sororities as fraternities.

Scholarship

A fraternity experience helps you make the academic transition from high school to college. Although the classes taken in high school are challenging, they'll be even harder in college. Fraternities usually require members to meet certain academic standards. Many hold mandatory study times, old class notes and exams are usually kept on file for study purposes, and personal tutors are often available. Members of a fraternity have a natural vested interest in seeing that other members succeed academically, so older members often assist younger members with their studies.

Friendship

Social life is an important component of Greek life. Social functions offer an excellent opportunity for freshmen to become better acquainted with others in the chapter. Whether it is a Halloween party or a formal dance, there are numerous chances for members to develop poise and confidence. By participating in these functions, students enrich friendships and build memories that will last a lifetime. Remember, social functions aren't only parties; they can include such activities as intramural sports and Homecoming.

Leadership

Because fraternities are self-governing organizations, leadership opportunities abound. Students are given hands-on experience in leading committees, managing budgets, and interacting with faculty members and administrators. Most houses have as many as ten officers, along with an array of committee members. By becoming actively involved in leadership roles, students gain valuable experience that is essential for a successful career. Interestingly, although Greeks represent less than 10 percent of the undergraduate student population, they hold the majority of leadership positions on campus.

Service

According to the North-American Interfraternity Council, fraternities are increasingly becoming involved in philanthropies and hands-on service projects. Helping less fortunate people has become a major focus of Greek life. This can vary from work with Easter Seals, blood drives, and food pantry collections to community upkeep, such as picking up trash, painting houses, or cleaning up area parks.

Greeks also get involved in projects with organizations such as Habitat for Humanity, the American Heart Association, and Children's Miracle Network. By being involved in philanthropic projects, students not only raise money for worthwhile causes, but they also gain a deeper insight into themselves and their responsibility to the community.

Roommates

When you arrive on campus, you will face a daunting task: to live peacefully with a stranger for the rest of the academic year.

To make this task easier, most schools use some type of room assignment survey. This can make roommate matches more successful. For example, two people who prefer to stay up late and play guitar can be matched, while two people who prefer to rise at dawn and hit the track can be a pair. Such differences are easy to ask about on a survey and easy for students to report. However, surveys cannot ask everything, and chances are pretty good that

HOMESICKNESS

Homesickness in its most basic form is a longing for the stuff of home: your parents, friends, bedroom, school, and all of the other familiar people and objects that make you comfortable. But on another level, homesickness is a longing to go back in time. Moving away to college forces you to take on new responsibilities and begin to act like an adult. This can be scary.

While this condition is often described as a "sickness," no pill will provide a quick fix. Instead, you need to acknowledge that your feelings are a normal reaction to a significant change in your life. Allow yourself to feel the sadness of moving on in life and be open to conversations about it that may crop up in your dorm or among your new friends. After all, everyone is dealing with this issue. Then, make an effort to create a new home and a new life on campus. Create new habits and routines so that this once-strange place becomes familiar. Join activities and engage in campus life. This will help you to create a feeling of belonging that will ultimately be the key to overcoming homesickness.

something about your roommate is going to get on your nerves.

In order to avoid conflict, plan ahead. When you first meet, work out some ground rules. Most schools have roommates write a contract together and sign it during the first week of school. Ground rules help eliminate conflict from the start by allowing each person to know what is expected. You should consider the following areas: privacy, quiet time, chores, and borrowing.

When considering privacy, think about how much time alone you need each day and how you and your roommate will arrange for private time. Class schedules usually give you some alone time. Be aware of this; if your class is cancelled, consider going for a cup of coffee or a browse in the bookstore instead of immediately rushing back to the room. Privacy also relates to giving your roommate space when he or she has had a bad day or just needs time to think. Set up clear hours for quiet time. Your dorm will already have some quiet hours established. You may choose to simply reiterate those or add additional time. Just be clear.

Two other potentially stormy issues are chores and borrowing. If there are cleaning chores that need to be shared, make a schedule and stick to it. No one appreciates a sink full of dirty dishes or a dingy shower. Remember the golden rule: do your chores as you wish your roommate would. When it comes to borrowing, set up clear rules. The safest bet is to not allow it; but if you do, limit when, for how long, and what will be done in case of damage.

Another issue many students confront is whether or not to live with a best friend from high school who is attending the same college. Generally, this is a bad idea for several reasons. First, you may think you know your best friend inside and out, but you may be surprised by her personal living habits. There is nothing like the closeness of a dorm room to reveal the annoying routines of your friend. Plus, personalities can change rapidly in college. Once you are away from home, you may be surprised at how you or your friend transforms from shy and introverted to late night partygoer. This can cause conflict. A final downfall is that the two of you will

stick together like glue in the first few weeks and miss out on opportunities to meet other people who are also new, vulnerable, and open to new friendships.

Armed with this information, you should have a smooth year with your new roommate. But just in case you are the exception, most colleges will allow students who absolutely cannot get along to move. Prior to moving, each student must usually go through a dispute resolution process. This typically involves your Resident Adviser, you, and your roommate trying to work through your problems in a structured way.

Living with a roommate can be challenging at times, but the ultimate rewards—meeting someone new, encountering new ideas, and learning how to compromise—will serve you well later in life. Enjoy your roommate and all the experiences you will have, both good and bad, for they are all part of the college experience.

Commuting from Home

For some students, home during the college years is the same house they grew up in. Whether you are in this situation because you can't afford to live on campus or because you'd just rather live at home with your family, some basic guidelines will keep you connected with campus life.

By all means, do not just go straight home after class. Spend some of your free time at school. Usually there is a student union or a coffee shop where students gather and socialize. Make it a point to go there and talk to people between classes. Also, get involved in extracurricular activities, and visit classmates in the dorms.

If you drive to school, find other students who want to carpool. Most schools have a commuter's office or club that will give you a list of people who live near you. Sharing a car ride will give you time to talk and form a relationship with someone else who knows about the challenges of commuting.

Commuters's clubs also sponsor a variety of activities throughout the year—give them a try! Be sure also to consider the variety of activities open to all members of the student body, ranging from student government to community service to intramural sports. You may find this takes a bit more effort on your part, but the payoff in the close friendships you'll form will more than make up for it.

WHAT IF YOU DON'T LIKE THE COLLEGE YOU PICK

In the best of all worlds, you compile a list of colleges, find the most compatible one, and are accepted. You have a great time, learn a lot, graduate, and head off to a budding career. However, you may find the college you chose isn't the best of all worlds. Imagine these scenarios:

1. Halfway through your first semester of college, you come to the distressing conclusion that you can't stand being there for whatever reason. The courses don't match your interests. The campus is out in the boonies, and you don't ever want to see another cow. The selection of extracurricular activities doesn't cut it.

2. You have methodically planned to go to a community college for two years and move to a four-year college to complete your degree. Transferring takes you nearer to your goal.

3. You thought you wanted to major in art, but by the end of the first semester, you find yourself more interested in English lit. Things get confusing, so you drop out of college to sort out your thoughts and now you want to drop back in, hoping to rescue some of those credits.

4. You didn't do that well in high school— socializing got in the way of studying. But you've wised up, have gotten serious about your future, and two years of community college have brightened your prospects of transferring to a four-year institution.

Circumstances shift, people change, and, realistically speaking, it's not all that uncommon to transfer. Many people do. The reasons why students transfer run the gamut, as do the institutional policies that govern them. The most common transfers are students who move from a two-year to a four-year university or the person who opts for a career change midstream.

Whatever reasons you might have for wanting to transfer, you will be doing more than just switching academic gears. Aside from potentially losing credits, time, and money, transferring means again adjusting to a new situation. This affects just about all transfer students, from those who made a mistake in choosing a college to those who planned to go to a two-year college and then transferred to a four-year campus. People choose colleges for arbitrary reasons. That's why admissions departments try to ensure a good match between the student and campus before classes begin. Unfortunately, sometimes students don't realize they've made a mistake until it's too late.

The best way to avoid transferring is to extensively research a college or university before choosing it. Visit the campus and stay overnight, talk to admissions and faculty members, and try to learn as much as you can.

10 Chapter

OTHER OPTIONS AFTER HIGH SCHOOL

Thirty years ago, most young people went directly to work after high school. Today, most young people first go to school for more training, but the majority don't go to traditional four-year colleges.

ACCORDING TO SHANNON MCBRIDE, Director of the Golden Crescent Tech Prep Partnership in Victoria, Texas, "Only 40 percent of high school graduates attempt to go to a four-year college, and of those, only 25 percent get their degree. And of that 25 percent, only 37 percent use the degree they got in that area."

So why aren't the remaining 60 percent of students choosing a traditional four-year college? The reasons are as varied as the students. Life events can often interfere with plans to attend college. Responsibilities to a family may materialize that make it impossible to delay earning an income for four years. One may have to work and go to school. And traditional colleges demand certain conventions, behaviors, and attitudes that don't fit every kind of person. Some people need a lot of physical activity to feel satisfied, while others just aren't interested in spending day after day sitting, reading, memorizing, and analyzing. Years of strict time management and postponed rewards are more than they can stand.

If any of these reasons ring true with you, there are still postsecondary options for you, all of which will not only allow you to pursue further education but also will train you for a career. Let's take a look at some of these educational directions you can follow.

DISTANCE LEARNING

As a future college student, can you picture yourself in any of these scenarios?

1. You need some information, but the only place to find it is at a big state university. Trouble is, it's hundreds of miles away. No problem. You simply go to your local community college and hook up electronically with the university. Voilà! The resources are brought to you.

2. That ten-page paper is due in a few days, but you still have some last-minute questions to ask the professor before you turn it in. Only one problem: you won't be able to see the professor until after the paper is due. Being a night owl, you also want to work on it when your roommate is asleep. Not to worry. Since you have the professor's e-mail address, just like all the other students in the class, you simply e-mail your question to her. She replies. You get your answer, finish the paper, and even turn it in electronically.

3. After graduating from high school, you can't go to college right away, but your employer has a neat hook up with a college that offers courses via the Internet. During your lunch hours, you and several of your work buddies log in to a class and get college credit.

Not too long ago, if you'd offered these scenarios to high school graduates as real possibilities, they would have thought you were a sci-fi freak. Distance education was not common at all—or if it was, it usually meant getting courses via snail mail or on videotape. Well, today you are in the right place at the right time. Distance education is a reality for countless high school graduates.

What distance education now means is that you can access educational programs and not have to physically be in a classroom on a campus. Through such technologies as cable or satellite television, videotapes and audiotapes, fax, computer modem, computer conferencing and videoconferencing, and other means of electronic delivery, the classroom comes to you—sometimes even if you're sitting in your room in your bunny slippers and it's 2 in the morning.

Distance learning expands the reach of the classroom by using various technologies to deliver university resources to off-campus sites, transmit college courses into the workplace, and enable you to view class lectures in the comfort of your home.

Where and How Can I Take Distance Learning Courses?

The technology for new, cheaper telecommunications technology is getting better all the time, and there is a growing demand for education by people who can't afford either the time or money to be a full-time, on-campus student. To fill that demand, educational networks also are growing and changing how and when you can access college courses.

Most states have established new distance learning systems to advance the delivery of instruction to schools, postsecondary institutions, and state government agencies. Colleges and universities are collaborating with commercial telecommunication entities, including online information services, such as America Online and cable and telephone companies, to provide education to far-flung student constituencies. Professions such as law, medicine, and accounting, as well as knowledge-based industries, are utilizing telecommunications networks for the transmission of customized higher education programs to working professionals, technicians, and managers.

Ways in Which Distance Learning May Be Offered:

- **Credit courses.** In general, if these credit courses are completed successfully, they may be applied toward a degree.

- **Noncredit courses and courses offered for professional certification.** These programs can help you acquire specialized knowledge in a concentrated, time-efficient manner and stay on top of the latest developments in your field. They provide a flexible way for you to prepare for a new career or study for professional licensure and certification. Many of these university programs are created in cooperation with professional and trade associations so that courses are based on real-life workforce needs, and the practical skills learned are immediately applicable in the field.

The Way Distance Learning Works

Enrolling in a distance learning course may simply involve filling out a registration form, making sure that you have access to the equipment needed, and paying the tuition and fees by check, money order, or credit card. In these cases, your applications may be accepted without entrance examinations or proof of prior educational experience.

Other courses may involve educational prerequisites and access to equipment not found in all geographic locations. Some institutions offer detailed information about individual courses, such as a course outline, upon request. If you have access to the Internet and simply wish to review course descriptions, you may be able to peruse an institution's course catalogs electronically by accessing the institution's home page on the Web.

Time Requirements

Some courses allow you to enroll at your convenience and work at your own pace. Others closely adhere to a traditional classroom schedule. Specific policies and time limitations pertaining to withdrawals, refunds, transfers, and renewal periods can be found in the institutional catalog.

Admission to a Degree Program

If you plan to enter a degree program, you should consult the academic advising department of the institution of your choice to learn about entrance requirements and application procedures. You may find it necessary to develop a portfolio of your past experiences and accomplishments that may have resulted in college-level learning.

How Do I Communicate with My Instructor?

Student-faculty exchanges occur using electronic communication (through fax and e-mail). Many institutions offer their distance learning students access to toll-free numbers so students can talk to their professors or teaching assistants without incurring any long-distance charges.

Responses to your instructor's comments on your lessons, requests for clarification of comments, and all other exchanges between you and your instructor will take time. Interaction with your instructor—whether by computer, phone, or letter—is important, and you must be willing to take the initiative.

What Else Does Distance Learning Offer?

Distance learning comes in a variety of colors and flavors. Along with traditional college degrees, you can earn professional certification or continuing education units (CEUs) in a particular field.

Professional Certification

Certificate programs often focus on employment specializations, such as hazardous waste management or electronic publishing, and can be helpful to those seeking to advance or change careers. Also, many states mandate continuing education for professionals such as teachers, nursing home administrators, or accountants. Distance learning offers a convenient way for many individuals to meet professional certification requirements. Health care, engineering, and education are just a few of the many professions that take advantage of distance learning to help their professionals maintain certification.

Many colleges offer a sequence of distance learning courses in a specific field of a profession. For instance, within the engineering profession, certificate programs in computer-integrated manufacturing, systems engineering, test and evaluation, waste management education, and research consortium are offered via distance learning.

Business offerings include distance learning certification in information technology, total quality management, and health services management.

Within the field of education, you'll find distance learning certificate programs in areas such as early reading instruction and special education for the learning handicapped. There are opportunities for you to earn degrees at a distance at the associate, baccalaureate, and graduate levels. Two-year community college students are now able to earn baccalaureate degrees—without relocating—by transferring to distance learning programs offered by four-year universities. Corporations are forming partnerships with universities to bring college courses to worksites and encourage employees to continue their education. Distance learning is especially popular among people who want to earn their degree part-time while continuing to work full-time. Although on-campus residencies are sometimes required for certain distance learning degree programs, they generally can be completed while employees are on short-term leave or vacation.

Continuing Education Units (CEUs)

If you choose to take a course on a noncredit basis, you may be able to earn continuing education units (CEUs). The CEU system is a nationally recognized system to provide a standardized measure for accumulating, transferring, and recognizing participation in continuing education programs. One CEU is defined as 10 contact hours of participation in an organized continuing education experience under responsible sponsorship, capable direction, and qualified instruction.

COMMUNITY COLLEGES

Two-year colleges or community colleges, are often called "the people's colleges." With their open-door policies (admission is open to individuals with a high school diploma or its equivalent), community colleges provide access to higher education for millions of Americans who might otherwise be excluded from higher education. Community college students are diverse, of all ages, races, and economic backgrounds. While many community college students enroll full-time, an equally large number attend on a part-time basis so they can fulfill employment and family commitments as they advance their education.

Today, there are more than 1,800 community colleges in the United States. They enroll more than 7.4 million students, who represent more than 50 percent of all undergraduates in the United States. As you can see, millions of first-time freshmen begin their higher education in a community college.

Community colleges are also referred to as either technical or junior colleges, and they may either be under public or independent control. What unites all two-year colleges is that they are regionally accredited, postsecondary institutions, whose highest credential awarded is the associate degree. With few exceptions, community colleges offer a comprehensive curriculum, which includes transfer, technical, and continuing education programs.

Important Factors in a Community College Education

The student who attends a community college can count on receiving quality instruction in a supportive learning community. This setting frees the student to pursue his or her own goals, nurture special talents, explore new fields of learning, and develop the capacity for lifelong learning.

From the student's perspective, four character-istics capture the essence of community colleges:

- They are community-based institutions that work in close partnership with high schools, community groups, and employers in extending high-quality programs at convenient times and places.

- Community colleges are cost effective. Annual tuition and fees at public community colleges average approximately half those at public four-year colleges and less than 15 percent of private four-year institutions. In addition, since most community colleges are generally close to their students' homes, these students can also save a significant amount of money on the room, board, and transportation expenses traditionally associated with a college education.

- They provide a caring environment, with faculty members who are expert instructors, known for excellent teaching and for meeting students at the point of their individual needs, regardless of age, sex, race, current job status, or previous academic preparation. Community colleges join a strong curriculum with a broad range of counseling and career services that are intended to assist students in making the most of their educational opportunities.

A SCHOLARSHIP FOR CAREER COLLEGE STUDENTS

The Imagine America Scholarship can help those who dream of a career but might not be able to achieve it through traditional college education.

What Is the Imagine America Scholarship?

Introduced in 1998 by the Career College Foundation, the Imagine America Scholarship aims to reduce the growing "skills gap" in America. Any graduating high school senior can be considered for selection for one of the two scholarships awarded to his or her high school. The Imagine America Scholarship gives 10,000 graduating high school seniors scholarships of $1,000 to be used at more than 300 participating career colleges and schools across the country.

You Can Participate in the Imagine America Scholarship If:

- You attend any private postsecondary institution that is accredited by an agency recognized by the U.S. Department of Education.

- You are graduating from high school this year.

To find out more about the Imagine America Scholarship Program, talk to your high school counselor or visit www.petersons.com/cca for more information.

- Many offer comprehensive programs, including transfer curricula in such liberal arts programs as chemistry, psychology, and business management, that lead directly to a baccalaureate degree and career programs that prepare students for employment or assist those already employed to upgrade their skills. For those students who need to strengthen their academic skills, community colleges also offer a wide range of developmental programs in mathematics, languages, and learning skills, designed to prepare the student for success in college studies.

Getting to Know Your Two-Year College

The best way to learn about your college is to visit in person. During a campus visit, be prepared to ask a lot of questions. Talk to students, faculty members, administrators, and counselors about the college and its programs, particularly those in which you have a special interest. Ask about available certificates and associate degrees. Don't be shy. Do what you can to dig below the surface. Ask college officials about the transfer rate to four-year colleges. If a college emphasizes student services, find out what particular assistance is offered, such as educational or career guidance. Colleges are eager to provide you with the information you need to make informed decisions.

The Money Factor

For many students, the decision to attend a community college is often based on financial factors. If you aren't sure what you want to do or what talents you have, community colleges allow you the freedom to explore different career interests at a low cost. For those students who can't afford the cost of university tuition, community colleges let them take care of their basic classes before transferring to a four-year institution. Many two-year colleges can now offer you instruction in your own home through cable television or public broadcast stations or through home study courses that can save both time and money. Look into all your options, and be sure to add up all the costs of attending various colleges before deciding which is best for you.

Working and Going to School

Many two-year college students maintain full-time or part-time employment while they earn their degrees. Over the past decades, a steadily growing number of students have chosen to attend community colleges while they fulfill family and employment responsibilities. To enable these students to balance the demands of home, work, and school, most community colleges offer classes at night and on weekends.

For the full-time student, the usual length of time it takes to obtain an associate degree is two years. However, your length of study will depend on the course load you take: the fewer credits you earn each term, the longer it will take you to earn a degree. To assist you in moving more quickly toward your degree, many community colleges now award credit through examination or for equivalent knowledge gained through relevant life experiences. Be certain to

MOST POPULAR MAJORS FOR COMMUNITY COLLEGE GRADS

The American Association of Community Colleges conducted a survey in the year 2000 to see what the most popular majors for community college students were. The top 15 majors and their average starting salaries follow:

MAJOR	AVERAGE STARTING SALARY
1. Registered Nursing	$32,757
2. General Computer Technologies	$34,242
3. Computer Networking	$38,767
4. Engineering–Electric/Electronics	$29,464
5. Computer Technician/Networking	$36,092
6. Manufacturing Technology	$30,291
7. Radiology Technology	$32,478
8. Digital Media	$35,409
9. Computer Programming	$30,838
10. General Skilled Trades	$25,598
11. Law Enforcement	$27,975
12. Dental Hygiene	$41,907
13. Computer-Aided Design	$27,968
14. Automotive	$29,305
15. General Allied Health	$24,781

find out the credit options that are available to you at the college in which you are interested. You may discover that it will take less time to earn a degree than you first thought.

Preparation for Transfer

Studies have repeatedly shown that students who first attend a community college and then transfer to a four-year college or university do at least as well academically as the students who entered the four-year institutions as freshmen. Most community colleges have agreements with nearby four-year institutions to make transfer of credits easier. If you are thinking of transferring, be sure to meet with a counselor or faculty adviser before choosing your courses. You will want to map out a course of study with transfer in mind. Make sure you also find out the credit-transfer requirements of the four-year institution you might want to attend.

New Career Opportunities

Community colleges realize that many entering students are not sure about the field in which they want to focus their studies or the career they would like to pursue. Community colleges have the resources to help students identify areas of career interest and to set challenging occupational goals.

Once a career goal is set, you can be confident that a community college will provide job-relevant, quality occupation and technical education. About half of the students who take courses for credit at community colleges do so to prepare for employment or to acquire or upgrade skills for their current job. Especially helpful in charting a career path is the assistance of a counselor or a faculty adviser, who can discuss job opportunities in your chosen field and help you map out your course of study.

In addition, since community colleges have close ties to their communities, they are in constant contact with leaders in business, industry, organized labor, and public life. Community colleges work with these individuals and their organizations to prepare students for direct entry into the world of work. For example, some community colleges have established partnerships with local businesses and industries to provide specialized training programs. Some also provide the academic portion of apprenticeship training, while others offer extensive job-shadowing and cooperative education opportunities. Be sure to examine all of the career-preparation opportunities offered by the community colleges in which you are interested.

VOCATIONAL/CAREER COLLEGES

Career education is important for every employee as technology continues to change. From the largest employers, such as the U.S. military, defense contractors, IBM, aviation, and health care, down to the company with one and two employees, issues of keeping up with technology and producing goods and services cheaper, faster, and at less cost requires—indeed demands—a skilled, world-class workforce. In good or bad economic times, you will always have a distinct advantage if you have a demonstrable skill and can be immediately productive while continuing to learn and improve. If you know how to use technology, work collaboratively, and find creative solutions, you will always be in demand.

Career colleges offer scores of opportunities to learn the technical skills required by many of today's and tomorrow's top jobs. This is especially true in the areas of computer and information technology, health care, and hospitality (culinary arts, travel and tourism, and hotel and motel management). Career colleges range in size from those with a handful of students to universities with thousands enrolled. They are located in every state in the nation and share one common objective—to prepare students for a successful career in the world of work through a focused, intensive curriculum.

America's career colleges are privately owned and operated for-profit companies. Instead of using tax support to operate, career colleges pay taxes. Because career colleges are businesses, they must be responsive to the workforce needs of their communities or they will cease to exist.

SNAPSHOT OF A CAREER COLLEGE STUDENT
Katrina Dew
Network Systems Administration
Silicon Valley College
Fremont, California

ABOUT KATRINA

Right after high school, Katrina headed for junior college, but she felt like she was spinning her wheels. She wanted something that was goal-oriented. Community college offered too many options. She needed to be focused in one direction.

At first, Katrina thought she would become a physical therapist. Then she realized how much schooling she would need to begin working. Turning to the computer field, she saw some definite benefits. For one, she had messed around with them in high school. She could get a degree and get out in two years. She saw that computer careers are big and getting bigger. Plus, there weren't a lot of women in that field, which signaled more potential for her. But before she switched schools, she visited the career college, talked to students, and sat in on lectures. She really liked the way the teachers related to their students. Along with her technical classes, she's taken algebra, psychology, English composition, and management communication.

WHAT I LIKE ABOUT BEING A CAREER STUDENT

"Career colleges are for fast-track-oriented students who want to get out in the work field and still feel that they have an appropriate education."

Nicholas Cecere
Automotive Techniques Management
Education America/Vale Technical Institute
Blairsville, Pennsylvania

ABOUT NICHOLAS

Nicholas has completely repainted his 1988 Mercury Topaz, redone all the brakes, put in a brand-new exhaust system, and lots of smaller stuff here and there. But he says that's nothing compared to the completely totaled cars some of his classmates haul into the school. Talk about hands-on: they're able to completely restore them while going through the program.

Nicholas didn't always have gasoline running through his veins. In fact, he just recently discovered how much he likes automotives. After graduating from high school, he went to a community college, and after one semester, he left to work at a personal care home. Standing over a sink of dirty dishes made him realize he wanted more than just a job. He started thinking about what he wanted to do and visited a few schools and the body shop where his brother worked. Where others saw twisted car frames, Nicholas saw opportunity and enrolled in the program.

WHAT I LIKE ABOUT BEING A CAREER STUDENT

"I compare career college to a magnifying glass that takes the sun and focuses it. You learn just what you need to learn."

Generally, career colleges prepare you for a specific career. Some will require you to take academic courses such as English or history. Others will relate every class you take to a specific job, such as computer-aided drafting or interior design. Some focus specifically on business or technical fields. Bob Sullivan, a career counselor at East Brunswick High School in East Brunswick, New Jersey, points out that the negative side to this kind of education is that if you haven't carefully researched what you want to do, you could waste a lot of time and money. "There's no room for exploration or finding yourself as opposed to a community college where you can go to find yourself and feel your way around," he explains.

So how do you find the right career college for you? A good place to start is knowing generally what you want to do. You don't have to know the fine details of your goals, but you should have a broad idea, such as a career in allied health or business or computing. Once you make that decision, most career colleges will help you define your initial decisions.

After you've crossed that hurdle, the rest is easy. Since professional training is the main purpose of career colleges, its graduates are the best measure of a school's success. Who hires the graduates? How do their jobs relate to the education they received? Career colleges should be able to provide that data to prospective students. "Career colleges have a different customer than other institutions," notes Stephen Friedheim, President of ESS College of Business in Dallas, Texas. In addition to focusing on the needs of their students, career colleges also want to ensure they meet the needs of the employers who are hiring their graduates. "The assumption is that if you can please the employer, you will please the student," Friedheim explains.

Checking the credentials of a career college is one of the most important steps you should take in your career college search. Though not every career college has to be accredited, it is a sign that the college has gone through a process that ensures quality. It also means that students can qualify for federal grant and loan programs. Furthermore, you should see if the college has met the standards from professional training organizations. In fields such as court reporting and health-related professions, those criteria are paramount.

FINANCIAL AID OPTIONS FOR CAREER AND COMMUNITY COLLEGES

The financial aid process is basically the same for students attending a community college, a career college, or a technical institute as it is for students attending a four-year college. However, there are some details that can make the difference between getting the maximum amount of financial aid and only scraping by.

As with four-year students, the federal government is still your best source of financial aid. Most community colleges and career and technical schools participate in federal financial aid programs. To get detailed information about federal financial aid programs and how to apply for them, read through Chapter 8: "Financial Aid Dollars and Sense." In the meantime, here are some quick tips on where to look for education money.

Investigate federal financial aid programs. You should definitely check out a Federal Pell Grant, which is a need-based grant available to those who can't pay the entire tuition themselves. The Federal Supplemental Educational Opportunity Grant (FSEOG) is for those students with exceptional financial need. You also can take advantage of the Federal Work-Study programs that provide jobs for students with financial aid eligibility in return for part of their tuition. Many two-year institutions offer work-study, but the number of jobs tends to be limited. Also, federal loans make up a substantial part of financial aid for two-year students. Student loans, which have lower interest rates, may be sponsored by the institution or federally sponsored, or they may be available through commercial financial institutions. They are basically the same as those for the traditional four-year college student, such as the Federal Perkins Loan and the Subsidized and Unsubsidized Federal Stafford or Direct Loans. In fact, some private career colleges and technical institutes only offer federal loans. You also can find more specific information about federal loans in Chapter 8.

Don't overlook scholarships. What many two-year students don't realize is that they could be eligible for scholarships. Regrettably, many make the assumption that scholarships are only for very smart students attending prestigious universities. You'd be surprised to learn how many community and career

WHAT TO LOOK FOR IN A CAREER COLLEGE

A tour of the college is a must! While visiting the campus, do the following:

- **Get a full explanation of the curriculum, including finding out how you will be trained.**

- **Take a physical tour of the classrooms and laboratories and look for cleanliness, modern equipment/computers, and size of classes. Observe the activity in classes: Are students engaged in class, and are lectures dynamic?**

- **Ask about employment opportunities after graduation. What are the placement rates (most current) and list of employers? Inquire about specific placement assistance: resume preparation, job leads, etc. Look for "success stories" on bulletin boards, placement boards, and newsletters.**

- **Find out about tuition and other costs associated with the program. Ask about the financial aid assistance provided to students.**

- **Find out if an externship is part of the training program. How are externships assigned? Does the student have any input as to externship assignment?**

- **Ask if national certification and registration in your chosen field is available upon graduation.**

- **Inquire about the college's accreditation and certification.**

- **Also find out the associations and organizations to which the college belongs. Ask what awards or honors the college has had bestowed.**

- **Ask if the college utilizes an advisory board to develop employer relationships.**

- **Ask about the rules and regulations. What GPA must be maintained? What is the attendance policy? What are grounds for termination? What is the refund policy if the student drops or is terminated? Is there a dress code? What are the holidays of the college?**

Source: Arizona College of Allied Health, Phoenix, Arizona

colleges offer scholarships. It's critical to talk to the financial aid officer of each school you plan to attend to find out what scholarships might be available.

Two-year students should find out how their state of residence can help them pay for tuition. Every state in the union has some level of state financial aid that goes to community college students. The amounts are dependent on which state you live in, and most aid is in the form of grants.

APPRENTICESHIPS

Some students like working with their hands and have the skill, patience, and temperament to become expert mechanics, carpenters, or electronic repair technicians. If you think you'd enjoy a profession like this and feel that college training isn't for you, then you might want to think about a job that requires apprenticeship training.

To stay competitive, America needs highly skilled workers. But if you're looking for a soft job, forget it. An apprenticeship is no snap. It demands hard work and has tough competition, so you've got to have the will to see it through. An apprenticeship is a program formally agreed upon between a worker and an employer where the employee learns a skilled trade through classroom work and on-the-job training. Apprenticeship programs vary in length, pay, and intensity among the various trades. A person completing an apprenticeship program generally becomes a journeyperson (skilled craftsperson) in that trade.

The advantages of apprenticeships are numerous. First and foremost, an apprenticeship leads to a lasting lifetime skill. As a highly trained worker, you can take your skill anywhere you decide to go. The more creative, exciting, and challenging jobs are put in the hands of the fully skilled worker, the all-around person who knows his or her trade inside out.

Skilled workers advance much faster than those who are semiskilled or whose skills are not broad enough to equip them to assume additional responsibilities in a career. Those who complete an apprenticeship have also acquired the skills and judgment that are necessary to go into business for themselves if they choose.

What to Do If You're Interested in an Apprenticeship

If you want to begin an apprenticeship, you have to be at least 16 years old, and you must fill out an application for employment. These applications may be available year-round or at certain times during the year, depending on the trade in which you're interested.

Federal regulations prohibit anyone under the age of 16 from being considered for an apprenticeship. Some programs require a high school degree or certain course work. Other requirements may include passing certain aptitude tests, proof of physical ability to perform the duties of the trade, and possession of a valid driver's license.

Once you have met the basic program entrance requirements, you'll be interviewed and awarded points on your interest in the trade, your attitude toward work in general, and personal traits, such as appearance, sincerity, character, and habits. Openings are awarded to those who have achieved the most points.

Because an apprentice must be trained in an area where work actually exists and where a certain pay scale is guaranteed upon completion of the program, the wait for application acceptance may be pretty long in areas of low employment. This standard works to your advantage, however. Just think: You wouldn't want to spend one to six years of your life learning a job where no work exists or where the wage is the same as, or just a little above, that of an unskilled or semiskilled laborer.

If you're considering an apprenticeship, the best sources of assistance and information are vocational or career counselors, local state employment security agencies, field offices of state apprenticeship agencies, and regional offices of the Bureau of Apprenticeship and Training (BAT). Apprenticeships are usually registered with the BAT or a state apprenticeship council. Some apprenticeships are not registered at all, although that doesn't necessarily mean that the program isn't valid. To find out if a certain apprenticeship is legitimate, contact your state's apprenticeship agency or a regional office of the BAT. Addresses and phone numbers for these regional offices are listed on the previous page. You can also visit the Bureau's Web site at www.doleta.gov/atels_bat/bat.cfm.

BUREAU OF APPRENTICESHIP AND TRAINING OFFICES

NATIONAL OFFICE:
U.S. Department of Labor
Frances Perkins Building
200 Constitution Avenue, NW
Washington, D.C. 20210

REGION I: BOSTON
Mr. John M. Griffin, Jr.
Regional Director
USDOL/ETA/ATELS
JFK Federal Building
Room E-370
Boston, MA 02203
Telephone: 617/788-0177
FAX: 617/788-0304
E-Mail: jgriffin@doleta.gov

Connecticut
Maine
Massachusetts
New Hampshire
Rhode Island
Vermont

REGION I: NEW YORK
Mr. Albert Hudanish
Regional Director
USDOL/ETA/ATELS
Room 602 - Federal Building
201 Varick Street
New York, NY 10014
Telephone: 212/337-2313
FAX: 212/337-2317
E-Mail: ahudanish@doleta.gov

New Jersey
New York
Puerto Rico
Virgin Islands

REGION II
Mr. Joseph T. Hersh
Regional Director
USDOL/ETA/ATELS
Suite 815-East
170 S. Independence Mall, West
Philadelphia, PA 19106-3315
Telephone: 215/861-4830
FAX: 215/861-4833
E-Mail: jhersh@doleta.gov

Delaware
Maryland
Pennsylvania
Virginia
West Virginia

REGION III
Mr. Garfield G. Garner, Jr
Regional Director
USDOL/ETA/ATELS
Room 6T71
61 Forsyth Street, S.W.
Atlanta, GA 30303
Telephone: 404/562-2335
FAX: 404/652-2329
E-Mail: ggarner@doleta.gov

Alabama
Florida
Georgia
Kentucky
Mississippi
North Carolina
South Carolina
Tennessee

REGION IV
Mrs. Betty Lucero-Turner
Regional Director
USDOL/ETA/ATELS
Federal Building
525 Griffin Street, Rm. 311
Dallas, TX 75202
Telephone: 214/767-4993
FAX: 214/767-4995
E-Mail: blucero-turner@doleta.gov

Arkansas
Louisiana
New Mexico
Oklahoma
Texas

Mrs. Betty Lucero-Turner
Associate Regional Director
USDOL/ETA/ATELS
1999 Broadway, Suite 1780
P. O. Box 46550
Denver, CO 80201-6550
Telephone: 303/844-4791
FAX: 303/844-1791
E-Mail: blucero-turner@doleta.gov

Colorado
Montana
North Dakota
South Dakota
Utah
Wyoming

REGION V
Mr. Terrence Benewich
Regional Director
USDOL/ETA/ATELS
230 South Dearborn Street, Rm. 656
Chicago, IL 60604
Telephone: 312/596-5500
FAX: 312/596-5501
E-Mail: tbenewich@doleta.gov

Illinois
Indiana
Michigan
Minnesota
Ohio
Wisconsin

Mrs. Sarah J. Clemens-Russell
Associate Regional Director
USDOL/ETA/ATELS
Suite 1040
1100 Main Street
Kansas City, MO 64105-2112
Telephone: 816/502-9090
FAX: 816/502-9091
E-Mail: sclemens@doleta.gov

Iowa
Kansas
Missouri
Nebraska

REGION VI
Mr. Ronald M. Johnson
Regional Director
USDOL/ETA/ATELS
71 Stevenson Street, Suite 815
San Francisco, CA 94105
Telephone: 415/975-4007
FAX: 415/975-4010
E-Mail:rjohnson@doleta.gov

Arizona
California
Hawaii
Nevada

Mr. Ronald M. Johnson
Associate Regional Director
USDOL/ETA/ATELS
1111 - Third Avenue, Suite 830
Seattle, WA 98101-3212
Phone: 206/553-5286
FAX: 206/553-1689
E-Mail: rjohnson@doleta.gov

Alaska
Idaho
Oregon
Washington

11 Chapter

THE MILITARY OPTION

Bet you didn't know that the United States military is the largest employer in the country. There's got to be a good reason that so many people get their paychecks from Uncle Sam.

SHOULD I OR SHOULDN'T I WORK FOR THE LARGEST EMPLOYER IN THE U.S.?

Every year, thousands of young people pursue a military career and enjoy the benefits it offers. Yet thousands more consider joining the military and decide against it. Their reasons vary, but many choose not to enlist because they lack knowledge of what a career in the military can offer. Others simply mistrust recruiters based on horror stories they've heard. Sadly, many make the decision against joining the military without ever setting foot in the recruiting office.

But if you are an informed "shopper," you will be able to make an informed choice about whether the military is right for you.

People rarely buy anything based on their needs: Instead, they buy based on their emotions. We see it on a daily basis in advertising, from automobiles to soft drinks. We rarely see an automobile commercial that gives statistics about how the car is engineered, how long it will last, the gas mileage, and other technical specifications. Instead, we see people driving around and having a good time.

The reason for this is that advertising agencies know that you will probably buy something based on how you feel rather than what you think. Because of this tendency to buy with emotion rather than reason, it is important to separate the feelings from the facts. That way, you can base your decision about whether to join the military primarily on the facts.

There are two big questions that you must answer before you can come to any conclusions. First, is the military right for me, and second, if the first answer is yes, which branch is right for me?

Suppose that you have to decide whether to buy a new car or repair your current car. The first choice you make will determine your next course of action. You will have to weigh the facts to determine if you will purchase a new car or not. Once you've decided to buy a car rather than repair your old one, you must then decide exactly what make and model will best suit your needs.

NO HYPE, JUST THE FACTS

So you didn't wake up one morning and know for sure that you're going to join the Navy. One minute you think you'd like the Army, but then you talk to your cousin who convinces you to follow him into the Air Force. But then the neighbor down the street is a Marine, and he's gung ho for you to join up with them. What to do?

Well, a helpful Web site is the answer. Go to www.spear.navy.mil/profile for some really straightforward and non-partisan information about each branch of the military. You'll be able to compare the benefits that each service offers plus pick up other helpful tips and information. The Web site is designed specifically for high school students considering the military.

"Normally the first question we get from people interested in the Air Force is 'What does the Air Force have to offer me?' But I back off and ask them about their qualifications. Sometimes it's easier to go to an Ivy League school than to join the Air Force because of our stringent requirements."
Master Sergeant Timothy Little
United States Air Force

You should make a list of the reasons why you want to join the military before you ever set foot in the recruiter's office. Whether your list is long—containing such items as money for college, job security, opportunity to travel, technical training, and good pay—or contains only one item, such as having full-time employment, the number of items on your list is not what's important. What is important is that you are able to satisfy those reasons, or primary motivators.

Whatever your list contains, the first course of action is to collect your reasons to join the military and put them in order of importance to you. This process, known as rank-ordering, will help you determine if you should proceed with the enlistment process.

"Take two people with the same qualifications who are looking for jobs. The person with the Army background will be that much more competitive. That's due to the fact that he or she is disciplined and knows how to act without being told what to do."
Staff Sergeant Max Burda
United States Army

Rank-ordering your list is a simple process of deciding which motivators are most important to you and then listing them in order of importance. List your most important motivator as number one, your next most important as number two, and so on.

If we apply the car-buying scenario here, your primary motivators may be finding a car that costs under $20,000, gets at least 30 miles to the gallon, has leather interior, is available in blue, and has a sunroof. If you put those motivators in rank order, your list might look something like this:

1. Costs under $20,000
2. Gets at least 30 mpg
3. Has a sunroof
4. Has leather interior
5. Available in blue

You'll notice that the number one, or most important, motivator in this case is cost, while the last,

or least important, motivator is color. The more important the motivator, the less likely you'll be willing to settle for something different or to live without it altogether.

After you've rank-ordered your motivators, go down your list and determine whether those motivators can be met by enlisting in the military. If you find that all your motivators can be met by enlisting, that's great; but even if only some of your motivators can be met, you may still want to consider enlisting. Seldom does a product meet all our needs and wants.

CHOOSING WHICH BRANCH TO JOIN

"If you like to travel, we offer more than anyone else. The longest you're underway is generally two to three weeks, with three to four days off in every port and one day on the ship. Prior to pulling in, you can even set up tours."
Chief Petty Officer Keith Horst
United States Navy

If you are seriously considering joining the military, you probably have checked out at least two of the branches. Check them all out, even if it means just requesting literature and reviewing it. A word of caution though: Brochures do not tell the complete story, and it is very difficult to base your decision either for or against a military branch on the contents of a brochure. Would you buy a car based solely on the information contained in a brochure? Probably not!

"I tell people that you get paid the same in all the services, and the benefits are the same. What's different about each branch is the environment."
Sergeant Ian Bonnell, Infantry Sergeant
United States Marines

The process of choosing the right branch of the military for you is basically the same process that you used to determine if joining the military was right for you. You should start with your list of primary

I'M JOINING THE AIR FORCE

It didn't take Brian Filipek long to decide he wanted to join the Air Force. But that's if you don't count the times he talked to people who had served in the Air Force or the research he did on the Internet to gather information—and that was before he even set foot inside the recruiter's office. By the time an Air Force recruiter responded to a card Brian had sent in, he was pretty sure he liked what he'd seen so far. "The recruiter didn't have to do any work to convince me," says Brian. After that, it was a matter of going through the pre-qualifying process, like whether he met the height and weight qualifications, and the security forms he had to fill out.

After he enlisted, Brian didn't stop gathering information. Long before he was sent to Basic Training, he found out about Warrior Week, which is held on one of the last weeks in Basic Training. He was already looking forward to it. "I'm an outdoors kind of person," he says. "I want to do the obstacle course and ropes course."

Though the idea of testing his endurance and strength appeals to him, being away from family will be hard. "Granted, your food is cooked for you, but you're still on your own," he says. However, he knows that it's worth it to achieve his goal of education and free job training. Brian acknowledges that the military is not for everyone, but as far as he's concerned, he's sure he's made the right choice.

Brian Filipek, Enlistee
U.S. Air Force

motivators and use the "yes/no" method to determine whether each branch can meet all or some of those motivators. Once you've determined which branch or branches can best meet your motivators, it's time to compare those branches. Remember to look for the negative aspects as well as the motivators of each of the branches as you compare.

After making your comparisons, you may still find yourself with more than one choice. What do you do then? You could flip a coin, but that's not the wisest idea! Instead, look at some of these factors:

Length of enlistment—Some branches may require a longer term for offering the same benefits that you could receive from another branch.

Advanced pay grade—You may be entitled to an advanced rank in some branches based on certain enlistment options.

"In the Army, you can get training in everything from culinary arts to truck driving and all the way to aviation mechanics, military intelligence, and computer networking."
Staff Sergeant Max Burda
United States Army

Length and type of training—How long will your training take? Usually the longer the training, the more in-depth and useful it is. You'll also want to consider how useful the training will be once you've left the military.

Enlistment bonuses—Be careful when using an enlistment bonus as the only factor in deciding which branch to choose. If it comes down to a tie between two branches and only one offers a bonus, it's not a bad reason to choose that branch.

Additional pay and allowances—There may be additional pay you'd be entitled to that can only be offered by a particular branch. For instance, if you join the Navy, you may be entitled to Sea Pay and Submarine Pay, something obviously not available if you join the Air Force.

Ability to pursue higher education—While all the military branches offer educational benefits, you must consider when you will be able to take advantage of these benefits. If your job requires 12-hour shifts and has you out in the field a lot, when will you be able to attend classes?

"Everyone in the Navy learns how to fight a fire. You get qualified in First Aid and CPR. That's mandatory for every sailor. The only jobs we don't have in the Navy are veterinarians, forest rangers, and rodeo stars."
Chief Petty Officer Keith Horst
United States Navy

Once you have considered these factors, and perhaps some of your own, you should be able to decide which branch is right for you. If you still haven't been able to select one branch over another, though, consider the following:

- Ask your recruiter if you can speak to someone who has recently joined.

- If there is a base nearby, you may be able to get a tour to look at its facilities.

- If you are well versed in Internet chat rooms, you may want to look for ones that cater to military members—then ask a lot of questions.

- Talk to friends and family members who are currently serving in the military. Be careful, however, not to talk to people who have been out of the military for a while, as they probably aren't familiar with today's military. Also, avoid people who left the military under less-than-desirable conditions (for example, someone who was discharged from Basic Training for no compatibility).

If you choose to continue with processing for enlistment, your next step will probably be to take the Armed Services Vocational Aptitude Battery (ASVAB).

THE ASVAB

The ASVAB, a multiple-aptitude battery designed for use with students in their junior or senior year in high school or in a postsecondary school, as well as those seeking military enlistment, was developed to yield results useful to both students and the military. The military uses the results to determine the qualifications of candidates for enlistment and to help place them in military occupational programs. Schools use ASVAB test results to assist their students in developing future educational and career plans.

Frequently Asked Questions about the ASVAB

What is the Armed Services Vocational Aptitude Battery (ASVAB)?

The ASVAB, sponsored by the Department of Defense, is a multi-aptitude test battery consisting of ten short individual tests covering Word Knowledge, Paragraph Comprehension, Arithmetic Reasoning, Mathematic Knowledge, General Science, Auto and Shop Information, Mechanical Comprehension, Electronics Information, Numerical Operations, and Coding Speed. Your ASVAB results provide scores for each individual test, as well as three academic composite scores—Verbal, Math, and Academic Ability—and two career exploration composite scores.

Why should I take the ASVAB?

As a high school student nearing graduation, you are faced with important career choices. Should you go on to college, technical, or vocational school? Would it be better to enter the job market? Should you consider a military career? Your ASVAB scores are measures of aptitude. Your composite scores measure your aptitude for higher academic learning and give you ideas for career exploration.

When and where is the ASVAB given?

ASVAB is administered annually or semiannually at more than 14,000 high schools and postsecondary schools in the United States.

Is there a charge or fee to take the ASVAB?

ASVAB is administered at no cost to the school or to the student.

How long does it take to complete the ASVAB?

ASVAB testing takes approximately 3 hours. If you miss class, it will be with your school's approval.

If I wish to take the ASVAB but my school doesn't offer it (or I missed it), what should I do?

See your school counselor. In some cases, arrangements may be made for you to take it at another high school. Your counselor should call 800-323-0513 (toll-free) for additional information.

How do I find out what my scores mean and how to use them?

Your scores will be provided to you on a report called the ASVAB Student Results Sheet. Along with your scores, you should receive a copy of *Exploring Careers: The ASVAB Workbook*, which contains information that will help you understand your

ASVAB results and show you how to use them for career exploration. Test results are returned to participating schools within thirty days.

What is a passing score on the ASVAB?

No one "passes" or "fails" the ASVAB. The ASVAB enables you to compare your scores to those of other students at your grade level.

If I take the ASVAB, am I obligated to join the military?

No. Taking the ASVAB does not obligate you to the military in any way. You are free to use your test results in whatever manner you wish. You may use the ASVAB results for up to two years for military enlistment if you are a junior, a senior, or a postsecondary school student. The military services encourage all young people to finish high school before joining the armed forces.

If I am planning to go to college, should I take the ASVAB?

Yes. ASVAB results provide you with information that can help you determine your capacity for advanced academic education. You can also use your ASVAB results, along with other personal information, to identify areas for career exploration.

Should I take the ASVAB if I plan to become a commissioned officer?

Yes. Taking the ASVAB is a valuable experience for any student who aspires to become a military officer. The aptitude information you receive could assist you in career planning.

Should I take the ASVAB if I am considering entering the Reserve or National Guard?

Yes. These military organizations also use the ASVAB for enlistment purposes.

What should I do if a service recruiter contacts me?

You may be contacted by a service recruiter before you graduate. If you want to learn about the many opportunities available through the military service, arrange for a follow-up meeting. However, you are under no obligation to the military as a result of taking the ASVAB.

Is the ASVAB administered other than in the school testing program?

Yes. ASVAB is also used in the regular military enlistment program. It is administered at approximately sixty-five Military Entrance Processing Stations located throughout the United States. Each year, hundreds of thousands of young men and women who are interested in enlisting in the uniformed services (Army, Navy, Air Force, Marines, and Coast Guard) but who did not take the ASVAB while in school are examined and processed at these military stations.

Is any special preparation necessary before taking the ASVAB?

Yes. A certain amount of preparation is required for taking any examination. Whether it is an athletic competition or a written test, preparation is a *must* in order to achieve the best results. Your test scores reflect not only your ability but also the time and effort in preparing for the test. The uniformed services use ASVAB to help determine a person's qualification for enlistment and to help indicate the vocational areas for which the person is best suited. Achieving your maximum score will increase your vocational opportunities. So take practice tests to prepare.

BASIC TRAINING: WHAT HAVE I GOTTEN MYSELF INTO?

The main objective of Basic Training is to transform civilians into well-disciplined military personnel in a matter of weeks. Performing such a monumental task takes a lot of hard work, both mentally and physically. For most people, Basic Training ends with a parade on graduation day. For others, though, it ends somewhere short of graduation. It is those "horror stories" that make Basic Training the one biggest fear, or anxiety-inducer, for those considering military enlistment.

Unlike the boot camp you may have heard about from your Uncle Louie or seen on television, today's Basic Training doesn't include the verbal and physical abuse of yesterday. All of the military branches are ensuring that new enlistees are treated fairly and with dignity. Not that enlistees aren't yelled at (because they are); however, the vulgarity and demeaning verbal attacks are a thing of the past. There are, from time to time, incidents involving instructors who contradict the military's policies. These violations, however, receive a lot of attention, are thoroughly investigated, and usually end up with disciplinary action taken against those involved in the abuse.

"A lot of kids are worried about Marine boot camp. They've seen movies or heard stories. Boot camp is not set up to make you fail. It's challenging, but that's the purpose of it. You're learning that no matter what life throws at you, you will be able to improvise, adapt, and overcome."

Sergeant Ian Bonnell, Infantry Sergeant
United States Marines

I SURVIVED BASIC TRAINING

Although Michael Hipszky was eager to join the Navy, it didn't take long for doubts about his decision to hit him. While he was riding the bus to the Navy's Basic Training facility, he asked himself THE QUESTION—"Why am I putting myself through this mess?" Recalls Michael, "It crosses everyone's mind. As far as I know, in my division, everyone had the same thought. 'I want to go home.' Those first few days are intense."

He figures it's because you lose control the minute you walk through the door on the first day of Basic Training. Someone's telling you (in a very loud voice) how to stand at attention, how to stand in line, how to do just about everything. "So many things go through your head," says Michael. He soon found that if he followed three rules, life got a whole lot easier:

1. KEEP YOUR MOUTH SHUT. "Your mouth is your biggest problem," he warns, "talking when you aren't supposed to and saying dumb things."

2. PAY ATTENTION TO DETAIL. "They'll say things like, 'Grab the door knob, turn it half to the right, and go through.' A lot of people will just pull it open and get yelled at. They teach you how to fold your clothes and clean the head (toilet). Everything is paying attention to detail," Michael advises.

3. DON'T THINK FOR YOURSELF. "Wait to be told what to do," Michael says, recalling the time his group was handed a form and told to wait until ordered to fill it out. Many saw that the form was asking for information like name, date, and division and began filling it out, only to get in trouble because they didn't wait.

Having been through Basic Training, Michael now knows that every little thing—from folding T-shirts the exact way he'd been told to do (arms folded in), to sweeping the floor, to marching—is all part of the training process. "You don't realize it until you're done," he says.

Despite all the yelling and push-ups, Michael values the training he got in the classes. He learned how to put out different kinds of fires, how to manage his money, how to identify aircraft—even etiquette. And that's just for starters.

His lowest point was about halfway through Basic, which, he found out, usually happens for everyone at the same time. "The first half of Basic, everything is so surreal. Then you get halfway through, and finishing up Basic seems so far away. You're always busy, whether you're stenciling your clothes or marching. You march a lot," he says. But then he reached his highest point, which was pass-in review at the end of the training and winning awards. He knew he'd done well. Looking into his future with the Navy, Michael says, "I want to see the world and have the experiences that the Navy can give you." Having finished Basic Training, he's well on his way.

Airman Michael Hipszky
United States Navy

If you are still uncertain of which branch you'd like to join, do not allow the type of Basic Training you'll receive to be your only deciding factor. If, for example, the Marine Corps meets all your needs and is clearly your first choice, do not select the Air Force because its Basic Training seems easier. Conversely, if the Air Force is clearly your first choice, do not select the Marine Corps because it has the "toughest" Basic Training, and you want to prove you are up to the challenge. Basic Training is a means of your transformation from civilian life to military life. It happens in a relatively short period of time compared to the entire length of your enlistment.

Some Words on Getting through Basic Training

No matter what you may have heard or read elsewhere, there are no secrets to getting through Basic Training; only common sense and preparation will get you through. Here are some do's and don'ts that should help you survive Basic Training for any of the services. Although following these guidelines will not ensure your success at Basic Training, your chances for success will be greatly improved by following them.

Before Arriving at Basic Training

DO:

- Start an exercise program.
- Maintain a sensible diet.
- Stay out of trouble (pay any traffic fines promptly before leaving for Basic Training).
- Ensure that all of your financial obligations are in order.
- Bring the required items that you are told to bring.
- Give up smoking.

DON'T:

- Skip preparing yourself physically because you think that Basic Training will whip you into shape.
- Abuse drugs and/or alcohol.
- Have a big send-off party and get drunk the night before you leave for Basic Training.
- Leave home with open tickets, summonses, or warrants.

- Get yourself into heavy debt (such as buying a new car).
- Bring any prohibited items.
- Have your hair cut in a radical manner. (This includes having your head shaved. Men will receive a "very close" haircut shortly after arriving at Basic Training.)
- Have any part of your body pierced, tattooed, or otherwise altered.

PAYING FOR COLLEGE THROUGH THE ARMED SERVICES

You can take any of the following three paths into the armed services—all of which provide opportunities for financial assistance for college.

Enlisted Personnel

All five branches of the armed services offer college-credit courses on base. Enlisted personnel can also take college courses at civilian colleges while on active duty.

"In the Air Force, you're not only getting an education, but also experience. You could go to school for a degree in avionics technology, but in the Air Force, you get the teaching and the experience— real-world, hands-on experience—that makes your education marketable."
Master Sergeant Timothy Little
United States Air Force

ROTC

More than 40,000 college students participate in Reserve Officers' Training Corps (ROTC). Two-, three-, and four-year ROTC scholarships are available to outstanding students. You can try ROTC at no obligation for two years or, if you have a four-year scholarship, for one year. Normally, all ROTC classes, uniforms, and books are free. ROTC graduates are required to serve in the military for a set period of time, either full-time on active duty or part-time in the Reserve or National Guard. Qualifying graduates can delay their service to go to graduate or professional school first.

Officer Candidate School

Openings at the U.S. service academies are few, so it pays to get information early. Every student is on a full scholarship, but free does not mean easy—these intense programs train graduates to meet the demands of leadership and success.

West Point. The U.S. Army Academy offers a broad-based academic program with twenty-two majors in twenty-five fields of study. Extensive training and leadership experience go hand in hand with academics.

Annapolis. The U.S. Naval Academy is a unique blend of tradition and state-of-the-art technology. Its core curriculum includes nineteen major fields of study, and classroom work is supported by practical experience in leadership and professional operations.

Air Force Academy. The U.S. Air Force Academy prepares and motivates cadets for careers as Air Force officers. The academy offers a B.S. degree in thirty majors. Graduates receive a reserve commission as a second lieutenant in the Air Force.

Coast Guard Academy. This broad-based education, which leads to a B.S. degree in eight technical or professional majors, includes a thorough grounding in the professional skills necessary for the Coast Guard's work.

Financing Higher Education through the U.S. Armed Forces

The U.S. military provides a number of options to help students and their parents get financial aid for postsecondary education.

The Montgomery GI Bill—Active Duty

The Montgomery GI Bill-Active Duty, called "MGIB" for short, provides up to 36 months of education benefits to eligible veterans for college, business, technical or vocational courses, correspondence courses, apprenticeship/job training, and flight training. You may be an eligible veteran if you got an Honorable Discharge, you have a High School

WHAT'S MY JOB?—OH, I JUST DRIVE AN ARMORED CARRIER AROUND

Justin Platt thought maybe he would join the Army, but first he had a few doubts to overcome. A big one was his reluctance to be away from friends and family. Another one was the overseas duty—something he definitely didn't want. But his desire to get his foot in the door of medical training won out. When he found out that he could get an education in the Army to become a nurse, his fears flew out the window, and Justin joined the Army. He's glad he did.

Stationed at Fort Carson in Colorado, Justin's been through Basic Training and is on his first stint of active duty working in—you guessed it—the medical field. "I work in an aid station, which is like a mini hospital," he says. He's the one who does the screening for anyone in his battalion who comes into sick call. Okay, it's from 5 a.m. to 7 a.m., but Justin doesn't mind.

Justin's job on active duty doesn't just consist of handing out Band-Aids and cough drops. He's also learning how to drive an armored carrier—not your usual medical training. But in the field, Army medics have to be able to pick up the wounded, which means knowing how to drive what he describes as a souped-up SUV—only instead of tires, it has tracks.

Justin plans to get enough rank to go from green to gold—enlisted to officer. "I'll have to take additional college courses to get a four-year degree," he says. It'll take him about seven years, including his Army duty. Not bad for someone who once had doubts about joining the military.

Private First Class Justin Platt
Fort Carson, Colorado

Diploma or GED, or, in some cases, 12 hours of college credit, AND you meet the necessary requirements related to military service. The monthly benefit paid to you is based on the type of training you take, length of your service, your category, and if the Department of Defense put extra money in your *MGI*B Fund (called "kickers"). You usually have ten years to use your *MGIB* benefits, but the time limit can be less, in some cases, and longer under certain circumstances.

Montgomery GI Bill—Selected Reserve

The Montgomery GI Bill—Selected Reserve program may be available to you if you are a member of the Selected Reserve. The Selected Reserve includes the Army Reserve, Navy Reserve, Air Force Reserve,

Marine Corps Reserve and Coast Guard Reserve, and the Army National Guard and the Air National Guard. You may use this education assistance program for degree programs, certificate or correspondence courses, cooperative training, independent study programs, apprenticeship/on-the-job training, and vocational flight training programs. Remedial, refresher, and deficiency training are available under certain circumstances. Eligibility for this program is determined by the Selected Reserve components. VA makes the payments for this program. You may be entitled to receive up to 36 months of education benefits. Your benefit entitlement ends fourteen years from the date of your eligibility for the program, or on the day you leave the Selected Reserve.

Call toll-free 1-888-GI-BILL-1 for more information, or visit the Web site at www.gibill.va.gov/education/benefits.htm.

The Department of Defense

The U.S. Department of Defense offers a large number of education benefits to those enrolled in the U.S. military or employed by the Department of Defense, including scholarships, grants, tuition assistance, and internships. Visit their Web site at http://web.lmi.org/edugate for complete information.

Tuition Assistance

All branches of the military pay up to 75 percent of tuition for full-time, active-duty enlistees who take courses at community colleges or by correspondence during their tours of duty. Details vary by service.

The Community College of the Air Force

Members of the armed forces can convert their technical training and military experience into academic credit, earning an associate degree, an occupational instructor's certificate, or a trade school certificate. Participants receive an official transcript from this fully accredited program. You can visit the Community College of the Air Force on line at www.au.af.mil/au/ccaf.

Educational Loan-Repayment Program

The Armed Services can help repay government-insured and other approved loans. One third of the loan will be repaid for each year served on active duty.

Other Forms of Tuition Assistance

Each branch of the military offers its own education incentives. To find out more, check with a local recruiting office.

Part 4

YOU AND THE WORKPLACE

SOME OF YOU WILL GO TO COLLEGE first and then look for jobs. Some of you might work for a few years and then go to college. And many of you will go immediately into the workplace and bypass college altogether. Whenever you become an employee, you'll want to know what you can do to succeed on the job and move to both higher levels of responsibility and more pay.

JUMP INTO WORK

Almost everyone ends up in the workplace at some point. No matter when you plan to receive that first full-time paycheck, there are some things you'll need to do to prepare yourself for the world of work.

AT EACH GRADE LEVEL, there are specific steps you should take regardless of whether or not you plan to attend college immediately following high school. In fact, college and career timelines should coincide, according to guidance counselors and career specialists, and students should take college-preparatory courses, even if they aren't planning on attending college.

THE CAREER TIMELINE

The following timeline will help you meet college requirements and help prepare you for work. In an effort to make sure that you are adequately preparing for both school and work, incorporate these five steps into your career/college timeline:

1. **Take an aptitude test.** You can do this as early as the sixth grade, but even if you do this in high school, it's not too late. By doing so, you will begin to get a feel for what areas you might be good at and enjoy. Your guidance counselor should have a test in his or her office for you to take, or you can try the ASVAB (see page 123). Thousands of high school students take this test every year to discover possible career paths—and taking the ASVAB doesn't require you to join the military!

2. **Beginning in middle school, you should start considering what your options are after high school.** However, if you're only starting to think about this in high school, that's okay, too. Keep a notebook of information gathered from field trips, job-shadowing experiences, mentoring programs, and career fairs to help you make sense of the possibilities open to you. This process should continue through high school. Many schools offer job shadowing and internship programs for students to explore different vocational avenues. Take advantage of these opportunities if you can. Too often, students don't explore the workplace until after they've taken the courses necessary to enter a particular profession, only to discover it wasn't the career they dreamed of after all.

3. **No later than the tenth grade, visit a vocational center to look at the training programs offered.** Some public school systems send students to vocational and career program centers for career exploration.

TAKING A BREAK BETWEEN HIGH SCHOOL AND COLLEGE

Because of the soaring costs of college tuition today, college is no longer a place to "find yourself." It is a costly investment in your future. The career you choose to pursue may or may not require additional education; your research will determine whether or not it's required or preferred. If you decide not to attend college immediately after high school, however, don't consider it to be a closed door. Taking some time off between high school and college is considered perfectly acceptable by employers. Many students simply need a break after thirteen years of schooling. Most experts agree that it's better to be ready and prepared for college; many adults get more out of their classes after they've had a few years to mature.

Source: Street Smart Career Guide: A Step-by-Step Program for Your Career Development.

4. **During your junior and senior years, be sure to create a portfolio of practice resumes, writing samples, and a list of work skills.** This portfolio should also include your high school transcript and letters of recommendation. It will serve as a valuable reference tool when it comes time to apply for jobs.

5. **By tenth or eleventh grade, you should begin focusing on a specific career path.** More employers today are looking for employees who have both the education and work experience that relates to the career field for which they're interviewing. If you are looking for part-time employment, you should consider jobs that pertain to your field of study. Until you start interacting with people in the field, you won't have a realistic feel of what's involved in that profession. If you're planning on heading into the workplace right after high school, take a look at the following pages for a list of careers that don't require a four-year degree.

WRITING YOUR RESUME

Resumes are a critical part of getting a job. A resume is an introduction of your skills to a potential employer. For that reason, your resume must stand out in a crowd because some employers receive dozens of resumes each week. A resume that is too long, cluttered, or disorganized may find its way to the "circular file," also known as the trash can. You can avoid this hazard by creating a resume that is short, presentable, and easy to read.

Remember that a resume is a summary of who you are and an outline of your experiences, skills, and goals. While writing it, you may discover some talents that you weren't aware you had and that will help boost your confidence for the job search.

Begin by collecting facts about yourself, including where you went to high school, your past and present jobs, activities, interests, and leadership roles. Next to the individual activities, write down

what responsibilities you had. For example, something as simple as babysitting requires the ability to settle disagreements and supervise others.

Next, decide on how you would like to format your resume. Most hiring managers expect to see one of two types of resumes: chronological or functional. The chronological resume is the most traditional, supplying the reader with a sequential listing (from present to past) of your accomplishments. Because the emphasis here is on past employment experience, high school and college students with little or no employment history might want to avoid this type. A functional resume, on the other hand, highlights a person's abilities rather than his or her work history. Entry-level candidates who want to focus on skills rather than credentials should consider using a functional resume.

CAREERS WITHOUT A FOUR-YEAR DEGREE

Some students spend a few years in the workplace before going to college. Others begin their career with a high school diploma, a vocational certificate, or up to two years of education or training after high school.

With that in mind, sometimes it's easier to know what you don't want rather than what you do want. Take a look at the list below, and check off the careers that interest you. Perhaps you've thought of something you'd like to do that isn't on this list. Well, don't dump your hopes. There are many different levels of training and education that can lead you to the career of your dreams. Since this list is not all-inclusive, you should check with your high school counselor or go on line to research the training you'll need to achieve the job or career you want—without a four-year degree. Then talk to your guidance counselor, teacher, librarian, or career counselor for more information about the careers on the list below or those you've researched on your own.

AGRICULTURE AND NATURAL RESOURCES
High school/vocational diploma
- ❑ Fisher
- ❑ Groundskeeper
- ❑ Logger
- ❑ Pest Controller

Up to two years beyond high school
- ❑ Fish and Game Warden
- ❑ Tree Surgeon

APPLIED ARTS (VISUAL)
High school/vocational diploma
- ❑ Floral Arranger
- ❑ Merchandise Displayer
- ❑ Painter (artist)

Up to two years beyond high school
- ❑ Cartoonist
- ❑ Commercial Artist
- ❑ Fashion Designer
- ❑ Interior Decorator
- ❑ Photographer

APPLIED ARTS (WRITTEN AND SPOKEN)
High school/vocational diploma
- ❑ Proofreader

Up to two years beyond high school
- ❑ Advertising copywriter
- ❑ Legal assistant

BUSINESS MACHINE/COMPUTER OPERATION
High school/vocational diploma
- ❑ Data Entry
- ❑ Statistical Clerk
- ❑ Telephone Operator
- ❑ Typist

Up to two years beyond high school
- ❑ Computer Operator
- ❑ Motion Picture Projectionist
- ❑ Word Processing Machine Operator

CONSTRUCTION AND MAINTENANCE
High school/vocational diploma
- ❑ Bricklayer
- ❑ Construction Laborer
- ❑ Elevator Mechanic
- ❑ Floor Covering Installer
- ❑ Heavy Equipment Operator
- ❑ Janitor
- ❑ Maintenance Mechanic

Up to two years beyond high school
- ❑ Building Inspector
- ❑ Carpenter
- ❑ Electrician

- ❑ Insulation Worker
- ❑ Lather
- ❑ Painter (construction)
- ❑ Pipefitter
- ❑ Plumber
- ❑ Roofer
- ❑ Sheet Metal Worker
- ❑ Structural Steel Worker
- ❑ Tile Setter

CRAFTS AND RELATED SERVICES
High school/vocational diploma
- ❑ Baker/Cook/Chef
- ❑ Butcher
- ❑ Furniture Upholsterer
- ❑ Housekeeper (hotel)
- ❑ Tailor/Dressmaker

Up to two years beyond high school
- ❑ Dry Cleaner
- ❑ Jeweler
- ❑ Locksmith
- ❑ Musical Instrument Repairer

CREATIVE/PERFORMING ARTS
High school/vocational diploma
- ❑ Singer
- ❑ Stunt Performer

Up to two years beyond high school
- ❑ Actor/Actress
- ❑ Dancer/Choreographer
- ❑ Musician
- ❑ Writer/Author

EDUCATION AND RELATED SERVICES
High school/vocational diploma
- ❑ Nursery School Attendant
- ❑ Teacher's Aide

ENGINEERING AND RELATED TECHNOLOGIES
High school/vocational diploma
- ❑ Biomedical Equipment Technician
- ❑ Laser Technician

Up to two years beyond high school
- ❑ Aerospace Engineer Technician
- ❑ Broadcast Technician
- ❑ Chemical Laboratory Technician
- ❑ Civil Engineering Technician
- ❑ Computer Programmer
- ❑ Computer Service Technician
- ❑ Electronic Technician
- ❑ Energy Conservation Technician
- ❑ Industrial Engineering Technician
- ❑ Laboratory Tester

- ❑ Mechanical Engineering Technician
- ❑ Metallurgical Technician
- ❑ Pollution Control Technician
- ❑ Quality Control Technician
- ❑ Robot Technician
- ❑ Surveyor (land)
- ❑ Technical Illustrator
- ❑ Tool Designer
- ❑ Weather Observer

FINANCIAL TRANSACTIONS
High school/vocational diploma
- ❑ Accounting Clerk
- ❑ Bank Teller
- ❑ Cashier
- ❑ Payroll Clerk
- ❑ Travel Agent

Up to two years beyond high school
- ❑ Bookkeeper
- ❑ Loan Officer

HEALTH CARE (GENERAL)
High school/vocational diploma
- ❑ Dental Assistant
- ❑ Medical Assistant
- ❑ Nursing/Psychiatric Aide

Up to two years beyond high school
- ❑ Dietetic Technician
- ❑ Nurse (practical)
- ❑ Nurse (registered)
- ❑ Optometric Assistant
- ❑ Physical Therapist's Assistant
- ❑ Physician's Assistant
- ❑ Recreation Therapist

HEALTH-CARE SPECIALTIES AND TECHNOLOGIES
High school/vocational diploma
- ❑ Dialysis Technician

Up to two years beyond high school
- ❑ Dental Hygienist
- ❑ Dental Laboratory Technician
- ❑ EEG Technologist
- ❑ EKG Technician
- ❑ Emergency Medical Technician
- ❑ Medical Laboratory Technician
- ❑ Medical Technologist
- ❑ Nuclear Medicine Technologist
- ❑ Operating Room Technician
- ❑ Optician
- ❑ Radiation Therapy Technologist
- ❑ Radiologic Technologist
- ❑ Respiratory Therapist
- ❑ Sonographer

HOME/BUSINESS EQUIPMENT REPAIR

High school/vocational diploma
- Air-Conditioning/Refrigeration/Heating Mechanic
- Appliance Servicer
- Coin Machine Mechanic

Up to two years beyond high school
- Communications Equipment Mechanic
- Line Installer/Splicer
- Office Machine Servicer
- Radio/TV Repairer
- Telephone Installer

INDUSTRIAL EQUIPMENT OPERATIONS AND REPAIR

High school/vocational diploma
- Assembler
- Blaster
- Boilermaker
- Coal Equipment Operator
- Compressor House Operator
- Crater
- Dock Worker
- Forging Press Operator
- Furnace Operator
- Heat Treater
- Machine Tool Operator
- Material Handler
- Miner
- Sailor
- Sewing Machine Operator

Up to two years beyond high school
- Bookbinder
- Compositor/Typesetter
- Electronic Equipment Repairer
- Electroplater
- Firefighter
- Instrument Mechanic
- Lithographer
- Machine Repairer
- Machinist
- Millwright
- Molder
- Nuclear Reactor Operator
- Patternmaker
- Photoengraver
- Power House Mechanic
- Power Plant Operator
- Printing Press Operator
- Stationery Engineer
- Tool and Die Maker
- Water Plant Operator
- Welder
- Wire Drawer

MANAGEMENT AND PLANNING

High school/vocational diploma
- Administrative Assistant
- Food Service Supervisor
- Postmaster
- Service Station Manager

Up to two years beyond high school
- Benefits Manager
- Building Manager
- Caterer
- Contractor
- Credit Manager
- Customer Service Coordinator
- Employment Interviewer
- Executive Housekeeper
- Funeral Director
- Hotel/Motel Manager
- Importer/Exporter
- Insurance Manager
- Manager (small business)
- Office Manager
- Personnel Manager
- Restaurant/Bar Manager
- Store Manager
- Supermarket Manager

MARKETING AND SALES

High school/vocational diploma
- Auctioneer
- Bill Collector
- Driver (route)
- Fashion Model
- Product Demonstrator
- Salesperson (general)
- Sample Distributor

Up to two years beyond high school
- Claims Adjuster
- Insurance Worker
- Manufacturer's Representative
- Real Estate Agent
- Sales Manager
- Travel Agent
- Travel Guide

PERSONAL AND CUSTOMER SERVICE

High school/vocational diploma
- Barber
- Bartender
- Beautician
- Child-Care Worker
- Counter Attendant
- Dining Room Attendant
- Electrologist
- Flight Attendant
- Host/Hostess
- Houseparent
- Manicurist
- Parking Lot Attendant
- Porter
- Private Household Worker
- Waiter/Waitress

RECORDS AND COMMUNICATIONS

High school/vocational diploma
- Billing Clerk
- Clerk (general)
- File Clerk
- Foreign Trade Clerk
- Hotel Clerk
- Meter Reader
- Postal Clerk
- Receptionist
- Stenographer

Up to two years beyond high school
- Court Reporter
- Legal Secretary
- Library Assistant
- Library Technician
- Medical Records Technician
- Medical Secretary
- Personnel Assistant
- Secretary
- Travel Clerk

SOCIAL AND GOVERNMENT

High school/vocational diploma
- Corrections Officer
- Police Officer
- Security Guard
- Store Detective

Up to two years beyond high school
- Detective (police)
- Hazardous Waste Technician
- Recreation Leader
- Personal/Customer Services

STORAGE AND DISPATCHING

High school/vocational diploma
- Dispatcher
- Mail Carrier
- Railroad Conductor
- Shipping/Receiving Clerk
- Stock Clerk
- Tool Crib Attendant
- Warehouse Worker

Up to two years beyond high school
- Warehouse Supervisor

VEHICLE OPERATION AND REPAIR

High school/vocational diploma
- Automotive Painter
- Bus Driver
- Chauffeur
- Diesel Mechanic
- Farm Equipment Mechanic
- Forklift Operator
- Heavy Equipment Mechanic
- Locomotive Engineer
- Railroad Braker
- Refuse Collector
- Service Station Attendant
- Taxicab Driver
- Truck Driver

Up to two years beyond high school
- Aircraft Mechanic
- Airplane Pilot
- Auto Body Repairer
- Automotive Mechanic
- Garage Supervisor
- Motorcycle Mechanic

Parts of a Resume

At the very least, your resume should include the following components:

Heading: Centered at the top of the page should be your name, address, phone number, and e-mail address.

Objective: In one sentence, tell the employer the type of work for which you are looking.

Education: Beginning with your most recent school or program, include the date (or expected date) of completion, the degree or certificate earned, and the address of the institution. Don't overlook any workshops or seminars, self-study, or on-the-job training in which you have been involved. If any courses particularly lend themselves to the type of work for which you are applying, include them. Mention grade point averages and class rank when they are especially impressive.

Skills and abilities: Until you've actually listed these on paper, you can easily overlook many of them. They may be as varied as the ability to work with computers or being captain of the girl's basketball team.

Work experience: If you don't have any, skip this section. If you do, begin with your most recent employer and include the date you left the job, your job title, the company name, and the company address. If you are still employed there, simply enter your start date and "to present" for the date. Include notable accomplishments for each job. High school and college students with little work experience shouldn't be shy about including summer, part-time, and volunteer jobs, such as lifeguarding, babysitting, delivering pizzas, or volunteering at local parks and recreation department.

Personal: Here's your opportunity to include your special talents and interests as well as notable accomplishments or experiences.

SAMPLE FUNCTIONAL RESUME

Michele A. Thomas
3467 Main Street
Atlanta, Georgia 30308
404-555-3423
E-mail: mthomas_987654321@yahoo.com

OBJECTIVE

Seeking a sales position in the wireless phone industry

EDUCATION

High School Diploma, June 2004

John F. Kennedy High School, Atlanta, Georgia

SKILLS

Computer literate, IBM: MS Works, MS Word, WordPerfect, Netscape; Macintosh: MS Word, Excel

ACTIVITIES/LEADERSHIP

Student Government secretary, 2003–2004

Key Club vice president, 2002–2003

Future Business Leaders of America

AWARDS

Varsity Swim Club (Captain; MVP Junior, Senior; Sportsmanship Award)
Outstanding Community Service Award, 2003

EXPERIENCE

Sales Clerk, The Limited, Atlanta, Georgia; part-time, September 2002 to present

Cashier, Winn-Dixie Supermarkets, Atlanta, Georgia, Summers 2001 and 2002

INTERESTS

Swimming, reading, computers

REFERENCES

Available upon request

References: Most experts agree that it's best to simply state that references are available upon request. However, if you do decide to list names, addresses, and phone numbers, limit yourself to no more than three. Make sure you inform any people whom you have listed that they may be contacted.

SAMPLE COVER LETTER

Take a look at how this student applied the facts outlined in her resume to the job she's applying for in the cover letter below. You can use this letter to help you get started on your own cover letters. Text that appears in all caps below indicates the kind of information you need to include in that section. Before you send your letter, proofread it for mistakes and ask a parent or friend you trust to look it over as well.

(DATE)
June 29, 2004

(YOUR ADDRESS)
3467 Main Street
Atlanta, Georgia 30308
E-mail: mthomas_987654321@yahoo.com
Phone: 404-555-3423

(PERSON—BY NAME—TO WHOM YOU'RE SENDING THE LETTER)
Mr. Charles E. Pence
Manager, Human Resources
NexAir Wireless
20201 East Sixth Street
Atlanta, Georgia 30372

Dear Mr. Pence:

(HOW YOU HEARD OF THE POSITION)
Your job announcement in the Atlanta Gazette for an entry-level sales position asked for someone who has both computer and sales skills. (SOMETHING EXTRA THAT WILL INTEREST THE READER) My training and past job experience fit both of those categories. I also bring an enthusiasm and desire to begin my career in a communications firm such as NexAir.

(WHAT PRACTICAL SKILLS YOU CAN BRING TO THE POSITION)
A few weeks ago, I graduated from John F. Kennedy High School here in Atlanta. While in school, I concentrated on gaining computer skills on both IBM and Macintosh machines and participated in organizations such as the Key Club, in which I was vice president, and the Future Business Leaders of America.

(RELATE PAST EXPERIENCE TO DESIRED JOB)
As you will see from my resume, I worked as a cashier at Winn-Dixie Supermarket for two summers and am currently employed as a sales clerk at The Limited. From these two positions, I have gained valuable customer service skills and an attention to detail, qualities which I am sure are of utmost importance to you as you make your hiring decision.

I would very much like to interview for the position and am available at your convenience. I look forward to hearing from you soon.

Sincerely,

Michele A. Thomas

Resume-Writing Tips

These tips will help as you begin constructing your resume:

- Keep the resume short and simple. Although senior executives may use as many as two or three pages, recent graduates should limit themselves to one page.

- Capitalize headings.

- Keep sentences short; avoid writing in paragraphs.

- Use language that is simple, not flowery or complex.

- Be specific, and offer examples when appropriate.

- Emphasize achievements.

- Be honest.

- Don't include information about salary or wages unless specifically requested.

- Use high-quality, white, beige, or gray, 8 ½" × 11" paper.

- Make good use of white space by leaving adequate side and top margins on the paper.

- Make what you write presentable, using good business style and typing it on a computer or word processor.

- Because your resume should be a reflection of your personality, write it yourself.

- Avoid gimmicks such as colored paper, photos, or clip art.

- Make good use of bullets or asterisks, underlining, and bold print.

- Proofread your work, and have someone you trust proofread it also.

- Be neat and accurate.

- Never send a resume without a cover letter.

The Cover Letter

Every resume should be accompanied by a cover letter. This is often the most crucial part of your job search because the letter will be the first thing that a potential employer reads. When you include a cover letter, you're showing the employer that you care enough to take the time to address him or her personally and that you are genuinely interested in the job.

Always call the company and verify the name and title of the person to whom you are addressing the letter. Although you will want to keep your letter brief, introduce yourself and begin with a statement that will catch the reader's attention. Indicate the position you are applying for and mention if someone referred you or if you are simply responding to a newspaper ad. Draw attention to yourself by including something that will arouse the employer's curiosity about your experience and accomplishments. A cover letter should request something, most commonly an interview. Sign and date your letter. Then follow up with a phone call a few days after you're sure the letter has been received. Persistence pays!

JOB HUNTING 101

High school is a time for taking classes and learning, developing relationships with others, becoming involved in extracurricular activities that teach valuable life skills, and generally preparing for college or a job. Regardless of where you're headed after high school, you need to learn how to create a favorable impression. That can mean setting some clear, attainable goals for yourself, putting them down on paper in the form of a resume and cover letter, and convincing interviewers that you are, indeed, the person for whom they are looking. In short, learn how to sell yourself. A brief course in Job Hunting 101 will help you do just that.

Marketing Yourself

You can use several approaches to market yourself successfully. Networking, the continual process of contacting friends and relatives, is a great way to get information about job openings. Seventy-five percent of the job openings in this country are not advertised but are filled by friends, relatives, and acquaintances of current employees. From the employer's perspective, there is less risk associated with hiring someone recommended by an employee than by hiring someone unknown. Networking is powerful. Everyone has a primary network of people they know and talk to frequently. Those acquaintances know and talk to networks of their own, thereby creating a secondary network for you and multiplying the number of individuals who know what you're looking for in a job.

Broadcasting is another marketing method in which you gather a list of companies that interest you and then mail them letters asking for job interviews. Although the rate of return on your mailings is small, two thirds of all job hunters use this approach, and half of those who use it find a job. You will increase your response rate by addressing your letter to a particular person—the one who has the power to hire you—and by following up with a phone call a few days after the letter has been received. To obtain the manager's name, simply call the company and ask the receptionist for the person's name, job title, and correct spelling. Good resources for finding potential employers include referrals, community agencies, job fairs, newspaper ads, trade directories, trade journals, state indexes, the local chamber of commerce, the Yellow Pages, and the Web. The following tips can help as you begin hunting for the perfect job:

- Job-hunting is time-intensive. Do your homework, and take it seriously by using every opportunity available to you.
- Prepare yourself for the fact that there will be far more rejections than acceptances.
- Consider taking a temporary job while you continue the job hunt. It will help pay the bills and give you new skills to boost your resume at the same time.
- Research the activities of potential employers, and show that you have studied them when you're being interviewed.
- Keep careful records of all contacts and follow-up activities.
- Don't ignore any job leads—act on every tip you get.
- Stay positive.

With all these thoughts in mind, you should be ready to begin the process of making people believe in you, and that's a major part of being successful in your job hunt.

THE JOB INTERVIEW

You can prevent some of the preinterview jitters by adequately preparing. Remember that you have nothing to lose and that you, too, are doing the choosing. Just as you are waiting and hoping to be offered a job, you have the option of choosing whether or not to accept an offer. It's all right to feel somewhat anxious, but keep everything in perspective. This is an adventure, and you are in control. Most important, remember to be yourself. With all of this in mind, consider some of the following points of the interview process:

- Speak up during the interview, and furnish the interviewer with the information he or she needs in order to make an informed decision. It is especially impressive if you can remember the names of people to whom you've been introduced. People like to be called by name, and it shows that you took the initiative to remember them.

- Always arrive a few minutes early for the interview, and look your best. The way you act and dress tells the interviewer plenty about your attitude and personality. Sloppy dress, chewing gum, and cigarettes have no place at an interview and will probably cut your interview short. Instead, dress professionally and appropriately for the job. Avoid heavy makeup, short skirts, jeans, and untidy or flashy clothing of any kind. Although a business suit may be appropriate for certain jobs, a person who is applying for an outdoor position should probably interview in clean, neatly pressed dress slacks and a golf shirt or a skirt and blouse.

The best way to prepare for the interview is to practice. Have a friend or relative play the role of the interviewer, and go over some of the most commonly asked questions. Learn as much as you can about the company you're interviewing with—it pays to do your homework. When you show a potential employer that you've taken the time and initiative to learn about his

or her company, you're showing that you will be a motivated and hardworking employee. Employers fear laziness and minimal effort, looking instead for workers who don't always have to be told what to do and when to do it.

Here is a list of interview questions you can expect to have to answer:

- **Tell me a little bit about yourself.** This is your chance to pitch your qualifications for the job in 2 minutes. Provide a few details about your education, previous jobs you've held, and extracurricular activities that relate to the position for which you're interviewing.

- **Are you at your best when working alone or in a group?** The safest answer is "Both." Most companies today cluster their employees into work groups, so you will need strong interpersonal skills. However, on occasion, you may be required to work on projects alone.

- **What did you like the most about your last job? What did you dislike the most about it?** Always accentuate the positives in an interview, so focus primarily on what you liked. Also be honest about what you disliked, but then explain how facing the negatives helped you grow as an employee.

- **What are your career goals?** Be sure you've done some research on the company and industry before your interview. When this question comes up, talk realistically about how far you believe your skills and talents will take you and what actions you plan to take to ensure this happens, such as pursuing more education.

Take the time to prepare some answers to these commonly asked questions. For instance, if you haven't set at least one career goal for yourself, do it now. Be ready to describe it to the interviewer. Likewise, you should be able to talk about your last job, including what you liked the most and the least. Adapt your answers so they apply to the job for which you are presently interviewing. Other questions that might be asked include:

FINDING JOBS ON THE WEB

As mentioned, you can find jobs through your network of friends, family, and acquaintances; through classified ads in the newspaper; and through career Web pages. Here is a listing of popular Web sites that not only offer job search technology but also information on resume writing, interviewing, and other important career advice.

www.monster.com   www.careerbuilder.com

www.hotjobs.com   www.vault.com

- What qualifications do you have?
- Why do you want to work for us?
- Do you enjoy school? Why or why not?
- Do you plan to continue your education?
- What do you plan to be doing five years from now?
- What motivates you to do a good job?

If you are seeking a job as a manager, you might respond by saying you liked the varied responsibilities of your past job. Recall that you enjoyed the unexpected challenges and flexible schedule. And when describing what you liked least, make sure you respond with some function or area of responsibility that has nothing to do with the responsibilities of the job you hope to get.

More than likely, the first question you'll be asked is to tell the interviewer something about yourself. This is your chance to "toot your horn," but don't ramble. You might ask the interviewer specifically what he or she would like to hear about: your educational background or recent experiences and responsibilities in your present or last job. After he or she chooses, stick to the basics; the next move belongs to the interviewer.

When asked about personal strengths and weaknesses, given that the question is two parts, begin with a weakness so you can end on a strong note with your strengths. Again, try to connect your description of a strength or weakness with the requirements for the job. Naturally, it wouldn't be wise to reveal a serious weakness about yourself, but you can mention how you have changed your shortcomings. You might say, "I like to get my work done fast, but I consciously try to slow down a little to make sure I'm careful and accurate." When it comes to strengths, don't exaggerate, but don't sell yourself short either.

Asking Questions

You can ask questions, too. In fact, the interviewer expects you to ask questions to determine if the job is right for you, just as he or she will be trying to find out if you'll be successful working for his or her company. When you ask questions, it shows that you're interested and want to learn more. When the type of question you ask indicates that you've done your homework regarding the job and the company, your interviewer will be impressed. Avoid asking questions about salary or fringe benefits, anything adversarial, or questions that show you have a negative opinion of the company. It's all right to list your questions on a piece of paper; it's the quality of the question that's important, not whether you can remember it. Here are a few sample questions that you should consider asking if the topics don't come up in your interview:

- What kind of responsibilities come with this job?
- How is the department organized?
- What will be the first project for the new hire to tackle?
- What is a typical career advancement path for a person in this position?
- Who will the supervisor be for this position, and can I meet him or her?
- What is the office environment like? Is it casual or corporate?
- When do you expect to reach a hiring decision?

Following Up

After the interview, follow up with a thank-you note to the interviewer. Not only is it a thoughtful gesture, it triggers the interviewer's memory about you and shows that you have a genuine interest in the job. Your thank-you note should be written in a business letter format and should highlight the key points in your interview.

During the interview process, remember that you will not appeal to everyone who interviews you. If your first experience doesn't work out, don't get discouraged. Keep trying.

SAMPLE THANK-YOU LETTER

After you've interviewed for a job, it's important to reiterate your interest in the position by sending a thank-you letter to those who interviewed you. Take a look at Michele's letter to the manager she interviewed with at NexAir. You can use this letter as a model when the time comes for you to write some thank-you letters.

July 17, 2004

Michele A. Thomas
3467 Main Street
Atlanta, Georgia 30308
E-mail: mthomas_987654321@yahoo.com
Phone: 404-555-3423

Mr. Charles E. Pence
Manager, Human Resources
NexAir Wireless
20201 East Sixth Street
Atlanta, Georgia 30372

Dear Mr. Pence:

It was a pleasure meeting with you Monday to discuss the sales opportunity at NexAir's downtown location. After learning more about the position, it is clear to me that with my background and enthusiasm, I would be an asset to your organization.

As we discussed, my experiences as a cashier at Winn-Dixie Supermarket and as a sales clerk at The Limited have provided me with the basic skills necessary to perform the responsibilities required of a sales representative at NexAir. I believe that with my ability to learn quickly and communicate effectively, I can help NexAir increase sales of its wireless products.

Thank you for the opportunity to interview with your organization. If there is any additional information I can provide about myself, please do not hesitate to call me. I look forward to hearing your decision soon.

Sincerely,

Michele A. Thomas

WHAT EMPLOYERS EXPECT FROM EMPLOYEES

As part of the National City Bank personnel team in Columbus, Ohio, Rose Graham works with Cooperative Business Education (CBE) coordinators in the area who are trying to place high school students in the workplace. When asked what skills she looks for in potential employees, she quickly replies that basic communication skills are at the top of her list. She stresses, "The ability to construct a sentence and put together words cannot be overemphasized." She cites knowledge of the personal computer, with good keyboarding skills, as essential.

In an article published in the *Nashville Business Journal*, Donna Cobble of Staffing Solutions outlined these basic skills for everyday life in the workplace:

Communication. Being a good communicator not only means having the ability to express oneself properly in the English language, but it also means being a good listener. If you feel inferior in any of these areas, it's a good idea to sign up for a public speaking class, read books on the subject, and borrow techniques from professional speakers.

Organization. Organization is the key to success in any occupation or facet of life. The ability to plan, prioritize, and complete a task in a timely fashion is a valuable skill. Check out Chapter 13 for tips on improving your time-management skills.

Problem solving. Companies are looking for creative problem solvers, people who aren't afraid to act on a situation and follow through with their decision. Experience and practice play a major role in your ability to determine the best solution. You can learn these techniques by talking with others about how they solve problems as well as observing others in the problem-solving process.

Sensitivity. In addition to being kind and courteous to their fellow workers, employees need to be sensitive to a coworker's perspective. That might mean putting yourself in the other person's shoes to gain a better understanding of that person's feelings. Employers look for individuals who are able to work on a team instead of those concerned only with their own personal gain.

Judgment. Although closely related to problem solving, good judgment shows up on many different levels in the workplace. It is the ability of a person to assess a situation, weigh the options, consider the risks, and make the necessary decision. Good judgment is built on experience and self-confidence.

Concentration. Concentration is the ability to focus on one thing at a time. Learning to tune out distractions and relate solely to the task at hand is a valuable asset for anyone.

Cooperation. Remember that you're being paid to do a job, so cooperate.

Honesty. Dishonesty shows up in many different ways, ranging from stealing time or property to divulging company secrets. Stay honest.

Initiative. Don't wait to be told exactly what to do. Show some initiative and look around to see what needs to be done next.

Willingness to learn. Be willing to learn how things are done at the company instead of doing things the way you want to do them.

Dependability. Arrive at work on time every day and meet your deadlines.

Enthusiasm. Although not every task you're assigned will be stimulating, show enthusiasm for your work at all times.

Acceptance of criticism. Constructive criticism is necessary for any employee to learn how things should be done. Employees who view criticism as a way to improve themselves will benefit from it.

Loyalty. There is no place for negativity in the workplace. You simply won't be happy working for an employer to whom you're not loyal.

Never fail to show pride in your work, the place where you work, and your appearance. By making these traits a part of your personality and daily performance, you will demonstrate that you are a cut above other employees with equal or better qualifications.

JUMPING ON THE SALARY FAST-TRACK

So the job offer comes, and it's time to talk about money. Unless you are an undiscovered genius, you most likely will start near the bottom of the salary scale if you're heading straight to the workplace after graduating from high school. There's not much room to negotiate a salary since you probably won't be able to say, "Well, I've done this, this, and this. I know what my experience is worth." You will find that most people hiring first-time employees will have a "take-it-or-leave-it" attitude about salary offers. However, according to Amryl Ward, a human resources consultant who has been hiring employees for more than twenty-five years in various human resource positions, there are some things that entry-level employees can do to make themselves more easily hired and, once hired, to get themselves on the fast-track toward more pay:

- **As you interview for the job, be prepared to tell a potential employer why you're worth hiring.** "Bring your skills to the table," says Ward. For instance, you might not think that the job you had during the summer at that big office supply store did anything more than earn you spending money. On the contrary, you learned valuable skills, such as how to be part of a team and how to deal with customers. What about that after-school office job you had? You learned how to answer the phones and how to work with certain software. Think carefully about the jobs you had in high school and what you learned from them. Those are called transferable skills.

- **Once you're hired, be willing to do more than just what the job requires.** Sure, you may be frying fries at the start. But if you come in early and stay late, if you pitch in to help another employee with his or her job, or if you voluntarily clean up the counters and sweep the floor, that says to management, "This employee is a winner. Let's keep him or her in mind the next time a promotion comes up." Soon, you might be managing a crew, then the store.

ON THE JOB

Once you snag that perfect job, there's no time to rest easy. You need to keep your manager happy and instill trust in your coworkers. And at the same time you're doing this, you'll want to watch out for yourself, keep yourself happy, and stay ahead of the learning curve. Here are some ways for you to do just that.

Minding Your Office Etiquette

Okay, so maybe you didn't know which was the salad fork at your cousin Sally's wedding reception. Most likely, though, you can name a few basic rules of etiquette, like not chewing with your mouth open at the dinner table. Now, what about when it comes to the manners you're supposed to have in the workplace? That usually draws a blank if you've never worked in an office setting. How would you know what's the right way to answer the phone or talk to your boss or customers?

Shannon McBride, of the Golden Crescent Tech-Prep Partnership in Victoria, Texas, has seen many students come through his program and land good jobs. He's also seen many of them succeed because they knew how to present themselves in a professional situation. Unfortunately, he can also relate stories of high school graduates who had no clue how to act in the workplace. They didn't realize that when they're working in an office with a group of people, they have to go out of their way to get along and follow the unwritten rules of that workplace. McBride says that means you'll have to size up how others are dressing and match what the office is geared to. For instance, if you work in a business office, most likely you'd wear slacks and a button-down shirt or a nice skirt and top. If you worked in a golf pro shop, you'd wear a golf shirt and shorts. "As much as you want to be an individual," says McBride, "you have to fit in when you're in a business setting. If you want an adult job, you have to act like an adult."

A lot of young people don't grasp how important office etiquette is and blow it off as just some silly rules imposed by adults. But McBride cautions that not following the norms of office etiquette can make or break a job. You can have all the technical talent and know all the latest software applications, but if you're not up on how people dress, talk, and conduct business, your job probably won't last very long. When it comes to getting a job, McBride warns, "First impressions are so important. Bad office etiquette can hurt that first impression." The best advice that we can give is that if you're not sure what the policy is about answering phones, using e-mail or the Internet on the job, or dress codes, ask your boss. He or she won't steer you wrong and will be pleased that you were concerned enough to ask.

Finding a Friendly Face at Work

There you are on the first day of a new job. Everyone looks like they know what they're doing while you stand there feeling really dumb. Even for the most seasoned employee, those first few weeks on the job are tough. Of course, everyone else looks like they know what they're doing because they've been doing it for quite some time. Wouldn't it be nice, though, if you had someone to help you adjust? Someone who would give you those little inside tips everyone else learns with experience. Someone to caution you about things that could go wrong or give you a heads-up when you're doing something that could lead to a reprimand. If you look around the office, you'll find such a person, says Robert Fait, Career Counselor and Instructional Specialist, who is associated with Career and Technology Education in the Katy Independent School district in Katy, Texas.

You might not realize that such a person is a mentor, but in the strict definition of the word, that's what he or she is. Or, as Fait puts it, "Mentors are role models who are willing to assist others with personal education and career goal setting and planning. This caring person shares a listening ear, a comforting shoulder, and an understanding heart." In other words, a mentor is someone who will make you feel comfortable in a new working environment, show you the procedures, and, in the end, help you become more productive.

Unless the company you're working for has a formal mentoring program, mentors don't come with huge signs around their necks that read, "Look here. I'm a mentor. Ask me anything." You have to look for them. Fait advises new employees to look closely at their coworkers and take notice of who demonstrates positive behavior, has strong work habits, and seems trustworthy. Those are the people to approach. "Such workers are usually willing to share their knowledge and insights with others," says Fait.

Who knows? Given some time, you could become a mentor yourself after you've been on the job for a while. Maybe you'll be able to help some new employee who looks kind of bewildered and in need of a friendly hand because you'll remember what it was like to be that new person.

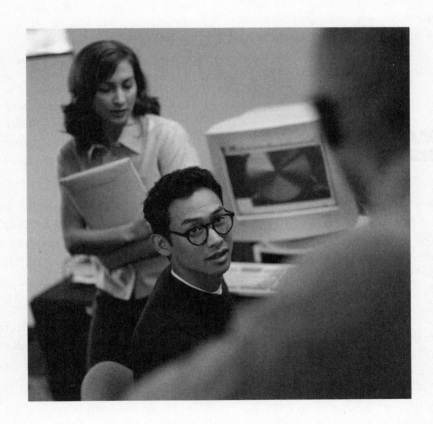

13 Chapter

SURVIVAL SKILLS

Whether you're headed to college or work, you're going to come face to face with some intimidating stuff after graduation.

YOUR LEVEL OF STRESS will most likely increase due to the demands of your classes or job and your exposure to alcohol or drugs. Various forms of conflict will arise, and you're going to have to keep up with your own health and nutrition. Seem daunting? It's really not if you keep a level head about you and stick to your core values. This chapter will help you work through the muddier side of life after high school.

SKILLS TO MAKE YOU STRESS-HARDY

Jump out of bed and into the shower. What to wear? Throw that on. Yuck—what's that stain? "Mom, where are my clean socks?" Tick, tock. No time to grab a bite if you want to make the homeroom bell. Skid around the corner and race for the classroom just as the final bell rings. Whoops, forgot your bio book. Sports, clubs, job, homework, friends on the internet, and finally (sigh) sleep.

Sound like your life? If you're like most high school students, that description probably hits pretty close to home. So now we'll take your already hectic schedule and throw in the fact that you'll soon be graduating and have to figure out what to do with your life. Can you say "stress"?

Some people say that stress actually motivates them to perform better, but we won't talk about those perfect people. For most of you, stress means that you may snap at the dog, slam a few doors, get mad at

your dad, and feel down. Maybe you'll even have physical symptoms—upset stomach, rapid heartbeat, sweaty palms, dizziness. The list goes on. Not a good place to be when you're dealing with a huge list of things to do, plus graduation is staring you in the face.

How to handle stress has been written about countless times, but out of all the advice that's out there, a few simple pointers can really help you prevent the sweaty palms and nauseated feeling in the pit of your stomach.

- **French fries out, good food in.** Eat at least one hot, balanced meal a day. Healthy, as in veggies, fruits, meats, cheese, grains. Read further along in this chapter for more information about nutrition and health.

- **Sleep.** 7, 8, 10 hours a day. Easier said than done, but well worth it. Sleep will not only get you through high school but also your college and career lives, and it will help you stop feeling like such a frazzled bunch of nerve endings.

- **Hug your dog, cat, rabbit, friend, or mom.** Loneliness breeds stress because then all you've got is yourself and those stressed-out thoughts zooming around in your head.

- **Hang out with friends.** That takes time, but being with people you like and doing fun things eases stress—as long as you don't overdo it.

- **Exercise.** This does not include running down the hall to make the bell. We're talking 20 minutes of heart-pounding perspiration at least three times a week. It's amazing what a little sweat can do to relax you. Believe it or not, good posture helps too.

- **Don't smoke, drink, or use excessive amounts of caffeine.** Whoever told you that partying is the way to relieve stress got it all wrong. Nicotine and alcohol actually take away the things your body needs to fight stress.

- **Simplify your expenses.** Money can be a big stress factor. Think of ways to eliminate where you're spending money so that the money you have doesn't have to be stretched so far. Be creative. Share resources. Sell items you no longer use. Maybe put off buying something you've been wanting.

- **Let your feelings out of your head.** It takes time and energy to keep them bottled up inside. Have regular conversations with your parents and siblings so that minor annoyances can be solved when they're still small.

- **Organize your time.** As in prioritizing and dealing with one small part of your life instead of trying to solve everything in one shot. Read on for more information about time management.

- **Lighten up.** When you've graduated and are into whatever it is you'll end up doing, you'll look back and realize that this was a teensy little part of your life. So look on the bright side. The decisions you'll be making about your future are heavy, but they won't be cut in stone. You can change them if they don't work out.

Stress Busters

Most people get stressed when things are out of control—too many things to do, too many decisions to make, or too much information to digest. If you add not having enough time, enough money, or enough energy to get it all done, you have the perfect recipe for stress.

In the space below, identify what's causing you stress:

_____

_____

_____

_____

_____

_____

Then, choose from these three stress-busting options:

1. **Alter the situation.** Some things you can't control, some things you can. Change the ones you can. If you have too much on your plate and can't possibly do it all, push a few things aside. There's got to be something on the list you can get rid of. (And no, homework is not a choice.) Maybe you need to be able to say no to extra demands. Concentrate on what is important. Make a list of your priorities from the most important to the least, and work your way down.

2. **Avoid the situation—for now.** Step back and ask, "Is this really a problem? Do I really need to solve it now?" This doesn't mean you should procrastinate on things that need to get done. Think of this stress buster as buying some time, taking a break, catching your breath, getting advice, and airing out the situation so that you can deal with it when you're better prepared to handle it.

3. **Accept the situation.** How you perceive your circumstances has a lot to do with how you make decisions about them. Put whatever is stressing you in the perspective of the big picture. How will this really affect me next year or even ten years from now? Look at your circumstances through the lens of your personal values. Think about what feels right to you, not someone else.

Quick Fixes for Stressful Moments

So, you've done all the things we talked about earlier in this chapter, and you're still feeling like you're being pulled in a million directions. If your stress thermometer has hit the top, use these quick fixes to help you calm down.

- Make the world slow down for a bit. Take a walk. Take a shower. Listen to some soothing music.

- Breathe deeply. Get in tune with the rhythm of your own breathing. Lie or sit down for 15 minutes and just concentrate on relaxing.

- Relax those little knots of tension. Start at your head and work down to your toes.

- Close your eyes and clear your mind. Oops, there comes that nagging thought. Out, out, out. Get rid of the clutter. Imagine yourself in your favorite place: the beach, under a tree, whatever works.

- Close the door to your bedroom, and let out a blood-curdling scream. Walt Whitman knew what he was talking about when he said, "I sound my barbaric yawp over the roofs of the world." Just let your family know what you're doing so they don't come running to your room in fear. You'll be amazed at how much better you feel.

- When all else fails, watch a funny movie. Read the comics. Get in a giggly frame of mind. Those big challenges will quickly be brought down to size.

WINNING THE TIME MANAGEMENT GAME

What is the value of time? Six dollars an hour? The price of a scholarship because the application is a day late? Time can be a very expensive resource or something you can use to your advantage. Even if you recognize the value of time, managing it is a challenge.

When you live with enough time, life is relaxed and balanced. In order to find that balance, you have to prioritize and plan. Decide what you want and what is important to you. Organize logically and schedule realistically. Overcome obstacles. Change bad habits. Simplify and streamline. Save time when you can.

Sound impossible? It's not easy, but you can do it. The secret is held in a Chinese proverb: The wisdom of life is the elimination of nonessentials.

It's All about Control

The good thing about time is that much of it is yours to do with as you wish. You may feel out of control and as if you must run to keep up with the conflicting demands and expectations of your life. But we all have the same number of hours in each day. The key is in how we spend them. The following tips are designed to help you spend your time wisely and to keep you in control of your life.

Prepare a list of your goals and the tasks necessary to accomplish them. This could be by day, week, month, semester, or even year. You may also want to break the list into sections, such as friends and family, school, work, sports, health and fitness, home, personal development, and college preparation.

Prioritize based on time-sensitive deadlines. Use a grading system to code how important each task is. A is "Do It Now," B is "Do It Soon," C is "Do It Later." Understand the difference between "important" and "urgent."

Be realistic about how much you can really do. Analyze how you spend your time now. What can you cut? How much time do you truly need for each task?

Think ahead. How many times have you underestimated how long it will take to do something? Plan for roadblocks, and give yourself some breathing space.

Accept responsibility. Once you decide to do something, commit yourself to it. That doesn't mean that a task that was on the "A" list can't be moved to the "C" list. But be consistent and specific about what you want to accomplish.

Divide and conquer. You may need to form a committee, delegate tasks to your parents, or ask for help from a friend. That is why it is called time management.

Take advantage of your personal prime time. Don't schedule yourself to get up and do homework at 6 a.m.

if you are a night owl. It won't work. Instead, plan complex tasks when you are most efficient.

Avoid procrastination. There are a million ways to procrastinate. And not one of them is a good reason if you really want to get something done. Have you ever noticed that you always find time to do the things you enjoy?

Do the most unpleasant task first. Get it over with. Then it will be all downhill from there.

Don't over-prepare. That is just another way to procrastinate.

Learn to say no to the demands on your time that you cannot afford.

Be enthusiastic, and share your goals with others.

If you set too many goals at once, you will overwhelm yourself from the start. Remember, what is important is the quality of the time you spend on a task, not the quantity. It doesn't make any difference if you study for 10 hours if you don't recall a thing you've reviewed. The overall goal is to be productive, efficient, and effective, not just busy. You'll also need to pace yourself. All work and no play makes for an unbalanced person.

Use all the benefits of modern technology to help you manage time. You can save lots of time by using a fax, e-mail, or voice mail. If you don't already use a day planner or calendar, you would be wise to invest in one. Write in all the important deadlines, and refer to it often. Block out commitments you know you have so you won't over-schedule yourself. When you do over-schedule yourself or underestimate the time it takes to accomplish a task, learn from your mistakes. But don't get too down on yourself. Give yourself a pep talk every now and then to keep yourself positive and motivated.

MOVING OUT ON YOUR OWN?

As you consider moving away from home either to a college dorm or your own place, some pretty wonderful expectations of what it will be like no doubt will come floating into your head. No more parental rules. On your own. Making your own

decisions. Hamburgers forever. Coming and going when you want to. Wait, what's this? Looks like you're out of clothes to wear. No more cereal bowls—they're all in the sink, and they're dirty. Out of milk and the refrigerator's empty. Yikes! What happened to all those warm, fuzzy thoughts about freedom?

Sure, it's nice to be able to come and go as you please, but before you get too far into that pleasant—and unrealistic—mind mode, here are some thoughts you might want to consider as you make plans to become independent. Ozzie Hashley, a guidance counselor at Clinton Community Schools in Clinton, Michigan, works with juniors and seniors in high school. Here is what he says to inform students about six realities of independent life.

1. If you rent your own place, have you thought about the extra charges in addition to the rent? Says Hashley, "Many students think only of paying the rent. They don't realize that they'll be responsible for utilities in many cases. Or the money it will take to wash and dry their clothes."

2. Subsisting on hamburgers and fries sounds yummy, but as you watch a fast food diet eat its way into your paycheck, you'll most likely think about cooking up something yourself. What will you cook? Who will buy the food? More importantly, who will do the dishes? Dividing up the responsibilities of preparing food is a big aspect of being on your own, especially when sharing a living space.

3. Medical insurance may not be on your mind as you prepare to graduate—you're probably on your parents' insurance plans right now. However, once you are established as independent at age 18 and you're living on your own, insurance becomes a big consideration. If you need health care and don't have medical insurance, the bills will be big. So when you get a job,

make sure that you have medical coverage. If you're going off to college after high school, you'll most likely be covered under your parents' insurance until age 23.

4. There's no one to tell you when to come home when you're on your own. There's also no one to tell you that you're really disorganized when it comes to managing your time. Time management might not sound like a big deal now, but when you have to juggle all the facets of being independent—your job, taking care of your living space and car, your social life—then being able to manage time becomes an important part of life.

5. Managing your money moves into a whole other realm when you are on your own. You have to make sure you have enough to pay the rent, your car loan, and insurance, not to mention that movie you wanted to see, the CD you wanted to buy, or those jeans you saw at the mall last week. If you want to eat at the end of the month, budgeting will become an important part of your new independent vocabulary. Ask your parents or an adult you trust to help you set up your budget. Also learn how to balance your checkbook. It's a lot easier to manage your money when you keep track of how much you have in your bank account and how much you spend!

DRUGS AND ALCOHOL: ARE YOU AT RISK?

At risk? Wait a minute. How could you be at risk when the legal drinking age in all fifty states is 21? Chances are, if you're reading this, you're not 21 yet. It's also illegal to smoke or buy any tobacco product before age 18, and possession of any drug for recreational use is illegal, period. So if you drink alcohol before age 21; smoke or buy cigarettes, cigars, or chewing tobacco before age 18; or take any illegal drugs, you could:

- Be arrested for driving under the influence (DUI)

- Be convicted

- Be required to pay steep fines

- Have your driving privileges suspended

- Get kicked out of school (that's any kind of school, college included)

- Get fired

- Go to jail

- Have a criminal record

A criminal record . . . so what?

Consider this true story. A 29-year-old man who recently received his graduate degree in business was offered a job with a major Fortune-100 corporation. We're talking big bucks, stock options, reserved parking space—the whole nine yards. When the company did a background check and found that he was arrested for a DUI during his freshman year of college, they rescinded their offer. The past can and will come back to haunt you. Let's not even think about what would happen down the line if you decide to run for public office.

Think about why you might want to try drinking or doing drugs. For fun? To forget your troubles? To be cool? Are your reasons good enough? Remember the consequences before you make a decision.

How Can I Say No Without Looking Like a Geek?

"It takes a lot more guts to stay sober, awake, and aware than to just get high, get numb, and learn nothing about life," says one former user. "Laugh at people who suggest you drink or take drugs, and then avoid them like the plague."

Friends worth having will respect your decision to say no. And girls—if a guy pressures you to drink or get high, ditch him pronto. You can vice-versa that for guys, too. According to the National Institute on Drug Abuse (NIDA), alcohol and club drugs like GHB or Rohypnol (roofies) make you an easy target for date rape.

The Nitty Gritty

Along with the temporary pleasure they may give you, all drugs (including club drugs, alcohol, and nicotine) have a downside. Alcohol, for example, is a depressant. Even one drink slows down the part of your brain that controls your reasoning. So your judgment gets dull just when you're wondering, "Should I drive my friends home? Should I talk to this guy? Should I have another drink?"

Your body needs about an hour to burn up the alcohol in one drink. Nothing, including coffee, will sober you up any faster. Here's what "one drink" means: one shot of hard liquor (straight or mixed in a cocktail), one glass of wine, one 12-ounce beer, or one wine cooler.

Alcohol helps smart people make bad decisions. In fact, many drugs make you believe that you're thinking even more clearly than usual. Well, guess what? You aren't. Depending on what drug you take, how much, and what you do while you're on it, you're also risking confusion, nausea, headache, sleep problems, depression, paranoia, rape (especially "date rape"), unwanted pregnancy, sexually transmitted diseases (STDs) ranging from herpes to HIV/AIDS, having a baby with a birth defect, memory impairment, persistent psychosis, lung damage, cancer, injuring or killing someone else, and death.

Take a moment now, when your brain is razor sharp, to decide if those consequences are worth the

DID YOU KNOW...

... that nicotine is as addictive as cocaine and heroin, according to the American Cancer Society?

... that drinking a lot of alcohol fast can kill you on the spot, according to Keystone College?

... that MDMA (Ecstasy, X, Adam, Clarity, Lover's Speed), according to NIDA, may permanently damage your memory?

DO I HAVE A PROBLEM?

Take the quiz below to see if you're in real trouble with drugs or alcohol.

1. Do you look forward to drinking or using drugs?
2. Do most of your friends drink or do drugs?
3. Do you keep a secret supply of alcohol or drugs?
4. Can you drink a lot without appearing drunk?
5. Do you "power-hit" to get high faster, by binge-drinking, funneling, or slamming?
6. Do you ever drink or do drugs alone, including in a group where no one else is doing so?
7. Do you ever drink or use drugs when you hadn't planned to?
8. Do you ever have blackouts where you can't remember things that happened when you were drunk or high?

If you answered yes to any of these questions, you probably need help. If you have a friend who fits the picture, find a respectful way to bring up your concerns. Don't be surprised if he or she tells you to back off—but don't give up, either. If someone in your family has an alcohol or drug problem, be aware that you may be prone to the same tendency.

Source: Keystone College, La Plume, Pennsylvania

escape you get for 20 minutes one night. You may be saying, "Oh, come on. Only addicts have problems like that." Getting drunk or high doesn't necessarily mean that you're an alcoholic or an addict—but it always means a loss of control.

"So much of addiction is about denial," says one member of Alcoholics Anonymous. "I just didn't think I looked or acted or thought or smelled or lied or cheated or failed like an alcoholic or addict. It was when the drugs and alcohol use started to cause problems in multiple areas of my life that I began to think the problem might reside with me. Friends leaving—in disgust—was what opened my eyes."

Where Can I Get Help?

If you think you have a problem, or if you think a friend has a problem, try Alcoholics Anonymous or Narcotics Anonymous. If you're not sure, ask yourself the questions in "Do I Have a Problem?" on the top of this page.

Talk to any adult you trust: maybe your doctor, a clergy member, a counselor, or your parents. Health clinics and hospitals offer information and treatment. The American Cancer Society can help you quit smoking. These are only a few places to turn—check out the Yellow Pages and the Web for more.

Alcoholics Anonymous
212-870-3400
www.aa.org

American Cancer Society
800-ACS-2345
www.cancer.org

Narcotics Anonymous
818-773-9999
www.na.org

So, that's the straight stuff. You're at a tough but wonderful age, when your life is finally your own and your decisions really matter. Think about what you value most—and then make your choices.

CONFLICT: HOW TO AVOID IT AND DEFUSE IT

You're walking along and you see a group of kids up ahead . . . and suddenly you're afraid. Or you're about to talk to someone you have a disagreement with, and already you're tense. Or your boyfriend's jealousy is spooking you. What should you do?

All of these situations involve potential conflicts that could get out of hand. Even if you never get into a violent situation, you'll face conflicts with others, as we all do. Learning to spot the warning signs of violence and to handle conflicts well will bring you lifelong benefits.

What's Your Style?

What do you do when you're faced with a potential conflict? Do you try to get away, no matter what? Do you find yourself bowing to pressure from others? Do you feel like you have to stand and fight, even if you don't want to? Do you wish you had some new ways to handle conflict?

Different situations call for different strategies. First, let's talk about situations where violence is a

real possibility. Most of us get a bad feeling before things get violent, but too often, we ignore the feeling. Trust your gut feeling! And whether you're on the street or in school, Fred Barfoot of the Crime Prevention Association of Philadelphia suggests that you keep in mind these tips for avoiding violence:

- Walk like you're in charge and you know where you're going.

- Stick to lighted areas.

- Travel with a trusted friend when possible. On campus, get an escort from security at night. Loners are targets.

- If a person or group up ahead makes you nervous, cross the street immediately—and calmly—as if you'd intended to anyway.

- Call out to an imaginary friend, "Hey, Joe! Wait up!" and then run toward your "friend," away from whoever is scaring you.

- Go right up to the nearest house and ring the bell. Pretend you're expected: "Hey Joe, it's me!" You can explain later.

- If someone threatens you physically, scream.

- If someone assaults you, scream, kick where it hurts, scratch—anything.

- Don't ever get in a car with someone you don't know well or trust, even if you've seen that person around a lot.

- Strike up a conversation with an innocent bystander if you feel threatened by someone else, just to make yourself less vulnerable for a few minutes.

- Wear a whistle around your neck or carry a personal alarm or pepper spray.

- If someone mugs you, hand over your purse, wallet, jewelry—whatever he or she asks for. None of it is worth your life.

- Don't go along with something your gut says is wrong, no matter who says it's okay.

Remember that it's not a sign of weakness to back down if someone's egging you on to fight. Bill Tomasco, principal of Furness High School in Philadelphia, says that pressure from other kids to fight creates much of the violence in schools. If you're being pushed to fight, show true strength: Know that your opponent has a good side too, speak only to that good side, and don't give in to the pressure of the crowd.

Are You Safe at Home?

Locking doors and windows makes sense—but sometimes the danger lies within. A lot of violence occurs in abusive relationships, says Amy Gottlieb, a marriage family therapist intern at the California Family Counseling Center in Encino. To find out if you're at risk, ask yourself whether your partner, roommate, or family member:

- Uses jealousy to justify controlling you
- Puts you down, humiliates you, or pulls guilt trips on you
- Threatens to reveal your secrets or tells lies about you
- Makes all the decisions
- Frightens you, especially if it's on purpose
- Threatens you in any way
- Makes light of abusive behavior or says you provoked it

If any of these things are going on in your relationship, talk about it to an adult you trust, and ask for help.

Talking It Out

If your instincts tell you to get away from a situation, do it. But you can resolve many actual or potential conflicts face to face and gracefully so that everyone walks away feeling good. Read on for some tips on handling conflict from Kare Anderson, a communications expert in Sausalito, California.

Most of us make the mistake of reacting quickly, thinking only of our own needs, and not listening, says

Anderson. Try doing the opposite. First and foremost, think about what you really want from the situation, and keep your goal in mind the whole time. But bring up the other person's concerns first. Then, discuss how the situation affects you both. Offer a solution that will benefit you both—and only then talk about how your solution addresses your own needs.

When the other person is talking, really listen—don't just come up with retorts in your head. Always show that you've heard the person before you give your response, especially if you're talking with someone of a different sex, size, or race. Those differences can distract us so much that we actually hear less. If you're female, you may need to s-l-o-w yourself down. Say less than you think you need to. Guys, don't shut down altogether—keep the communication going.

Even if the other person acts like a jerk, be gracious and respectful. Ask questions instead of criticizing. Let someone save face instead of looking like a fool. If you insult or embarrass someone, you may never have that person's full attention again. In short, treat the other person as you'd like to be treated.

What should you do if you're really angry? One teen said, "Thinking about things calms me down." Another said, "Once in a while, we have to cool off for a day and then come back to the discussion." Anger almost always covers up fear. What are you afraid of? Is the reward you want out of this negotiation bigger than your fear? Focus on that reward. Don't forget to breathe—long, slow breaths.

Think about these strategies often, so you'll be more likely to use them when a situation gets hot, instead of just reacting blindly. Use them to plan for negotiations ahead of time, too. Learning to resolve problems with people takes most of us a lifetime—get a jump on it now!

THE LOWDOWN ON SEXUAL HARASSMENT

Has someone ever looked at you, talked to you, or touched you in a way that gave you the creeps, made you self-conscious about your body, or created a sexual mood when it wasn't appropriate? And did you begin to dread seeing this person because he or she just wouldn't quit?

If so, you've encountered sexual harassment. Sexual harassment is inappropriate behavior that

- is happening to you because of your sex,

- is unwanted (you don't like it),

- is objectively offensive (to a hypothetical "reasonable" man or woman),

- is either severe, persistent, or pervasive, and

- interferes with your work or school experience.

Paul Edison, a domestic and sexual violence prevention educator in Portland, Oregon, says that mostly—just as with crimes like rape—men harass women. But teenage girls are a bit more likely than older women to sexually harass someone, more girl-on-girl harassment goes on with teens, and guys get harassed, too. In some of the most brutal cases coming to light, gay men (or men perceived to be gay) are the targets.

People who sexually harass others fall into three camps, says Edison. Some just seem to be misguided and insensitive. Others get turned on by harassing someone. And a third group does it to intimidate—for example, to drive someone away from a job or just to make him or her feel bad about himself or herself.

So What Do I Do if Someone's Harassing Me?

Experts in self-defense say the best technique is to name the behavior that's bugging you and request that it stop. You might say, "Your hand is on my knee. Please remove it." If the person doesn't quit, you might try writing a letter spelling out what's bothering you and requesting that the person stop—this way, you've confronted the situation directly and you also have a record of your complaint.

But here's the good news, says Edison: You are not expected to handle harassment on your own, especially if the person harassing you is in a position of authority over you, such as a teacher, sergeant, or boss. The authorities at your school or your job should handle it—but they can't do that unless you tell them what's going on.

If you file a complaint, be prepared to describe what happened, when, and where. And make sure you report your concerns to someone who has clear authority to handle sexual harassment complaints, such as the principal or the personnel director.

Often, the person harassing you will stop as soon as he or she gets the clear message that the behavior isn't okay with you, especially if your complaint goes to someone higher up as well. Edison notes that most harassment cases don't end up involving lawyers and lawsuits. You may choose, in serious cases, to register your complaint with the Office of Civil Rights (if you're being harassed at school) or the Equal Employment Opportunity Commission (if you're being harassed at work). You can also file your complaint on different levels at the same time: for example, with your school and the police.

You have the legal right to a school and workplace free from discrimination based on your race, color, religion, sex, national origin, and—depending on where you live, as state and local laws vary—your sexual orientation. You have the right to protection from retaliation if you file a complaint of harassment. So don't be afraid to report a situation if it truly offends you and interferes with your life.

What if I'm Just Being Hypersensitive?

If someone's words or actions make you uncomfortable, that's all the reason you need to ask that person to stop the behavior, no matter how innocent the behavior may be. Trust your feelings—especially if you find you're trying to convince yourself that nothing is wrong.

What Will Happen to the Person Who Has Been Harassing Me?

If your complaint is successfully handled, says Edison, the main thing that will happen is that the person will stop harassing you. People aren't "charged" with sexual harassment unless their behavior includes criminal conduct. But your harasser may face disciplinary action, loss of privileges, suspension, expulsion, lawsuits, or criminal action, depending on the severity of his or her behavior.

How Can I Avoid Harassing Someone?

Sometimes the line between harmless flirting, joking, or complimenting and harassment is pretty thin. How can you stay on the right side of that line?

First, pay attention to your own motives. Be honest with yourself. Do you enjoy watching someone get uncomfortable when you say or do certain things? Do you feel angry with the person for some reason? Do you enjoy exercising your authority over this person in some way? Do you find yourself obsessing about the person? If any of these are true, whatever you're saying or doing probably isn't harmless.

Even if your motives seem harmless to you, be extraordinarily careful about whom and how you touch. You may be comfortable touching people casually—perhaps you'll touch someone's hand or shoulder in conversation—but remember that other people's boundaries may differ from yours.

Pay attention to the person's reactions to you. Are you getting clear green signals when you do or say things around this person, or does the person seem to shrink away from you? Does the person shut down or seem upset when you do or say certain things? If someone's told you clearly that she or he doesn't like it when you do or say certain things, apologize and stop at once. And remember, no means no.

So, if you're faced with something that feels like sexual harassment, remember to trust your feelings, convey them clearly, and get help promptly if you need it.

STAYING HEALTHY IN SPITE OF YOURSELF

When someone—like your mom—asks if you're eating right, do you ever want to say, "Hey, have you looked at my life lately? Do you see a lot of time there for eating right?" Well, how about exercise—are you getting enough? "Yeah, right. I bench-press my backpack when I'm not doing wind sprints to my next class," may be how you reply.

If you're feeling like you can't escape your stress and fatigue, you might be surprised by how much better you'll feel if you keep active and don't just eat junk. Your workload will seem easier. You'll sleep better. You'll look fantastic. And you can stay healthy—even if your time and money are in short supply.

But Really, Who Has Time to Exercise?

As one teen says, "Schoolwork gets in the way, and then I want to relax when I have a moment that isn't filled with schoolwork." You can make time for anything, if you choose to. But if you aren't athletic by nature or your school or work keeps you going nonstop, exercise is the first thing to go out the window.

However, you don't have to become a gym rat or run miles to get enough exercise. Longer workouts are great if you do them consistently, but you're better off getting little bits of regular exercise than just doing a huge workout every so often or never doing anything. And by "little bits," we mean 15- to 20-minute chunks. Add that to a fast walk to the bus, a frenzied private dance session in your room, or running up the stairs instead of taking the elevator, and you're exercising!

Regardless of how you choose to pump that muscle in the middle of your chest, the important thing is that you're doing something. You'll not only

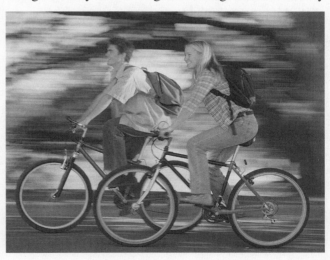

feel better about yourself, but you'll have increased energy to do other things, like study, go to work, or go out with friends.

What Does "Eating Right" Mean Anyway?

Eating right means eating a balance of good foods in moderate amounts. Your diet needn't be complicated or expensive. Dr. Michele Wilson, a specialist in adolescent medicine at the Children's Hospital of Philadelphia, notes that a teen's diet should be heavy in grains—especially whole grains—and light in sugars and fats. It should include a lot of fruits and vegetables and provide you with plenty of protein, calcium, vitamin A, B vitamins, iron, and zinc. Sound complicated?

Well, what's complicated about a bean burrito with cheese? How about pasta with vegetables, meat, or both in the sauce? A banana or some cantaloupe? Stir-fried vegetables with tofu? Carrot sticks with peanut butter? Yogurt? Cereal with milk and fruit? All of these are cheap, quick to make, and great for you.

One teen swears by microwaveable veggie burgers and adds, "Staying away from deep-fried anything is a good plan." Try to avoid things like chips and sweets, says Dr. Wilson, adding that if you're a vegetarian—and especially if you don't eat dairy products or fish—you should make sure you're getting enough protein and iron. And no matter what your diet, drink water—eight glasses a day.

As Long as I'm in Control of What I Eat, I'm Okay, Right?

That depends. Of course, having no control over what you eat is a problem. But "in control" can be good or bad. How severely do you control what and how you eat? Are you obsessed with getting thinner? Do people who love you tell you that you're too thin, and do you take that as a compliment? Do you ever binge secretly or make yourself throw up after a meal? If any of these are true, you may be suffering from anorexia or bulimia.

According to the National Association of Anorexia Nervosa and Associated Disorders (ANAD), eating disorders affect about 7 million women and 1 million men in this country and can lead to serious health problems—even death. "The thing that convinced me to get help was fear—I had to be hospitalized, as I was literally dying from my anorexia," says one woman. Most Americans who are anorexic or bulimic developed their eating disorders in their teens.

We asked some women being treated for eating disorders what they used to see when they looked in the mirror. "Total ugliness," said one. "The smallest dimple in my flesh looked immense," said another. And a third said, "I got rid of the mirrors because they would set me off to where I wouldn't eat for days." Their advice to teens struggling with an eating disorder? "Treat yourself as you wish your parents had treated you," "Ask people you feel close to not to discuss your weight with you," and "Find ways outside of yourself to feel in control." Above all—get help! That means going to someone you trust, whether it be a parent, relative, sibling, friend, doctor, or teacher. Or call ANAD's national hotline at 847-831-3438 for a listing of support groups and referrals in your area.

So if I Eat Right and Exercise, I'm Healthy?

Well, probably. But Dr. Wilson suggests that you keep a few other things in mind too. If you smoke, drink, or do drugs, you're asking for trouble. Aside from their many scarier side effects, all these habits can steal nutrients that you need. If all this sounds like the recipe for a dull and totally uncool life, remember that feeling and looking great are never boring and that vomiting (or dying) after downing the most tequilas in the fastest time looks really uncool. If you're making short-term decisions that will hurt you in the long run, take some time to figure out why. Good health is priceless—just ask any grandparent.

APPENDICES

Now that you have decided what types of opportunities you wish to pursue after graduation, you need a jumping-off point for getting more information. The **Appendices** that follow will provide you with a sampling of additional data to help you with your decision-making process.

NOTE: Because of Peterson's comprehensive editorial review and because all material comes directly from institution or organization officials, we believe that the information presented in these **Appendices** is accurate. Nonetheless, errors and omissions are possible in a data collection and processing endeavor of this scope. You should check with the specific institution or organization at the time of application to verify pertinent data that may have changed since the publication of this book.

HIGH SCHOOL DIPLOMA TEST REQUIREMENTS

Delaware

The Delaware Student Testing Program (DSTP) was implemented in spring 1998 in English language arts (reading and writing) and math. Science and social studies were added to the testing program in spring 2000. Students in the tenth grade are tested in English language arts (reading and writing) and math. Students in the eleventh grade are tested in science and social studies. Beginning with the class of 2004 (students who took the DSTP in spring 2002 as tenth graders), students will receive one of three types of diplomas based on their DSTP performance levels on the tenth grade test: Distinguished, Standard, or Basic. Students will have multiple opportunities to retake the test in order to improve their performance and upgrade the type of diploma. Local districts also will have the option of awarding a Certificate of Completion to students who do not meet all state and/or local requirements for a diploma but who have completed a program of study. Beginning with the class of 2006, science and social studies will also affect the type of diploma a student is eligible for. For more information, see the Delaware Department of Education Web site at www.doe.state.de.us or call 302-739-6700.

District of Columbia

The District of Columbia currently does not require high school students to pass a proficiency test in order to receive a high school diploma.

Maryland

Currently, Maryland requires students to pass functional tests in reading, writing, and mathematics as one condition for graduation from high school. The functional test requirements are expected to be phased out when high school assessments begin for the graduating class of 2007. Students will be tested in English, government, algebra, geometry, and biology. For more information, see the Maryland Department of Education Web site at www.msde.state.md.us or call 410-767-0100.

New Jersey

The High School Proficiency Assessment (HSPA) was implemented in March 2002 for the class of 2003. Students are tested in language arts literacy and math. In March 2005, science will be added. HSPA data are used to satisfy a part of the graduation requirements, determine a student's needs for remediation, and identify areas for improvement. A released version of the HSPA is available at each high school. Senior students who fail any section of the HSPA are required to demonstrate mastery through a special review assessment (SRA 11) they can take in English or a combination of English and a native language. Districts are required to provide remediation. For more information, see the New Jersey Department of Education Web site at www.state.nj.us/education or call 609-292-8736 or 609-292-8739.

New York

High school students must show successful completion on five Regents Examinations to graduate. Subjects tested are English language arts, global history and geography, U.S. history and government, math, science (living environment and/or physical setting), and a second language. In general, students in the tenth grade are tested in science, math, and global history and geography. Students in the eleventh grade are tested in English Language arts, U.S. history, and government. In addition, students must complete 20.5 credits, including physical education, to graduate. For more information, visit the New York Department of Education Web site at www.emsc.nysed.gov/part100/pages/1005a.html.

Pennsylvania

Pennsylvania currently does not require high school students to pass a proficiency test in order to receive a high school diploma.

Virginia

Standards of Learning (SOL) Tests are currently being phased in and will be fully implemented for the class of 2004. Students will be tested in English, math, science, history, and 1 test of their own chosing. For more information, see the Virginia Department of Education Web site at www.vipnet.org/vipnet/edu-ent/k-12.html or call 804-225-2102.

West Virginia

West Virginia currently does not require high school students to pass a proficiency test in order to receive a high school diploma.

FOUR-YEAR COLLEGES AND UNIVERSITIES

Delaware

Delaware State University
1200 North DuPont Hwy
Dover, DE 19901-2277
302-739-4924
www.dsc.edu

Goldey-Beacom College
4701 Limestone Rd.
Wilmington, DE 19808-1999
302-998-8814
www.goldey.gbc.edu

United States Open University
6 Denny Rd., Ste. 301
Wilmington, DE 19809
302-778-0300
www.open.edu

University of Delaware
Newark, DE 19716
302-831-2000
www.udel.edu

Wesley College
120 North State St.
Dover, DE 19901-3875
302-736-2300
www.wesley.edu

Wilmington College
320 DuPont Hwy
New Castle, DE 19720-6491
302-328-9401
www.wilmcoll.edu

District of Columbia

American University
4400 Massachusetts Ave., NW
Washington, DC 20016-8001
202-885-1000
www.american.edu

Corcoran College of Art and Design
500 17th St. NW
Washington, DC 20006-4804
202-639-1800
www.corcoran.edu

Gallaudet University
800 Florida Ave., NE
Washington, DC 20002-3625
202-651-5000
www.gallaudet.edu

Georgetown University
37th and O St., NW
Washington, DC 20057
202-687-5055
www.georgetown.edu

Howard University
2400 Sixth St., NW
Washington, DC 20059-0002
202-806-6100
www.howard.edu

Potomac College
4000 Chesapeake St., NW
Washington, DC 20016
202-686-0876
www.potomac.edu

Southeastern University
501 I St., SW
Washington, DC 20024-2788
202-488-8162
www.seu.edu

Strayer University
1025 15th St., NW
Washington, DC 20005-2603
202-408-2400
www.strayer.edu

The Catholic University of America
Cardinal Station
Washington, DC 20064
202-319-5000
www.cua.edu

The George Washington University
2121 Eye St., NW
Washington, DC 20052
202-994-1000
www.gwu.edu

Trinity College
125 Michigan Ave., NE
Washington, DC 20017-1094
202-884-9000
www.trinitydc.edu

University of the District of Columbia
4200 Connecticut Ave., NW
Washington, DC 20008-1175
202-274-5000
www.udc.edu

Maryland

Baltimore Hebrew University
5800 Park Heights Ave.
Baltimore, MD 21215-3996
410-578-6900
www.bhu.edu

Baltimore International College
Commerce Exchange,
17 Commerce St.
Baltimore, MD 21202-3230
410-752-4710
www.bic.edu

Bowie State University
14000 Jericho Park Rd.
Bowie, MD 20715-9465
301-860-4000
www.bowiestate.edu

Capitol College
11301 Springfield Rd.
Laurel, MD 20708-9759
301-369-2800
www.capitol-college.edu

College of Notre Dame of Maryland
4701 North Charles St.
Baltimore, MD 21210-2476
410-435-0100
www.ndm.edu

Columbia Union College
7600 Flower Ave.
Takoma Park, MD 20912-7796
301-891-4000
www.cuc.edu

Coppin State College
2500 West North Ave.
Baltimore, MD 21216-3698
410-383-5400
www.coppin.edu

Frostburg State University
101 Braddock Rd.
Frostburg, MD 21532-1099
301-687-4000
www.frostburg.edu

Goucher College
1021 Duln.y Valley Rd.
Baltimore, MD 21204-2794
410-337-6000
www.goucher.edu

Griggs University
PO Box 4437,
12501 Old Columbia Pk
Silver Spring,
MD 20914-4437
301-680-6570
www.griggs.edu

Hood College
401 Rosemont Ave.
Frederick, MD 21701-8575
301-663-3131
www.hood.edu

Johns Hopkins University
3400 North Charles St.
Baltimore, MD 21218-2699
410-516-8000
www.jhu.edu

Loyola College in Maryland
4501 North Charles St.
Baltimore, MD 21210-2699
410-617-2000
www.loyola.edu

Maple Springs Baptist Bible College and Seminary
4130 Belt Rd.
Capitol Heights, MD 20743
301-736-3631

Maryland Institute, College of Art
1300 Mount Royal Ave.
Baltimore, MD 21217-4191
410-669-9200
www.mica.edu

Morgan State University
1700 East Cold Spring Ln.
Baltimore, MD 21251
443-885-3333
www.morgan.edu

Mount Saint Mary's College and Seminary
16300 Old Emmitsburg Rd.
Emmitsburg, MD 21727-7799
301-447-6122
www.msmary.edu

Ner Israel Rabbinical College
Mount Wilson Ln.
Baltimore, MD 21208
410-484-7200

Peabody Conservatory of Music of The Johns Hopkins University
1 East Mount Vernon Pl.
Baltimore, MD 21202-2397
410-659-8150
www.peabody.jhu.edu

Salisbury University
1101 Camden Ave.
Salisbury, MD 21801-6837
410-543-6000
www.ssu.edu

Sojourner-Douglass College
500 North Caoline St.
Baltimore, MD 21205-1814
410-276-0306
www.sdc.edu

St. John's College
PO Box 2800
Annapolis, MD 21404
410-263-2371
www.sjca.edu

St. Mary's College of Maryland
18952 East Fisher Rd.
St. Mary's City,
MD 20686-3001
301-862-0200
www.smcm.edu

Towson University
8000 York Rd.
Towson, MD 21252-0001
410-704-2000
www.towson.edu

United States Naval Academy
121 Blake Rd.
Annapolis, MD 21402-5000
410-293-1000
www.usna.edu

University of Baltimore
1420 North Charles St.
Baltimore, MD 21201-5779
410-837-4200
www.ubalt.edu

University of Maryland
Eastern Shore
Princess Anne,
MD 21853-1299
410-651-2200
www.umes.edu

University of Maryland
University College
3501 University Blvd East
Adelphi, MD 20783
301-985-7000
www.umuc.edu

University of Maryland,
Baltimore County
1000 Hilltop Cr.
Baltimore, MD 21250-5398
410-455-1000
www.umbc.edu

University of Maryland,
College Park
College Park, MD 20742
301-405-1000
www.maryland.edu

University of Phoenix-
Maryland Campus
8830 Stanford Blvd, Ste. 100
Columbia, MD 21045
410-536-7144
www.phoenix.edu

Villa Julie College
Green Spring Valley Rd.
Stevenson, MD 21153
410-486-7000
www.vjc.edu

Washington Bible College
6511 Princess Garden Pkwy
Lanham, MD 20706-3599
301-552-1400
www.bible.edu

Washington College
300 Washington Ave.
Chestertown, MD 21620-1197
410-778-2800
www.washcoll.edu

Western Maryland College
2 College Hill
Westminster, MD 21157-4390
410-848-7000
www.wmdc.edu

New Jersey

Beth Medrash Govoha
617 Sixth St.
Lakewood, NJ 08701-2797
732-367-1060

Bloomfield College
467 Franklin St.
Bloomfield, NJ 07003-9981
973-748-9000
www.bloomfield.edu

Caldwell College
9 Ryerson Ave.
Caldwell, NJ 07006-6195
973-618-3000
www.caldwell.edu

Centenary College
400 Jefferson St.
Hackettstown, NJ 07840-2100
908-852-1400
www.centenarycollege.edu

College of Saint Elizabeth
2 Convent Rd.
Morristown, NJ 07960-6989
973-290-4000
www.st-elizabeth.edu

DeVry College of Technology
630 US Hwy 1
North Brunswick,
NJ 08902-3362
732-435-4880
www.nj.devry.edu

Drew University
36 Madison Ave.
Madison, NJ 07940-1493
973-408-3000
www.drew.edu

Fairleigh Dickinson
University, Florham-
Madison Campus
285 Madison Ave.
Madison, NJ 07940-1099
973-443-8500
www.fdu.edu

Fairleigh Dickinson
University, Teaneck-
Hackensack Campus
1000 River Rd.
Teaneck, NJ 07666-1914
201-692-2000
www.fdu.edu

Felician College
262 South Main St.
Lodi, NJ 07644-2198
201-559-6000
www.felician.edu

Georgian Court College
900 Lakewood Ave.
Lakewood, NJ 08701-2697
732-364-2200
www.georgian.edu

Kean University
1000 Morris Ave.
Union, NJ 07083
908-527-2000
www.kean.edu

Monmouth University
400 Cedar Ave.
West Long Branch,
NJ 07764-1898
732-571-3400
www.monmouth.edu

Montclair State University
1 Normal Ave.
Upper Montclair,
NJ 07043-1624
973-655-4000
www.montclair.edu

New Jersey City University
2039 Kennedy Blvd
Jersey City, NJ 07305-1597
201-200-2000
www.njcu.educore.htm

New Jersey Institute of
Technology
University Heights
Newark, NJ 07102-1982
973-596-3000
www.njit.edu

Princeton University
Princeton, NJ 08544-1019
609-258-3000
www.princeton.edu

Rabbinical College of
America
226 Sussex Ave.,
PO Box 1996
Morristown, NJ 07962-1996
973-267-9404

Ramapo College of New
Jersey
505 Ramapo Valley Rd.
Mahwah, NJ 07430-1680
201-684-7500
www.ramapo.edu

Rider University
2083 Lawrenceville Rd.
Lawrenceville,
NJ 08648-3001
609-896-5000
www.rider.edu

Rowan University
201 Mullica Hill Rd.
Glassboro, NJ 08028-1701
856-256-4500
www.rowan.edu

Rutgers, The State
University of New Jersey,
Camden
311 North Fifth St.
Camden, NJ 08102-1401
856-225-1766
www.rutgers.edu

Rutgers, The State
University of New Jersey,
New Brunswick
New Brunswick,
NJ 08901-1281
732-932-4636
www.rutgers.edu

Rutgers, The State
University of New Jersey,
Newark
Newark, NJ 07102
973-353-1766
www.info.rutgers.edu/newark

Saint Peter's College
2641 Kennedy Blvd
Jersey City, NJ 07306-5997
201-915-9000
www.spc.edu

Seton Hall University
400 South Orange Ave.
South Orange,
NJ 07079-2697
973-761-9000
www.shu.edu

Stevens Institute of Technology
Castle Point on Hudson
Hoboken, NJ 07030
201-216-5000
www.stevens-tech.edu

Talmudical Academy of
New Jersey
Rt. 524
Adelphia, NJ 07710
732-431-1600

The College of New Jersey
PO Box 7718
Ewing, NJ 08628
609-771-1855
www.tcnj.edu

The Richard Stockton
College of New Jersey
PO Box 195, Jimmie Leeds Rd.
Pomona, NJ 08240-0195
609-652-1776
www.stockton.edu

Thomas Edison State College
101 West State St.
Trenton, NJ 08608-1176
609-984-1100
www.tesc.edu

Westminster Choir College
of Rider University
101 Walnut Ln.
Princeton, NJ 08540-3899
609-921-7100
www.westminster.rider.edu

William Paterson University
of New Jersey
300 Pompton Rd.
Wayne, NJ 07470-8420
973-720-2000
www.wpunj.edu

New York

Adelphi University
South Ave.
Garden City, NY 11530
516-877-3000
www.adelphi.edu

Albany College of Pharmacy
of Union University
106 New Scotland Ave.
Albany, NY 12208-3425
518-445-7200
www.acp.edu

Alfred University
One Saxon Dr.
Alfred, NY 14802-1205
607-871-2111
www.alfred.edu

Audrey Cohen College
75 Varick St.
New York, NY 10013-1919
212-343-1234
www.audreycohen.edu

Bard College
Ravine Rd., PO Box 5000
Annandale-on-Hudson,
NY 12504
845-758-6822
www.bard.edu

Barnard College
3009 Brd.way
New York, NY 10027-6598
212-854-5262
www.barnard.edu

Bernard M. Baruch College
of the City University of
New York
17 Lexington Ave.
New York, NY 10010-5585
212-802-2000
www.baruch.cuny.edu

Beth HaMedrash Shaarei
Yosher Institute
4102-10 Sixteenth Ave.
Brooklyn, NY 11204
718-854-2290

Beth Hatalmud Rabbinical
College
2127 Eighty-second St.
Brooklyn, NY 11214
718-259-2525

Boricua College
3755 Brd.way
New York, NY 10032-1560
212-694-1000

Briarcliffe College
1055 Stewart Ave.
Bethpage, NY 11714
516-918-3600
www.briarcliffe.edu

Brooklyn College of the City
University of New York
2900 Bedford Ave.
Brooklyn, NY 11210-2889
718-951-5000
www.brooklyn.cuny.edu

Canisius College
2001 Main St.
Buffalo, NY 14208-1098
716-883-7000
www.canisius.edu

Cazenovia College
22 Sullivan St.
Cazenovia, NY 13035-1084
315-655-7000
www.cazcollege.edu

Central Yeshiva Tomchei
Tmimim-Lubavitch
841-853 Ocean Pkwy
Brooklyn, NY 11230
718-434-0784

City College of the City
University of New York
160 Convent Ave.
New York, NY 10031-9198
212-650-7000
www.ccny.cuny.edu

Clarkson University
Potsdam, NY 13699
315-268-6400
www.clarkson.edu

Colgate University
13 Oak Dr.
Hamilton, NY 13346-1386
315-228-1000
www.colgate.edu

College of Aeronautics
8601 23rd Ave.
Flushing, NY 11369-1037
718-429-6600
www.aero.edu

College of Mount Saint Vincent
6301 Riverdale Ave.
Riverdale, NY 10471-1093
718-405-3200
www.cmsv.edu

College of Staten Island of the
City University of New York
2800 Victory Blvd
Staten Island, NY 10314-6600
718-982-2000
www.csi.cuny.edu

Columbia College
116th St. and Brd.way
New York, NY 10027
212-854-1754
www.columbia.edu

Columbia University, School
of General Studies
2970 Brd.way
New York, NY 10027-6939
212-854-2772

Columbia University, The Fu
Foundation School of
Engineering and Applied
Science
500 West 120th St.
New York, NY 10027
212-854-1754
www.columbia.edu

Concordia College
171 White Plains Rd.
Bronxville, NY 10708-1998
914-337-9300
www.concordia-ny.edu

Cooper Union for the
Advancement of Science
and Art
30 Cooper Square
New York, NY 10003-7120
212-353-4100
www.cooper.edu

Cornell University
Ithaca, NY 14853-0001
607-255-2000
www.cornell.edu

D'Youville College
320 Porter Ave.
Buffalo, NY 14201-1084
716-881-3200
www.dyc.edu

Daemen College
4380 Main St.
Amherst, NY 14226-3592
716-839-3600
www.daemen.edu

Darkei Noam Rabbinical
College
2822 Ave. J
Brooklyn, NY 11210
718-338-6464

DeVry Institute of Technology
30-20 Thomson Ave.
Long Island City, NY 11101
718-361-0004
www.ny.devry.edu

Dominican College
470 Western Hwy
Orangeburg, NY 10962-1210
845-359-7800
www.dc.edu

Dowling College
Idle Hour Blvd
Oakdale, NY 11769-1999
631-244-3000
www.dowling.edu

Elmira College
One Park Pl.
Elmira, NY 14901
607-735-1800
www.elmira.edu

Eugene Lang College, New
School University
65 West 11th St.
New York, NY 10011-8601
212-229-5600
www.newschool.edu

Excelsior College
7 Columbia Cr.
Albany, NY 12203-5159
518-464-8500
www.excelsior.edu

Fashion Institute of
Technology
Seventh Ave. at 27th St.
New York, NY 10001-5992
212-217-7999
www.fitnyc.suny.edu

Five Towns College
305 North Service Rd.
Dix Hills, NY 11746-6055
631-424-7000
www.fivetowns.edu

Fordham University
441 East Fordham Rd.
New York, NY 10458
718-817-1000
www.fordham.edu

Globe Institute of
Technology
291 Brd.way, Second Floor
New York, NY 10007
212-349-4330
www.globe.edu

Hamilton College
198 College Hill Rd.
Clinton, NY 13323-1296
315-859-4011
www.hamilton.edu

Hartwick College
West St., PO Box 4020
Oneonta, NY 13820-4020
607-431-4200
www.hartwick.edu

Hilbert College
5200 South Park Ave.
Hamburg, NY 14075-1597
716-649-7900
www.hilbert.edu

Hobart and William Smith
Colleges
Geneva, NY 14456-3397
315-781-3000
www.hws.edu

Hofstra University
100 Hofstra University
Hempstead, NY 11549
516-463-6600
www.hofstra.edu

Holy Trinity Orthodox
Seminary
PO Box 36
Jordanville, NY 13361
315-858-0945
www.hts.edu

Houghton College
One Willard Ave.
Houghton, NY 14744
716-567-9200
www.houghton.edu

Hunter College of the City
University of New York
695 Park Ave.
New York, NY 10021-5085
212-772-4000
www.hunter.cuny.edu

Iona College
715 North Ave.
New Rochelle, NY 10801-
1890
914-633-2000
www.iona.edu

Ithaca College
100 Job Hall
Ithaca, NY 14850-7020
607-274-3011
www.ithaca.edu

Jewish Theological
Seminary of America
3080 Brd.way
New York, NY 10027-4649
212-678-8000
www.jtsa.edu

John Jay College of
Criminal Justice of the City
University of New
899 Tenth Ave.
New York, NY 10019-1093
212-237-8000
www.jjay.cuny.edu

Kehilath Yakov Rabbinical
Seminary
206 Wilson St.
Brooklyn, NY 11211-7207
718-963-1212

Keuka College
Keuka Park, NY 14478-0098
315-279-5000
www.keuka.edu

Kol Yaakov Torah Center
29 West Maple Ave.
Monsey, NY 10952-2954
914-425-3863
www.horizons.edu

Laboratory Institute of
Merchandising
12 East 53rd St.
New York, NY 10022-5268
212-752-1530
www.limcollege.edu

Le Moyne College
1419 Salt Springs Rd.
Syracuse, NY 13214-1399
315-445-4100
www.lemoyne.edu

Lehman College of the City
University of New York
250 Bedford Park Blvd West
Bronx, NY 10468-1589
718-960-8000
www.lehman.cuny.edu

Long Island University,
Brentwood Campus
100 Second Ave.
Brentwood, NY 11717
631-273-5112
www.liunet.edu/cwis/brent/
brent.htm

Long Island University,
Brooklyn Campus
One University Plaza
Brooklyn, NY 11201-8423
718-488-1000
www.liu.edu

Long Island University, C.W.
Post Campus
720 Northern Blvd
Brookville, NY 11548-1300
516-299-2000
www.cwpost.liunet.edu/cwis
/cwp/post.html

Long Island University,
Southampton College
239 Montauk Hwy
Southampton, NY 11968-
4198
631-283-4000
www.southampton.liu.edu

Long Island University,
Southampton College,
Friends World
239 Montauk Hwy
Southampton, NY 11968
631-287-8464
www.southampton.liu.edu/fw/

Machzikei Hadath Rabbinical
College
5407 Sixteenth Ave.
Brooklyn, NY 11204-1805
718-854-8777

Manhattan College
Manhattan College Pkwy
Riverdale, NY 10471
718-862-8000
www.manhattan.edu

Manhattan School of Music
120 Claremont Ave.
New York, NY 10027-4698
212-749-2802
www.msmnyc.edu

Manhattanville College
2900 Purchase St.
Purchase, NY 10577-2132
914-694-2200
www.mville.edu

Mannes College of Music,
New School University
150 West 85th St.
New York, NY 10024-4402
212-580-0210
www.mannes.edu

Marist College
3399 North Rd.
Poughkeepsie, NY 12601-1387
845-575-3000
www.marist.edu

Marymount College
100 Marymount Ave.
Tarrytown, NY 10591-3796
914-631-3200
www.marymt.edu

Marymount Manhattan
College
221 East 71st St.
New York, NY 10021-4597
212-517-0400
www.marymount.mmm.edu

Medaille College
18 Agassiz Cr.
Buffalo, NY 14214-2695
716-884-3281
www.medaille.edu

Medgar Evers College of the
City University of New York
1650 Bedford Ave.
Brooklyn, NY 11225-2298
718-270-4900
www.mec.cuny.edu

Mercy College
555 Brd.way
Dobbs Ferry, NY 10522-1189
914-693-4500
www.mercynet.edu

Mesivta of Eastern Pkwy
Rabbinical Seminary
510 Dahill Rd.
Brooklyn, NY 11218-5559
718-438-1002

Mesivta Tifereth Jerusalem
of America
145 East Brd.way
New York, NY 10002-6301
212-964-2830

Mesivta Torah Vodaath
Rabbinical Seminary
425 East Ninth St.
Brooklyn, NY 11218-5299
718-941-8000

Mirrer Yeshiva
1795 Ocean Pkwy
Brooklyn, NY 11223-2010
718-645-0536

Molloy College
1000 Hempstead Ave.
Rockville Centre,
NY 11571-5002
516-678-5000

Mount Saint Mary College
330 Powell Ave.
Newburgh, NY 12550-3494
845-561-0800
www.msmc.edu

Nazareth College of
Rochester
4245 East Ave.
Rochester, NY 14618-3790
716-389-2525
www.naz.edu

New School Bachelor of
Arts, New School University
66 West 12th St.
New York, NY 10011-8603
212-229-5600
www.newschool.edu

New York Institute of
Technology
PO Box 8000
Old Westbury, NY 11568-8000
516-686-7516
www.nyit.edu

New York School of Interior
Design
170 East 70th St.
New York, NY 10021-5110
212-472-1500
www.nysid.edu

New York University
70 Washington Square South
New York, NY 10012-1019
212-998-1212
www.nyu.edu

Niagara University
Niagara University, NY 14109
716-285-1212
www.niagara.edu

Nyack College
One South Blvd
Nyack, NY 10960-3698
845-358-1710
www.nyackcollege.edu

Ohr Hameir Theological
Seminary
Furnace Woods Rd.
Peekskill, NY 10566
914-736-1500

Ohr Somayach/Joseph
Tanenbaum Educational
Center
PO Box 334, 244 Rt. 306
Monsey, NY 10952-0334
914-425-1370

Pace University
One Pace Plaza
New York, NY 10038
212-346-1200
www.pace.edu

Parsons School of Design,
New School University
66 Fifth Ave.
New York, NY 10011-8878
212-229-8900
www.parsons.edu

Paul Smith's College of Arts
and Sciences
PO Box 265
Paul Smiths, NY 12970-0265
518-327-6000
www.paulsmiths.edu

Plattsburgh State University
of New York
101 Brd. Steet
Plattsburgh, NY 12901-2681
518-564-2000
www.plattsburgh.edu

Polytechnic University,
Brooklyn Campus
Six Metrotech Center
Brooklyn, NY 11201-2990
718-260-3600
www.poly.edu

Practical Bible College
PO Box 601
Bible School Park,
NY 13737-0601
607-729-1581
www.practical.edu

Pratt Institute
200 Willoughby Ave.
Brooklyn, NY 11205-3899
718-636-3600
www.pratt.edu

Purchase College, State
University of New York
735 Anderson Hill Rd.
Purchase, NY 10577-1400
914-251-6000
www.purchase.edu

Queens College of the City
University of New York
65-30 Kissena Blvd
Flushing, NY 11367-1597
718-997-5000
www.qc.edu

Rabbinical Academy Mesivta
Rabbi Chaim Berlin
1605 Coney Island Ave.
Brooklyn, NY 11230-4715
718-377-0777

Rabbinical College Beth
Shraga
28 Saddle River Rd.
Monsey, NY 10952-3035
914-356-1980

Rabbinical College Bobover
Yeshiva B'nei Zion
1577 Forty-eighth St.
Brooklyn, NY 11219
718-438-2018

Rabbinical College Ch'san
Sofer
1876 Fiftieth St.
Brooklyn, NY 11204
718-236-1171

Rabbinical College of Long
Island
201 Magnolia Blvd
Long Beach, NY 11561-3305
516-431-7414

Rabbinical Seminary Adas
Yereim
185 Wilson St.
Brooklyn, NY 11211-7206
718-388-1751

Rabbinical Seminary M'kor
Chaim
1571 Fifty-fifth St.
Brooklyn, NY 11219
718-851-0183

Rabbinical Seminary of
America
92-15 Sixty-ninth Ave.
Forest Hills, NY 11375
718-268-4700

Rensselaer Polytechnic
Institute
110 8th St.
Troy, NY 12180-3590
518-276-6000
www.rpi.edu

Roberts Wesleyan College
2301 Westside Dr.
Rochester, NY 14624-1997
716-594-6000
www.roberts.edu

Rochester Institute of
Technology
One Lomb Memorial Dr.
Rochester, NY 14623-5698
716-475-2411
www.rit.edu

Russell Sage College
45 Ferry St.
Troy, NY 12180-4115
518-244-2000
www.sage.edu/html/rsc/
welcome.html

Sarah Lawrence College
1 Mead Way
Bronxville, NY 10708
914-337-0700
www.slc.edu

School of Visual Arts
209 East 23rd St.
New York, NY 10010-3994
212-592-2000
www.schoolofvisualarts.edu

Sh'or Yoshuv Rabbinical
College
1526 Central Ave.
Far Rockaway, NY 11691-4002
718-327-2048

Siena College
515 Loudon Rd.
Loudonville, NY 12211-1462
518-783-2300
www.siena.edu

Skidmore College
815 North Brd.way
Saratoga Springs,
NY 12866-1632
518-580-5000
www.skidmore.edu

St. Bonaventure University
Rt. 417
St. Bonaventure,
NY 14778-2284
716-375-2000
www.sbu.edu

St. Francis College
180 Remsen St.
Brooklyn Heights,
NY 11201-4398
718-522-2300
www.stfranciscollege.edu

St. John Fisher College
3690 East Ave.
Rochester, NY 14618-3597
716-385-8000
www.sjfc.edu

St. John's University
8000 Utopia Pkwy
Jamaica, NY 11439
718-990-6161
www.stjohns.edu

St. Joseph's College,
New York
245 Clinton Ave.
Brooklyn, NY 11205-3688
718-636-6800
www.sjcnj.edu

St. Joseph's College, Suffolk
Campus
155 West Roe Blvd
Patchogue, NY 11772-2399
631-447-3200
www.sjcny.edu

St. Lawrence University
Canton, NY 13617-1455
315-229-5011
www.stlawu.edu

St. Thomas Aquinas College
125 Rt. 340
Sparkill, NY 10976
845-398-4000
www.stac.edu

State University of New York
at Albany
1400 Washington Ave.
Albany, NY 12222-0001
518-442-3300
www.albany.edu

State University of New York
at Binghamton
PO Box 6000
Binghamton, NY 13902-6000
607-777-2000
www.binghamton.edu

State University of New York
at Farmingdale
Rt. 110
Farmingdale, NY 11735
631-420-2000
www.farmingdale.edu

State University of New York
at New Paltz
75 South Manheim Blvd
New Paltz, NY 12561
845-257-2121
www.newpaltz.edu

State University of New York
at Oswego
Oswego, NY 13126
315-312-2500
www.oswego.edu

State University of New York
College at Brockport
350 New Campus Dr.
Brockport, NY 14420-2997
716-395-2211
www.brockport.edu

State University of New York
College at Buffalo
1300 Elmwood Ave.
Buffalo, NY 14222-1095
716-878-4000
www.buffalostate.edu

State University of New York
College at Cortland
PO Box 2000
Cortland, NY 13045
607-753-2011
www.cortland.edu

State University of New York
College at Fredonia
Fredonia, NY 14063-1136
716-673-3111
www.fredonia.edu

State University of New York
College at Geneseo
1 College Cr.
Geneseo, NY 14454-1401
716-245-5211
www.geneseo.edu

State University of New York
College at Old Westbury
PO Box 210
Old Westbury, NY 11568-0210
516-876-3000
www.oldwestbury.edu

State University of New York
College at Oneonta
Ravine Pkwy
Oneonta, NY 13820-4015
607-436-3500
www.oneonta.edu

State University of New York
College at Potsdam
44 Pierrepont Ave.
Potsdam, NY 13676
315-267-2000
www.potsdam.edu

State University of New York
College of Agriculture and
Technology
at Cobleskill
Cobleskill, NY 12043
518-255-5011
www.cobleskill.edu

State University of New York
College of Environmental
Science and Forestry
1 Forestry Dr.
Syracuse, NY 13210-2779
315-470-6500
www.esf.edu

State University of New York
College of Technology at
Canton
Cornell Dr.
Canton, NY 13617
315-386-7011
www.canton.edu

State University of New York
Empire State College
1 Union Ave.
Saratoga Springs,
NY 12866-4391
518-587-2100
www.esc.edu

State University of New York
Health Science Center at
Brooklyn
450 Clarkson Ave.
Brooklyn, NY 11203-2098
718-270-1000
www.downstate.edu

State University of New York
Institute of Technology at
Utica/Rome
PO Box 3050
Utica, NY 13504-3050
315-792-7100
www.sunyit.edu

State University of New York
Maritime College
6 Pennyfield Ave.
Throggs Neck,
NY 10465-4198
718-409-7200
www.sunymaritime.edu

State University of New York
Upstate Medical University
750 East Adams St.
Syracuse, NY 13210-2334
315-464-5540
www.upstate.edu

Stony Brook University,
State University of New York
Nicolls Rd.
Stony Brook, NY 11794
631-689-6000
www.sunysb.edu

Syracuse University
Syracuse, NY 13244-0003
315-443-1870
www.syracuse.edu

Talmudical Institute of
Upstate New York
769 Park Ave.
Rochester, NY 14607-3046
716-473-2810

Talmudical Seminary Oholei
Torah
667 Eastern Pkwy
Brooklyn, NY 11213-3310
718-774-5050

The College of Insurance
101 Murray St.
New York, NY 10007-2165
212-962-4111
www.tci.edu

The College of New Rochelle
29 Castle Pl.
New Rochelle,
NY 10805-2308
914-632-5300
www.cnr.edu

The College of Saint Rose
432 Western Ave.
Albany, NY 12203-1419
518-454-5111
www.strose.edu

The Culinary Institute of
America
1946 Campus Dr.
Hyde Park, NY 12538-1499
845-452-9600
www.ciachef.edu

The Juilliard School
60 Lincoln Center Plaza
New York, NY 10023-6588
212-799-5000
www.juilliard.edu

Torah Temimah Talmudical
Seminary
507 Ocean Pkwy
Brooklyn, NY 11218-5913
718-853-8500

Touro College
27-33 West 23rd St.
New York, NY 10010
212-463-0400
www.touro.edu

Union College
Schenectady, NY 12308-2311
518-388-6000
www.union.edu

United States Merchant
Marine Academy
300 Steamboat Rd.
Kings Point, NY 11024-1699
516-773-5000
www.usmma.edu

United States Military
Academy
600 Thayer Rd.
West Point, NY 10996
845-938-4011
www.usma.edu

United Talmudical Seminary
82 Lee Ave.
Brooklyn, NY 11211-7900
718-963-9260

University at Buffalo, The
State University of New York
Capen Hall
Buffalo, NY 14260
716-645-2000
www.buffalo.edu

University of Rochester
Wilson Blvd
Rochester, NY 14627-0250
716-275-2121
www.rochester.edu

Utica College of Syracuse
University
1600 Burrstone Rd.
Utica, NY 13502-4892
315-792-3111
www.utica.edu

Vassar College
124 Raymond Ave.
Poughkeepsie, NY 12604
845-437-7000
www.vassar.edu

Wadhams Hall Seminary-
College
6866 State Hwy 37
Ogdensburg, NY 13669
315-393-4231
www.wadhams.edu

Wagner College
1 Campus Rd.
Staten Island, NY 10301-4495
718-390-3100
www.wagner.edu

Webb Institute
Crescent Beach Rd.
Glen Cove, NY 11542-1398
516-671-2213
www.webb-institute.edu

Wells College
Aurora, NY 13026
315-364-3266
www.wells.edu

Yeshiva Derech Chaim
1573 39th St.
Brooklyn, NY 11218
718-438-3070

Yeshiva Karlin Stolin
Rabbinical Institute
1818 Fifty-fourth St.
Brooklyn, NY 11204
718-232-7800

Yeshiva of Nitra Rabbinical
College
Pines Bridge Rd.
Mount Kisco, NY 10549
718-384-5460

Yeshiva Shaar Hatorah
Talmudic Research Institute
117-06 84th Ave.
Kew Gardens, NY 11418-1469
718-846-1940

Yeshiva University
500 West 185th St.
New York, NY 10033-3201
212-960-5400
www.yu.edu

Yeshivat Mikdash Melech
1326 Ocean Pkwy
Brooklyn, NY 11230-5601
718-339-1090

Yeshivath Viznitz
Phyllis Terrace, PO Box 446
Monsey, NY 10952
914-356-1010

Yeshivath Zichron Moshe
Laurel Park Rd.
South Fallsburg, NY 12779
914-434-5240

York College of the City
University of New York
94-20 Guy R Brewer Blvd
Jamaica, NY 11451-0001
718-262-2000
www.york.cuny.edu

Pennsylvania

Albright College
13th and Bern Sreets,
PO Box 15234
Reading, PA 19612-5234
610-921-2381
www.albright.edu

Allegheny College
520 North Main St.
Meadville, PA 16335
814-332-3100
www.allegheny.edu

Alvernia College
400 Saint Bernardine St.
Reading, PA 19607-1799
610-796-8200
www.alvernia.edu

Arcadia University
450 South Easton Rd.
Glenside, PA 19038-3295
215-572-2900
www.arcadia.edu

Baptist Bible College of
Pennsylvania
538 Venard Rd.
Clarks Summit,
PA 18411-1297
570-586-2400
www.bbc.edu

Bloomsburg University of
Pennsylvania
400 East Second St.
Bloomsburg, PA 17815-1905
570-389-4000
www.bloomu.edu

Bryn Athyn College of the
New Church
PO Box 717
Bryn Athyn, PA 19009-0717
215-938-2543
www.newchurch.edu/
college/

Bryn Mawr College
101 North Merion Ave.
Bryn Mawr, PA 19010-2899
610-526-5000
www.brynmawr.edu

Bucknell University
Lewisburg, PA 17837
570-577-2000
www.bucknell.edu

Cabrini College
610 King of Prussia Rd.
Radnor, PA 19087-3698
610-902-8100
www.cabrini.edu

California University of
Pennsylvania
250 University Ave.
California, PA 15419-1394
724-938-4000
www.cup.edu

Carlow College
3333 Fifth Ave.
Pittsburgh, PA 15213-3165
412-578-6005
www.carlow.edu

Carnegie Mellon University
5000 Forbes Ave.
Pittsburgh, PA 15213-3891
412-268-2000
www.cmu.edu

Cedar Crest College
100 College Dr.
Allentown, PA 18104-6196
610-437-4471
www.cedarcrest.edu

Chatham College
Woodland Rd.
Pittsburgh, PA 15232-2826
412-365-1100
www.chatham.edu

Chestnut Hill College
9601 Germantown Ave.
Philadelphia, PA 19118-2693
215-248-7000
www.chc.edu

Cheyney University of
Pennsylvania
Cheyney and Creek Rd.s
Cheyney, PA 19319
610-399-2000
www.cheyney.edu

Clarion University of
Pennsylvania
Clarion, PA 16214
814-393-2000
www.clarion.edu

College Misericordia
301 Lake St.
Dallas, PA 18612-1098
570-674-6400
www.miseri.edu

Delaware Valley College
700 East Butler Ave.
Doylestown, PA 18901-2697
215-345-1500
www.devalcol.edu

DeSales University
2755 Station Ave.
Center Valley, PA 18034-9568
610-282-1100
www.desales.edu

Dickinson College
PO Box 1773
Carlisle, PA 17013-2896
717-243-5121
www.dickinson.edu

Drexel University
3141 Chestnut St.
Philadelphia, PA 19104-2875
215-895-2000
www.drexel.edu

Duquesne University
600 Forbes Ave.
Pittsburgh, PA 15282-0001
412-396-6000
www.duq.edu

East Stroudsburg University
of Pennsylvania
200 Prospect St.
East Stroudsburg,
PA 18301-2999
570-422-3211
www.esu.edu

Eastern College
1300 Eagle Rd.
St. Davids, PA 19087-3696
610-341-5800
www.eastern.edu

Edinboro University of
Pennsylvania
Edinboro, PA 16444
814-732-2000
www.edinboro.edu

Elizabethtown College
1 Alpha Dr.
Elizabethtown,
PA 17022-2298
717-361-1000
www.etown.edu

Franklin and Marshall
College
PO Box 3003
Lancaster, PA 17604-3003
717-291-3911
www.fandm.edu

Gannon University
University Square
Erie, PA 16541-0001
814-871-7000
www.gannon.edu

Geneva College
3200 College Ave.
Beaver Falls, PA 15010-3599
724-846-5100
www.geneva.edu

Gettysburg College
300 North Washington St.
Gettysburg, PA 17325-1483
717-337-6000
www.gettysburg.edu

Gratz College
7605 Old York Rd.
Melrose Park, PA 19027
215-635-7300
www.gratzcollege.edu

Grove City College
100 Campus Dr.
Grove City, PA 16127-2104
724-458-2000
www.gcc.edu

Gwynedd-Mercy College
Sumneytown Pike
Gwynedd Valley,
PA 19437-0901
215-646-7300
www.gmc.edu

Haverford College
370 Lancaster Ave.
Haverford, PA 19041-1392
610-896-1000
www.haverford.edu

Holy Family College
Grant and Frankford Ave.s
Philadelphia, PA 19114-2094
215-637-7700
www.hfc.edu

Immaculata College
1145 King Rd., Box 500
Immaculata, PA 19345-0500
610-647-4400
www.immaculata.edu

Indiana University of
Pennsylvania
Indiana, PA 15705-1087
724-357-2100
www.iup.edu

Juniata College
1700 Moore St.
Huntingdon, PA 16652-2119
814-641-3000
www.juniata.edu

King's College
133 North River St.
Wilkes-Barre, PA 18711-0801
570-208-5900
www.kings.edu

Kutztown University of
Pennsylvania
PO Box 730
Kutztown, PA 19530-0730
610-683-4000
www.kutztown.edu

La Roche College
9000 Babcock Blvd
Pittsburgh, PA 15237-5898
412-367-9300
www.laroche.edu

La Salle University
1900 West Olney Ave.
Philadelphia, PA 19141-1199
215-951-1000
www.lasalle.edu

Lafayette College
Easton, PA 18042-1798
610-330-5000
www.lafayette.edu

Lancaster Bible College
901 Eden Rd.,
PO Box 83403
Lancaster, PA 17608-3403
717-569-7071
www.lbc.edu

Lebanon Valley College
101 North College Ave.
Annville, PA 17003-1400
717-867-6100
www.lvc.edu

Lehigh University
27 Memorial Dr. West
Bethlehem, PA 18015-3094
610-758-3000
www.lehigh.edu

Lincoln University
PO Box 179
Lincoln University, PA 19352
610-932-8300
www.lincoln.edu

Lock Haven University of
Pennsylvania
North Fairview St.
Lock Haven, PA 17745-2390
570-893-2011
www.lhup.edu

Lycoming College
700 College Pl.
Williamsport, PA 17701-5192
570-321-4000
www.lycoming.edu

Mansfield University of
Pennsylvania
Academy St.
Mansfield, PA 16933
570-662-4000
www.mansfield.edu

Marywood University
2300 Adams Ave.
Scranton, PA 18509-1598
570-348-6211
www.marywood.edu

MCP Hahnemann University
245 North 15th St.
Philadelphia, PA 19102-1192
215-762-7000
www.mcphu.edu

Mercyhurst College
501 East 38th St.
Erie, PA 16546
814-824-2000
www.mercyhurst.edu

Messiah College
One College Ave.
Grantham, PA 17027
717-766-2511
www.messiah.edu

Millersville University of
Pennsylvania
PO Box 1002
Millersville, PA 17551-0302
717-872-3011
www.millersville.edu

Moore College of Art and
Design
20th and the Pkwy
Philadelphia, PA 19103
215-568-4515
www.moore.edu

Moravian College
1200 Main St.
Bethlehem, PA 18018-6650
610-861-1300
www.moravian.edu

Mount Aloysius College
7373 Admiral Peary Hwy
Cresson, PA 16630-1999
814-886-4131
www.mtaloy.edu

Muhlenberg College
2400 Chew St.
Allentown, PA 18104-5586
484-664-3100
www.muhlenberg.edu

Neumann College
One Neumann Dr.
Aston, PA 19014-1298
610-459-0905
www.neumann.edu

Peirce College
1420 Pine St.
Philadelphia, PA 19102-4699
215-545-6400
www.peirce.edu

Pennsylvania College of
Technology
One College Ave.
Williamsport, PA 17701-5778
570-326-3761
www.pct.edu

Pennsylvania School of Art
& Design
204 North Prince St.,
PO Box 59
Lancaster, PA 17608-0059
717-396-7833
www.psad.edu

Philadelphia Biblical
University
200 Manor Ave.
Langhorne, PA 19047-2990
215-752-5800
www.pbu.edu

Philadelphia University
School House Ln. and
Henry Ave.
Philadelphia, PA 19144-5497
215-951-2700
www.philau.edu

Point Park College
201 Wood St.
Pittsburgh, PA 15222-1984
412-391-4100
www.ppc.edu

Robert Morris University
881 Narrows Run Rd.
Moon Township,
PA 15108-1189
412-262-8200
www.rmu.edu

Rosemont College
1400 Montgomery Ave.
Rosemont, PA 19010-1699
610-527-0200
www.rosemont.edu

Saint Francis University
PO Box 600, 117 Evergreen Dr.
Loretto, PA 15940-0600
814-472-3000
www.sfcpa.edu

Saint Joseph's University
5600 City Ave.
Philadelphia, PA 19131-1395
610-660-1000
www.sju.edu

Saint Vincent College
300 Fraser Purchase Rd.
Latrobe, PA 15650-2690
724-539-9761
www.stvincent.edu

Seton Hill College
Seton Hill Dr.
Greensburg, PA 15601
724-834-2200
www.setonhill.edu

Shippensburg University of
Pennsylvania
1871 Old Main Dr.
Shippensburg, PA 17257-2299
717-477-7447
www.ship.edu

Slippery Rock University of
Pennsylvania
Slippery Rock, PA 16057
724-738-9000
www.sru.edu

St. Charles Borromeo
Seminary, Overbrook
100 East Wynnewood Rd.
Wynnewood, PA 19096
610-667-3394

Susquehanna University
514 University Ave.
Selinsgrove, PA 17870
570-374-0101
www.susqu.edu

Swarthmore College
500 College Ave.
Swarthmore, PA 19081-1397
610-328-8000
www.swarthmore.edu

Talmudical Yeshiva of
Philadelphia
6063 Drexel Rd.
Philadelphia, PA 19131-1296
215-473-1212

Temple University
1801 North Brd. St.
Philadelphia, PA 19122-6096
215-204-7000
www.temple.edu

The Curtis Institute of Music
1726 Locust St.
Philadelphia, PA 19103-6107
215-893-5252

The Pennsylvania State
University Abington College
1600 Woodland Rd.
Abington, PA 19001-3918
215-881-7300
www.psu.edu

The Pennsylvania State
University Altoona College
3000 Ivyside Park
Altoona, PA 16601-3760
814-949-5000
www.psu.edu

The Pennsylvania State
University at Erie, The
Behrend College
Station Rd.
Erie, PA 16563
814-898-6000
www.psu.edu

The Pennsylvania State
University Berks Campus of the
Berks-Lehigh Valley College
Tulpehocken Rd., PO Box 7009
Reading, PA 19610-6009
610-396-6000
www.psu.edu

The Pennsylvania State
University Harrisburg Campus
of the Capital College
777 West Harrisburg Pike
Middletown, PA 17057-4898
717-948-6000
www.psu.edu

The Pennsylvania State
University Lehigh Valley
Campus of the Berks-Lehigh
Valley College
8380 Mohr Ln.
Fogelsville, PA 18051-9999
610-285-5000
www.psu.edu

The Pennsylvania State
University Schuylkill Campus of
the Capital College
200 University Dr.
Schuylkill Haven, PA 17972-2208
570-385-6000
www.psu.edu

The Pennsylvania State
University University Park
Campus
201 Old Main
University Park, PA 16802-1503
814-865-4700
www.psu.edu

The University of Scranton
Scranton, PA 18510
570-941-7400
www.scranton.edu

The University of the Arts
320 South Brd. St.
Philadelphia, PA 19102-4944
215-717-6000
www.uarts.edu

Thiel College
75 College Ave.
Greenville, PA 16125-2181
724-589-2000
www.thiel.edu

Thomas Jefferson University
Eleventh and Walnut St.s
Philadelphia, PA 19107
215-955-6000
www.tju.edu

University of Pennsylvania
34th and Walnut St.s
Philadelphia, PA 19104
215-898-5000
www.upenn.edu

University of Phoenix-
Philadelphia Campus
170 South Warner Rd., Ste. 200
Wayne, PA 19087
610-989-0880
www.phoenix.edu

University of Phoenix-
Pittsburgh Campus
Penn Center West Four, Ste. 100,
Mail Stop: 10-1651
Pittsburgh, PA 15276
412-747-9000
www.phoenix.edu

University of Pittsburgh
4200 Fifth Ave.
Pittsburgh, PA 15260
412-624-4141
www.pitt.edu

University of Pittsburgh at
Bradford
300 Campus Dr.
Bradford, PA 16701-2812
814-362-7500
www.upb.pitt.edu

University of Pittsburgh at
Greensburg
1150 Mount Pleasant Rd.
Greensburg, PA 15601-5860
724-837-7040
www.pitt.edu~upg/

University of Pittsburgh at
Johnstown
450 Schoolhouse Rd.
Johnstown, PA 15904-2990
814-269-7000
www.info.pitt.edu~upjweb/

University of the Sciences in
Philadelphia
600 South 43rd St.
Philadelphia, PA 19104-4495
215-596-8800
www.usip.edu

Ursinus College
Box 1000, Main St.
Collegeville, PA 19426-1000
610-409-3000
www.ursinus.edu

Valley Forge Christian College
1401 Charlestown Rd.
Phoenixville, PA 19460-2399
610-935-0450
www.vfcc.edu

Villanova University
800 Lancaster Ave.
Villanova, PA 19085-1699
610-519-4500
www.villanova.edu

Washington & Jefferson
College
60 South Lincoln St.
Washington, PA 15301-4801
724-222-4400
www.washjeff.edu

Waynesburg College
51 West College St.
Waynesburg, PA 15370-1222
724-627-8191
www.waynesburg.edu

West Chester University of
Pennsylvania
University Ave. and High St.
West Chester, PA 19383
610-436-1000
www.wcupa.edu

Westminster College
319 South Market St.
New Wilmington,
PA 16172-0001
724-946-8761
www.westminster.edu

Widener University
One University Pl.
Chester, PA 19013-5792
610-499-4000
www.widener.edu

Wilkes University
170 South Franklin St,
PO Box 111
Wilkes-Barre, PA 18766-0002
570-408-5000
www.wilkes.edu

Wilson College
1015 Philadelphia Ave.
Chambersburg, PA 17201-1285
717-264-4141
www.wilson.edu

Yeshiva Beth Moshe
930 Hickory St., PO Box 1141
Scranton, PA 18505-2124
717-346-1747

York College of Pennsylvania
York, PA 17405-7199
717-846-7788
www.ycp.edu

Virginia

American Military University
9104-P Manassas Dr.
Manassas, VA 20111
703-330-5398
www.amunet.edu

Averett University
420 West Main St.
Danville, VA 24541-3692
434-791-5600
www.averett.edu

Bluefield College
3000 College Dr.
Bluefield, VA 24605-1799
540-326-3682
www.bluefield.edu

Bridgewater College
402 East College St.
Bridgewater, VA 22812-1599
540-828-8000
www.bridgewater.edu

Christendom College
134 Christendom Dr.
Front Royal, VA 22630-5103
540-636-2900
www.christendom.edu

Christopher Newport
University
1 University Pl.
Newport News, VA 23606-2998
757-594-7000
www.cnu.edu

Community Hospital of
Roanoke Valley-College of
Health Sciences
PO Box 13186
Roanoke, VA 24031-3186
540-985-8483
www.chs.edu

DeVry Institute of
Technology
Century Building II, Ste. 1100,
2361 Jefferson Davis Hwy
Arlington, VA 22202
866-338-7932
www.crys.devry.edu

Eastern Mennonite
University
1200 Park Rd.
Harrisonburg, VA 22802-2462
540-432-4000
www.emu.edu

Emory & Henry College
PO Box 947
Emory, VA 24327-0947
540-944-4121
www.ehc.edu

Ferrum College
PO Box 1000
Ferrum, VA 24088-9001
540-365-2121
www.ferrum.edu

George Mason University
4400 University Dr.
Fairfax, VA 22030-4444
703-993-1000
www.gmu.edu

Hampden-Sydney College
PO Box 667
Hampden-Sydney, VA 23943
804-223-6000
www.hsc.edu

Hampton University
Hampton, VA 23668
757-727-5000
www.hamptonu.edu

Hollins University
PO Box 9603
Roanoke, VA 24020-1603
540-362-6000
www.hollins.edu

James Madison University
800 South Main St.
Harrisonburg, VA 22807
540-568-6211
www.jmu.edu

Liberty University
1971 University Blvd
Lynchburg, VA 24502
804-582-2000
www.liberty.edu

Longwood College
201 High St.
Farmville, VA 23909-1800
804-395-2000
www.longwood.edu

Lynchburg College
1501 Lakeside Dr.
Lynchburg, VA 24501-3199
804-544-8100
www.lynchburg.edu

Mary Baldwin College
201 East Frederick St.
Staunton, VA 24401-3610
540-887-7000
www.mbc.edu

Mary Washington College
1301 College Ave.
Fredericksburg,
VA 22401-5358
540-654-1000
www.mwc.edu

Marymount University
2807 North Glebe Rd.
Arlington, VA 22207-4299
703-522-5600
www.marymount.edu

Norfolk State University
700 Park Ave.
Norfolk, VA 23504
757-823-8600
www.nsu.edu

Old Dominion University
5215 Hampton Blvd
Norfolk, VA 23529
757-683-3000
www.odu.edu

Radford University
PO Box 6890, RU Station
Radford, VA 24142
540-831-5000
www.radford.edu

Randolph-Macon College
PO Box 5005
Ashland, VA 23005-5505
804-752-7200
www.rmc.edu

Randolph-Macon Woman's
College
2500 Rivermont Ave.
Lynchburg, VA 24503-1526
804-947-8000
www.rmwc.edu

Roanoke College
221 College Ln.
Salem, VA 24153-3794
540-375-2500
www.roanoke.edu

Saint Paul's College
115 College Dr.
Lawrenceville, VA 23868-1202
804-848-3111
www.saintpauls.edu

Shenandoah University
1460 University Dr.
Winchester, VA 22601-5195
540-665-4500
www.su.edu

Southern Virginia College
One College Hill Dr.
Buena Vista, VA 24416
540-261-8400
www.southernvirginia.edu

Sweet Briar College
US Rt. 29 North
Sweet Briar, VA 24595
804-381-6100
www.sbc.edu

The Art Institute of
Washington
1820 North Fort Meyer Dr.,
Ground Floor
Arlington, VA 22209
703-358-9550
www.aiw.artinstitutes.edu

The College of William and
Mary
PO Box 8795
Williamsburg, VA 23187-8795
757-221-4000
www.wm.edu

The University of Virginia's
College at Wise
1 College Ave.
Wise, VA 24293
540-328-0100
www.uvawise.edu

University of Richmond
28 Westhampton Way
University of Richmond,
VA 23173
804-289-8000
www.richmond.edu

University of Virginia
Charlottesville, VA 22903
434-924-0311
www.virginia.edu

Virginia Commonwealth
University
901 West Franklin St.
Richmond, VA 23284-9005
804-828-0100
www.vcu.edu

Virginia Intermont College
1013 Moore St.
Bristol, VA 24201-4298
540-669-6101
www.vic.edu

Virginia Military Institute
Lexington, VA 24450
540-464-7207
www.vmi.edu

Virginia Polytechnic Institute
and State University
Blacksburg, VA 24061
540-231-6000

Virginia State University
1 Hayden Dr.
Petersburg, VA 23806-0001
804-524-5000
www.vsu.edu

Virginia Union University
1500 North Lombardy St.
Richmond, VA 23220-1170
804-257-5600

Virginia Wesleyan College
1584 Wesleyan Dr.
Norfolk, VA 23502-5599
757-455-3200
www.vwc.edu

Washington and Lee
University
Lexington, VA 24450-0303
540-463-8400
www.wlu.edu

World College
5193 Shore Dr., Ste. 105
Virginia Beach,
VA 23455-2500
757-464-4600

West Virginia

Alderson-Brd.dus College
1 College Hill
Philippi, WV 26416
304-457-1700
www.ab.edu

Appalachian Bible College
PO Box ABC
Bradley, WV 25818
304-877-6428
www.abc.edu

Bethany College
Main St.
Bethany, WV 26032
304-829-7000
www.bethanywv.edu

Bluefield State College
219 Rock St.
Bluefield, WV 24701-2198
304-327-4000
www.bluefield.wvnet.edu

Concord College
Vermillion St.,
PO Box 1000
Athens, WV 24712-1000
304-384-3115
www.concord.edu

Davis & Elkins College
100 Campus Dr.
Elkins, WV 26241-3996
304-637-1900
www.dne.edu

Fairmont State College
1201 Locust Ave.
Fairmont, WV 26554
304-367-4000
www.fscwv.edu

Glenville State College
200 High St.
Glenville, WV 26351-1200
304-462-7361
www.glenville.edu

Marshall University
400 Hal Greer Blvd
Huntington, WV 25755
304-696-3170
www.marshall.edu

Mountain State University
PO Box AG
Beckley, WV 25802-2830
304-253-7351
www.mountainstate.edu

Ohio Valley College
One Campus View Dr.
Vienna, WV 26105-8000
304-865-6000
www.ovc.edu

Salem International
University
223 West Main St.,
PO Box 500
Salem, WV 26426-0500
304-782-5011
www.salemiu.edu

Shepherd College
PO Box 3210
Shepherdstown,
WV 25443-3210
304-876-5000
www.shepherd.edu

University of Charleston
2300 MacCorkle Ave., SE
Charleston, WV 25304-1099
304-357-4800
www.uchaswv.edu

West Liberty State College
PO Box 295
West Liberty, WV 26074
304-336-5000
www.wlsc.wvnet.edu

West Virginia State College
Post Office Box 1000
Institute, WV 25112-1000
304-766-3000
www.wvsc.edu

West Virginia University
University Ave.
Morgantown, WV 26506
304-293-0111
www.wvu.edu

West Virginia University
Institute of Technology
405 Fayette Pike
Montgomery, WV 25136
304-442-3071
www.wvutech.edu

West Virginia Wesleyan
College
59 College Ave.
Buckhannon, WV 26201
304-473-8000
www.wvwc.edu

Wheeling Jesuit University
316 Washington Ave.
Wheeling, WV 26003-6295
304-243-2000
www.wju.edu

TWO-YEAR COLLEGES AND UNIVERSITIES

Delaware

Delaware Technical &
Community College, Jack F.
Owens Campus
PO Box 610, Rt. 18
Georgetown, DE 19947
302-856-5400
www.dtcc.edu/

Delaware Technical &
Community College,
Stanton/Wilmington Campus
400 Stanton-Christiana Rd.
Newark, DE 19713
302-454-3900
www.dtcc.edu/

Delaware Technical &
Community College, Terry
Campus
100 Campus Dr.
Dover, DE 19901
302-857-1000
www.dtcc.edu/terry/

Maryland

Allegany College of
Maryland
12401 Willowbrook Rd., SE
Cumberland, MD 21502-2596
301-784-5000
www.ac.cc.md.us/

Anne Arundel Community
College
101 College Pkwy
Arnold, MD 21012-1895
410-647-7100
www.aacc.cc.md.us/

Baltimore City Community
College
2901 Liberty Heights Ave.
Baltimore, MD 21215-7893
410-462-8000
www.bccc.state.md.us/

Carroll Community College
1601 Washington Rd.
Westminster, MD 21157
410-386-8000
www.carroll.cc.md.us/

Cecil Community College
One Seahawk Dr.
North East, MD 21901-1999
410-287-6060
www.cecil.cc.md.us/

Chesapeake College
PO Box 8
Wye Mills, MD 21679-0008
410-822-5400
www.chesapeake.edu/

College of Southern
Maryland
8730 Mitchell Rd., PO Box 910
La Plata, MD 20646-0910
301-934-2251
www.csm.cc.md.us/

Frederick Community
College
7932 Opossumtown Pike
Frederick, MD 21702-2097
301-846-2400
www.fcc.cc.md.us/

Garrett Community College
687 Mosser Rd., PO Box 151
McHenry, MD 21541-0151
301-387-3000
www.garrett.gcc.cc.md.us/

Hagerstown Business
College
18618 Crestwood Dr.
Hagerstown, MD 21742-2797
301-739-2670
www.hagerstown
businesscol.org

Hagerstown Community
College
11400 Robinwood Dr.
Hagerstown, MD 21742-6590
301-790-2800
www.hcc.cc.md.us/

Harford Community College
401 Thomas Run Rd.
Bel Air, MD 21015-1698
410-836-4000
www.harford.cc.md.us/

Howard Community College
10901 Little Patuxent Pkwy
Columbia, MD 21044-3197
410-772-4800
www.howardcc.edu/

Maryland College of Art and
Design
10500 Georgia Ave.
Silver Spring, MD 20902-4111
301-649-4454
www.mcadmd.org/

Montgomery College
900 Hungerford Dr.
Rockville, MD 20850
301-279-5000
www.montgomerycollege.org/

Prince George's Community
College
301 Largo Rd.
Largo, MD 20774-2199
301-336-6000
www.pg.cc.md.us/

The Community College of
Baltimore County-
Catonsville Campus
800 South Rolling Rd.
Baltimore, MD 21228-5381
410-455-6050
www.ccbc.cc.md.us/

The Community College of
Baltimore County-Dundalk
Campus
7200 Sollers Point Rd.
Baltimore, MD 21222-4694
410-282-6700
www.ccbc.cc.md.us/

The Community College of
Baltimore County-Essex
Campus
7201 Rossville Blvd
Baltimore, MD 21237-3899
410-682-6000
www.ccbc.cc.md.us/

Wor-Wic Community College
32000 Campus Dr.
Salisbury, MD 21804
410-334-2800
www.worwic.cc.md.us/

New Jersey

Assumption College for
Sisters
350 Bernardsville Rd.
Mendham, NJ 07945-0800
973-543-6528
www.acscollegeforsisters.org/

Atlantic Cape Community
College
5100 Black Horse Pike
Mays Landing,
NJ 08330-2699
609-625-1111
www.atlantic.edu/

Bergen Community College
400 Paramus Rd.
Paramus, NJ 07652-1595
201-447-7100
www.bergen.cc.nj.us/

Berkeley College
44 Rifle Camp Rd., PO Box 440
West Paterson,
NJ 07424-3353
973-278-5400
www.berkeleycollege.edu/

Brookdale Community
College
765 Newman Springs Rd.
Lincroft, NJ 07738-1597
732-842-1900
www.brookdale.cc.nj.us/

Burlington County College
Rt. 530
Pemberton, NJ 08068-1599
609-894-9311
www.bcc.edu/

Camden County College
PO Box 200
Blackwood, NJ 08012-0200
856-227-7200
www.camdencc.edu/

County College of Morris
214 Center Grove Rd.
Randolph, NJ 07869-2086
973-328-5000
www.ccm.edu/

Cumberland County College
PO Box 1500, College Dr.
Vineland, NJ 08362-1500
856-691-8600
www.cccnj.net/

Essex County College
303 University Ave.
Newark, NJ 07102-1798
973-877-3000
www.essex.edu/

Gibbs College
33 Plymouth St.
Montclair, NJ 07042-2699
973-744-2010
www.njgibbscollege.net

Gloucester County College
1400 Tanyard Rd.
Sewell, NJ 08080
856-468-5000
www.gccnj.edu/

Hudson County Community
College
25 Journal Square
Jersey City, NJ 07306
201-656-2020
www.hudson.cc.nj.us/

Mercer County Community
College
1200 Old Trenton Rd.,
PO Box B
Trenton, NJ 08690-1004
609-586-4800
www.mccc.edu/

Middlesex County College
2600 Woodbridge Ave.,
PO Box 3050
Edison, NJ 08818-3050
732-548-6000
www.middlesex.cc.nj.us/

Ocean County College
College Dr., PO Box 2001
Toms River, NJ 08754-2001
732-255-0400
www.ocean.cc.nj.us/

Passaic County Community
College
One College Blvd
Paterson, NJ 07505-1179
973-684-6800
www.pccc.cc.nj.us/

Raritan Valley Community
College
PO Box 3300
Somerville, NJ 08876-1265
908-526-1200
www.raritanval.edu/

Salem Community College
460 Hollywood Ave.
Carneys Point,
NJ 08069-2799
856-299-2100
www.salem.cc.nj.us/

Somerset Christian College
10 Liberty Square
Zarephath, NJ 08890-9035
732-356-1595
www.zarephath.edu

Sussex County Community
College
1 College Hill
Newton, NJ 07860
973-300-2100
www.sussex.cc.nj.us/

Union County College
1033 Springfield Ave.
Cranford, NJ 07016-1528
908-709-7000
www.ucc.edu/

Warren County Community
College
475 Rt. 57 West
Washington, NJ 07882-4343
908-689-1090
www.warren.cc.nj.us/

New York

Adirondack Community
College
640 Bay Rd.
Queensbury, NY 12804
518-743-2200
www.sunyacc.edu/

American Academy
McAllister Institute of
Funeral Service
450 West 56th St.
New York, NY 10019-3602
212-757-1190

American Academy of
Dramatic Arts
120 Madison Ave.
New York, NY 10016-7004
212-686-9244
www.aada.org/

Berkeley College
3 East 43rd St.
New York, NY 10017-4604
212-986-4343
www.berkeleycollege.edu/

Berkeley College
99 Church St.
White Plains, NY 10601
914-694-1122
www.berkeleycollege.edu/

Borough of Manhattan
Community College of the
City University of
New York
199 Chambers St.
New York, NY 10007-1097
212-346-8000
www.bmcc.cuny.edu/

Bramson ORT College
69-30 Austin St.
Forest Hills, NY 11375-4239
718-261-5800
www.bramsonort.org/

Bronx Community College
of the City University of
New York
University Ave. & West 181st St.
Bronx, NY 10453
718-289-5100
www.bcc.cuny.edu/

Broome Community College
PO Box 1017
Binghamton, NY 13902-1017
607-778-5000
www.sunybroome.edu/

Bryant and Stratton
Business Institute
150 Bellwood Dr.
Rochester, NY 14606
716-720-0660
www.bryantstratton.edu/

Bryant and Stratton
Business Institute
953 James St.
Syracuse, NY 13203-2502
315-472-6603
www.bryantstratton.edu/

Bryant and Stratton
Business Institute
1225 Jefferson Rd.
Rochester, NY 14623-3136
716-292-5627
www.bryantstratton.edu/

Bryant and Stratton
Business Institute
Ste. 400, 465 Main St.
Buffalo, NY 14203
716-884-9120
www.bryantstratton.edu/

Bryant and Stratton
Business Institute
1214 Abbott Rd.
Lackawanna, NY 14218-1989
716-821-9331
www.bryantstratton.edu/

Bryant and Stratton
Business Institute
1259 Central Ave.
Albany, NY 12205-5230
518-437-1802
www.bryantstratton.edu/

Bryant and Stratton
Business Institute, Amherst
Campus
40 Hazelwood Dr.
Amherst, NY 14228
716-691-0012
www.bryantstratton.edu/

Bryant and Stratton
Business Institute, North
Campus
8687 Carling Rd.
Liverpool, NY 13090-1315
315-652-6500
www.bryantstratton.edu/

Catholic Medical Center of
Brooklyn and Queens
School of Nursing
175-05 Horace Harding Expwy
Fresh Meadows, NY 11365
718-357-0500

Cayuga County Community
College
197 Franklin St.
Auburn, NY 13021-3099
315-255-1743
www.cayuga-cc.edu/

Clinton Community College
136 Clinton Point Dr.
Plattsburgh, NY 12901-9573
518-562-4200
www.clintoncc.suny.edu/

Cochran School of Nursing
967 North Brd.way
Yonkers, NY 10701
914-964-4283
www.riversidehealth.org/

Columbia-Greene
Community College
4400 Rt. 23
Hudson, NY 12534-0327
518-828-4181
www.sunycgcc.edu/

Corning Community College
One Academic Dr.
Corning, NY 14830-3297
607-962-9011
www.corning-cc.edu/

Crouse Hospital School of
Nursing
736 Irving Ave.
Syracuse, NY 13210
315-470-7481
www.crouse.org/son/home.htm

Dorothea Hopfer School of
Nursing at The Mount Vernon
Hospital
53 Valentine St.
Mount Vernon, NY 10550
914-664-8000

Dutchess Community
College
53 Pendell Rd.
Poughkeepsie,
NY 12601-1595
845-431-8000
www.sunydutchess.edu/

Ellis Hospital School of
Nursing
1101 Nott St.
Schenectady, NY 12308
518-243-4471
www.ehson.org

Elmira Business Institute
303 North Main St.
Elmira, NY 14901
607-733-7177
www.ebi-college.com/

Erie Community College,
City Campus
121 Ellicott St.
Buffalo, NY 14203-2698
716-851-1001
www.sunyerie.edu/

Erie Community College,
North Campus
6205 Main St.
Williamsville, NY 14221-7095
716-851-1002
www.sunyerie.edu/

Erie Community College,
South Campus
4041 Southwestern Blvd
Orchard Park, NY 14127-2199
716-851-1003
www.sunyerie.edu/

Eugenio Mar&,ia de Hostos
Community College of the
City University of New York
500 Grand Concourse
Bronx, NY 10451
718-518-4444
www.hostos.cuny.edu/

Finger Lakes Community
College
4355 Lakeshore Dr.
Canandaigua, NY 14424-8395
716-394-3500
www.flcc.edu/

Fiorello H. LaGuardia
Community College of the City
University of New York
31-10 Thomson Ave.
Long Island City,
NY 11101-3071
718-482-7200
www.lagcc.cuny.edu/

Fulton-Montgomery
Community College
2805 State Hwy 67
Johnstown, NY 12095-3790
518-762-4651
www.fmcc.suny.edu/

Genesee Community
College
1 College Rd.
Batavia, NY 14020-9704
716-343-0055
www.sunygenesee.cc.ny.us/

Helene Fuld College of
Nursing of North General
Hospital
1879 Madison Ave.
New York, NY 10035-2709
212-423-1000

Herkimer County
Community College
Reservoir Rd.
Herkimer, NY 13350
315-866-0300
www.hccc.ntcnet.com/

Hudson Valley Community
College
80 Vandenburgh Ave.
Troy, NY 12180-6096
518-629-4822
www.hvcc.edu/

Institute of Design and
Construction
141 Willoughby St.
Brooklyn, NY 11201-5317
718-855-3661
www.idcbrooklyn.org/

Interboro Institute
450 West 56th St.
New York, NY 10019-3602
212-399-0091
www.interboro.com/

Island Drafting and Technical
Institute
128 Brd.way
Amityville, NY 11787
631-691-8733
www.islanddrafting.com/

ITT Technical Institute
13 Airline Dr.
Albany, NY 12205
518-452-9300
www.itt-tech.edu/

ITT Technical Institute
235 Greenfield Pkwy
Liverpool, NY 13088
315-461-8000
www.itt-tech.edu/

ITT Technical Institute
2295 Millersport Hwy,
PO Box 327
Getzville, NY 14068
716-689-2200
www.itt-tech.edu/

Jamestown Business
College
7 Fairmount Ave., Box 429
Jamestown, NY 14702-0429
716-664-5100
www.jbcny.org/

Jamestown Community
College
525 Falconer St.
Jamestown, NY 14701-1999
716-665-5220
www.sunyjcc.edu/

Jefferson Community
College
1220 Coffeen St.
Watertown, NY 13601
315-786-2200
www.sunyjefferson.edu/

Katharine Gibbs School
200 Park Ave.
New York, NY 10166-0005
212-867-9300
www.katharinegibbs.com/

Katharine Gibbs School
320 South Service Rd.
Melville, NY 11747-3785
631-370-3300
www.gibbsmelville.com/

Kingsborough Community
College of the City
University of New York
2001 Oriental Blvd,
Manhattan Beach
Brooklyn, NY 11235
718-368-5000
www.kbcc.cuny.edu/

Long Island Business
Institute
6500 Jericho Turnpike
Commack, NY 11725
631-499-7100
www.libinstitute.com

Long Island College Hospital
School of Nursing
397 Hicks St.
Brooklyn, NY 11201-5940
718-780-1953

Maria College
700 New Scotland Ave.
Albany, NY 12208-1798
518-438-3111
www.mariacollege.org

Mildred Elley
800 New Louden Rd.
Latham, NY 12110
518-786-0855

Mohawk Valley Community
College
1101 Sherman Dr.
Utica, NY 13501-5394
315-792-5400
www.mvcc.edu/

Monroe College
Monroe College Way
Bronx, NY 10468-5407
718-933-6700
www.monroecoll.edu/

Monroe College
434 Main St.
New Rochelle, NY 10801
914-632-5400
www.monroecoll.edu/

Monroe Community College
1000 East Henrietta Rd.
Rochester, NY 14623-5780
716-292-2000
www.monroecc.edu/

Nassau Community College
1 Education Dr.
Garden City, NY 11530-6793
516-572-7500
www.sunynassau.edu/

New York Career Institute
15 Park Row, 4th Floor
New York, NY 10038-2301
212-962-0002
www.nyci.com/

New York City Technical
College of the City
University of New York
300 Jay St.
Brooklyn, NY 11201-2983
718-260-5000
www.nyctc.cuny.edu/

New York Restaurant School
75 Varick St., 16th Floor
New York, NY 10013
212-226-5500
www.nyrs.artinstitutes.edu/

Niagara County Community
College
3111 Saunders Settlement Rd.
Sanborn, NY 14132-9460
716-614-6222

North Country Community
College
20 Winona Ave., PO Box 89
Saranac Lake, NY 12983-0089
518-891-2915
www.nccc.edu/

Olean Business Institute
301 North Union St.
Olean, NY 14760-2691
716-372-7978

Onondaga Community
College
4941 Onondaga Rd.
Syracuse, NY 13215-2099
315-498-2622
www.sunyocc.edu/

Orange County Community
College
115 South St.
Middletown, NY 10940-6437
914-344-6222
www.orange.cc.ny.us

Phillips Beth Israel School of
Nursing
310 East 22nd St., 9th Floor
New York, NY 10010-5702
212-614-6110
www.wehealny.org/bischool
of nursing/

Plaza Business Institute
74-09 37th Ave.
Jackson Heights,
NY 11372-6300
718-779-1430
www.plazacollege.edu/

Queensborough Community
College of the City
University of New York
222-05 56th Ave.
Bayside, NY 11364
718-631-6262 Fax: 718-281-5189
www.qcc.cuny.edu/

Rochester Business Institute
1630 Portland Ave.
Rochester, NY 14621
716-266-0430
www.rochester-
institute.com/

Rockland Community
College
145 College Rd.
Suffern, NY 10901-3699
914-574-4000
www.sunyrockland.edu/

Sage College of Albany
140 New Scotland Ave.
Albany, NY 12208-3425
518-292-1730
www.sage.edu/SCA/

Saint Joseph's Hospital Health
Center School of Nursing
206 Prospect Ave.
Syracuse, NY 13203
315-448-5040
www.sjhsyr.org/nursing/

Samaritan Hospital School
of Nursing
2215 Burdett Ave.
Troy, NY 12180
518-271-3285

Schenectady County
Community College
78 Washington Ave.
Schenectady, NY 12305-2294
518-381-1200
www.sunysccc.edu

Simmons Institute of
Funeral Service
1828 South Ave.
Syracuse, NY 13207
315-475-5142
www.simmonsinstitute.com/

State University of New York
College of Agriculture and
Technology at Morrisville
PO Box 901
Morrisville, NY 13408-0901
315-684-6000
www.morrisville.edu/

State University of New York
College of Environmental
Science & Forestry, Ranger
School
PO Box 48,
257 Ranger School Rd.
Wanakena, NY 13695
315-848-2566
www.esf.edu/

State University of New York
College of Technology at Alfred
Alfred, NY 14802
607-587-4111
www.alfredstate.edu

State University of New York
College of Technology at Delhi
Main St.
Delhi, NY 13753
607-746-4000
www.delhi.edu/

Suffolk County Community
College
533 College Rd.
Selden, NY 11784-2899
631-451-4110
www.sunysuffolk.edu/

Sullivan County Community
College
112 College Rd.
Loch Sheldrake, NY 12759
845-434-5750
www.sullivan.suny.edu/

Taylor Business Institute
269 West 40th St.
New York, NY 10018
212-643-2020

TCI-The College for
Technology
320 West 31st St.
New York, NY 10001-2705
212-594-4000
www.tciedu.com/

The New York College for
Wholistic Health Education
& Research
6801 Jericho Turnpike, Ste. 300
Syosset, NY 11791-4413
516-364-0808
www.nycollege.edu/

Tompkins Cortland
Community College
170 North St., PO Box 139
Dryden, NY 13053-0139
607-844-8211
www.sunytccc.edu/

Trocaire College
360 Choate Ave.
Buffalo, NY 14220-2094
716-826-1200
www.trocaire.edu/

Ulster County Community
College
Stone Ridge, NY 12484
914-687-5000
www.ulster.cc.ny.us/

Utica School of Commerce
201 Bleecker St.
Utica, NY 13501-2280
315-733-2307
www.uscny.com/

Villa Maria College of
Buffalo
240 Pine Ridge Rd.
Buffalo, NY 14225-3999
716-896-0700
www.villa.edu/

Westchester Business
Institute
325 Central Ave., PO Box 710
White Plains, NY 10602
914-948-4442
www.wbi.org/

Westchester Community
College
75 Grasslands Rd.
Valhalla, NY 10595-1698
914-785-6600
www.sunywcc.edu/

Wood Tobe-Coburn School
8 East 40th St.
New York, NY 10016
212-686-9040
www.woodtobecoburn.com/

Pennsylvania

Academy of Medical Arts
and Business
2301 Academy Dr.
Harrisburg, PA 17112-1012
717-545-4747
www.acadcampus.com/

Allentown Business School
1501 Lehigh St.
Allentown, PA 18103-3880
610-791-5100
www.chooseabs.com/

Antonelli Institute
300 Montgomery Ave.
Erdenheim, PA 19038
215-836-2222
www.antonelli.org/

Berean Institute
1901 West Girard Ave.
Philadelphia, PA 19130-1599
215-763-4833

Berks Technical Institute
2205 Ridgewood Rd.
Wyomissing, PA 19610-1168
610-372-1722
www.berkstech.com/

Bradford School
707 Grant St., Gulf Tower
Pittsburgh, PA 15219
412-391-6710
www.bradfordschoolpgh.com

Bradley Academy for the
Visual Arts
1409 Williams Rd.
York, PA 17402-9012
717-755-2300
www.bradley-acad.com/

Bucks County Community
College
275 Swamp Rd.
Newtown, PA 18940-1525
215-968-8000
www.bucks.edu/

Business Institute of
Pennsylvania
335 Boyd Dr.
Sharon, PA 16146
724-983-0700
www.biop.com

Butler County Community
College
College Dr., PO Box 1203
Butler, PA 16003-1203
724-287-8711
www.bc3.cc.pa.us/

Cambria County Area
Community College
PO Box 68
Johnstown, PA 15907-0068
814-532-5300
www.ccacc.cc.pa.us/

Cambria-Rowe Business
College
221 Central Ave.
Johnstown, PA 15902-2494
814-536-5168
www.crbc.net/

Central Pennsylvania College
College Hill Rd.
Summerdale, PA 17093-0309
717-732-0702 Fax: 717-732-5254
www.centralpenn.edu/

CHI Institute
520 St. Rd.
Southampton, PA 18966-3747
215-357-5100
www.chitraining.com

CHI Institute, RETS Campus
1991 Lawrence Rd., Ste. 42
Broomall, PA 19008
610-353-7630

Churchman Business School
355 Spring Garden St.
Easton, PA 18042-3592
610-258-5345
www.churchman4u.com/

Commonwealth Technical
Institute
727 Goucher St.
Johnstown, PA 15905-3092
814-255-8200
www.hgac.org/

Community College of
Allegheny County
800 Allegheny Ave.
Pittsburgh, PA 15233-1894
412-323-2323
www.ccac.edu/

Community College of
Beaver County
One Campus Dr.
Monaca, PA 15061-2588
724-775-8561
www.ccbc.cc.pa.us/

Community College of
Philadelphia
1700 Spring Garden St.
Philadelphia, PA 19130-3991
215-751-8000
www.ccp.cc.pa.us/

Consolidated School of
Business
1605 Clugston Rd.
York, PA 17404
717-764-9550
www.csb.edu/

Consolidated School of
Business
2124 Ambassador Cr.
Lancaster, PA 17603
717-394-6211
www.csb.edu/

Dean Institute of Technology
1501 West Liberty Ave.
Pittsburgh, PA 15226-1103
412-531-4433
www.home.earthlink.net/~
deantech

Delaware County
Community College
901 South Media Line Rd.
Media, PA 19063-1094
610-359-5000
www.dccc.edu/

Douglas School of Business
130 Seventh St.
Monessen, PA 15062
724-684-3684
www.douglas-school.com/

DuBois Business College
1 Beaver Dr.
DuBois, PA 15801-2401
814-371-6920
www.dbcollege.com/

Duff's Business Institute
110 Ninth St.
Pittsburgh, PA 15222-3618
412-261-4520
www.cci.edu

Education America, Vale
Technical Institute
135 West Market St.
Blairsville, PA 15717-9989
724-459-9500
www.educationamerica.com

Electronic Institutes
19 Jamesway Plaza
Middletown, PA 17057-4851
717-944-2731
www.ei.tec.pa.us/

Erie Business Center South
170 Cascade Galleria
New Castle, PA 16101-3950
724-658-9066
www.eriebc.com/

Erie Business Center, Main
246 West Ninth St.
Erie, PA 16501-1392
814-456-7504
www.eriebc.com/

Erie Institute of Technology
2221 Peninsula Dr.
Erie, PA 16506-2954
814-838-2711
www.erieinst.com/

Harcourt Learning Direct
Center for Degree Studies
925 Oak St.
Scranton, PA 18515
570-342-7701
www.harcourt-learning.com/

Harcum College
750 Montgomery Ave.
Bryn Mawr, PA 19010-3476
610-525-4100
www.harcum.edu/

Harrisburg Area Community
College
1 HACC Dr.
Harrisburg, PA 17110-2999
717-780-2300
www.hacc.edu/

Hussian School of Art
1118 Market St.
Philadelphia, PA 19107-3679
215-981-0900
www.hussianart.edu/

ICM School of Business &
Medical Careers
10 Wood St. at Fort Pitt Blvd
Pittsburgh, PA 15222-1977
412-261-2647
www.icmschools.com

Information Computer
Systems Institute
2201 Hangar Pl.
Allentown, PA 18103-9504
610-264-8029
www.icsinstitute.com/

International Academy of
Design & Technology
555 Grant St.
Pittsburgh, PA 15219
412-391-4197
www.iadtpitt.com/

ITT Technical Institute
105 Mall Blvd
Monroeville, PA 15146
412-856-5920
www.itt-tech.edu/

ITT Technical Institute
5020 Louise Dr.
Mechanicsburg, PA 17055
717-691-9263
www.itt-tech.edu/

ITT Technical Institute
Eight Pkwy Centre
Pittsburgh, PA 15220
412-937-9150
www.itt-tech.edu/

Johnson Technical Institute
3427 North Main Ave.
Scranton, PA 18508-1495
570-342-6404
www.jti.org/

Keystone College
One College Green
La Plume, PA 18440
570-945-5141
www.keystone.edu/

Lackawanna College
501 Vine St.
Scranton, PA 18509
570-961-7810
www.ljc.edu/

Lansdale School of Business
201 Church Rd.
North Wales, PA 19454-4148
215-699-5700
www.lsbonline.com/

Laurel Business Institute
11-15 Penn St.
Uniontown, PA 15401
724-439-4900
www.laurelbusiness.net/

Lehigh Carbon Community
College
4525 Education Park Dr.
Schnecksville, PA 18078-2598
610-799-2121
www.lccc.edu/

Lincoln Technical Institute
5151 Tilghman St.
Allentown, PA 18104-3298
610-398-5300
www.lincolntech.com/

Lincoln Technical Institute
9191 Torresdale Ave.
Philadelphia, PA 19136-1595
215-335-0800

Luzerne County Community
College
1333 South Prospect St.
Nanticoke, PA 18634-9804
570-740-0300
www.luzerne.edu/

Manor College
700 Fox Chase Rd.
Jenkintown, PA 19046
215-885-2360
www.manor.edu/

McCann School of Business
Main and Pine St.s
Mahanoy City, PA 17948
717-773-1820
www.mccannschool.com/

Median School of Allied
Health Careers
125 7th St.
Pittsburgh, PA 15222-3400
412-391-7021
www.medianschool.com/

Montgomery County
Community College
340 DeKalb Pike
Blue Bell, PA 19422-0796
215-641-6300
www.mc3.edu

New Castle School of Trades
New Castle Youngstown Rd.,
Rt. 422 RD1
Pulaski, PA 16143-9721
724-964-8811
www.ncstrades.com/

Newport Business Institute
945 Greensburg Rd.
Lower Burrell, PA 15068-3929
724-339-7542
www.akvalley.com/newport/

Newport Business Institute
941 West Third St.
Williamsport, PA 17701-5855
570-326-2869
www.akvalley.com/newport/

Northampton County Area
Community College
3835 Green Pond Rd.
Bethlehem, PA 18020-7599
610-861-5300
www.northampton.edu/

Northwest Pennsylvania
Technical Institute
150 East Front St., Ste. 200
Erie, PA 16507
814-452-1122
www.penn.org/

Oakbridge Academy of Arts
1250 Greensburg Rd.
Lower Burrell, PA 15068
724-335-5336
www.akvalley.com/
oakbridge/

Orleans Technical Institute-
Center City Campus
1845 Walnut St., Ste. 700
Philadelphia, PA 19103-4707
215-854-1853
www.jevs.org/

Pace Institute
606 Court St.
Reading, PA 19601
610-375-1212
www.paceinstitute.com/

Penn Commercial Business
and Technical School
82 South Main St.
Washington, PA 15301-6822
724-222-5330
www.penn-commercial.com

Pennco Tech
3815 Otter St.
Bristol, PA 19007-3696
215-824-3200

Pennsylvania Institute of
Culinary Arts
717 Liberty Ave.
Pittsburgh, PA 15222-3500
412-566-2433
www.paculinary.com/

Pennsylvania Institute of
Technology
800 Manchester Ave.
Media, PA 19063-4098
610-892-1500
www.pit.edu/

Pittsburgh Institute of
Aeronautics
PO Box 10897
Pittsburgh, PA 15236-0897
412-462-9011
www.piainfo.org/

Pittsburgh Institute of
Mortuary Science,
Incorporated
5808 Baum Blvd
Pittsburgh, PA 15206-3706
412-362-8500
www.p-i-m-s.com/

Pittsburgh Technical Institute
635 Smithfield St.
Pittsburgh, PA 15222-2560
412-809-5100
www.pittsburghtechnical.com

Reading Area Community
College
PO Box 1706
Reading, PA 19603-1706
610-372-4721
www.racc.cc.pa.us/

Schuylkill Institute of
Business and Technology
171 Red Horse Rd.
Pottsville, PA 17901
570-622-4835
www.sibtinpa.com/

South Hills School of
Business & Technology
480 Waupelani Dr.
State College, PA 16801-4516
814-234-7755
www.southhills.edu/

South Hills School of
Business & Technology
508 58th St.
Atloona, PA 16602
814-944-6134
www.southhills.edu/

Thaddeus Stevens College
of Technology
750 East King St.
Lancaster, PA 17602-3198
717-299-7730
www.stevenstech.org/

The Art Institute of
Philadelphia
1622 Chestnut St.
Philadelphia, PA 19103-5198
215-567-7080
www.aiph.artinstitutes.edu/

The Art Institute of
Pittsburgh
420 Blvd of the Allies
Pittsburgh, PA 15219
412-263-6600
www.aip.aii.edu/

The Pennsylvania State
University Beaver Campus of
the Commonwealth College
100 University Dr.
Monaca, PA 15061
724-773-3500
www.psu.edu/

The Pennsylvania State
University Delaware County
Campus of the
Commonwealth College
25 Yearsley Mill Rd.
Media, PA 19063-5596
610-892-1350
www.psu.edu/

The Pennsylvania State
University DuBois Campus of
the Commonwealth College
College Pl.
DuBois, PA 15801-3199
814-375-4700
www.psu.edu/

The Pennsylvania State
University Fayette Campus of
the Commonwealth College
1 University Dr., PO Box 519
Uniontown, PA 15401-0519
724-430-4100
www.psu.edu/

The Pennsylvania State
University Hazleton Campus of
the Commonwealth College
Hazleton, PA 18201-1291
570-450-3000
www.psu.edu/

The Pennsylvania State
University McKeesport
Campus of the
Commonwealth College
4000 University Dr.
McKeesport, PA 15132-7698
412-675-9000
www.psu.edu/

The Pennsylvania State
University Mont Alto
Campus of the
Commonwealth College
Campus Dr.
Mont Alto, PA 17237-9703
717-749-6000
www.psu.edu/

The Pennsylvania State
University New Kensington
Campus of the
Commonwealth College
3550 7th St. Rd., RT 780
New Kensington,
PA 15068-1798
724-334-5466
www.nk.psu.edu/

The Pennsylvania State
University Shenango
Campus of the
Commonwealth College
147 Shenango Ave.
Sharon, PA 16146-1537
724-983-2814
www.psu.edu/

The Pennsylvania State
University Wilkes-Barre
Campus of the
Commonwealth College
PO PSU
Lehman, PA 18627-0217
570-675-2171
www.psu.edu/

The Pennsylvania State
University Worthington
Scranton Campus of the
Commonwealth College
120 Ridge View Dr.
Dunmore, PA 18512-1699
570-963-2500
www.psu.edu/

The Pennsylvania State
University York Campus of
the Commonwealth College
1031 Edgecomb Ave.
York, PA 17403-3298
717-771-4000
www.psu.edu/

The Restaurant School
4207 Walnut St.
Philadelphia, PA 19104-3518
215-222-4200
www.therestaurantschool.com

The Williamson Free School
of Mechanical Trades
106 South New Middletown Rd.
Media, PA 19063
610-566-1776
www.libertynet.org/wiltech/

Thompson Institute
5650 Derry St.
Harrisburg, PA 17111-3518
717-564-4112
www.thompsoninstitute.org/

Tri-State Business Institute
5757 West 26th St.
Erie, PA 16506
814-838-7673

Triangle Tech, Inc.
1940 Perrysville Ave.
Pittsburgh, PA 15214-3897
412-359-1000
www.triangle-tech.com/

Triangle Tech, Inc.-DuBois
School
PO Box 551
DuBois, PA 15801-0551
814-371-2090
www.triangle-tech.com/

Triangle Tech, Inc.-Erie
School
2000 Liberty St.
Erie, PA 16502-2594
814-453-6016
www.triangle-tech.com

Triangle Tech, Inc.-
Greensburg Center
222 East Pittsburgh St., Ste. A
Greensburg, PA 15601-3304
724-832-1050
www.triangle-tech.com

University of Pittsburgh at
Titusville
PO Box 287
Titusville, PA 16354
814-827-4400
www.upt.pitt.edu/

Valley Forge Military College
1001 Eagle Rd.
Wayne, PA 19087-3695
610-989-1200
www.vfmac.edu/

Western School of Health
and Business Careers
421 Seventh Ave.
Pittsburgh, PA 15219-1907
412-281-2600
www.westernschool.com/

Westmoreland County
Community College
400 Armbrust Rd.
Youngwood, PA 15697-1895
724-925-4000
www.westmoreland.cc.pa.us

York Technical Institute
1405 Williams Rd.
York, PA 17402-9017
717-757-1100
www.yti.edu/

Yorktowne Business Institute
West Seventh Ave.
York, PA 17404
717-846-5000
www.ybi.edu/

Virginia

Blue Ridge Community College
PO Box 80
Weyers Cave, VA 24486-0080
540-234-9261
www.br.cc.va.us/

Bryant and Stratton College,
Richmond
8141 Hull St. Rd.
Richmond, VA 23235-6411
804-745-2444
www.bryantstratton.edu/

Bryant and Stratton College,
Virginia Beach
301 Centre Pointe Dr.
Virginia Beach,
VA 23462-4417
757-499-7900
www.bryantstratton.edu/

Central Virginia Community
College
3506 Wards Rd.
Lynchburg, VA 24502-2498
804-832-7600
www.cv.cc.va.us/

Dabney S. Lancaster
Community College
100 Dabney Dr., PO Box 1000
Clifton Forge, VA 24422
540-863-2800
www.dl.cc.va.us/

Danville Community College
1008 South Main St.
Danville, VA 24541-4088
804-797-2222
www.dc.cc.va.us/

Dominion College
933 Reservoir St.
Harrisonburg, VA 22801
540-433-6977
www.dominioncollege.com/

Dominion College
5372 Fallowater Ln., Ste. B
Roanoke, VA 24014
540-776-8381
www.dominioncollege.org/

Eastern Shore Community
College
29300 Lankford Hwy
Melfa, VA 23410-3000
757-787-5900
www.es.cc.va.us/

ECPI College of Technology
1919 Commerce Dr.
Hampton, VA 23666
757-838-9191
www.ecpi.edu/

ECPI College of Technology
5555 Greenwich Rd.
Virginia Beach, VA 23462
757-671-7171
www.ecpi.edu/

ECPI Technical College
5234 Airport Rd.
Roanoke, VA 24012
540-563-8080
www.ecpi.edu/

ECPI Technical College
800 Moorefield Park Dr.
Richmond, VA 23236
804-330-5533
www.ecpi.edu/

Germanna Community
College
2130 Germanna Hwy
Locust Grove, VA 22508-2102
540-727-3000
www.so.cc.va.us/

ITT Technical Institute
300 Gateway Centre Pkwy
Richmond, VA 23235
804-330-4992
www.itt-tech.edu/

ITT Technical Institute
863 Glenrock Rd., Ste. 100
Norfolk, VA 23502-3701
757-466-1260
www.itt-tech.edu

J. Sargeant Reynolds
Community College
PO Box 85622
Richmond, VA 23285-5622
804-371-3000
www.jsr.cc.va.us/

John Tyler Community
College
13101 Jefferson Davis Hwy
Chester, VA 23831-5316
804-796-4000
www.jt.cc.va.us/

Johnson & Wales University
2428 Almeda Ave., Ste. 316
Norfolk, VA 23513
757-853-3508
www.jwu.edu/

Lord Fairfax Community
College
PO Box 47
Middletown, VA 22645-0047
540-868-7000
www.lf.cc.va.us/

Mountain Empire
Community College
PO Drawer 700
Big Stone Gap,
VA 24219-0700
540-523-2400
www.me.cc.va.us/

National College of Business
& Technology
51 B Burgess Rd.
Harrisonburg, VA 22801-9709
540-432-0943
www.ncbt.edu

National College of Business
& Technology
100 Logan St., PO Box 629
Bluefield, VA 24605-1405
540-326-3621
www.ncbt.edu/

National College of Business
& Technology
10 Church St., PO Box 232
Martinsville, VA 24114
540-632-5621
www.ncbt.edu

National College of Business
& Technology
1813 East Main St.
Salem, VA 24153
540-986-1800
www.ncbt.edu/index2.shtml

National College of Business
& Technology
734 Main St.
Danville, VA 24541-1819
804-793-6822
www.ncbt.edu/

National College of Business
& Technology
104 Candlewood Court
Lynchburg, VA 24502-2653
804-239-3500
www.ncbt.edu/index2.shtml

National College of Business
& Technology
300A Piedmont Ave.
Bristol, VA 24201
540-669-5333
www.ncbt.edu/index2.shtml

National College of Business
& Technology
1819 Emmet St.
Charlottesville, VA 22901
804-295-0136
www.ncbt.edu/

New River Community
College
PO Box 1127
Dublin, VA 24084-1127
540-674-3600
www.nr.cc.va.us/

Northern Virginia
Community
College
4001 Wakefield Chapel Rd.
Annandale, VA 22003-3796
703-323-3000
www.nv.cc.va.us/

Patrick Henry Community
College
PO Box 5311
Martinsville, VA 24115-5311
540-638-8777
www.ph.cc.va.us/

Paul D. Camp Community
College
PO Box 737,
100 North College Dr.
Franklin, VA 23851-0737
757-569-6700
www.pc.cc.va.us/

Piedmont Virginia
Community College
501 College Dr.
Charlottesville,
VA 22902-7589
804-977-3900
www.pvcc.cc.va.us/

Rappahannock Community
College
12745 College Dr.
Glenns, VA 23149-2616
804-758-6700
www.rcc.cc.va.us/

Richard Bland College of The
College of William and Mary
11301 Johnson Rd.
Petersburg, VA 23805-7100
804-862-6100
www.rbc.edu/

Southside Virginia
Community College
109 Campus Dr.
Alberta, VA 23821-9719
804-949-1000
www.sv.cc.va.us/

Southwest Virginia
Community College
PO Box SVCC
Richlands, VA 24641-1101
540-964-2555
www.sw.vccs.edu

Stratford University
7777 Leesburg Pike,
Ste. 100 South
Falls Church, VA 22043
703-821-8570
www.stratford.edu/

Thomas Nelson Community
College
PO Box 9407
Hampton, VA 23670-0407
757-825-2700
www.tncc.cc.va.us/

Tidewater Community
College
121 College Pl.
Norfolk, VA 23510
757-822-1122
www.tc.cc.va.us/

Virginia Highlands
Community College
PO Box 828
Abingdon, VA 24212-0828
540-676-5484
www.vh.cc.va.us/

Virginia Western Community
College
PO Box 14007
Roanoke, VA 24038
540-857-7311
www.vw.cc.va.us/

Wytheville Community
College
1000 East Main St.
Wytheville, VA 24382-3308
540-223-4700
www.wd.dd.va.us/

West Virginia

Huntington Junior College
of Business
900 Fifth Ave.
Huntington, WV 25701-2004
304-697-7550
www.htgnjrcollege.com

Mountain State College
1508 Spring St.
Parkersburg, WV 26101-3993
304-485-5487
www.mountainstate.org/

National Institute of
Technology
5514 Big Tyler Rd.
Cross Ln.s, WV 25313-1390
304-776-6290

Potomac State College of
West Virginia University
Fort Ave.
Keyser, WV 26726-2698
304-788-6800
www.pscvax.psc.wvnet.edu

Southern West Virginia
Community and Technical
College
PO Box 2900
Mount Gay, WV 25637-2900
304-792-7098
www.southern.wvnet.edu/

West Virginia Business
College
1052 Main St.
Wheeling, WV 26003
304-232-0361

West Virginia Junior College
1000 Virginia St. East
Charleston, WV 25301-2817
304-345-2820
www.wvjc.com/
West Virginia Junior College
148 Willey St.
Morgantown, WV 26505-
5521
304-296-8282

West Virginia Northern
Community College
1704 Market St.
Wheeling, WV 26003-3699
304-233-5900
www.northern.wvnet.edu/

West Virginia University at
Parkersburg
300 Campus Dr.
Parkersburg, WV 26101-9577
304-424-8000
www.wvup.wvnet.edu/

VOCATIONAL/CAREER COLLEGES

Delaware

Delaware College of Art and
Design
600 North Market St.
Wilmington, DE 19801
302-622-8867 Ext. 118
www.dcad.edu

Delaware Technical &
Community College,
Stanton/Wilmington Campus
400 Stanton-Christiana Rd.
Newark, DE 19713
302-454-3954
www.dtcc.edu

Schilling-Douglas School of
Hair Design
70 Amstel Ave.
Newark, DE 19711
302-737-5100 Ext. 11
www.schillingdouglas.com

Star Technical Institute
631 West Newport Pike,
Graystone Plaza
Wilmington, DE 19804
302-999-7827

Maryland

Aaron's Academy of Beauty
340 Post Office Rd.
Waldorf, MD 20602
301-645-3681

Aesthetics Institute of
Cosmetology
15958C Shady Grove Rd.
Gaithersburg, MD 20877
301-330-9252

All-State Career School
2200 Broening Hwy, Ste. 160
Baltimore, MD 21224
410-631-1818 Ext. 227

Allegany College of Maryland
12401 Willowbrook Rd., SE
Cumberland, MD 21502-2596
301-784-5199
www.allegany.edu

Anne Arundel Community
College
101 College Pkwy
Arnold, MD 21012-1895
410-777-2246
www.aacc.edu

Baltimore School of
Massage
6401 Dogwood Rd.
Baltimore, MD 21207
410-944-8855
www.bsom.com

Blades School of Hair Design
22576-316 MacArthur Blvd
California, MD 20619
301-862-9797

Carroll Community College
1601 Washington Rd.
Westminster, MD 21157
410-386-8430
www.carrollcc.edu

Diesel Institute of America
Route 40, Box 69
Grantsville, MD 21536
301-895-5138

Hair Academy, Inc.-New
Carrollton
8435 Old Annapolis Rd.
New Carrollton, MD 20784

Howard Community College
10901 Little Patuxent Pkwy
Columbia, MD 21044-3197
410-772-4856
www.howardcc.edu

International Beauty School 3
227 Archer St.
Bel Air, MD 21014
410-838-0845

International Beauty School 5
PO Box 1597
Cumberland, MD 21501-1597
301-777-3020

L'Academie de Cuisine
16006 Industrial Drive
Gaithersburg, MD 20877
301-670-8670
www.lacademie.com

Lincoln Technical Institute
9325 Snowden River Pkwy
Columbia, MD 21046
410-290-7100 Ext. 202

Maryland Beauty Academy
of Essex
505 Eastern Blvd
Essex, MD 21221
410-686-4477

Maryland College of Art and
Design
10500 Georgia Ave.
Silver Spring, MD 20902-4111
301-649-4454 Ext. 311
www.mcadmd.org

Montgomery Beauty School
8736 Arliss St.
Silver Spring, MD 20901
301-588-7666

New Creations Academy of
Hair Design
3930 Bexley Place
Suitland, MD 20746
301-899-9100

Prince George's Community
College
301 Largo Rd.
Largo, MD 20774-2199
301-322-0866
www.pgcc.edu

Strayer University at White
Marsh Campus
9409 Philadelphia Rd.
Baltimore, MD 21237
410-238-9000
www.strayer.edu

TESST College of
Technology
1520 South Caton Ave.
Baltimore, MD 21227-1063
410-644-6400
www.tesst.com

TESST College of
Technology
4600 Powder Mill Rd.
Beltsville, MD 20705
301-937-8448
www.tesst.com

The Community College of
Baltimore County-
Catonsville Campus
800 South Rolling Rd.
Baltimore, MD 21228-5381
410-869-1250
www.ccbc.cc.md.us

Ultrasound Diagnostic School
8401 Corporate Drive, #500
Landover, MD 20785
301-918-8221
www.ultrasounddiagnostic
school.comdefault.htm

New Jersey

Academy of Computer Careers
2 Sindoni Lane
Hammonton, NJ 8037
609-561-4424

Academy of Computer
Careers
150 Delsea Drive
Sewell, NJ 8080
856-881-6555

Artistic Academy of Hair
Design
2121 Brd.way
Fairlawn, NJ 7410
201-794-3502 Ext. 253

Associated College Group, Inc.
1410 Main Ave.
Clifton, NJ 7011
973-772-9393

Associated College Group, Inc.
121-125 Newark Ave.
Jersey City, NJ 7302
201-435-5111

Associated College Group, Inc.
100 Bayard St.
New Brunswick, NJ 8901

Atlantic Cape Community
College
5100 Black Horse Pike
Mays Landing, NJ 08330-2699
609-343-5000
www.atlantic.edu

Bergen Community College
400 Paramus Rd.
Paramus, NJ 07652-1595
201-447-7195
www.bergen.edu

Berkeley College
44 Rifle Camp Rd.
West Paterson, NJ 07424-3353
973-278-5400
www.berkeleycollege.edu

Brick Computer Science
Institute
515 Route 70
Brick, NJ 8723
800-585-3523 Ext. 2221
www.brickcomputer.com

Brookdale Community
College
765 Newman Springs Rd.
Lincroft, NJ 07738-1597
732-224-2375
www.brookdalecc.edu

Burlington County College
Route 530
Pemberton, NJ 08068-1599
609-894-9311 Ext. 7282
www.bcc.edu

Business Training Institute
365 West Passaic St., 6th Fl
Rochelle Park, NJ 07662-3017
201-845-9300

Capri Institute of Hair Design
268 Brick Blvd
Brick, NJ 8723
908-920-3600

Capri Institute of Hair Design
1595 Main Ave.
Clifton, NJ 7011
201-772-4610

Concorde School of Hair
Design-Bloomfield
9-15 Ward St.
Bloomfield, NJ 7003
973-680-0099

Cooper Health System Center
For Allied Health Education
1 Cooper Plaza
Camden, NJ 8103
856-342-2734

Cumberland County College
PO Box 1500, College Dr.
Vineland, NJ 08362-1500
856-690-9155
www.cccnj.net

Divers Academy International
of the Eastern Seaboard
2500 South Brd.way
Camden, NJ 08104-2431
856-966-1871
www.diversacademy.com

Engine City Technical Institute
2365 Route 22 West
Union, NJ 7083
800-305-3487
www.enginecitytech.com

Essex County College
303 University Ave.
Newark, NJ 07102-1798
973-877-3100
www.essex.edu

Gordon Phillips School of
Beauty Culture
729 Haddon Ave.
Collingswood, NJ 8108
570-429-1800

Gordon Phillips School of
Beauty Culture
1305 Blackwood-Clementon Rd.
Commerce Plaza 2
Laurel Springs, NJ 8021
856-435-8100

HoHoKus Hackensack School
of Business and Medical
Sciences
66 Moore St.
Hackensack, NJ 7601
201-488-9400
www.hohokushackensack.com

Mercer County Community
College
1200 Old Trenton Rd.,
PO Box B
Trenton, NJ 08690-1004
609-586-0505
www.mccc.edu

Natural Motion Institute of
Hair Design
2800 Kennedy Blvd
Jersey City, NJ 7306
201-659-0303

New Horizon Institute of
Cosmetology, Inc.
5518 Bergenline Ave.
West New York, NJ 7093
201-866-4000

Omega Institute
7050 Route 38, E
Pennsauken, NJ 8109
856-663-4299

Pennco Tech
99 Erial Rd.
PO Box 1427
Blackwood, NJ 08012-9961
856-232-0310
www.penncotech.com

Raritan Valley Community
College
PO Box 3300
Somerville, NJ 08876-1265
908-526-1200 Ext. 8217
www.raritanval.edu

Reignbow Hair Fashion
Institute
121 Watchung Ave.
North Plainfield, NJ 7060
908-754-4247

Roman Academy of Beauty
Culture
431 Lafayette Ave.
Hawthorne, NJ 7506
973-423-2223

Somerset County Technical
Institute
North Bridge St. and Vogt Dr
Bridgewater, NJ 08807-0350
908-526-8900 Ext. 7268
www.scti.org

Star Technical Institute
1255 Route 70
Ste. 12, North
Lakewood, NJ 08701-5947
732-901-9710

Star Technical Institute
2 Carnegie Rd.
Lawrenceville, NJ 8648
609-406-1505

Star Technical Institute-
Deptford
1450 Clements Bridge Rd.
Deptford, NJ 8096
609-384-2888

Steno Tech Career Institute
20 Just Rd.
Fairfield, NJ 07004-3413
973-882-4875

Stuart School of Business
Administration
2400 Belmar Blvd
Wall, NJ 7719
732-681-7200
www.stuartschool.com

Sussex County Community
College
1 College Hill
Newton, NJ 7860
973-300-2218
www.sussex.edu

The Chubb Institute
40 Journal Square, 1st Floor
Jersey City, NJ 7306
201-876-3800
www.chubbinstitute.com/

The Cittone Institute
1697 Oak Tree Rd.
Edison, NJ 8820
732-548-2651
www.cittone.com

Warren County Community
College
475 Route 57 West
Washington, NJ 07882-4343
908-835-9222
www.warren.edu

New York

Adirondack Beauty School
108 Dix Ave.
Glens Falls, NY 12801
518-745-1646

American Academy
McAllister Institute of
Funeral Service
450 West 56th St.
New York, NY 10019-3602
212-757-1190
www.a-a-m-i.org

Austin Beauty School
527 Central Ave.
Albany, NY 12206
518-438-7879

Beauty School of
Middletown
225 Dolson Ave.
Middletown, NY 10940
845-343-2171

Bryant and Stratton College
1259 Central Ave.
Albany, NY 12205-5230
518-437-1802
www.bryantstratton.edu

Bryant and Stratton College,
North Campus
8687 Carling Rd.
Liverpool, NY 13090-1315
315-652-6500
www.bryantstratton.edu

Buffalo Vocational Technical
Center-Practical Nursing
820 Northhampton St.
Buffalo, NY 14211
716-897-8108

Cattaraugus County BOCES-
School of Practical Nursing
1825 Windfall Rd.
Olean, NY 14760
716-376-8217

Charles Stuart School of
Diamond Setting
1420 Kings Hwy, 2nd Floor
Brooklyn, NY 11229
718-339-2640

Cheryl Fells School of
Business
2541 Military Rd.
Niagara Falls, NY 14304
716-297-2750

Continental School of
Beauty Culture
1050 Union Rd.
West Seneca, NY 14224
716-675-8205

Continental School of
Beauty Culture-Jefferson
633 Jefferson Rd.
Rochester, NY 14623
716-272-8060

Continental School of
Beauty Culture-Kenmore
326 Kenmore Ave.
Buffalo, NY 14223
716-833-5016

Continental School of
Beauty Culture-Olean
515 North Union St.
Olean, NY 14760
716-372-5095

Dutchess BOCES School of
Practical Nursing
578 Salt Point Turnpike
Poughkeepsie, NY 12601-6599
845-486-8045

FEGS Trades and Business
School
199 Jay St.
Brooklyn, NY 11201
212-366-8450

Finger Lakes Community
College
4355 Lakeshore Drive
Canandaigua, NY 14424-8395
716-394-3500
www.flcc.edu

Global Business Institute
1931 Mott Ave.
Far Rockaway, NY 11691
718-327-2220

Global Business Institute
209 West 125th St.
New York, NY 10027
212-663-1500

Hair Design Institute at
Fifth Avenue
6711 5th Ave.
Brooklyn, NY 11220
718-745-1000 Ext. 100

Hamilton-Fulton-
Montgomery BOCES
212 County Hwy 103
Johnstown, NY 12095

Herkimer County BOCES
Practical Nursing Program
352 Gros Blvd
Herkimer, NY 13350
315-867-2040

Hudson Valley Community
College
80 Vandenburgh Ave.
Troy, NY 12180-6096
518-629-7309
www.hvcc.edu

Jamestown Community
College
525 Falconer St.
Jamestown, NY 14701-1999
716-665-5220
www.sunyjcc.edu

Jefferson-Lewis BOCES
Program of Practical Nursing
20104 New York State Rt. 3
Watertown, NY 13601
315-779-7200

Jon Louis School of Beauty
210 East 188th St.
Bronx, NY 10458
718-733-2828

Jon Louis School of Beauty
91-14 Merrick Blvd
Jamaica, NY 11435
718-658-6240

Learning Institute for Beauty
Sciences
38-15 Brd.way
Astoria, NY 11103
718-726-8383

Learning Institute for Beauty
Sciences
2384 86th St.
Brooklyn, NY 11214
718-373-2400
www.libs.org

Learning Institute for Beauty
Sciences
173A Fulton Ave.
Hempstead, NY 11550
516-483-6259

Lynn Educational Alternative
Program
Route 28, Box 1159
Old Forge, NY 13420-1159
315-369-2740

Midway Paris Beauty School
54-40 Myrtle Ave.
Ridgewood, NY 11385
718-418-2790

National Tractor Trailer
School, Inc.
PO Box 208
Liverpool, NY 13088-0208
315-451-2430

National Tractor Trailer
School, Inc.-Buffalo Campus
175 Katherine St.
Buffalo, NY 14210-2007
716-849-6887

New School of Radio and
Television
50 Colvin Ave.
Albany, NY 12206
518-438-7682
www.nsrt.org

New York Institute of
Massage
4701 Transit Rd.
Box 645
Buffalo, NY 14231
716-633-0355 Ext. 214
www.nyinstituteofmassage.com

New York International
Beauty School, Ltd.
210 West 50 St.
New York, NY 10019
212-868-7171

New York School of Interior
Design
170 East 70th St.
New York, NY 10021-5110
212-472-1500 Ext. 202
www.nysid.edu

North Country Community
College
20 Winona Ave., PO Box 89
Saranac Lake, NY 12983-0089
518-891-2915
www.nccc.edu

Paul Smith's College of Arts
and Sciences
PO Box 265
Paul Smiths, NY 12970-0265
518-327-6227
www.paulsmiths.edu

Samaritan Hospital School
of Nursing
2215 Burdett Ave.
Troy, NY 12180
518-271-3285

Schuyler-Chemung-Tioga
Practical Nursing Program
459 Philo Rd.
Elmira, NY 14903
607-739-8170

Shear Ego International
School of Hair Design
525 Titus Ave.
Rochester, NY 14617
716-342-0070

State University of New York
College of Agriculture and
Technology at Cobleskill
Cobleskill, NY 12043
518-234-5525
www.cobleskill.edu

State University of New York
College of Technology at
Alfred
Alfred, NY 14802
607-587-4215
www.alfredstate.edu

Steuben-Allegany BOCES
School of Practical Nursing-
Coopers
1 Vocational Drive, Coopers
Education Center
Painted Post, NY 14870
607-962-3523

Steuben-Allegany BOCES
School of Practical Nursing-
Warsaw
422 North Main St.
Warsaw, NY 14569
877-238-5833

Studio Jewelers
32 East 31 St.
New York, NY 10016-4112

Suburban Technical School
175 Fulton Ave.
Hempstead, NY 11550
516-481-9775

The Culinary Institute of
America
1946 Campus Drive
Hyde Park, NY 12538-1499
845-451-1327
www.ciachef.edu

Tompkins Cortland
Community College
170 North St., PO Box 139
Dryden, NY 13053-0139
607-844-8211
www.sunytccc.edu

Triple Cities School of
Beauty Culture
5 Court St.
Binghamton, NY 13901
607-722-1279

Trocaire College
360 Choate Ave.
Buffalo, NY 14220-2094
716-826-1200
www.trocaire.edu

Willsey Institute
120 Stuyvesant Place
Staten Island, NY 10301
718-422-5706

Pennsylvania

Academy of Creative Hair
Design
252 West Side Mall Office
Complex
Kingston, PA 18704
717-288-4574

All State Career School
97 Second St.
North Versailles, PA 15137
412-823-1818 Ext. 28

Allentown School of
Cosmetology, Inc.
1921 Union Blvd
Allentown, PA 18103-1629
610-437-4626
www.asc-ssc.com

Allied Medical and Technical
Careers
166 Slocum St.
Forty Fort, PA 18704-2936
570-288-8400
www.alliedteched.com

Allied Medical and Technical
Careers
571 Ash St.
Scranton, PA 18509-2903
570-558-1818

Alternative Conjunction
Clinic and School of
Massage Therapy
716 State St.
Lemoyne, PA 17403
717-737-7180

Ambler Beauty Academy
50 East Butler Pike
Ambler, PA 19002
215-643-5994

Bucks County School of
Beauty Culture, Inc.
1761 Bustleton Pike
Feasterville, PA 19647
215-322-0666
www.bcsbc.com

Business Institute of
Pennsylvania
628 Arch St., Ste. B105
Meadville, PA 16335
814-724-0700
www.biop.com

Butler Beauty School
233 South Main St.
Butler, PA 16001
724-287-0708

Cambria-Rowe Business
College
422 South 13th St.
Indiana, PA 15701
724-463-0222
www.crbc.net

Cambria-Rowe Business
College
221 Central Ave.
Johnstown, PA 15902-2494
814-536-5168
www.crbc.net

Career Training Academy-
Monroeville Campus
105 Mall Blvd, W, Ste. 300
Monroeville, PA 15146
412-372-3900
www.careerta.com

CHI Institute, RETS Campus
1991 Lawrence Rd., Ste. 42
Broomall, PA 19008
610-353-7630

Clearfield Beauty Academy
22 North Third St.
Clearfield, PA 16830
814-765-2022

Computer Learning Network
2900 Fairway Drive
Altoona, PA 16602
814-944-5643
www.clnaltoona.com

Conemaugh Valley Memorial
Hospital
1086 Franklin St.
Johnstown, PA 15905-4398
814-534-9844

Court Reporting Institute of
Orleans Technology Institute
1845 Walnut St., 7th Floor
Philadelphia, PA 19103-4707
215-854-1853

CSC Institute
1111 St. Rd., Ste. 222
Southhampton, PA 18966
215-396-7921

Dean Institute of Technology
1501 West Liberty Ave.
Pittsburgh, PA 15226-1103
412-531-4433
www.home.earthlink.net/~de
antech

Delaware County Technical
School
Delmar Drive and
Henderson Blvd
Folcroft, PA 19032-1998
610-583-2934

Empire Beauty School
171 Cedar Ave. Southgate
Shopping Center
Chambersburg, PA 17201
717-264-6300

Empire Beauty School
Clearview Shopping Center,
Carlisle St.
Hanover, PA 17331
717-633-6201

Empire Beauty School
3941 Jonestown Rd.
Harrisburg, PA 17109
570-652-8500

Empire Beauty School
124 West Brd. St.
Hazleton, PA 18201
570-454-8461

Empire Beauty School
1801 Columbia Ave.
Wheatland Shopping Center
Lancaster, PA 17603
717-394-8561

Empire Beauty School
1776 Quentin Rd., Cedar
Crest Square
Lebanon, PA 17042
717-272-3323

Empire Beauty School
5103 Carlisle Pike
Mechanicsburg, PA 17055
570-429-1800

Empire Beauty School
4026 Woodhaven Rd.
Philadelphia, PA 19154
215-637-3700
www.empirebeauty.com

Empire Beauty School
141 High St.
Pottstown, PA 19464
610-327-1313

Empire Beauty School
324 N. Centre St.
Pottsville, PA 17901
570-622-6060
www.empirebeauty.com

Empire Beauty School
2302 North 5th St.
Reading, PA 19605
610-372-2777

Empire-Lackawanna Beauty
School
219 Lackawanna Ave.
Scranton, PA 18503
570-346-1465

Franklin County Career and
Technology Center
2463 Loop Rd.
Chambersburg, PA 17201
717-263-5667

Gordon Phillips Beauty School
The Plaza on Mall Blvd
Monroeville, PA 15146
412-373-7727

Gordon Phillips Beauty School
1522 Chestnut St.
Philadelphia, PA 19102
215-568-3980

Gordon Phillips Beauty
School
7248 Frankford Ave.
Philadelphia, PA 19135
215-331-4444

Gordon Phillips School of
Beauty Culture
108 West Germantown Pike,
Hillcrest Plaza
Norristown, PA 19401
610-272-1555

Gwynedd-Mercy College
Sumneytown Pike
PO Box 901
Gwynedd Valley, PA
19437-0901
215-641-5530
www.gmc.edu

Hanover Public School
District-Practical Nursing
Program
403 Moul Ave.
Hanover, PA 17331
717-637-2111

Hazleton Area Career Center
Practical Nursing Program
1451 West 23rd St.
Hazleton, PA 18201
570-459-3178

Information Computer
Systems Institute
2201 Hangar Place
Allentown, PA 18103-9504
610-264-8029
www.icsinstitute.com

Institute for Career Training-
School of Welding
100 Pennsylvania Ave.
Selinsgrove, PA 17870-9339
570-743-5500

Jean Madeline Education
Center
315a Bainbridge St.
Philadelphia, PA 19147
215-574-9670 Ext. 19

JNA Institute of Culinary Arts
1212 South Brd. St.
Philadelphia, PA 19146
215-468-8800
www.culinaryarts.com

Keystone College
One College Green
La Plume, PA 18440
800-824-2764
www.keystone.edu

L.T. International Beauty
School
1238 Spring Garden St.
Philadelphia, PA 19123
215-922-4478

Lackawanna College
501 Vine St.
Scranton, PA 18509
570-961-7841
www.lackawanna.edu

Lansdale School of Business
201 Church Rd.
North Wales, PA 19454-4148
215-699-5700
www.lsbonline.com

Laurel Business Institute
11-15 Penn St.
Uniontown, PA 15401
724-439-4900
www.laurelbusiness.net

Lebanon County Area
Vocational Technical School
833 Metro Drive
Lebanon, PA 17042
717-273-8551

McCann School of Business
2650 Woodglen Rd.
Pottsville, PA 17901
570-622-7622
www.mccannschool.com

Mercer County Area
Vocational Technical School
776 Greenville Rd.
Mercer, PA 16137-0152
724-662-3000 Ext. 1410

Mercyhurst College
501 East 38th St.
Erie, PA 16546
814-824-2202
www.mercyhurst.edu

Metropolitan Career Center
100 South Brd. St.
Philadelphia, PA 19110
215-568-9215 Ext. 306
www.metropolitancareer-
center.org

Newport Business Institute
945 Greensburg Rd.
Lower Burrell, PA 15068-3929
724-339-7542
www.newportbusiness.com

Newport Business Institute
941 West Third St.
Williamsport, PA 17701-5855
570-326-2869
www.newportbusiness.com

Northern Tier Career Center-
Practical Nursing Program
RR 1
Box 157A
Towanda, PA 18848-9731
570-265-8113

Penn State Cosmetology
Academy
2200 East State St.
Hermitage, PA 16148
724-347-4503

Pennsylvania Academy of
Cosmetology and Sciences
2445 Bedford St.
Johnstown, PA 15904
814-269-3444

Pennsylvania College of
Technology
One College Ave.
Williamsport, PA 17701-5778
570-327-4761
www.pct.edu

Pennsylvania Institute of
Taxidermy, Inc.
118 Industrial Park Rd.
Ebensberg, PA 15931
814-472-4510

Pittsburgh Beauty Academy
313 Fifth Ave.
Charleroi, PA 15022
724-483-3551

Pittsburgh Institute of
Mortuary Science,
Incorporated
5808 Baum Blvd
Pittsburgh, PA 15206-3706
412-362-8500
www.p-i-m-s.com

Pittsburgh Technical Institute
635 Smithfield St.
Pittsburgh, PA 15222-2560
412-809-5100
www.pittsburghtechnical.com

Presbyterian Medical Center,
University of Pennsylvania
Health System, School of
Practical
39th and Market St.s
Philadelphia, PA 19104
215-662-9165

Pruonto's Hair Design
Institute
705 12th St.
Altoona, PA 16602
814-944-4494
www.pruontos.com

Punxy Beauty School
222 Findley St.
Punxsutawney, PA 15767
814-938-8811

Schuylkill Institute of
Business and Technology
171 Red Horse Rd.
Pottsville, PA 17901
570-622-4835

South Hills Beauty Academy
3269 West Liberty Ave.
Pittsburgh, PA 15216
412-561-3381

Star Technical Institute
844 West Market St.
Kingston, PA 18704
570-331-2006

Star Technical Institute
1619 Walnut St., 3rd Floor
Philadelphia, PA 19103
215-640-0177

Star Technical Institute-
Allentown
2102 Union Blvd
Allentown, PA 18103
610-434-9963

Star Technical Institute-
Scranton Campus
1636 Nay Aug Ave.
Green Ridge Plaza
Scranton, PA 18509
201-222-1700
www.startechinstitute.com

Stroudsburg School of
Cosmetology
100 North Eighth St.
Stroudsburg, PA 18360-1720
570-421-3387
www.asc-ssc.com

The Art Institute of
Pittsburgh
420 Blvd of the Allies
Pittsburgh, PA 15219
800-275-2470
www.aip.aii.edu

The Chubb Institute
965 Baltimore Pike
Springfield, PA 19064-3957
610-338-2300

The PJA School
7900 West Chester Pike
Upper Darby, PA 19082-1926
610-789-6700
www.pjaschool.com

Thompson Institute
2593 Philadelphia Ave.
Chambersburg, PA 17201
717-709-9400
www.thompsoninstitute.com

Thompson Institute
5650 Derry St.
Harrisburg, PA 17111-3518
717-564-4112
www.thompsoninstitute.org

Triangle Tech, Inc.-
Greensburg Center
222 East Pittsburgh St., Ste. A
Greensburg, PA 15601-3304
724-832-1050
www.triangle-tech.com

Ultrasound Diagnostic
School
Pittsburgh, PA 15232
412-362-9404

Ultrasound Diagnostic
School
3 Neshaminy Interplex,
Ste. 117
Trevose, PA 19053
215-244-4906

Venango County Area
Vocational Technical School
1. Vo-Tech Drive
Oil City, PA 16301
814-677-3097 Ext. 207

Wilma Boyd Career Schools,
Inc.
1412 Beers School Rd.
Moon Township, PA
15108-2549
412-299-2200
www.boydschool.com

York County Area Vocational
Tech School-Practical
Nursing Program
2179 South Queen St.
York, PA 17402
717-741-0820 Ext. 2302

York Technical Institute
1405 Williams Rd.
York, PA 17402-9017
717-757-1100
www.yti.edu

Virginia

Americas Computers
Training Source
3333 Virginia Beach Blvd,
Ste. 28
Virginia Beach, VA 23452
757-340-1111 Ext. 330

Applied Career Training, Inc.
1100 Wilson Blvd, Mall Level
Arlington, VA 22209
703-527-6660
www.healthtraining.com

Beta Tech
7914 Midlothian Turnpike
Richmond, VA 23235
804-330-0111
www.tidetech.com

Blue Ridge Community
College
PO Box 80
Weyers Cave, VA 24486-0080
540-234-9261 Ext. 2287
www.brcc.edu

Bryant and Stratton College,
Virginia Beach
301 Centre Pointe Drive
Virginia Beach, VA
23462-4417
757-499-7900
www.bryantstratton.edu

Center For Employment
Training-Alexandria
2762 Duke St.
Alexandria, VA 22301
408-287-7924

Central School of Practical
Nursing
1330 North Military Hwy
Norfolk, VA 23502
757-892-3300

Central Virginia Community
College
3506 Wards Rd.
Lynchburg, VA 24502-2498
804-832-7633
www.cvcc.vccs.edu

Colonial Heights Beauty
Academy
1851 Southpark Blvd
Colonial Heights, VA 23834
804-526-6363

Dabney S. Lancaster
Community College
100 Dabney Drive,
PO Box 1000
Clifton Forge, VA 24422
540-863-2815
www.dl.vccs.edu

Dominion College
5372 Fallowater Lane, Ste. B
Roanoke, VA 24014
540-776-8381
www.dominioncollege.org

Eastern Shore Community
College
29300 Lankford Hwy
Melfa, VA 23410-3000
757-787-5913
www.es.cc.va.us

ECPI College of Technology
5555 Greenwich Rd.
Virginia Beach, VA 23462
757-671-7171
www.ecpi.edu

ECPI Technical College
800 Moorefield Park Drive
Richmond, VA 23236
804-330-5533
www.ecpi.net

ECPI Technical College
5234 Airport Rd.
Roanoke, VA 24012
540-563-8080
www.ecpi.net

Germanna Community
College
2130 Germanna Hwy
Locust Grove, VA 22508-2102
540-727-3030
www.so.cc.va.us

Ghent Beauty Academy
2811 Lafayette Blvd
Norfolk, VA 23509
757-855-2107
www.ghentbeauty.qpg.com

Graham Webb International
Academy of Hair
2625 Wilson Blvd
Arlington, VA 22201
703-243-9322 Ext. 113

Hampton Rd.s School of
Hair Technology
3535f Tidewater Drive
Norfolk, VA 23509
Hampton University
Hampton, VA 23668
757-727-5328
www.hamptonu.edu

Henrico County-Saint Marys
Hospital School of Practical
Nursing
201 East Nine Mile Rd.
Highland Springs, VA 23075
804-328-4095

Hicks Academy of Beauty
Culture
436 Boush St.
Norfolk, VA 23510
757-399-7677

Indian River Beauty
Academy
6528 Indian River Rd.
Virginia Beach, VA 23464
757-420-1645

J. Sargeant Reynolds
Community College
PO Box 85622
Richmond, VA 23285-5622
804-371-3029
www.jsr.vccs.edu

John Tyler Community
College
13101 Jefferson Davis Hwy
Chester, VA 23831-5316
804-796-4362
www.jt.cc.va.us

Johnsons Beauty Academy
402 North Second St.
Richmond, VA 23219-1704
804-649-2572

Lord Fairfax Community
College
173 Skirmisher Lane
PO Box 47
Middletown, VA 22645-0047
540-868-7150
www.lf.vccs.edu

Medical Careers Institute
11790 Jefferson Ave.
Newport News, VA 23606
757-873-2423
www.medicalcareers
institute.com

Miller-Motte Technical
College
1912 Memorial Ave.
Lynchburg, VA 24501
804-847-7701
www.millermotte.net

Mountain Empire
Community College
PO Drawer 700
Big Stone Gap, VA
24219-0700
276-523-7474
www.me.vccs.edu

New Horizons Regional
Education Center School of
Practical Nursing
520 Butler Farm Rd.
Hampton, VA 23666
757-766-1100 Ext. 336

New River Community
College
PO Box 1127
Dublin, VA 24084-1127
540-674-3603
www.nr.cc.va.us

NNPS RRMC School of
Practical Nursing
12420 Warwick Blvd, Ste. 6G
Newport News, VA 23606
757-594-2722

Norfolk Skills Center
922 West 21st St.
Norfolk, VA 23517-1516
757-628-3300

Paul D. Camp Community
College
PO Box 737,
100 North College Drive
Franklin, VA 23851-0737
757-569-6725
www.pc.vccs.edu

Potomac Academy of Hair
Design
350 South Washington St.
Falls Church, VA 22046
703-532-5050 Ext. 110
www.naccas.org/
potomacacademy

Rappahannock Community
College
12745 College Drive
Glenns, VA 23149-2616
804-758-6740
www.rcc.vccs.edu

Riverside School of Health
Occupations
12420 Warwick Blvd
Ste. 6G
Newport News, VA 23606
757-594-2722

Sentara Norfolk General
Hospital School of Health
Professions
600 Gresham Drive,
Jenkins Hall
Norfolk, VA 23507
757-668-2666

Southside School of
Practical Nursing
800 Oak St.
Farmville, VA 23901
804-315-2630

Southside Virginia
Community College
109 Campus Drive
Alberta, VA 23821-9719
434-949-1014
www.sv.vccs.edu

Southwest Virginia
Community College
PO Box SVCC
Richlands, VA 24641-1101
276-964-2555 Ext. 238
www.sw.edu

Staunton School of
Cosmetology, Inc.
128 East Beverly St.
PO Box 2385
Staunton, VA 24401
540-885-0808

Stratford University
7777 Leesburg Pike,
Ste. 100 South
Falls Church, VA 22043
800-444-0804 Ext. 3260
www.stratford.edu

Strayer University at
Henrico Campus
11551 Nuckols Rd., #D
Glen Allen, VA 23059
804-527-1000
www.strayer.edu

Suffolk Beauty School
860 Portsmouth Blvd
Suffolk, VA 23434-3020
757-934-0656

The School of Hair Design
3535 D Franklin Rd., SW
Roanoke, VA 24014
540-343-0153

Tidewater Tech
932 Ventures Way
Chesapeake, VA 23320
757-549-2121

Tidewater Tech
7020 North Military Hwy
Norfolk, VA 23518
757-853-2121 Ext. 206

Tidewater Tech
1429 Miller Store Rd.
Virginia Beach, VA 23455
757-363-2121

Tidewater Tech-Newport
News Campus
616 Denbigh Blvd
Newport News, VA 23608
757-874-2121
www.tidetech.com

Virginia School of Hair
Design
101 West Queens Way
Hampton, VA 23669
757-722-0211

Virginia School of Massage
2008 Morton Drive
Charlottesville, VA 22903
434-293-4031
www.vasom.com

Virginia Western Community
College
PO Box 14007
Roanoke, VA 24038
540-857-7231
www.vw.vccs.edu

Wards Corner Beauty
Academy
216 East Little Creek Rd.
Norfolk, VA 23505
757-583-3300

Washington County Adult
Skill Center
848 Thompson Drive
Abingdon, VA 24210
703-676-1948
www.wcskillcenter.org

Wytheville Community
College
1000 East Main St.
Wytheville, VA 24382-3308
276-223-4755
www.wcc.vccs.edu

West Virginia

B. M. Spurr School of
Practical Nursing
800 Wheeling Ave.
Glen Dale, WV 26038
304-843-3255

Beckley Beauty Academy
109 South Fayette St.
Beckley, WV 25801
304-253-8326

Clarksburg Beauty Academy
120 South 3rd St.
Clarksburg, WV 26301
304-624-6475

Fred W. Eberle School of
Practical Nursing
Route 5
Box 2
Buckhannon, WV 26201
304-472-1259

Human Resource
Development and Training
1644 Mileground
Morgantown, WV 26505
304-296-8223
www.stanleytechnical.com

Human Resources
Development and
Employment
120 South Linden Ave.
Clarksburg, WV 26301-2270
304-623-6367

Human Resources
Development and Employment
278c Spruce St.
Morgantown, WV
26505-7525
304-296-3548

Human Resources
Development and
Employment
800 Camden Ave.
Parkersburg, WV 26101
304-422-3331

Huntington School of Beauty
Culture-Main Campus
5185 Route 60, East Hills Mall
Huntington, WV 25705-2030
304-736-6289

Morgantown Beauty
College, Inc.
276 Walnut St.
Morgantown, WV 26505
304-292-8475 Ext. 4

Mountaineer Beauty College
700 Sixth Ave.
PO Box 547
St. Albans, WV 25177
304-727-9999

Scott College of
Cosmetology
1502 Market St.
Wheeling, WV 26003
304-232-7798

Valley College of Technology
330 Harper Park Drive
Beckley, WV 25801
304-252-9547
www.valleycollege.com

Valley College of Technology
2600 Aikens Center
Edwin Miller Blvd
Martinsburg, WV 25401
304-263-0979
www.vct.edu

West Virginia Junior College
176 Thompson Drive
Bridgeport, WV 26330
304-363-8824

Wood County Vocational
School of Practical Nursing
1515 Blizzard Drive
Parkersburg, WV 26101-6424
304-420-9651

SCHOLARSHIPS AND FINANCIAL AID

Delaware

Christa McAuliffe Teacher Scholarship Loan

Award for Delaware residents who are pursuing teaching careers. Must agree to teach in Delaware public schools as repayment of loan. Minimum award is $1000 and is renewable for up to four years. Available only at Delaware colleges. Based on academic merit. Must be ranked in upper half of class, and have a score of 1050 on SAT or 25 on the ACT Assessment. **Award:** Forgivable loan for use in freshman, sophomore, junior, or senior years; renewable. **Number:** 1-60. **Amount:** $1000-$5000. **Eligibility Requirements:** Applicant must be enrolled or expecting to enroll full-time at a four-year institution or university; resident of Delaware and studying in Delaware. Applicant must have 2.5 GPA or higher. Available to U.S. citizens. **Application Requirements:** Application, essay, test scores, transcript. **Application deadline:** March 31. **Contact:** Donna Myers, Higher Education Analyst, Delaware Higher Education Commission, 820 North French St., 5th Floor, Wilmington, DE 19711-3509. **Phone:** 302-577-3240. **E-mail:** dhec@doe.k12.de.us

Delaware Nursing Incentive Scholarship Loan

Award for Delaware residents pursuing a nursing career. Must be repaid with nursing practice at a Delaware state-owned hospital. Based on academic merit. Must have minimum 2.5 GPA. Renewable for up to four years. Academic Fields/Career Goals Nursing. **Award:** Forgivable loan for use in freshman, sophomore, junior, or senior years; renewable. **Number:** 1-40. **Amount:** $1000-$5000. **Eligibility Requirements:** Applicant must be enrolled or expecting to enroll full-time at a two-year or four-year institution or university and resident of Delaware. Applicant must have 2.5 GPA or higher. Available to U.S. citizens. **Application Requirements:** Application, essay, test scores, transcript. **Application Deadline:** March 31. **Contact:** Donna Myers, Higher Education Analyst, Delaware Higher Education Commission, 820 North French St., 5th Floor, Wilmington, DE 19711-3509. **Phone:** 302-577-3240. **E-mail:** dhec@doe.k12.de.us

Delaware Solid Waste Authority Scholarship

Scholarships given to residents of Delaware who are high school seniors or freshmen or sophomores in college. Must be majoring in either environmental engineering or environmental sciences in a Delaware college. Must file the Free Application for Federal Student Aid (FAFSA). Scholarships are automatically renewed for three years if a 3.0 GPA is maintained. **Award:** Scholarship for use in freshman or sophomore years; renewable. **Amount:** $2000. **Eligibility Requirements:** Applicant must be enrolled or expecting to enroll full-time at a two-year or four-year institution or university; resident of Delaware and studying in Delaware. Applicant must have 3.0 GPA or higher. **Application Requirements:** Financial need analysis, FAFSA. **Application Deadline:** March 15. **Contact:** Donna Myers, Higher Education Analyst, Delaware Higher Education Commission, 820 North French St., 5th Floor, Wilmington, DE 19711-3509. **Phone:** 302-577-3240. **E-mail:** dhec@doe.k12.de.us

Diamond State Scholarship

Renewable award for Delaware high school seniors enrolling full-time at an accredited college or university. Must be ranked in upper quarter of class and score 1200 on SAT or 27 on the ACT Assessment. **Award:** Scholarship for use in freshman year; renewable. **Number:** 50-200. **Amount:** $1250. **Eligibility Requirements:** Applicant must be high school student; planning to enroll or expecting to enroll full-time at a four-year institution or university and resident of Delaware. Applicant must have 3.5 GPA or higher. Available to U.S. citizens. **Application Requirements:** Application, essay, test scores, transcript. **Application Deadline:** March 31. **Contact:** Donna Myers, Higher Education Analyst, Delaware Higher Education Commission, 820 North French St., 5th Floor, Wilmington, DE 19711-3509. **Phone:** 302-577-3240. **E-mail:** dhec@doe.k12.de.us

Educational Benefits for Children of Deceased Military and State Police

Renewable award for Delaware residents who are children of state or military police who were killed in the line of duty. Must attend a Delaware institution unless program of study is not available. Funds cover tuition and fees at Delaware institutions. The amount varies at non-Delaware institutions. Must submit proof of service and related death. Must be ages 16-24 at time of application. Deadline is three weeks before classes begin. **Award:** Grant for use in freshman, sophomore, junior, or senior years; renewable. **Number:** 1-10. **Amount:** $6255. **Eligibility Requirements:** Applicant must be age 16-24; enrolled or expecting to enroll full-time at a two-year or four-year institution or university and resident of Delaware. Applicant or parent of applicant must have employment or volunteer experience in police/firefighting. Available to U.S. citizens. Applicant or parent must meet one or more of the following requirements: general military experience; retired from active duty; disabled or killed as a result of military service; prisoner of war; or missing in action. **Application Requirements:** Application, verification of service-related death. **Application Deadline:** Continuous. **Contact:** Donna Myers, Higher Education Analyst Delaware Higher Education Commission, 820 North French St. 5th Floor, Wilmington, DE 19711-3509. **Phone:** 302-577-3240. **E-mail:** dhec@doe.k12.de.us

Legislative Essay Scholarship

Must be a senior in high school and Delaware resident. Submit an essay of 500 to 2000 words on a designated historical topic (changes annually). For more information visit: www.doe.state.de.us/high-ed. **Award:** Scholarship for use in freshman year; not renewable. **Number:** 62. **Amount:** $500-$5500. **Eligibility Requirements:** Applicant must be high school student; planning to enroll or expecting to enroll full or part-time at a two-year, four-year, or technical institution or university and resident of Delaware. Available to U.S. citizens. **Application Requirements:** Application, applicant must enter a contest, essay. **Application Deadline:** November 16. **Contact:** Donna Myers, Higher Education Analyst, Delaware Higher Education Commission, 820 North French St. 5th Floor, Wilmington, DE 19711-3509. **Phone:** 302-577-3240. **E-mail:** dhec@doe.k12.de.us

Scholarship Incentive Program

One-time award for Delaware residents with financial need. May be used at an institution in Delaware or Pennsylvania, or at another out-of-state institution if a program is not available at a publicly-supported school in Delaware. Must have minimum 2.5 GPA. **Award:** Grant for use in freshman, sophomore, junior, or senior years; not renewable. **Number:** 1000-1300. **Amount:** $700-$2200. **Eligibility Requirements:** Applicant must be enrolled or expecting to enroll full-time at a two-year or four-year institution or university; resident of Delaware and studying in Delaware or Pennsylvania. Applicant must have 2.5 GPA or higher. Available to U.S. citizens. **Application Requirements:** Application, financial need analysis, transcript. **Application Deadline:** April 15. **Contact:** Donna Myers, Higher Education Analyst, Delaware Higher Education Commission, 820 North French St. 5th Floor, Wilmington, DE 19711-3509. **Phone:** 302-577-3240. **E-mail:** dhec@doe.k12.de.us

State Tuition Assistance

Award providing tuition assistance for any member of the Air or Army National Guard attending a Delaware two-year or four-year college. Awards are renewable. Applicant's minimum GPA must be 2.0. For full- or part-time study. Amount of award varies. **Award:** Scholarship for use in freshman, sophomore, junior, or senior years; renewable. **Eligibility Requirements:** Applicant must be enrolled or expecting to enroll full or part-time at a two-year or four-year institution and studying in Delaware. Available to U.S. citizens. Applicant must have served in the Air Force National Guard or Army National Guard. **Application Requirements:** **Application Deadline:** Continuous. **Contact:** TSgt. Robert Csizmadia, State Tuition Assistance Manager, Delaware National Guard, First Regiment Rd., Wilmington, DE 19808-2191. **Phone:** 302-326-7012. **E-mail:** robert.csizmadi@de.ngb.army.mil

District of Columbia

American Council of the Blind Scholarships

Merit-based award available to undergraduate, graduate, vocational or technical students who are legally blind in both eyes. Submit certificate of legal blindness and proof of acceptance at an accredited postsecondary institution. **Award:** Scholarship for use in freshman, sophomore, junior, senior, or graduate years; not renewable. **Number:** 30. **Amount:** $500-$5000. **Eligibility Requirements:** Applicant must be

enrolled or expecting to enroll full-time at a two-year, four-year, or technical institution or university. Applicant must be visually impaired. Applicant must have 3.5 GPA or higher. **Application Requirements:** Application, autobiography, essay, references, transcript. **Application Deadline:** March 1. **Contact:** Terry Pacheco, Affiliate and Membership Services, American Council of the Blind, 1155 15th St., NW, Ste. 1004, Washington, DC 20005. **Phone:** 202-467-5081. **E-mail:** info@acb.org

DC Leveraging Educational Assistance Partnership Program (LEAP)

Available to Washington, D.C. residents who have financial need. Must also apply for the Federal Pell Grant. Must attend an eligible college at least half-time. Contact financial aid office or local library for more information. Proof of residency may be required. Deadline is last Friday in June. Award Scholarship for use in freshman, sophomore, junior, or senior years; not renewable. **Number:** 1200-1500. **Amount:** $500-$1500. **Eligibility Requirements:** Applicant must be enrolled or expecting to enroll full or part-time at a two-year, four-year, or technical institution or university and resident of District of Columbia. Available to U.S. citizens. **Application Requirements:** Application, financial need analysis, Student Aid Report (SAR). **Application Deadline:** June 28. **Contact:** Angela March, Program Manager, District of Columbia State Education Office, 441 4th St. NW, Ste. 350 North, Washington, DC 20001. **Phone:** 202-727-6436. **E-mail:** angela.march@dc.gov

Maryland

Child Care Provider Program

Forgivable loan provides assistance for Maryland undergraduates attending a Maryland institution and pursuing studies in a child development program or an early childhood education program. Must serve as a professional day care provider in Maryland for one year for each year award received. Must maintain minimum 2.0 GPA. Contact for further information. **Award:** Forgivable loan for use in freshman, sophomore, junior, or senior years; renewable. **Number:** 100-150. **Amount:** $500-$2000. **Eligibility Requirements:** Applicant must be enrolled or expecting to enroll full or part-time at a two-year or four-year institution or university; resident of

Maryland and studying in Maryland. Available to U.S. citizens. **Application Requirements:** Application, transcript. **Application Deadline:** June 15. **Contact:** Margaret Crutchley, Office of Student Financial Assistance, Maryland Higher Education Commission, 839 Bestgate Rd., Ste. 400, Annapolis, MD 21401-3013. **Phone:** 410-260-4545. **E-mail:** ofsamail@mhec.state.md.us

Delegate Scholarship Program

Delegate scholarships help Maryland residents attending Maryland degree-granting institutions, certain career schools, or nursing diploma schools. May attend out-of-state institution if Maryland Higher Education Commission deems major to be unique and not offered at a Maryland institution. Free Application for Federal Student Aid may be required. Students interested in this program should apply by contacting their legislative district delegate. **Award:** Scholarship for use in freshman, sophomore, junior, senior, or graduate years; not renewable. **Number:** up to 3500. **Amount:** $200-$12,981. **Eligibility Requirements:** Applicant must be enrolled or expecting to enroll full or part-time at a two-year, four-year, or technical institution or university; resident of Maryland and studying in Maryland. Available to U.S. citizens. **Application Requirements:** Application, financial need analysis. **Application Deadline:** Continuous. **Contact:** Barbara Fantom, Office of Student Financial Assistance, Maryland Higher Education Commission, 839 Bestgage Rd., Ste. 400, Annapolis, MD 21401-3013. **Phone:** 410-260-4547. **E-mail:** osfamail@mhec.state.md.us

Developmental Disabilities and Mental Health Workforce Tuition Assistance Program

Provides tuition assistance to students who are service employees that provide direct support or care to individuals with developmental disabilities or mental disorders. Must be a Maryland resident attending a Maryland college. Minimum 2.0 GPA. **Award:** Forgivable loan for use in freshman, sophomore, junior, senior, or graduate years; renewable. **Number:** 300-400. **Amount:** $500-$3000. **Eligibility Requirements:** Applicant must be enrolled or expecting to enroll full or part-time at a two-year or four-year institution or university; resident of Maryland and studying in Maryland. Applicant or parent of applicant must have employment or volunteer experience in designated career field. Available to U.S. citizens. **Application Requirements:** Application, transcript. **Application Deadline:** July 1.

Contact: Gerrie Rogers, Office of Student Financial Assistance, Maryland Higher Education Commission, 839 Bestgate Rd., Ste. 400, Annapolis, MD 21401. **Phone:** 410-260-4574. **E-mail:** osfamail@mhec.state.md.us

Distinguished Scholar Award

Renewable award for Maryland students enrolled full-time at Maryland institutions. National Merit Scholar Finalists automatically offered award. Others may qualify for the award in satisfying criteria of a minimum 3.7 GPA or in combination with high test scores, or for Talent in Arts competition in categories of music, drama, dance, or visual arts. Must maintain annual 3.0 GPA in college for award to be renewed. Contact for further details. **Award:** Scholarship for use in freshman, sophomore, junior, or senior years; renewable. **Number:** up to 2000. **Amount:** up to $3000. **Eligibility Requirements:** Applicant must be high school student; planning to enroll or expecting to enroll full-time at a two-year or four-year institution or university; resident of Maryland and studying in Maryland. Available to U.S. citizens. **Application Requirements:** Application, test scores, transcript. **Application Deadline:** March 1. **Contact:** Monica Tipton, Office of Student Financial Assistance, Maryland Higher Education Commission, 839 Bestgate Rd., Ste. 400, Annapolis, MD 21401-3013. **Phone:** 410-260-4568. **E-mail:** ofsamail@mhec.state.md.us

Distinguished Scholar-Teacher Education Awards

Up to $3,000 award for Maryland high school seniors who have received the Distinguished Scholar Award. Recipient must enroll as a full-time undergraduate in a Maryland institution and pursue a program of study leading to a Maryland teaching certificate. Must maintain annual 3.0 GPA for renewal. Must teach in a Maryland public school one year for each year award is received. **Award:** Forgivable loan for use in freshman, sophomore, junior, or senior years; renewable. **Number:** 20-80. **Amount:** up to $3000. **Eligibility Requirements:** Applicant must be high school student; planning to enroll or expecting to enroll full-time at a two-year or four-year institution or university; resident of Maryland and studying in Maryland. Applicant must have 3.0 GPA or higher. Available to U.S. citizens. **Application Requirements:** Application, test scores, transcript, must be recipient of the Distinguished

Scholar Award. **Application Deadline:** Continuous. **Contact:** Monica Tipton, Office of Student Financial Assistance, Maryland Higher Education Commission, 839 Bestgate Rd., Ste. 400, Annapolis, MD 21401-3013. **Phone:** 410-260-4568. **E-mail:** ofsamail@mhec.state.md.us

Educational Assistance Grants

Award for Maryland residents accepted or enrolled in a full-time undergraduate degree or certificate program at a Maryland institution or hospital nursing school. Must submit financial aid form by March 1. Must earn 2.0 GPA in college to maintain award. **Award:** Grant for use in freshman, sophomore, junior, or senior years; renewable. **Number:** 11,000-20,000. **Amount:** $400-$2700. **Eligibility Requirements:** Applicant must be enrolled or expecting to enroll full-time at a two-year or four-year institution or university; resident of Maryland and studying in Maryland. Available to U.S. citizens. **Application Requirements:** Application, financial need analysis. **Application Deadline:** March 1. **Contact:** Barbara Fantom, Office of Student Financial Assistance, Maryland Higher Education Commission, 839 Bestgate Rd., Ste. 400, Annapolis, MD 21401-3013. **Phone:** 410-260-4547. **E-mail:** osfamail@mhec.state.md.us

Edward T. Conroy Memorial Scholarship Program

Scholarship for dependents of deceased or 100% disabled U.S. Armed Forces personnel, the son, daughter, or surviving spouse of a victim of the September 11, 2001, terrorist attacks who died as a result of the attacks on the World Trade Center in New York City, the attack on the Pentagon in Virginia, or the crash of United Airlines Flight 93 in Pennsylvania; a POW/MIA of the Vietnam Conflict or his/her son or daughter; the son, daughter or surviving spouse (who has not remarried),of a state or local public safety employee or volunteer who died in the line of duty; or a state or local public safety employee or volunteer who was 100% disabled in the line of duty. Must be Maryland resident at time of disability. Submit applicable VA certification. Must be at least 16 years of age and attend Maryland institution. **Award:** Scholarship for use in freshman, sophomore, junior, senior, or graduate years; renewable. **Number:** up to 70. **Amount:** up to $12,981. **Eligibility Requirements:** Applicant must be age 16-24; enrolled or expecting to enroll full or part-time at a two-year or four-year institution or university; resident of Maryland and studying in

Maryland. Available to U.S. citizens. **Application Requirements:** Application, birth and death certificate, and disability papers. **Application Deadline:** July 30. **Contact:** Margaret Crutchley, Office of Student Financial Assistance, Maryland Higher Education Commission, 839 Bestgate Rd., Ste. 400, Annapolis, MD 21401-3013. **Phone:** 410-260-4545. **E-mail:** osfamail@mhec.state.md.us

Firefighter, Ambulance, and Rescue Squad Member Tuition Reimbursement Program

Award intended to reimburse members of rescue organizations serving Maryland communities for tuition costs of course work towards a degree or certificate in fire service or medical technology. Must attend a two- or four-year school in Maryland. Minimum 2.0 GPA. **Award:** Scholarship for use in freshman, sophomore, junior, or senior years; not renewable. **Number:** 100-300. **Amount:** $200-$4000. **Eligibility Requirements:** Applicant must be enrolled or expecting to enroll full or part-time at a two-year or four-year institution or university; resident of Maryland and studying in Maryland. Applicant or parent of applicant must have employment or volunteer experience in police/firefighting. Available to U.S. citizens. **Application Requirements:** Application, transcript. **Application Deadline:** July 1. **Contact:** Gerrie Rogers, Office of Student Financial Assistance Maryland Higher Education Commission, 839 Bestgate Rd., Ste. 400, Annapolis, MD 21401-3013. **Phone:** 410-260-4574. **E-mail:** ofsamail@mhec.state.md.us

Graduate and Professional Scholarship Program

Graduate and professional scholarships provide need-based financial assistance to students attending a Maryland school of medicine, dentistry, law, pharmacy, social work, or nursing. Funds are provided to specific Maryland colleges and universities. Students must demonstrate financial need and be Maryland residents. Contact institution financial aid office for more information. **Award:** Scholarship for use in freshman, sophomore, junior, senior, graduate, or postgraduate years; renewable. **Number:** 40-200. **Amount:** $1000-$5000. **Eligibility Requirements:** Applicant must be enrolled or expecting to enroll full or part-time at a four-year institution or university; resident of Maryland and studying in Maryland. Available to U.S. citizens. **Application Requirements:** Application, financial need analysis.

Application Deadline: March 1. **Contact:** Maryland Higher Education Commission, 839 Bestgate Rd., Ste. 400, Annapolis, MD 21401-3013.

Guaranteed Access Grant

Award for Maryland resident enrolling full-time in an undergraduate program at a Maryland institution. Must be under 22 at time of first award and begin college within one year of completing high school in Maryland with a minimum 2.5 GPA. Must have an annual family income less than 130% of the federal poverty level guideline. **Award:** Grant for use in freshman, sophomore, junior, or senior years; renewable. **Number:** up to 1000. **Amount:** $400-$10,200. **Eligibility Requirements:** Applicant must be enrolled or expecting to enroll full-time at a two-year or four-year institution or university; resident of Maryland and studying in Maryland. Applicant must have 2.5 GPA or higher. Available to U.S. citizens. **Application Requirements:** Application, financial need analysis, transcript. **Application Deadline:** Continuous. **Contact:** Theresa Lowe, Office of Student Financial Assistance, Maryland Higher Education Commission, 839 Bestgate Rd., Ste. 400, Annapolis, MD 21401-3013. **Phone:** 410-260-4555. **E-mail:** osfamail@mhec.state.md.us

Hope for Nontraditional Students-Community College Transfer Scholarship Program

Award available to students who transfer with minimum 3.0 GPA and 60 credits from a Maryland two-year college to a Maryland four-year college. Annual family income limit is $95,000. Must agree to work in Maryland for up to three years. Funds are limited. **Award:** Forgivable loan for use in junior or senior years; renewable. **Amount:** up to $3000. **Eligibility Requirements:** Applicant must be enrolled or expecting to enroll full-time at a four-year institution or university; resident of Maryland and studying in Maryland. Applicant must have 3.0 GPA or higher. Available to U.S. citizens. **Application Requirements:** Application, financial need analysis, transcript. **Application Deadline:** March 1. **Contact:** Office of Student Financial Assistance, Maryland Higher Education Commission, 839 Bestgate Rd., Ste. 400, Annapolis, MD 21401. **Phone:** 410-260-4565. **E-mail:** osfamail@mhec.state.md.us

Hope Scholarship

Student must be a high school senior at the time of application and must enroll in an eligible major. Family income may not exceed $95,000 annu-ally. Recipients must agree to work in the state of Maryland for one year for each year they accept the award. Funds are limited. **Award:** Forgivable loan for use in freshman, sophomore, junior, or senior years; renewable. **Amount:** $1000-$3000. **Eligibility Requirements:** Applicant must be high school student; planning to enroll or expecting to enroll full-time at a two-year or four-year institution or university; resident of Maryland and studying in Maryland. Applicant must have 3.0 GPA or higher. Available to U.S. citizens. **Application Requirements:** Application, financial need analysis, transcript. **Application Deadline:** March 1. **Contact:** Office of Financial Assistance, Maryland Higher Education Commission, 839 Bestgate Rd., Ste. 400, Annapolis, MD 21401. **Phone:** 410-260-4565. **E-mail:** osfamail@mhec.state.md.us

J.F. Tolbert Memorial Student Grant Program

Available to Maryland residents attending a private career school in Maryland with at least 18 clock hours per week. **Award:** Grant for use in freshman or sophomore years; not renewable. **Number:** 1000. **Amount:** up to $300. **Eligibility Requirements:** Applicant must be enrolled or expecting to enroll at a technical institution; resident of Maryland and studying in Maryland. Available to U.S. citizens. **Application Requirements:** Application, financial need analysis. **Application Deadline:** Continuous. **Contact:** Carla Rich, Office of Student Financial Assistance Maryland Higher Education Commission, 839 Bestgate Rd., Ste. 400, Annapolis, MD 21401-3013. **Phone:** 410-260-4513. **E-mail:** osfamail@mhec.state.md.us

Janet L. Hoffmann Loan Assistance Repayment Program

Provides assistance for repayment of loan debt to Maryland residents working full-time in non-profit organizations and state or local governments. Must submit Employment Verification Form and Lender verification form. **Award:** Grant for use in freshman, sophomore, junior, senior, or graduate years; not renewable. **Number:** up to 400. **Amount:** up to $7500. **Eligibility Requirements:** Applicant must be enrolled or expecting to enroll at an institution or university; resident of Maryland and studying in Maryland. Available to U.S. citizens. **Application Requirements:** Application, transcript, IRS 1040 form. **Application Deadline:** September 30. **Contact:** Marie Janiszewski, Office of Student Financial Assistance, Maryland Higher Education Commission, 839 Bestgate Rd., Ste. 400, Annapolis, MD 21401. **Phone:** 410-260-4569. **E-mail:** osfamail@mhec.state.md.us

Maryland State Nursing Scholarship and Living Expenses Grant

Renewable grant for Maryland residents enrolled in a two- or four-year Maryland institution nursing degree program. Recipients must agree to serve as a full-time nurse in a Maryland shortage area and must maintain a 3.0 GPA in college. Application deadline is June 30. Submit Free Application for Federal Student Aid. **Award:** Forgivable loan for use in freshman, sophomore, junior, senior, or graduate years; renewable. **Number:** up to 600. **Amount:** $200-$3000. **Eligibility Requirements:** Applicant must be enrolled or expecting to enroll full or part-time at a two-year or four-year institution or university; resident of Maryland and studying in Maryland. Applicant must have 3.0 GPA or higher. Available to U.S. citizens. **Application Requirements:** Application, financial need analysis, transcript. **Application Deadline:** June 30. **Contact:** Marie Janiszewski, Office of Student Financial Assistance, Maryland Higher Education Commission, 839 Bestgate Rd., Ste. 400, Annapolis, MD 21401-3013. **Phone:** 410-260-4569. **E-mail:** ofsamail@mhec.state.md.us

Maryland Teacher Scholarship

Available to Maryland residents attending a college in Maryland with a major in teacher education. Must be seeking initial teaching certification. Must work as public school teacher within the state of Maryland. Funds are limited. **Award:** Forgivable loan for use in freshman, sophomore, junior, senior, graduate, or postgraduate years; renewable. **Amount:** $1000-$5000. **Eligibility Requirements:** Applicant must be enrolled or expecting to enroll full or part-time at a two-year or four-year institution or university; resident of Maryland and studying in Maryland. Applicant must have 3.0 GPA or higher. Available to U.S. citizens. **Application Requirements:** Application, transcript. **Application Deadline:** March 1. **Contact:** Scholarship Administration, Maryland Higher Education Commission, 839 Bestgate Rd., Ste. 400, Annapolis, MD 21401. **Phone:** 410-260-4565. **E-mail:** osfamail@mhec.state.md.us

Part-time Grant Program

Funds provided to Maryland colleges and universities. Eligible students must be enrolled on a part-time basis (6-11 credits) in an undergraduate degree program. Must demonstrate financial need and also be Maryland resident. Contact financial aid office at institution for more information. **Award:** Grant for use in freshman, sophomore, junior, or senior years; renewable. **Number:** 1800-9000. **Amount:** $200-$1000. **Eligibility Requirements:** Applicant must be enrolled or expecting to enroll part-time at a two-year or four-year institution or university; resident of Maryland and studying in Maryland. Available to U.S. citizens. **Application Requirements:** Application, financial need analysis. **Application Deadline:** March 1. **Contact:** Maryland Higher Education Commission, 839 Bestgate Rd., Ste. 400, Annapolis, MD 21401-3013.

Physical and Occupational Therapists and Assistants Grant Program

For Maryland residents training as physical, occupational therapists or therapy assistants at Maryland postsecondary institutions. Recipients must provide one year of service for each full, or partial, year of award. Service must be to handicapped children in a Maryland facility that has, or accommodates and provides services to, such children. Minimum 2.0 GPA. **Award:** Forgivable loan for use in freshman, sophomore, junior, senior, or graduate years; renewable. **Number:** up to 10. **Amount:** up to $2000. **Eligibility Requirements:** Applicant must be enrolled or expecting to enroll full-time at a two-year or four-year institution or university; resident of Maryland and studying in Maryland. Available to U.S. citizens. **Application Requirements:** Application, transcript. **Application Deadline:** July 1. **Contact:** Gerrie Rogers, Office of Student Financial Assistance, Maryland Higher Education Commission, 839 Bestgate Rd., Ste. 400, Annapolis, MD 21401. **Phone:** 410-260-4574. **E-mail:** ssamail@mhec.state.md.us

Science and Technology Scholarship

Provides assistance to full-time students in an academic program that will address career shortage areas in the state (computer science, engineering, biological sciences, mathematics, and physical sciences). Must be Maryland resident. Must have cumulative unweighted 3.0 GPA in grades 9-first semester of senior year if applying as a high school student. College applicants must have a cumulative average of 3.0 or greater to apply. Funds are limited. **Award:** Forgivable loan for use in freshman, sophomore, junior, or senior years; renewable. **Amount:** $1000-$3000. **Eligibility Requirements:**

Applicant must be enrolled or expecting to enroll full-time at a two-year or four-year institution or university; resident of Maryland and studying in Maryland. Applicant must have 3.0 GPA or higher. Available to U.S. citizens. **Application Requirements:** Application, transcript. **Application Deadline:** March 1. Scholarship Administration. **Contact:** Maryland Higher Education Commission, 839 Bestgate Rd., Ste. 400, Annapolis, MD 21401. **Phone:** 410-260-4565. **E-mail:** ssamail@mhec.state.md.us

Senatorial Scholarships

Renewable award for Maryland residents attending a Maryland degree-granting institution, nursing diploma school, or certain private career schools. May be used out-of-state only if Maryland Higher Education Commission deems major to be unique and not offered at Maryland institution. Award Scholarship for use in freshman, sophomore, junior, senior, or graduate years; renewable. **Number:** up to 7000. **Amount:** $200-$2000. **Eligibility Requirements:** Applicant must be enrolled or expecting to enroll full or part-time at a two-year, four-year, or technical institution or university; resident of Maryland and studying in Maryland. Available to U.S. citizens. **Application Requirements:** Financial need analysis, test scores, application to Legislative District Senator. **Application Deadline:** March 1. **Contact:** Barbara Fantom, Office of Student Financial Assistance, Maryland Higher Education Commission, 839 Bestgate Rd., Ste. 400, Annapolis, MD 21401-3013. **Phone:** 410-260-4547. **E-mail:** osfamail@mhec.state.md.us

Sharon Christa McAuliffe Teacher Education-Critical Shortage Grant Program

Renewable awards for Maryland residents who are college juniors, seniors, or graduate students enrolled in a Maryland teacher education program. Must agree to enter profession in a subject designated as a critical shortage area. Must teach in Maryland for one year for each award year. Renewable for one year. **Award:** Forgivable loan for use in junior, senior, or graduate years; renewable. **Number:** up to 137. **Amount:** $200-$12,981. **Eligibility Requirements:** Applicant must be enrolled or expecting to enroll full or part-time at a four-year institution or university; resident of Maryland and studying in Maryland. Applicant must have 3.0 GPA or higher. Available to U.S. citizens. **Application Requirements:** Application, essay, tran-

script. **Application Deadline:** December 31. **Contact:** Margaret Crutchley, Office of Student Financial Assistance, Maryland Higher Education Commission, 839 Bestgate Rd., Ste. 400, Annapolis, MD 21401-3013. **Phone:** 410-260-4545. **E-mail:** ofsamail@mhec.state.md.us

William Kapell International Piano Competition and Festival

Quadrennial international piano competition for ages 18-33. $80 application fee. Competition takes place at the Clarice Smith Performing Arts Center at the University of Maryland July 16-25, 2003. Next competition will be in 2007. **Award:** Prize for use in freshman, sophomore, junior, senior, graduate, or postgraduate years; not renewable. **Number:** up to 12. **Amount:** $1000-$20,000. **Eligibility Requirements:** Applicant must be age 18-33; enrolled or expecting to enroll at an institution or university and must have an interest in music. Available to U.S. and non-U.S. citizens. **Application Requirements:** Application, applicant must enter a contest, autobiography, photo, portfolio, references, CD or audiocassette of performance. Fee: $80. **Application Deadline:** February 1. **Contact:** Dr. Christopher Patton, Coordinator, Clarice Smith Performing Arts Center at Maryland, Ste. 3800, University of Maryland, College Park, MD 20742-1625. **Phone:** 301-405-8174. **E-mail:** kapell@deans.umd.edu

New Jersey

Dana Christmas Scholarship for Heroism
One-time, non-renewable college scholarship will recognize and honor young for exceptional acts of heroism. The scholarship may be used for undergraduate or graduate higher education expenses. Must be current New Jersey resident and at time of act of heroism. **Award:** Scholarship for use in freshman, sophomore, junior, senior, or graduate years; not renewable. **Number:** up to 5. **Amount:** up to $10,000. **Eligibility Requirements:** Applicant must be age 21 or under; enrolled or expecting to enroll at a four-year institution or university and resident of New Jersey. Available to U.S. citizens. **Application Requirements:** Application. **Application Deadline:** October 15. **Contact:** New Jersey Higher Education Student Assistance Authority, PO Box 540, Trenton, NJ 08625-0540. **Phone:** 800-792-8670.

Edward J. Bloustein Distinguished Scholars

Renewable scholarship for students who place in the top 10% of their classes and have a minimum combined SAT score of 1260, or are ranked first, second or third in their class as of the end of the junior year. Must be New Jersey resident. Must attend a New Jersey two-year college, four-year college or university, or approved programs at proprietary institutions. Deadline for Spring term is March 1 and for Fall term is October 1.**Award:** Scholarship for use in freshman, sophomore, junior, or senior years; renewable. **Amount:** $1000. **Eligibility Requirements:** Applicant must be high school student; planning to enroll or expecting to enroll full-time at a two-year or four-year institution or university; resident of New Jersey and studying in New Jersey. Available to U.S. citizens. **Application Requirements:** Application, test scores. **Contact:** New Jersey Higher Education Student Assistance Authority, PO Box 540, Trenton, NJ 08625-0540. **Phone:** 800-792-8670.

New Jersey Educational Opportunity Fund Grants

Grants up to $4150 per year. Must be a New Jersey resident for at least twelve consecutive months and attend a New Jersey institution. Must be from a disadvantaged background as defined by EOF guidelines. EOF grant applicants must also apply for financial aid. EOF recipients may qualify for the Martin Luther King Physician/Dentistry Scholarships for graduate study at a professional institution. Academic Fields/Career Goals Dental Health/Services; Health and Medical Sciences. **Award:** Grant for use in freshman, sophomore, junior, senior, or graduate years; renewable. **Amount:** up to $4150. **Eligibility Requirements:** Applicant must be enrolled or expecting to enroll full-time at a four-year institution or university; resident of New Jersey and studying in New Jersey. Available to U.S. citizens. **Application Requirements:** Application, financial need analysis. **Contact:** Sandra Rollins, Associate Director of Financial Aid, University of Medicine and Dentistry of NJ School of Osteopathic Medicine, 40 East Laurel Rd., Primary Care Center 119, Stratford, NJ 08084. **Phone:** 856-566-6008. **E-mail:** rollins@umdnj.edu

NJSA Scholarship Program

One-time award for legal residents of New Jersey enrolled in an accredited architecture program. Minimum 2.5 GPA required. Must show evidence of financial need, scholarship, and promise in architecture. Submit portfolio and $5 application fee. **Award:** Scholarship for use in sophomore, junior, senior, or graduate years; not renewable. **Amount:** $1500-$3000. **Eligibility Requirements:** Applicant must be enrolled or expecting to enroll full-time at a four-year, or technical institution or university and resident of New Jersey. Applicant must have 2.5 GPA or higher. Available to U.S. citizens. **Application Requirements:** Application, essay, financial need analysis, portfolio, references, transcript. Fee: $5. **Application Deadline:** April 25. **Contact:** Robert Zaccone, President, AIA New Jersey Scholarship Foundation, Inc., 212 White Ave., Old Tappan, NJ 07675-7411

New Jersey War Orphans Tuition Assistance

Renewable award for New Jersey residents who are high school seniors ages 16-21 and who are children of veterans killed or disabled in duty, missing in action, or prisoner-of-war. For use at a two- or four-year college or university. Write for more information. Deadlines: October 1 for fall semester and March 1 for spring semester. **Award:** Scholarship for use in freshman, sophomore, junior, or senior years; renewable. **Amount:** $2000-$5000. **Eligibility Requirements:** Applicant must be high school student; age 16-21; planning to enroll or expecting to enroll full-time at a two-year or four-year institution or university and resident of New Jersey. Applicant or parent must meet one or more of the following Requirements: general military experience; retired from active duty; disabled or killed as a result of military service; prisoner of war; or missing in action. **Application Requirements:** Application, transcript. **Contact:** Patricia Richter, Grants Manager, New Jersey Department of Military and Veterans Affairs, PO Box 340, Trenton, NJ 08625-0340. **Phone:** 609-530-6854. **E-mail:** patricia.richter@njdmava.state.nj.us

Outstanding Scholar Recruitment Program

Students who meet the Eligibility criteria and enroll as first-time freshmen at participating New Jersey institutions receive annual scholarship awards of up to $7500. The award amounts vary on a sliding scale depending on class rank and combined SAT scores. Must maintain a B average for renewal. Deadline March 1 for Spring term, October 1 for Fall term. **Award:** Scholarship for use in freshman, sophomore, junior, or senior years; renewable. **Amount:** up to $7500. **Eligibility Requirements:** Applicant must be high school student; planning to enroll or expecting to enroll at an institution or university and studying in New Jersey. **Application Requirements:** Test scores. **Contact:** New Jersey Higher Education Student Assistance Authority, PO Box 540, Trenton, NJ 08625-0540. **Phone:** 800-792-8670.

Survivor Tuition Benefits Program

Provides tuition for spouses and dependents of law enforcement officers, fire, or emergency services personnel killed in the line of duty. Recipients must be enrolled in an undergraduate degree program at a college or university in New Jersey as either half-time or full-time students. Deadline March 1 for Spring term, October 1 for Fall term. **Award:** Scholarship for use in freshman, sophomore, junior, or senior years; renewable. **Eligibility Requirements:** Applicant must be enrolled or expecting to enroll full or part-time at a four-year institution or university; resident of New Jersey and studying in New Jersey. Applicant or parent of applicant must have employment or volunteer experience in police/firefighting. Available to U.S. citizens. **Application Requirements:** Application. **Contact:** New Jersey Higher Education Student Assistance Authority, PO Box 540, Trenton, NJ 08625-0540. **Phone:** 800-792-8670.

Tuition Assistance for Children of POW/MIAs

Assists children of military service personnel declared missing in action or prisoner-of-war after January 1, 1960. Must be a resident of New Jersey. Renewable grants provide tuition for undergraduate study in New Jersey. Apply by October 1 for fall, March 1 for spring. Must be high school senior to apply. **Award:** Scholarship for use in freshman, sophomore, junior, or senior years; renewable. **Eligibility Requirements:** Applicant must be high school student; planning to enroll or expecting to enroll full-time at a two-year or four-year institution; resident of New Jersey and studying in New Jersey. Available to U.S. citizens. Applicant or parent must meet one or more of the following requirements: general military experience; retired from active duty; disabled or killed as a result of military service; prisoner of war; or missing in action. **Application Requirements:** Application, transcript. **Contact:** Patricia Richter, Grants Manager, New Jersey Department of Military and Veterans Affairs,

PO Box 340, Trenton,
NJ 08625-0340. **Phone:** 609-530-6854.
E-mail:
patricia.richter@njdmava.state.nj.us

Urban Scholars

Renewable scholarship to high achieving students attending public secondary schools in the State's urban and
economically distressed areas of New
Jersey. Students must rank in the top
10% of their class and have a GPA of at
least 3.0 at the end of their junior year.
Must be New Jersey resident. Must
attend a New Jersey two-year college,
four-year college or university, or
approved programs at proprietary institutions. Students do not apply directly
for scholarship consideration. Deadline
March 1 for Spring term, October 1 for
Fall term. **Award:** Scholarship for use in
freshman, sophomore, junior, or senior
years; renewable. **Amount:** $1000.
Eligibility Requirements: Applicant must
be high school student; planning to
enroll or expecting to enroll full-time at
a two-year or four-year institution or
university; resident of New Jersey and
studying in New Jersey. Applicant must
have 3.0 GPA or higher. Available to
U.S. citizens. **Application Requirements:**
Application, test scores. **Contact:** New
Jersey Higher Education Student
Assistance Authority, PO Box 540,
Trenton, NJ 08625-0540. **Phone:** 800-
792-8670.

Veterans' Tuition Credit Program

Award for veterans who served in the
armed forces between December 31,
1960, and May 7, 1975. Must have been
a New Jersey resident at time of induc-
tion or discharge or for one year prior
to application. Apply by October 1 for
fall, March 1 for spring. Renewable
award of $200-$400. **Award:**
Scholarship for use in freshman, sophomore, junior, or senior years; renewable. **Amount:** $200-$400. **Eligibility
Requirements:** Applicant must be
enrolled or expecting to enroll full or
part-time at a two-year, four-year, or
technical institution or university and
resident of New Jersey. Available to
U.S. citizens. Applicant must have general military experience. **Application
Requirements:** Application. **Contact:**
Patricia Richter, Grants Manager, New
Jersey Department of Military and
Veterans Affairs, PO Box 340, Trenton,
NJ 08625-0340. **Phone:** 609-530-6854.
E-mail:
patricia.richter@njdmava.state.nj.us

New York

New York Council for the Humanities-Young Scholars Contest

The Young Scholars Contest is a
research essay competition on a pre-
determined theme in the humanities.
New York State high school students
who are legal residents of the state are
eligible. Further information, guidelines
and deadlines are available at Web site
www.nyhumanities.org. **Award:**
Scholarship for use in freshman year;
not renewable. **Number:** 6-18. **Amount:**
$250-$5000. **Eligibility Requirements:**
Applicant must be high school student;
planning to enroll or expecting to
enroll full-time at a two-year or four-
year institution or university and resident of New York. Available to U.S. and
non-U.S. citizens. **Application
Requirements:** Applicant must enter a
contest, essay. **Contact:** New York
Council for the Humanities,
150 Brd.way, Ste. 1700,
New York, NY 10038

New York Educational Opportunity Program (EOP)

Renewable award for New York resident
attending New York college/university
for undergraduate study. For education-
ally and economically disadvantaged
students; includes educational assistance such as tutoring. Contact
prospective college for information.
Award: Scholarship for use in freshman, sophomore, junior, or senior
years; renewable. **Eligibility
Requirements:** Applicant must be
enrolled or expecting to enroll full-time
at a two-year or four-year institution or
university; resident of New York and
studying in New York. Available to U.S.
citizens. **Application Requirements:**
Application, financial need analysis,
transcript. **Contact:** Student Information
New York State Higher Education
Services Corporation, 99 Washington
Ave., Room 1320, Albany, NY 12255.

New York Lottery Leaders of Tomorrow (Lot) Scholarship

The goal of this program is to reinforce
the lottery's education mission by
awarding four-year scholarships, $1000
per year for up to four years. One
scholarship is available to every New
York high school, public or private, that
awards a high school diploma. **Award:**
Scholarship for use in freshman, sophomore, junior, or senior years; renewable. **Amount:** $1000. **Eligibility
Requirements:** Applicant must be high
school student; planning to enroll or

expecting to enroll full-time at a two-
year, four-year, or technical institution
or university; resident of New York and
studying in New York. Applicant must
have 3.0 GPA or higher. Available to
U.S. citizens.
Application Requirements: Application,
essay, transcript. **Application Deadline:**
March 19. **Contact:** Betsey Morgan,
Program Coordinator, CASDA-LOT
(Capital Area School Development
Association), The University at Albany
East Campus, One University Place - A-
409, Rensselaer, NY 12144-3456.
Phone: 518-525-2788. **E-mail:**
asdalot@uamail.albany.edu

New York State Aid to Native Americans

Award for enrolled members of a New
York State tribe and their children who
are attending or planning to attend a
New York State college and who are
New York State residents. Award for
full-time-students up to $1550 annually;
part-time awards approximately $65
per credit hour. **Award:** Scholarship for
use in freshman, sophomore, junior, or
senior years; not renewable. **Amount:**
up to $1550. **Eligibility Requirements:**
Applicant must be American
Indian/Alaska Native; enrolled or
expecting to enroll full or part-time at a
two-year, four-year, or technical institution or university; resident of New York
and studying in New York. **Application
Requirements:** Application. **Application
Deadline:** July 15. **Contact:** Native
American Education Unit, New York
State Education Department, New York
State Higher Education Services
Corporation, EBA Room 374, Albany,
NY 12234. **Phone:** 518-474-0537.

New York State Higher Education Services Corporation-New York Aid for Part-time Study

Renewable scholarship provides tuition
assistance to part-time students who
are New York residents attending New
York-accredited institutions. Deadlines
and award amounts vary. Must be U.S.
citizen. **Award:** Grant for use in freshman, sophomore, junior, or senior
years; renewable. **Amount:** up to $2000.
Eligibility Requirements: Applicant must
be enrolled or expecting to enroll part-
time at a two-year or four-year institution; resident of New York and studying
in New York. Available to U.S. citizens.
Application Requirements: Application.
Contact: Student Information, New York
State Higher Education Services
Corporation, 99 Washington Ave.,
Room 1320, Albany, NY 12255.
Phone: 518-473-3887.

New York State Tuition Assistance Program

Award for New York state residents attending New York postsecondary institution. Must be full-time student in approved program with tuition over $200 per year. Must show financial need and not be in default in any other state program. Renewable award of $500-$5000. **Award:** Grant for use in freshman, sophomore, junior, or senior years; renewable. **Number:** 300,000-320,000. **Amount:** $500-$5000. **Eligibility Requirements:** Applicant must be enrolled or expecting to enroll full-time at a two-year or four-year institution or university; resident of New York and studying in New York. **Application Requirements:** Application, financial need analysis. **Application Deadline:** May 1. **Contact:** Student Information, New York State Higher Education Services Corporation, 99 Washington Ave., Room 1320, Albany, NY 12255.

New York Vietnam Veterans Tuition Awards

Scholarship for veterans who served in Vietnam. Must be a New York resident attending a New York institution. Renewable award of $500-$1000. Deadline: May 1. Must establish Eligibility by September 1. **Award:** Scholarship for use in freshman, sophomore, junior, or senior years; renewable. **Amount:** $500-$1000. **Eligibility Requirements:** Applicant must be enrolled or expecting to enroll full or part-time at a two-year, four-year, or technical institution or university; resident of New York and studying in New York. Applicant must have served in the Air Force, Army, Marine Corp, or Navy. **Application Requirements:** Application, financial need analysis. **Application Deadline:** May 1. **Contact:** Student Information, New York State Higher Education Services Corporation, 99 Washington Ave., Room 1320, Albany, NY 12255.

Regents Award for Child of Veteran

Award for students whose parent, as a result of service in U.S. Armed Forces during war or national emergency, died; suffered a 40% or more disability; or is classified as missing in action or a prisoner of war. Veteran must be current New York State resident or have been so at time of death. Must be New York resident attending, or planning to attend, college in New York State. Must establish eligibility before applying for payment. **Award:** Scholarship for use in freshman, sophomore, junior, or senior years; not renewable. **Amount:** $450. **Eligibility Requirements:** Applicant must

be enrolled or expecting to enroll full-time at a two-year or four-year institution or university; resident of New York and studying in New York. Available to U.S. citizens. Applicant or parent must meet one or more of the following requirements: general military experience; retired from active duty; disabled or killed as a result of military service; prisoner of war; or missing in action. **Application Requirements:** Application, proof of Eligibility. **Application Deadline:** May 1. **Contact:** Student Information, New York State Higher Education Services Corporation, 99 Washington Ave., Room 1320, Albany, NY 12255.

Regents Professional Opportunity Scholarships

Award for New York State residents pursuing career in certain licensed professions. Must attend New York State college. Priority given to economically disadvantaged members of minority group underrepresented in chosen profession and graduates of SEEK, College Discovery, EOP, and HEOP. Must work in New York State in chosen profession one year for each annual payment. **Award:** Forgivable loan for use in freshman, sophomore, junior, senior, or graduate years; not renewable. **Amount:** $1000-$5000. **Eligibility Requirements:** Applicant must be enrolled or expecting to enroll full-time at a two-year or four-year institution or university; resident of New York and studying in New York. Available to U.S. citizens. **Application Requirements:** Application. **Application Deadline:** May 1. **Contact:** Scholarship Processing Unit-New York State Education Department, New York State Higher Education Services Corporation, EBA Room 1078, Albany, NY 12234. **Phone:** 518-486-1319.

Scholarships for Academic Excellence

Renewable awards of up to $1500 for academically outstanding New York State high school graduates planning to attend an approved postsecondary institution in New York State. For full-time study only. Contact high school guidance counselor to apply. **Award:** Scholarship for use in freshman, sophomore, junior, or senior years; renewable. **Number:** 8000. **Amount:** $500-$1500. **Eligibility Requirements:** Applicant must be high school student; planning to enroll or expecting to enroll full-time at a four-year institution or university; resident of New York and studying in New York. Available to U.S. citizens. **Application Requirements:** Application. **Contact:** Student Information, New York State Higher Education Services Corporation, 99 Washington Ave., Room 1320, Albany, NY 12255.

World Trade Center Memorial Scholarship

Renewable awards of up to the average cost of attendance at a State University of New York four-year college. Available to the families and financial dependents of victims who died or were severely and permanently disabled as a result of the Sept. 11, 2001 terrorist attacks on the U.S.A and the rescue and recovery efforts. **Award:** Scholarship for use in freshman, sophomore, junior, or senior years; renewable. **Eligibility Requirements:** Applicant must be enrolled or expecting to enroll full-time at a two-year or four-year institution or university and resident of New York. Available to U.S. citizens. **Application Requirements:** Application. **Application Deadline:** May 1. **Contact:** HESC Scholarship Unit, New York State Higher Education Services Corporation, 99 Washington Ave., Room 1320, Albany, NY 12255. **Phone:** 518-402-6494

Pennsylvania

Educational Gratuity Program

This program is for eligible dependents of 100% disabled or deceased veteran whose disability was incurred during a period or war or armed conflict. Must be a Pennsylvania resident attending a Pennsylvania school. **Award:** Grant for use in freshman, sophomore, junior, or senior years; renewable. **Amount:** up to $500. **Eligibility Requirements:** Applicant must be age 16-23; enrolled or expecting to enroll full-time at a two-year, four-year, or technical institution or university; resident of Pennsylvania and studying in Pennsylvania. Available to U.S. citizens. Applicant must have general military experience. **Application Requirements:** Application, driver's license, financial need analysis, transcript. **Application Deadline:** Continuous. **Contact:** Michelle Zimmerman, Clerk Typist, Pennsylvania Bureau for Veterans Affairs, Fort Indiantown Gap, Annville, PA 17003-5002. **Phone:** 717-861-8910. **E-mail:** michzimmer@state.pa.us

New Economy Technology Scholarships

Renewable award for Pennsylvania residents pursuing a degree in science or technology at a PHEAA-approved Pennsylvania school. Must maintain minimum 3.0 GPA. Must commence employment in Pennsylvania in field related to student's program within one year after completion of studies. Must work one year for each year scholarship was awarded. **Award:** Scholarship for use in freshman, sophomore, junior, or senior years; renewable. **Amount:** up to $3000. **Eligibility Requirements:** Applicant must be enrolled or expecting to enroll full or part-time at a two-year, four-year, or technical institution; resident of Pennsylvania and studying in Pennsylvania. Applicant must have 3.0 GPA or higher. **Application Requirements:** Application, FAFSA. **Application Deadline:** December 31. **Contact:** PHEAA State Grant and Special Programs Division, Pennsylvania Higher Education Assistance Agency, 1200 North Seventh St., Harrisburg, PA 17102-1444. **Phone:** 800-692-7392.

Pennsylvania State Grant

Award for Pennsylvania residents attending an approved postsecondary institution as undergraduates in a program of at least two years duration. Renewable for up to eight semesters if applicants show continued need and academic progress. Submit Free Application for Federal Student Aid. **Award:** Grant for use in freshman, sophomore, junior, or senior years; renewable. **Number:** up to 151,000. **Amount:** $300-$3300. **Eligibility Requirements:** Applicant must be enrolled or expecting to enroll full or part-time at a two-year, four-year, or technical institution or university and resident of Pennsylvania. Available to U.S. and Canadian citizens. **Application Requirements:** Application, financial need analysis. **Application Deadline:** May 1. **Contact:** Keith New, Director of Communications and Press Office, Pennsylvania Higher Education, Assistance Agency, 1200 North Seventh St., Harrisburg, PA 17102-1444. **Phone:** 717-720-2509 **E-mail:** knew@pheaa.org

Postsecondary Education Gratuity Program

Waiver of tuition and fees for children of Pennsylvania police officers, firefighters, rescue or ambulance squad members, corrections facility employees or National Guard members who died in the line of duty after January 1, 1976. Must be a resident of Pennsylvania 25 years old or younger and enrolled full time as an undergraduate student at a Pennsylvania community college, state-owned institution or state-related institution. Award is for a maximum of 5 years. Application deadline March 31. **Award:** Grant for use in freshman, sophomore, junior, or senior years; renewable. **Eligibility Requirements:** Applicant must be age 25 or under; enrolled or expecting to

enroll full-time at a two-year or four-year institution or university; resident of Pennsylvania and studying in Pennsylvania. **Application Requirements:** Application. **Application Deadline:** March 31. **Contact:** PHEAA State Grant and Special Programs Division, Pennsylvania Higher Education, Assistance Agency, 1200 North Seventh St., Harrisburg, PA 17102-1444. **Phone:** 800-692-7392.

Veterans Grant

Renewable awards for Pennsylvania residents who are qualified veterans attending an approved undergraduate program full-time. Up to $3300 for in-state study or $800 for out-of-state study. Deadlines: May 1 for all renewal applicants, new applicants who plan to enroll in an undergraduate baccalaureate degree program, and those in college transfer programs at two-year public or junior colleges; August 1 for all first-time applicants who plan to enroll in a business, trade, or technical school; a hospital school of nursing; or a two-year terminal program at a community, junior, or four-year college. **Award:** Grant for use in freshman, sophomore, junior, or senior years; renewable. **Amount:** $800-$3300. **Eligibility Requirements:** Applicant must be enrolled or expecting to enroll full-time at a two-year, four-year, or technical institution or university and resident of Pennsylvania. Available to U.S. citizens. Applicant must have general military experience. **Application Requirements:** Application. **Contact:** Keith New, Director of Communications and Press Office, Pennsylvania Higher Education Assistance Agency, 1200 North Seventh St., Harrisburg, PA 17102-1444. **Phone:** 717-720-2509. **E-mail:** knew@pheaa.org

Virginia

Walter Reed Smith Scholarship

Award for full-time female undergraduate student who is a descendant of a Confederate soldier, studying nutrition, home economics, nursing, business administration, or computer science. Must carry a minimum of 12 credit hours each semester and have a minimum 3.0 GPA. Submit letter of endorsement from sponsoring chapter of the United Daughters of the Confederacy. **Award:** Scholarship for use in freshman, sophomore, junior, or senior years; renewable. **Number:** 1-2. **Amount:** $800-$1000. **Eligibility Requirements:** Applicant must be

enrolled or expecting to enroll full-time at a four-year institution or university and female. Applicant or parent of applicant must be member of United Daughters of the Confederacy. Applicant must have 3.0 GPA or higher. Available to U.S. citizens. **Application Requirements:** Application, essay, financial need analysis, photo, references, self-addressed stamped envelope, transcript. **Application Deadline:** February 15. **Contact:** Second Vice President General, United Daughters of the Confederacy, 328 North Blvd., Richmond, VA 23220-4057. **Phone:** 804-355-1636.

General Mills Scholars Program/Internship

Scholarships and paid summer internships awarded to college sophomores and juniors majoring in accounting, business (sales interest), computer science, engineering, finance, human resources, information systems, information technology or marketing at a UNCF member college or university. Minimum 3.5 GPA required. Prospective applicants should complete the Student Profile found at **Web site:** www.uncf.org. **Award:** Scholarship for use in sophomore or junior years; not renewable. **Amount:** $5000. **Eligibility Requirements:** Applicant must be Black (non-Hispanic) and enrolled or expecting to enroll full-time at a four-year institution or university. Applicant must have 3.5 GPA or higher. Available to U.S. citizens. **Application Requirements:** Application, financial need analysis, test scores. **Application Deadline:** February 14. **Contact:** Program Services Department, United Negro College Fund, 8260 Willow Oaks Corporate Dr., Fairfax, VA 22031.

Mary Marshall Practical Nursing Scholarships

Award for practical nursing students who are Virginia residents. Must attend a nursing program in Virginia. Recipient must agree to work in Virginia after graduation. Minimum 3.0 GPA required. Recipients may reapply up to three years for an award. **Award:** Scholarship for use in freshman, sophomore, junior, or senior years; not renewable. **Amount:** $150-$500. **Eligibility Requirements:** Applicant must be enrolled or expecting to enroll full or part-time at a two-year or technical institution; resident of Virginia and studying in Virginia. Applicant must have 3.0 GPA or higher. Available to U.S. citizens. **Application Requirements:** Application, financial need analysis, references, transcript. **Application Deadline:** June 30. **Contact:** Norma

Marrin, Business Manager/Policy Analyst, Virginia Department of Health, Office of Health Policy and Planning, PO Box 2448, Richmond, VA 23218-2448. **Phone:** 804-371-4090. **E-mail:** nmarrin@vdh.state.va.us

Mary Marshall Registered Nursing Program Scholarships

Award for registered nursing students who are Virginia residents. Must attend a nursing program in Virginia. Recipient must agree to work in Virginia after graduation. Minimum 3.0 GPA required. Recipient may reapply up to three years for an award. **Award:** Scholarship for use in freshman, sophomore, junior, or senior years; not renewable. **Number:** 60-100. **Amount:** $1200-$2000. **Eligibility Requirements:** Applicant must be enrolled or expecting to enroll full or part-time at a two-year or four-year institution or university; resident of Virginia and studying in Virginia. Applicant must have 3.0 GPA or higher. Available to U.S. citizens. **Application Requirements:** Application, financial need analysis, references, transcript. **Application Deadline:** June 30. **Contact:** Norma Marrin, Business Manager/Policy Analyst, Virginia Department of Health, Office of Health Policy and Planning, PO Box 2448, Richmond, VA 23218-2448. **Phone:** 804-371-4090. **E-mail:** nmarrin@udh.state.va.us

Virginia Tuition Assistance Grant Program (Private Institutions)

Renewable awards of approximately $3,000 each for undergraduate, graduate, and first professional degree students attending an approved private, nonprofit college within Virginia. Must be a Virginia resident and be enrolled full-time. Not to be used for religious study. Preferred deadline July 31. Others are wait-listed. Contact college financial aid office. The application process is handled by the participating colleges' financial aid office. **Award:** Grant for use in freshman, sophomore, junior, senior, or graduate years; renewable. **Number:** 15,000. **Amount:** $3000. **Eligibility Requirements:** Applicant must be enrolled or expecting to enroll full-time at a four-year institution; resident of Virginia and studying in Virginia. **Application Requirements:** Application. **Application Deadline:** July 31. **Contact:** Financial Aid Office at participating institution, State Council of Higher Education for Virginia, James Monroe Building, 10th Floor, 101 North 14th St., Richmond, VA 23219.

Virginia War Orphans Education Program

Grant is equal to tuition-free education for up to 48 months. One of the applicant's parents must have served in the armed forces of the United States and be permanently and totally disabled due to war or other armed conflict, died as a result of war or other armed conflict or be listed as a prisoner of war (POW) or missing in action (MIA). Must be a resident of Virginia studying in Virginia. **Award:** Grant for use in freshman, sophomore, junior, or senior years; renewable. **Eligibility Requirements:** Applicant must be age 16-25; enrolled or expecting to enroll at an institution or university; resident of Virginia and studying in Virginia. Available to U.S. citizens. Applicant or parent must meet one or more of the following Requirements: general military experience; retired from active duty; disabled or killed as a result of military service; prisoner of war; or missing in action. **Application Requirements:** Application. **Contact:** Commonwealth of Virginia Department of Veterans' Affairs, 270 Franklin Rd. SW, Room 503, Poff Federal Building, Roanoke, VA 24011-2215.

Virginia War Orphans Education Program

Scholarships for postsecondary students between ages 16 and 25 to attend Virginia state supported institutions. Must be child or surviving child of veteran who has either: been permanently or totally disabled due to war or other armed conflict; died as a result of war or other armed conflict; or been listed as a POW or MIA. Parent must also meet Virginia residency requirements. Contact for application procedures and deadline. **Award:** Scholarship for use in freshman, sophomore, junior, senior, or graduate years; renewable. **Eligibility Requirements:** Applicant must be age 16-25; enrolled or expecting to enroll at a two-year, four-year, or technical institution or university and studying in Virginia. Applicant or parent must meet one or more of the following Requirements: general military experience; retired from active duty; disabled or killed as a result of military service; prisoner of war; or missing in action. **Application Requirements:** Application. **Contact:** Beth Tonn, Administrative Assistant, Virginia Department of Veterans' Affairs, Poff Federal Building, 270 Franklin Rd., S.W., Room 503, Roanoke, VA 24011-2215. **Phone:** 540-857-7104

West Virginia Division of Veterans' Affairs War Orphans Education Program

Renewable waiver of tuition award for West Virginia residents who are children of deceased veterans. Parent must have died of war-related service-connected disability. Must be ages 16-23. Minimum 2.5 GPA required. Must attend a state-supported West Virginia postsecondary institution. Deadline: July 1 and December 1. **Award:** Scholarship for use in freshman, sophomore, junior, senior, or graduate years; renewable. **Eligibility Requirements:** Applicant must be age 16-23; enrolled or expecting to enroll full or part-time at a two-year, four-year, or technical institution or university; resident of West Virginia and studying in West Virginia. Applicant must have 2.5 GPA or higher. Available to U.S. citizens. Applicant or parent must meet one or more of the following requirements: general military experience; retired from active duty; disabled or killed as a result of military service; prisoner of war; or missing in action. **Application Requirements:** Application, references. **Contact:** Ms. Linda Walker, Secretary, West Virginia Division of Veterans' Affairs, 1321 Plaza East, Ste. 101, Charleston, WV 25301-1400. **Phone:** 304-668-3661. **E-mail:** wvdva@state.wv.us

West Virginia

Higher Education Adult Part-time Student Grant Program

Program to assist needy adult students to continue their education on a part-time basis. Also has a component in which 25% of the funding may be utilized for students enrolled in workforce and skill development programs. Contact institution financial aid office for more information and deadlines. **Award:** Grant for use in freshman, sophomore, junior, or senior years; not renewable. **Eligibility Requirements:** Applicant must be enrolled or expecting to enroll full or part-time at a two-year, four-year, or technical institution or university; resident of West Virginia and studying in West Virginia. Available to U.S. citizens. **Application Requirements:** Application, financial need analysis. **Contact:** Judy Kee, Financial Aid Manager, West Virginia Higher Education Policy Commission-Office of Financial Aid and Outreach Services, 1018 Kanawha Blvd., East, Ste. 700, Charleston, WV 25301. **Phone:** 304-558-4618. **E-mail:** kee@hepc.wvnet.edu

Promise Scholarship

Renewable award for West Virginia residents. Minimum 3.0 GPA and combined ACT score of 21 or 1000 on the SAT. Provides full-tuition scholarship to a state college or university in West Virginia or an equivalent scholarship to an in-state private college. Financial resources are not a factor. **Award:** Scholarship for use in freshman, sophomore, junior, or senior years; renewable. **Number:** 3500. **Amount:** $3000. **Eligibility Requirements:** Applicant must be high school student; planning to enroll or expecting to enroll full-time at a two-year or four-year institution or university; resident of West Virginia and studying in West Virginia. Applicant must have 3.0 GPA or higher. Available to U.S. citizens. **Application Requirements:** Application, financial need analysis, test scores, transcript. **Application Deadline:** January 31. **Contact:** Robert Morgenstern, Executive Director, West Virginia Higher Education Policy Commission-Office of Financial Aid and Outreach Services, Promise Scholarship, 1018 Kanawha Blvd., Ste. 700, Charleston, WV 25301. **Phone:** 304-558-4417. **E-mail:** morgenstern@hepc.wvnet.edu

Underwood-Smith Teacher Scholarship Program

For West Virginia residents at West Virginia institutions pursuing teaching careers. Must have a 3.25 GPA after completion of two years of course work. Must teach two years in West Virginia public schools for each year the award is received. Recipients will be required to sign an agreement acknowledging an understanding of the program's requirements and their willingness to repay the award if appropriate teaching service is not rendered. **Award:** Scholarship for use in junior, senior, or graduate years; renewable. **Number:** 53. **Amount:** up to $5000. **Eligibility Requirements:** Applicant must be enrolled or expecting to enroll full-time at a four-year institution or university; resident of West Virginia and studying in West Virginia. Available to U.S. citizens. **Application Requirements:** Application, essay, references. **Application Deadline:** March 1. **Contact:** Michelle Wicks, Scholarship Coordinator, West Virginia Higher Education Policy Commission-Office of Financial Aid and Outreach Services, 1018 Kanawha Blvd. East, Ste. 700, Charleston, WV 25301. **Phone:** 304-558-4618. **E-mail:** wicks@hepc.wvnet.edu

West Virginia Engineering, Science & Technology Scholarship Program

For students attending West Virginia institutions full time pursuing a career in engineering, science or technology. Must have a 3.0 GPA on a 4.0 scale. Must work in the fields of engineering, science or technology in West Virginia one year for each year the award is received. **Award:** Scholarship for use in freshman, sophomore, junior, or senior years; renewable. **Number:** 300. **Amount:** up to $3000. **Eligibility Requirements:** Applicant must be enrolled or expecting to enroll full-time at a two-year, four-year, or technical institution or university and studying in West Virginia. Applicant must have 3.0 GPA or higher. Available to U.S. citizens. **Application Requirements:** Application, essay, test scores, transcript. **Application Deadline:** March 1. **Contact:** Michelle Wicks, Scholarship Coordinator, West Virginia Higher Education Policy Commission-Office of Financial, Aid and Outreach Services, 1018 Kanawha Blvd. East, Ste. 700, Charleston, WV 25301. **Phone:** 304-558-4618. **E-mail:** wicks@hepc.wvnet.edu

West Virginia Higher Education Grant Program For West Virginia

Residents attending an approved non-profit degree-granting college or university in West Virginia or Pennsylvania. Must be enrolled full-time. Based on financial need and academic merit. Award covers tuition and fees. **Award:** Grant for use in freshman, sophomore, junior, or senior years; renewable. **Number:** 10,500-10,800. **Amount:** $350-$2718. **Eligibility Requirements:** Applicant must be enrolled or expecting to enroll full-time at a two-year or four-year institution or university; resident of West Virginia and studying in Pennsylvania or West Virginia. Available to U.S. citizens. **Application Requirements:** Application, financial need analysis, test scores, transcript. **Application Deadline:** March 1. **Contact:** Robert Long, Grant Program Coordinator, West Virginia Higher Education Policy Commission-Office of Financial Aid and Outreach Services, 1018 Kanawha Blvd. East, Ste. 700, Charleston, WV 25301-2827. **Phone:** 888-825-5707. **E-mail:** long@hepc.wvnet.edu

INTERNSHIPS

Delaware

Historical Society of Delaware
General Information: Historical society with research library, urban museums, historic house museum, publications, and outreach programs
Contact: Barbara Benson, Executive Director, 505 Market St. Wilmington, DE 19801
Fax: 302-655-7844
E-mail: hsd@hsd.org
Web site: www.hsd.org

Quiet Resorts Public Relations
General Information: Public relations firm operating weekly and seasonal newspapers in local resort towns and providing publicity services
Contact: Paul Jankovic, PO Box 505, Bethany Beach, DE 19930
Phone: 410-524-5351
Fax: 302-539-1232
E-mail: ecprg@aol.com
Web site: www.ecusa.com

WRDX-Clear Channel Communications
General Information: Radio brd.casting company
Contact: Rich Gallo, Assistant Promotions Director, 3001 Philadelphia Pike, Claymont, DE 19703
Phone: 302-793-4200, Ext. 302
Fax: 302-793-4204
E-mail: richatwrdx@aol.com
Web site: www.wrdx.com

District of Columbia

Accuracy in Academia
General Information: Nonprofit organization dedicated to fighting political correctness and defending free speech on college campuses nationwide
Contact: Executive Director, 4455 Connecticut Ave., Washington, DC 20008
Phone: 202-364-3085
Fax: 202-364-4098
E-mail: aimintern@yahoo.com
Web site: www.academia.org

Accuracy in Media
General Information: Nonprofit educational organization whose purpose is to monitor bias and inaccuracies in the news media through a newsletter and news column
Contact: Don Irvine, Executive Director, 4455 Connecticut Ave. NW, Ste. 330, Washington, DC 20008
Fax: 202-364-4098
E-mail: aimintern@yahoo.com
Web site: www.aim.org

Americans for Democratic Action
General Information: Nation's oldest liberal lobbying group that combines grassroots organizing with lobbying on various issues at local, state, and national levels
Contact: Valerie Dulk-Jacobs, Special Assistant to the Director, 1625 K St., NW, Ste. 210, Washington, DC 20006
Phone: 202-785-5980
Fax: 202-785-5969
E-mail: valerie@adaction.com
Web site: www.adaction.org

American Youth Work Center/Youth Today
General Information: National monthly newspaper for professionals concerned with youth, especially at-risk, out-of-school youth; topics may include child welfare, juvenile justice, child labor, and substance abuse
Contact: John Kelly, Intern Coordinator, 1200 17th St., NW, 4th Floor, Washington, DC 20036
Phone: 202-785-0764, Ext. 110
Fax: 202-728-0657
E-mail: jkelly@youthtoday.org

Amnesty International USA, Washington Office
General Information: Organization conducting a worldwide movement working impartially for the release of prisoners of conscience, fair and prompt trials for political prisoners, and an end to torture and executions
Contact: Toni Coverton, Acting Office Manager, 600 Pennsylvania Ave., SE, 5th Floor, Washington, DC 20003
Phone: 202-544-0200
Fax: 202-546-7142
E-mail: tcoverto@aiusa.org
Web site: www.amnesty-usa.org

Campaign for Tobacco-Free Kids
General Information: Organization dedicated to protecting children from tobacco addiction and exposure to secondhand smoke
Contact: 1400 Eye St., NW, Ste. 1200, Washington, DC 20005
Fax: 202-296-5427
E-mail: jobs@tobaccofreekids.org
Web site: www.tobaccofreekids.org

Center for Folklife & Cultural Heritage
General Information: Center that engages in cultural conservation and representation activities that promote continuity, integrity, and equity for traditional ethnic, tribal, regional, minority, and working-class cultures in the U.S. and abrd. through scholarly research, professional advocacy, and public programs
Contact: Arlene Reiniger, Program Specialist, Intern Coordinator, 750 9th St., NW, Ste. 4100 Washington, DC 20560
Phone: 202-275-1180
Fax: 202-275-1119
E-mail: arlene@folklife.si.edu
Web site: www.sss.si.edu/folklife

Children's Defense Fund
General Information: Advocacy organization that exists to provide a strong voice for children; goals are achieved by educating the public about children's needs and encouraging preventive investment in children before they get sick, get into trouble, drop out of school, or suffer from family breakdown
Contact: Kristin Peterson, Internship Coordinator, 25 E St., NW, Washington, DC 20001
Phone: 202-628-8787
Fax: 202-662-3570
E-mail: kpeterson@childrensdefense.org
Web site: www.childrensdefense.org

Climate Institute
General Information: Organization serving as a link between scientists and policymakers on the issues of climate change and stratospheric ozone depletion
Contact: John Topping, President, 333 1/2 Pennsylvania Ave., SE, Washington, DC 20003
Fax: 202-547-0111
E-mail: jtopping@climate.org
Web site: www.climate.org

Common Cause
General Information: Nonprofit, nonpartisan citizens' lobbying group working to promote honesty, accountability, and ethics in government

Contact: Kathleen Grant, Director of Outreach and Youth Initiatives, 1250 Connecticut Ave., NW, Washington, DC 20036
Phone: 202-833-1200
Fax: 202-659-3716
E-mail: kgrant@commoncause.org
Web site: www.commoncause.org

Creative Management Services
General Information: Communications company producing advertising, marketing, public relations, video productions, and event planning for large and small companies and the government
Contact: Anne Schwab, President, 906 D St., NE, Washington, DC 20002
Phone: 202-333-3560
Fax: 202-544-2856
E-mail: crmgtser@aol.com

D.C. Rape Crisis Center
General Information: Private nonprofit agency offering 24-hour crisis counseling, companion services, and community education programs on related issues
Contact: Karen Bailey, Executive Assistant, PO Box 34125, Washington, DC 20043
Phone: 202-232-0789, Ext. 221
Fax: 202-387-3812
E-mail: dcrccintern@hotmail.com
Web site: www.dcrcc.org

Discovery Creek Children's Museum of Washington
General Information: Children's museum focusing on the environment and education, located on 12-acre site that includes the only remaining one-room schoolhouse in Washington, D.C. as well as a renovated historic stable at Glen Echo Park in Glen Echo, MD and a mobile exhibition "The Rolling Rainforest"
Contact: Anne Knight, Intern Program Manager, 2233 Wisconsin Ave., Ste. 410, Washington, DC 20007
Phone: 202-337-5111
Fax: 202-337-5344
E-mail: aknight@discoverycreek.org
Web site: www.discoverycreek.org

Empower Program
General Information: Nonprofit educational organization that works with youth, ages 10-21, to prevent gender-based violence, such as sexual harassment, sexual assault, dating violence, and bullying
Contact: Sydney Campbell, Office Manager, 1312 8th St., NW, Washington, DC 20001
Phone: 202-232-8200

Fax: 202-234-1901
E-mail: empower@empowered.org
Web site: www.empowered.org

Federation of American Scientists
General Information: Nonprofit, privately funded organization engaged in analysis and advocacy on the consequences of science and technology on public policy
Contact: Sarah Mason, Organization Manager, 1717 K St. NW, Ste. 209, Washington, DC 20036
Fax: 202-675-1010
E-mail: fas@fas.org
Web site: www.fas.org

International Arts and Artists
General Information: Nonprofit arts management services organization
Contact:
Elaine Yan, Internship Program Manager
3061 M St., NW, 2nd Floor
Washington, DC 20007
Phone: 202-338-0680
Fax: 202-333-0758
E-mail: elainey@artsandartists.org
Web site: www.artsandartists.org

International Trade Administration
General Information: International trade organization that assists small and medium-sized businesses in exporting overseas and formulates and implements U.S. foreign trade policy
Contact: Tina James, Human Resources Specialist, 14th St. and Constitution Ave., NW, Room 7417, Washington, DC 20230
Fax: 202-482-1903
E-mail: tina_james@ita.doc.gov

Jobs with Justice
General Information: National coalition of labor unions and religious, civil rights, women's, student, farm, and community organizations working together at the local level to defend and expand the rights of working people
Contact: Sian Lewis, Office Coordinator, 501 Third St., NW, Washington, DC 20001-2797
Phone: 202-434-1106
Fax: 202-434-1477
E-mail: sian@jwj.org
Web site: www.jwj.org

Meridian International Center-Educational and Visitor Services
General Information: Service promoting international understanding through exchange of people, ideas, and the arts
Contact: Intern Coordinator, 1630

Crescent Place, NW, Washington, DC 20009
Fax: 202-667-1475
Web site: www.meridian.org

National Asian Pacific American Legal Consortium
General Information: Civil rights organization that advances the legal and civil rights of Asian-Pacific Americans through litigation, advocacy, public education, and public policy development
Contact: Vincent Eng, Legal Director, 1140 Connecticut Ave., NW, Ste. 1200, Washington, DC 20036
Phone: 202-296-2300
Fax: 202-296-2318
E-mail: veng@napalc.org
Web site: www.napalc.org

National Crime Prevention Council
General Information: Organization that helps focus the power of the individual and the community in the fight against crime
Contact: Vernell Banks, Human Resources Assistant, 1000 Connecticut Ave., NW, 13th Floor, Washington, DC 20036
Phone: 202-466-6272
Fax: 202-296-1356
E-mail: hr-intern@ncpc.org
Web site: www.ncpc.org

National Museum of American History
General Information: Museum that investigates, interprets, collects, preserves, exhibits, and honors the heritage of the American people
Contact: Suzanne McLaughlin, Intern Manager, 14th St. and Constitution Ave., NW, Room 1040, MRC 0605 Washington, DC 20560-0605
Phone: 202-357-1606
Fax: 202-786-2851
E-mail: intern@nmah.si.edu
Web site: www.americanhistory.si.edu/interns

National Organization for Victim Assistance (NOVA)
General Information: Private, nonprofit, 501(c)(3) organization of victim and witness assistance programs and practitioners, criminal justice agencies and professionals, mental health professionals, researchers, former victims and survivors, and others committed to the recognition and implementation of victim rights and services
Contact: Cheryl Tyiska, Director of Victim Services, 1730 Park Rd., NW,

Washington, DC 20010
Phone: 202-232-6682
Fax: 202-462-2255
E-mail: cheryl@trynova.org
Web site: www.trynova.org

National Organization for Women (National Action Center)
General Information: Feminist organization working to ensure full equality for women and to end discrimination
Contact: Intern Coordinator, 733 15th St., NW, 2nd Floor, Washington, DC 20005
Phone: 202-628-8669
Fax: 202-785-8576
E-mail: nowinterns@aol.com
Web site: www.now.org

Naval Historical Center
General Information: Museum that undertakes historical research and writing, archival management, documentary editing, museum exhibits, educational and public programs, collections management, and library services for the Navy and the public
Contact: Edward M. Furgol, Curator, 805 Kidder Breese St., SE, Washington Navy Yard, DC 20374-5060
Phone: 202-433-6901
Fax: 202-433-8200
E-mail: edward.furgol@navy.mil
Web site: www.history.navy.mil

Peace Action and Peace Action Education Fund
General Information: Grassroots peace and justice organization that seeks to promote global security by converting to a peace economy and stopping the nuclear arms race and conventional arms trade
Contact: Carrie Benzschawel, Program Associate, 1819 H St., NW, Room 425, Washington, DC 20006
Phone: 202-862-9740, Ext. 3041
Fax: 202-862-9762
Web site: www.peace-action.org

Progressive Action Network (East Coast and Midwest Interns)
General Information: Network providing stable funding for progressive political organizations, mobilizing mass numbers of people to participate in the political process, and developing activism and membership development careers
Contact: Barbara Helmick, Executive Director, 1341 G St., NW, Ste. 600, Washington, DC 20005
Phone: 202-624-1720
Fax: 202-737-9197
Web site: www.progressiveaction.org

Smithsonian Institution, National Museum of Natural History
General Information: Museum that employs curatorial and scientific staff to collect specimens, conduct research, and study in the natural sciences
Contact: Mary Sangrey, Program Director, 10th St. and Constitution Ave., NW
Washington, DC 20560-0166
Phone: 202-357-4548
Fax: 202-786-2563
E-mail: sangrey.mary@nmnh.si.edu
Web site: www.nmnh.si.edu/rtp/

Smithsonian Institution, Office of Sponsored Projects
General Information: Unit that provides assistance to Smithsonian staff who are seeking, or have obtained, grants or other external funding for sponsored projects
Contact: Karen Otiji, Internship Coordinator, 750 Ninth St., NW, Ste. 9200, Washington, DC 20001
Phone: 202-275-0677
Fax: 202-275-0497
E-mail: kareno@osp.si.edu
Web site: www.si.edu

Smithsonian Institution, Office of the Chief Technology Officer
General Information: Unit that provides Smithsonian's central computing and telecommunications services and training as well as leadership in information technology
Contact: Sherri Manning, Internship Coordinator, Arts and Industries Building, 900 Jefferson Drive, SW, Washington, DC 20560-0433
Fax: 202-633-9466
E-mail: mannings@oit.si.edu
Web site:
www.si.edu/organiza/offices/oit/start.htm

Maryland

Affiliated Sante Group and the Rock Creek Foundation
General Information: Behavioral health-care company utilizing students and volunteers seeking to fulfill academic and personal community service roles
Contact: Beth Albaneze, Director of Students and Volunteers, 700 Roeder Rd., 4th Floor, Silver Spring, MD 20910
Phone: 301-589-8303, Ext. 417
Fax: 301-589-5861
E-mail: balbaneze@santegroup.org
Web site: www.thesantegroup.org

Catoctin Mountain Park
General Information: Park dedicated to the preservation and protection of historical objects and wildlife
Contact: Chief Ranger, 6602 Foxville Rd., Thurmont, MD 21788-1598
Phone: 301-663-9388
Web site: www.nps.gov/cato

Frederick County Department of Parks and Recreation
General Information: Parks and recreation department
Contact: Jeremy Kortright, Recreation Superintendent, 118 North Market St., Frederick, MD 21701
Phone: 301-696-2936
Fax: 301-694-2595
E-mail: parksandrecreation@fredco-md.net
Web site:
www.co.frederick.md.us/govt/parks

Fund for Animals, Inc.
General Information: Nonprofit animal protection organization that focuses on companion animal and wildlife issues
Contact: Jennifer Allen, Program Coordinator, 8121 Georgia Ave., Ste. 301, Silver Spring, MD 20910
Phone: 301-585-2591, Ext. 206
Fax: 301-585-2595
E-mail: jallen@fund.org
Web site: www.fund.org

Genesee Valley Outdoor Learning Center
General Information: Experiential learning center that offers ropes course and environmental programs for school children, those with special needs, at-risk youth, and corporations
Contact: Marcia Denmark, Supervisor of Program and Personnel, 1717 Rayville Rd., Parkton, MD 21120
Phone: 410-343-0101
Fax: 410-343-1451
E-mail: info@geneseevalley.org
Web site: www.geneseevalley.org

HARBEL Prevention and Recovery Center
General Information: State-certified substance abuse prevention and treatment program that provides early intervention/prevention/treatment services through individual, family, and group counseling, school outreach, and tutoring
Contact: Patricia Stabile, Director, 5807 Harford Rd., Baltimore, MD 21214
Phone: 410-444-2100
Fax: 410-426-1140
E-mail: harbelprc@yahoo.com
Web site: www.phoenix.goucher.edu/~harbel/hprc.htm

Harvey Property Management Company, Inc.

General Information: Commercial property management and development company
Contact: Avi Halpert, Vice President, Property Management, 6931 Arlington Rd., Ste. 500, Bethesda, MD 20814
Fax: 301-907-0394
E-mail: avih@harveycompanies.com

National 4-H Center

General Information: Conference center that teaches political awareness and the history of Washington, D.C.
Contact: Joel Hawthorne, Sales Director, 7100 Connecticut Ave., Chevy Chase, MD 20815
Phone: 301-961-2801
Fax: 301-961-2922
E-mail: jhawthorne@fourhcouncil.edu
Web site: www.n4h.org

Shore Facts Marketing Research

General Information: Firm that provides market research for clients in resort retail industries by using psychographic and demographic data, focus group interviews, videotape analysis, and extensive mail and personal interviews
Contact: Paul Jankovic, Owner/Publisher, PO Box 1759, Ocean City, MD 21843
Phone: 410-524-5351
Fax: 302-539-1232
E-mail: ecprg@aol.com
Web site: www.ecusa.com

New Jersey

Alice Paul Centennial Foundation

General Information: Nonprofit corporation created to celebrate Alice Paul's birth in 1885; goals are to enhance public awareness of the life and work of Alice Paul and to educate women and girls to accept leadership challenges in their lives, communities, and work places
Contact: Rhonda Carboni, President, 128 Hooten Rd., Mt. Laurel, NJ 08054
Phone: 856-231-1885
Fax: 856-231-4223
E-mail: info@alicepaul.org
Web site: www.alicepaul.org

Big Brothers Big Sisters of Salem County

General Information: Organization that provides positive opportunities for growth and development for children and at-risk youth through one-to-one matches with volunteers, educational programs, and recreational activities
Contact: Lori Tesauro, Executive Director, 29 South Main St., Woodstown, NJ 08098
Phone: 856-769-3556
Fax: 856-769-3566
E-mail: salemcountybbbs@hotmail.com

Boys & Girls Clubs of Newark

General Information: Youth development agency
Contact: John Mack, Executive Director, 155 Washington St., Ste. 202, Newark, NJ 07102-2001
Phone: 973-242-1200
Fax: 973-242-8629
E-mail: jmack@bgcn.org
Web site: www.bgcn.org

Family Service Bureau of Newark

General Information: Behavioral health organization providing counseling to all ages concerning most mental health issues; psychiatrist available; substance abuse programs
Contact: Linda Combs, Training Director, 393 Central Ave., Newark, NJ 07103
Fax: 732-484-3452
E-mail: lcombs@newcommunity.org
Web site: www.newcommunity.org

Metuchen-Edison YMCA

General Information: Community-based YMCA that offers membership privileges and programming services to build body, mind, and spirit for all persons in the community
Contact: Megan Powers, Branch Executive Director, 65 High St., Metuchen, NJ 08840
Phone: 732-548-2044
Fax: 732-549-0910
E-mail: mpmetedisonymca1@aol.com

Montclair Art Museum

General Information: Art museum with a permanent collection spanning 3 centuries of American art with strengths in 19th-century American landscapes, Hudson River School, and American impressionist paintings, in addition to a Native American collection of almost 4000 objects which represent nearly every North American indigenous culture
Contact: Rachel Wynne, Associate Educator, 3 South Mountain Ave., Montclair, NJ 07042
Fax: 973-746-0536
E-mail: rachel@montclair-art.org

Morris Area Girl Scout Council

General Information: Agency that recruits and retains girls and adults into the Girl Scouting organization and provides fun and interesting programs so that girls can become happy, resourceful citizens
Contact: Martha Krall, Membership Services Director, 1579 Sussex Turnpike, Randolph, NJ 07869
Fax: 973-927-7683
E-mail: gsboard@magsc.org
Web site: www.magsc.org

Rutgers Cooperative Extension of Hunterdon County

General Information: Program that provides information to commercial farmers to allow them to make good pest control decisions
Contact: Meredith Compton, IPM Program Associate, PO Box 2900, 4 Gauntt Place, Flemington, NJ 08822
Phone: 908-788-1338
Fax: 908-806-4735
E-mail: macompton@aesop.rutgers.edu
Web site: www.rce.rutgers.edu

Somerset County Park Commission Environmental Education Center

General Information: Environmental education center/park providing leisure learning opportunities for the public, schools, and scouting groups
Contact: Kurt Bender, Environmental Science Supervisor, 190 Lord Stirling Rd., Basking Ridge, NJ 07920
Phone: 908-766-2489, Ext. 332
Fax: 908-766-2687
E-mail: kbbender@parks.co.somerset.nj.us
Web site: www.park.co.somerset.nj.us

New York

Accredited Care, Inc.

General Information: Provider of home health-care services
Contact: Fred Press, Director, 106 West Third St., Ste. 707, Jamestown, NY 14701
Phone: 212-517-8110
E-mail: acihomehealth@aol.com

Alternatives Federal Credit Union

General Information: Community development credit union that focuses services toward low income residents of Tompkins County, New York
Contact: Sharon Kinnan, Human Resource Manager, 125 North Fulton St., Ithaca, NY 14850
Phone: 607-273-4611, Ext. 821
Fax: 607-277-6391
E-mail: skinnan@alternatives.org
Web site: www.alternatives.org

American & International Designs, Inc.
General Information: Interior design firm that specializes in restaurant, healthcare, medical, corporate facilities and the luxury home market
Contact: Alex Reyes, Internship Coordinator, 1100 South Ave., Ste. 2, Staten Island, NY 10314
Fax: 718-317-9627
E-mail: susanharann@aol.com
Web site: www.designamericanyc.com

American Society of Composers, Authors, and Publishers
General Information: Membership organization of over 70,000 composers, songwriters, lyricists, and music publishers; ASCAP's function is to protect the rights of its members by licensing and paying royalties for the public performances of their copyrighted works
Contact: Manny Valderas, Human Resources Administrator, 1 Lincoln Plaza, Floor 6, New York, NY 10023-7129
Fax: 212-874-8480
E-mail: jobline@ascap.com
Web site: www.ascap.com

The Arch, Inc.
General Information: Organization that provides human services through diversity education and arts outreach programs; assists at-risk communities, families, and individuals with arts performance/classes/workshops, food distribution, advocacy, stress relief, and multimedia services (by-donation)
Contact: Craig Kaufman, Director, 175-43 Hillside Ave., Jamaica, NY 11432
Phone: 718-883-7770
Fax: 718-262-8234
E-mail: kaufman@thearch.org
Web site: www.thearch.org

Archive of Contemporary Music
General Information: Nonprofit music library and research center, with over one million recordings, dedicated to the collection and preservation of all types of popular music from around the world, 1950 to the present
Contact: Bob George, Director, 54 White St., New York, NY 10013
Phone: 212-226-6967
Fax: 212-226-6540
E-mail: arcmusic@inch.com
Web site: www.arcmusic.org

Association of Independent Video and Filmmakers-Foundation for Independent Video and Film
General Information: Trade association of 5000 independent media professionals that provides advocacy and information services; also an educational nonprofit organization offering informational and networking events for filmmakers, and the publisher of a national magazine, The Independent
Contact: Bo Mehrad, Information Services Associate, 304 Hudson St., 6th Floor, New York, NY 10013
Fax: 212-463-8519
E-mail: bo@aivf.org
Web site: www.aivf.org

Bailey House, Inc
General Information: Nonprofit agency that provides housing and supportive services for families living with HIV and AIDS
Contact: Tamesha Harper, Placement Services Manager, 275 7th Ave., 12th Floor, New York, NY 10001
Phone: 212-633-2500, Ext. 215
Fax: 212-633-2932
E-mail: tharper@baileyhouse.org
Web site: www.baileyhouse.org

Barrow Group
General Information: Theater performing full-length new works
Contact: Eric Paeper, Managing Director, 312 West 36th St., New York, NY 10018
E-mail: barrowgroup@earthlink.net
Web site: www.barrowgroup.org

Battery Dance Company
General Information: Dance company that tours internationally, works extensively in the public schools, and produces an annual free public dance festival in New York City's financial district; also organizes domestic tours by foreign dance troupes
Contact: Jonathan Hollander, Artistic/Executive Director, 380 Brd.way, 5th Floor, New York, NY 10013-3518
Phone: 212-219-3910
Fax: 212-219-3911
E-mail: jonathan@batterydanceco.com
Web site: www.batterydanceco.com

Boys & Girls Clubs of Albany
General Information: Organization that promotes the social, educational, and vocational development of at-risk boys and girls by building self-esteem, values, and skills during youth and adolescence
Contact: Doretha Holmes, Deputy Executive Director, 21 Delaware Ave., Albany, NY 12210
Phone: 518-462-5528
Fax: 518-462-5540

Boys & Girls Clubs of East Aurora
General Information: Youth service organization
Contact: Gary Schutrum, Executive Director, 24 Paine St., East Aurora, NY 14052
Phone: 716-652-1060
Fax: 716-652-0212
E-mail: gschutrum@bgcea.org
Web site: www.bgcea.org

Brett Singer & Associates, LLC/David Gersten & Associates, Inc.
General Information: Entertainment publicity office focusing mostly on theater (Brd.way, off-Brd.way, tours)
Contact: Brett Singer, President, 240 West 44th St., New York, NY 10036
Phone: 212-575-0263
Fax: 212-575-2240
E-mail: interns@brettsinger.com
Web site: www.brettsinger.com

Brooklyn Botanic Garden
General Information: Botanical garden
Contact: Rochelle Cabiness, Director of Human Resources, 1000 Washington Ave., Brooklyn, NY 11225
Phone: 718-623-7216
Fax: 718-622-7826
E-mail: rochellecabiness@bbg.org
Web site: www.bbg.org

Buzzco Associates, Inc.
General Information: Traditional animation company specializing in all forms of 2-D animation with projects ranging from corporate sales films, cable network IDs, network public service announcements, and national and regional commercials
Contact: Candy Kugel, Director, Producer, 33 Bleecker St., New York, NY 10012
Phone: 212-473-8800
Fax: 212-473-8891
E-mail: info@buzzzco.com
Web site: www.buzzzco.com

Carolyn Ray
General Information: Manufacturer of fabrics and wallcoverings for interior designers and architects
Contact: Rachael Zumbo, Internship Coordinator, 578 Nepperhan Ave., Yonkers, NY 10701
Fax: 914-476-0677
E-mail: carolyn-ray@msn.com

Central Park SummerStage
General Information: New York's premier free performing arts festival that presents productions of superior artistic caliber

Contact: Carter Angus, Internship Coordinator, 830 Fifth Ave., New York, NY 10021
Fax: 212-360-2754
E-mail: info@summerstage.org
Web site: www.summerstage.org

City Lights Youth Theatre
General Information: Nonprofit theater arts education program for students K-12, offering process-oriented classes, workshops, and residencies that engage New York youth from diverse backgrounds in the performance of theater
Contact: Warren Baumgart, Artistic Director, 300 West 43rd St., Ste. 402, New York, NY 10036
Fax: 212-262-1888
E-mail: citylights@clyouththeatre.org
Web site: www.clyouththeatre.org

Coalition for the International Criminal Court
General Information: Program promoting a fair, effective, and independent International Criminal Court; ratification and implementation of the Rome Statute for the ICC; NGO network building
Contact: Joydeep Sengupta, Outreach/Communications Associate, 777 United Nations Plaza, 12th Floor, New York, NY 10017
Fax: 212-599-1332
E-mail: cicc6@icgnow.org
Web site: www.iccnow.org

Community Environmental Center
General Information: Not-for-profit energy conservation and environmental education center
Contact: Lynn Grace, Director of the Learning Center/Outreach, 43-10 11th St., Long Island City, NY 11101
Phone: 718-784-1444, Ext. 107
Fax: 718-784-8347
E-mail: lgrace@cecenter.org

Director's Company
General Information: Theater that specializes in the development of the director
Contact: Veronica Bainbridge, Internship Coordinator, 311 West 43rd St., Ste. 307, New York, NY 10036
Fax: 212-246-5882
Web site: www.thedirectorscompany.org

The Edelman Group
General Information: Firm that specializes in design, advertising, and marketing for corporate clients
Contact: Sandra Gibbs, Office Administrator
50 Brd. St., Ste. 2001
New York, NY 10004
Fax: 212-825-1900
E-mail: sandy@edelmangroup.com
Web site: www.edelmangroup.com

Elizabeth Dow
General Information: Manufacturer of handpainted wallcoverings and interior decorative painting
Contact: Xavier Santana, Internship Coordinator, 155 6th Ave., 4th Floor, New York, NY 10013
Phone: 212-463-0144
Fax: 212-463-0824
E-mail: edowltd@aol.com
Web site: www.elizabethdow.com

Farm Sanctuary
General Information: National, nonprofit organization dedicated to ending animal agriculture abuses through public education programs, legislation, farm animal cruelty investigations, and campaigns, in addition to running shelters that provide 24-hour emergency rescue, rehabilitation, and permanent care for hundreds of animals
Contact: Michelle Waffner, Education Program Manager
3100 Aikens Rd.
Watkins Glen, NY 14891
Phone: 607-583-4512
Fax: 607-583-4349
E-mail: education@farmsanctuary.org
Web site: www.farmsanctuary.org

The 52nd St. Project
General Information: Nonprofit organization that serves inner-city children by putting them together with adult actors to create original theater
Contact: Megan Sandberg-Zakian, Associate Artistic Director, 500 West 52nd St., 2nd Floor, New York, NY 10019
Phone: 212-333-5252
Fax: 212-333-5598
E-mail: intern@52project.org
Web site: www.52project.org

Fools Company, Inc.
General Information: Not-for-profit cultural and educational organization whose mission is to produce and present innovative and unconventional works and workshops in all areas of the performing arts
Contact: Jill Russell, Executive Director, 423 West 46th St., New York, NY 10036-3510
Phone: 212-307-6000
E-mail: foolsco@nyc.rr.com

Franklin Furnace Archive, Inc.
General Information: Presenters of live art on the Internet
Contact: Harley Spiller, Internship Coordinator, 45 John St., Ste. 611, New York, NY 10038-3706
Phone: 212-766-2606
Fax: 212-766-2740
E-mail: harley@franklinfurnace.org
Web site: www.franklinfurnace.org

Girl Scouts of Southwestern New York
General Information: Organization that provides girls with contemporary developmental experiences to inspire the highest ideals of character and conduct and fosters development into happy, resourceful, and contributing adult women
Contact: Lisa Lane-Gniewecki, Executive Director, 2661 Horton Rd., Jamestown, NY 14701
Phone: 716-665-2225
Fax: 716-661-9704
E-mail: gsswny@yahoo.com

Hearts and Minds Network, Inc.
General Information: Nonprofit organization addressing poverty, the environment, human rights, addictions, and other major issues and providing a clearinghouse of information for the public, locally, nationally, and internationally
Contact: Volunteer/Internship Manager, 3074 Brd.way, New York, NY 10027
Phone: 212-280-0333
Fax: 212-280-0336
E-mail: help@change.net
Web site: www.change.net

Here Arts Center
General Information: Theater and gallery that develop new works
Contact: David Winitsky, Internship Coordinator, 145 Ave. of the Americas, Ground Floor, New York, NY 10013
Fax: 212-647-0257
E-mail: david@here.org
Web site: www.here.org

International Center of Photography
General Information: Museum and school dedicated to the understanding and appreciation of photography
Contact: Greg Murphy, Internship Coordinator, 1114 Ave. of the Americas, School and Administration Offices, New York, NY 10036
Phone: 212-857-0022
Fax: 212-857-0090
E-mail: info@icp.org
Web site: www.icp.org

Jean Cocteau Repertory Theater

General Information: Permanent residential acting company performing in repertory presenting classical plays
Contact: Ernest Johns, Production Director, 330 Bowery, New York, NY 10012
Fax: 212-777-6151
E-mail: cocteau@jeancocteaurep.org
Web site: www.jeancocteaurep.org

John Drew Theater of Guild Hall

General Information: Performing arts presenter and Equity theater associated with art museum
Contact: Josh Gladstone, Artistic Director, 158 Main St., East Hampton, NY 11937
Fax: 631-324-2722
E-mail: joshgladstone@guildhall.org
Web site: www.GuildHall.org

Manhattan Class Company

General Information: Off-Brd.way theater
Contact: Eric Bornemann, Office Manager, 145 West 28th St., 8thFloor, New York, NY 10001
Phone: 212-727-7722
Fax: 212-727-7780
E-mail: ebornemann@mcctheater.org
Web site: www.mcctheater.org

Maysles Films, Inc.

General Information: Leading force in non-fiction film, making over a dozen documentaries as well as producing reality commercials and infomercials
Contact: Internship Coordinator, 250 West 54th St., PH, New York, NY 10019
Phone: 212-582-6050
Fax: 212-586-2057
Web site: www.mayslesfilms.com

Metro Justice of Rochester

General Information: Multi-issue community organization focusing on economic justice, antiracism, Latin American solidarity, health care, labor, women's issues, and environmental issues
Contact: Jon Greenbaum, Organizer, 36 St. Paul St., Room 112, Rochester, NY 14604
Phone: 585-325-2560
Fax: 585-325-2561
E-mail: metroj@frontiernet.net
Web site: www.metrojustice.org

Michael Perez Gallery

General Information: Art gallery showing only the owner's work
Contact: Allison Schneider, Partner, 49 Jobs Lane, Southampton, NY 11968
E-mail: mperezgallery@aol.com
Web site: www.michaelperez-artist.com

The Museum of Television & Radio

General Information: Museum that collects, preserves, and exhibits radio and television programs
Contact: Robert Eng, Director, 25 West 52nd St., New York, NY 10019
Phone: 212-621-6620
Fax: 212-621-6700
E-mail: reng@mtr.org
Web site: www.mtr.org

Nassau County Office of Cinema and Television Promotion

General Information: Film commission that scouts locations and facilitates film production, commercials, videos, and still photography; also runs the Long Island International Film Expo
Contact: Debra Markowitz, Director 400 County Seat Drive Mineola, NY 11501
Phone: 516-571-3168
Fax: 516-571-5801
E-mail: debfilm@aol.com

Web site: www.nassaucountynyde-velopment.org
New York Botanical Garden
General Information: Internationally recognized center for botanical research, dedicated to environmental education and the conservation of plant diversity; operations at this facility include scientific research, horticulture, and education
Contact: Claribel Irizarry, Human Resources Representative, 200th St. and Kazimiroff Blvd, Bronx, NY 10458-5126
Phone: 718-817-8872
Fax: 718-220-6504
E-mail: hr2@nybg.org
Web site: www.nybg.org

New York State Theatre Institute

General Information: Professional theater company and statewide arts-in-education program that develops one new musical theater production a season for family audiences, and performs a range of classical, modern, contemporary, and new works for school, family, and general audiences
Contact: Arlene Leff, Intern Program Administrator/Education Director, Russell Sage Campus, 37 First St., Troy, NY 12180
Phone: 518-274-3573
Fax: 518-274-3815
E-mail: nysti@capital.net
Web site: www.nysti.org

Operation Crossrd.s Africa

General Information: International nonprofit, nongovernmental volunteer organization
Contact: Willis Logan, Chairman, 34 Mount Morris Park, New York, NY 10027
Phone: 212-289-1949
Fax: 212-289-2526
E-mail: oca@igc.org
Web site: www.igc.org/oca

The Poetry Project

General Information: Literary center with an arts program featuring readings, performances, workshops, and publications
Contact: Maureen Owen, Program Coordinator, 131 East 10th St., New York, NY 10003
Phone: 212-674-0910
Fax: 212-529-2318
E-mail: poproj@poetryproject.com
Web site: www.poetryproject.com

Queens Theater in the Park

General Information: Performing arts center
Contact: Gail Koelln, Development Director, PO Box 520069, Flushing, NY 11352
Phone: 718-760-0686
Fax: 718-760-5092
E-mail: qtipgail@aol.com
Web site: www.queenstheatre.org

Rainforest Relief

General Information: Rainforest preservation/conservation organization working to reduce the demand for rainforest-destructive materials through education and direct action
Contact: Tim Keating, Executive Director, 338 Prospect Place, Brooklyn, NY 11238
Phone: 718-398-3760
Fax: 718-398-3760
E-mail: relief@igc.org
Web site: www.rainforestrelief.org

Richard P. Dieguez, Attorney and Counsellor at Law

General Information: Entertainment law practice and entertainment industry educational organization
Contact: Richard Dieguez, 192 Garden St., Ste. 2, Roslyn Heights, NY 11577-1012
Phone: 516-621-6424
E-mail: rpdieguez@rpdieguez.com
Web site: www.rpdieguez.com

Socialist Party USA

General Information: Political party
Contact: Greg Pason, National Secretary, 339 Lafayette St., Room 303,

New York, NY 11001
Phone: 212-982-4586
Fax: 212-982-4586
E-mail: natsec@sp-usa.org
Web site: www.votesocialist.org

South St. Seaport Museum

General Information: Maritime history museum, located in a 12-block historic district in downtown Manhattan, that interprets the role of the seaport in the development of the city, the state, and the nation through education programs, exhibitions, and the preservation of buildings and ships
Contact: Richard Dorfman, Director of Volunteers and Community Outreach, 207 Front St.
New York, NY 10038
Phone: 212-748-8727
Fax: 212-748-8610
E-mail: rdorfman@southstseaport.org
Web site: www.southstseaport.org

Staten Island Institute of Arts and Sciences

General Information: Organization that focuses on Staten Island and its people and has strong collections in these subjects
Contact: Bart Bland, Director of Exhibitions, 75 Stuyvesant Place, Staten Island, NY 10301-1998
Phone: 718-727-1135
Fax: 718-273-5683
E-mail: blandsiias@aol.com
Web site: www.siiasmuseum.org

The Theatre-Studio, Inc.

General Information: Studio theater that focuses on growth of theater arts for the community
Contact: A. M. Raychel, Producing/Artistic Director, 750 Eighth Ave., Ste. 200, New York, NY 10036
Phone: 212-719-0500
Fax: 212-719-0537
E-mail: arayche@attglobal.net
Web site: www.theatrestudio.org

Thirteenth St. Repertory Company
General Information: Nonprofit off-off-Brd.way theater that operates 52 weeks per year and performs full-length plays every 3 months, children's plays every Saturday and Sunday, Sunday Reading Series, and other ongoing projects
Contact: Sandra Nordgren, General Manager, 50 West 13th St., New York, NY 10011
Phone: 917-363-2369
E-mail: sandranord@aol.com
Web site: www.13thSt.Rep.org

United Nations Association of the USA

General Information: Nonprofit, nonpartisan, national organization dedicated to strengthening the United Nations system and to enhancing U.S. participation in the UN and other international institutions
Contact: Gary Su, Intern Coordinator, 801 2nd Ave., New York, NY 10017
Fax: 212-682-9185
E-mail: gsu@unausa.org
Web site: www.unausa.org

Untitled Theater Company #61

General Information: Nonprofit producer of experimental and philosophic plays off-Brd.way
Contact: Edward Einhorn, Artistic Director, 235 West 102nd St., Ste. 16-S, New York, NY 10025
Phone: 212-866-1073
E-mail: utc61@hotmail.com
Web site: www.untitledtheater.com

Vineyard Theater

General Information: Theater that specializes in developing and producing new dramatic and musical theater
Contact: Rebecca Habel, Business Manager, 108 East 15th St., New York, NY 10003-9689
Fax: 212-353-3803
E-mail: rhabel@vineyardtheatre.org
Web site: www.vineyardtheatre.org

Visiting Neighbors, Inc.

General Information: Organization that fosters independence for senior citizens living in their homes through neighbor assistance and an escort and shopping program
Contact: Cynthia Maurer, Executive Director, 611 Brd.way, 5th Floor, Ste. 510, New York, NY 10012
Phone: 212-260-6200
Fax: 212-260-2962
E-mail: hsquarevn@aol.com
Web site: www.visitingneighbors.org

WALK FM/AM

General Information: Commercial FM/AM radio station offering programming to Long Island's adult audiences
Contact: Bill Terry, Intern Coordinator, 66 Colonial Drive, Patchogue, NY 11772
Phone: 631-475-5200
Fax: 631-475-9016
E-mail: bterry@walkradio.com
Web site: www.WALKRADIO.com

Women's Project and Productions

General Information: Nonprofit theater organization that seeks to develop and produce original works written and directed by women in the off-Brd.way theater and to promote women in the theater nationally
Contact: Cory Hinkle, Assistant to Artistic Director/Intern Coordinator, 55 West End Ave., New York, NY 10023
Phone: 212-765-1706
Fax: 212-765-2024
E-mail: info@womensproject.org
Web site: www.womensproject.org

Yeshiva University Museum

General Information: Museum that preserves, exhibits, and interprets Jewish life, art history, and culture through multidisciplinary exhibitions, contemporary shows, and scholarly catalogs
Contact: Mary Kiplok, Internship Coordinator, 15 West 16th St., New York, NY 10011
Fax: 212-294-8335
E-mail: mkiplok@yum.cjh.org
Web site: www.yu.edu/museum

Pennsylvania

The Andy Warhol Museum

General Information: Museum that features extensive permanent collections of art and archives and presents the work of one of the most influential American artists of the second half of the 20th century
Contact: Rachel Baron, Administrative and Financial Coordinator, 117 Sandusky St., Pittsburgh, PA 15212
Web site: www.warhol.org

Arden Theatre Company

General Information: Nonprofit, professional theater company whose mission is to tell the greatest stories by the greatest storytellers of all time, stories that arouse, provoke, illuminate, and inspire
Contact: Intern or Apprentice Coordinator, 40 North Second St., Philadelphia, PA 19106
Fax: 215-922-7011
Web site: www.ardentheatre.org

Audubon YMCA

General Information: Organization that provides the community with services that promote healthy spirits, minds, and bodies
Contact: Janet Genuardi, 2460 Blvd of the Generals, Norristown, PA 19403
Phone: 610-539-0900
Fax: 610-539-2975
E-mail: jlg@net-thing.net
Web site: www.phoenixvilleareaymca.org

Big Brothers Big Sisters of Bucks County

General Information: Organization that provides mentoring services to youth
Contact: Susan Bartels, Director of Program Development, 2875 Old York Rd., Jamison, PA 18929
Phone: 215-343-8260, Ext. 15
Fax: 215-343-8265
E-mail: bartels@bbbsbc.org
Web site: www.bbbsbc.org

Fort Necessity National Battlefield

General Information: Site commemorating the start of the French and Indian War in 1754
Contact: Carney Rigg, Volunteer Coordinator, 1 Washington Pkwy, Farmington, PA 15437
E-mail: carney_rigg@nps.gov
Web site: www.nps.gov/fone

Great Valley Nature Center

General Information: Center that provides environmental education and recreational experience for school children, organized groups, and the general public
Contact: Janet Zeis, Intern Coordinator, PO Box 82, Devault, PA 19432
Phone: 610-935-9777
Fax: 610-935-0130
E-mail: gvncee@nni.com
Web site: www.gvnc.org

Greenwood Furnace State Park

General Information: State park that offers a full range of camping and activities, including a visitor center offering historical interpretation of the former iron furnace
Contact: Paul Fagley, Cultural Educator, RR 2, Box 118, Huntingdon, PA 16652-9006
Phone: 814-667-1805
Fax: 814-667-1802
E-mail: greenwoodfurnacesp@state.pa.us
Web site: www.dcnr.state.pa.us

Greer Lange Talent Agency

General Information: Full-service talent agency representing union and non-union actors, models, and extras
Contact: Stacy Bell, Vice President, Sales and Marketing, 40 Lloyd Ave., Ste. 104, Malvern, PA 19355
Fax: 610-889-3097
E-mail: info@greerlange.com
Web site: www.greerlange.com

Hopewell Furnace National Historic Site

General Information: Historic site preserving a 19th-century ironmaking community and a 200,000-object museum collection on 848 acres
Contact: Frank Hebblethwaite, Volunteer Coordinator, 2 Mark Bird Lane, Elverson, PA 19520
Phone: 610-582-8773, Ext. 229
Fax: 610-582-2768
E-mail: hofu_superintendent@nps.gov
Web site: www.nps.gov/hofu

Philadelphia Magazine

General Information: City magazine covering local politics, news, and entertainment
Contact: Victor Fiorillo, Research Editor, 1818 Market St., 36th Floor, Philadelphia, PA 19103
Fax: 215-656-3502
E-mail: victor@phillymag.com
Web site: www.phillymag.com

Riverbend Environmental Education Center

General Information: Environmental education center emphasizing awareness, appreciation, and understanding of the environment
Contact: Stacy Carr, Director of Children's Programs, 1950 Spring Mill Rd., Gladwyne, PA 19035
Phone: 610-527-5234
Fax: 610-527-1161
E-mail: scarr@riverbendeec.org
Web site: www.gladwyne.com/riverbend

Sarah Heinz House

General Information: Youth recreation center for children ages 7-18
Contact: Jennifer Roberts, Program Director, One Heinz St., Pittsburgh, PA 15212
Phone: 412-231-2377
Fax: 412-231-2428
E-mail: roberts@sarahheinzhouse.com
Web site: www.sarahheinzhouse.org

Waynesboro YMCA

General Information: Worldwide fellowship united by a common loyalty to Jesus Christ for the purpose of building Christian personality and a Christian society
Contact: H. Smith, Associate Executive Director, 810 East Main St., Waynesboro, PA 17268
Phone: 717-762-6012
Fax: 717-762-4368
E-mail: alansmith@wboy.org
Web site: www.wboy.org

Women's International League for Peace and Freedom

General Information: Organization devoted to ending sexism, racism, classism, oppression, militarism, and all forms of violence
Contact: Jody Dodd, Leadership/Outreach Coordinator, 1213 Race St., Philadelphia, PA 19107-1691
Phone: 215-563-7110
Fax: 215-563-5527
E-mail: jdodd@wilpf.org
Web site: www.wilpf.org

YWCA of Greater Harrisburg

General Information: Organization that actively serves as an advocate and resource to the community on issues that impact women and children and provides services to empower women, including violence intervention and prevention, child care, and housing
Contact: Jennifer Cooper, Assistant Director of Violence and Prevention Services, 1101 Market St., Harrisburg, PA 17103
Phone: 717-238-7273
Fax: 717-238-4533
E-mail: jcooper@ywcahbg.org

Virginia

Alternative House

General Information: Shelter and outreach program that builds on the innate strengths and resiliency of children, youth, and families through individual, group, and family interaction
Contact: Volunteer Coordinator, 2136 Gallows Rd., Ste. E, Dunn Loring, VA 22027
Phone: 703-820-9039
Fax: 703-820-0788

Ash Lawn Opera Festival

General Information: Summer festival producing 2 operas and 1 musical theater production for a total of 28 performances; hosts additional musical and theatrical productions for all ages
Contact: Assistant to the General Director, 1941 James Monroe Pkwy, Charlottesville, VA 22902-8722
Phone: 434-293-4500
Fax: 434-293-0736
E-mail: opera@ave..org
Web site: www.ashlawnopera.org

Booker T. Washington National Monument

General Information: National park service site where Booker T. Washington was born in 1856; focuses on interpretive programs about the influence of slavery on Washington's life
Contact: Betsy Haynes, 12130 Booker T. Washington Hwy, Hardy, VA 24101
E-mail: betsy_haynes@nps.gov
Web site: www.nps.gov/bowa

Children's Hospice International

General Information: Organization that provides advocacy and outreach services for children with life-threatening conditions and their families
Contact: Ann Armstrong-Dailey, Founding Director, 901 North Pitt St., Ste. 230, Alexandria, VA 22314
Phone: 703-684-0330
Fax: 703-684-0226
E-mail: chiorg@aol.com
Web site: www.chionline.org

Children's Museum of Richmond (CMOR)

General Information: Cultural art center
Contact: Irene Luu, Volunteer Resources Coordinator, 2626 West Brd. St., Richmond, VA 23220-1904
Phone: 804-474-7029
Fax: 804-474-7099
E-mail: iluu@c-mor.org
Web site: www.c-mor.org

Fairfax Symphony Orchestra

General Information: Nonprofit, professional symphony orchestra that performs year-round in northern Virginia and greater metropolitan Washington, D.C
Contact: Rachael Garrity, Executive Director, PO Box 1300, Annandale, VA 22003
Fax: 703-642-7205
E-mail: rgarrity@fairfaxsymphony.org
Web site: www.fairfaxsymphony.org

Grobit Media

General Information: Digital media contact design and development firm specializing in consumer products
Contact: Greg Schraff, Managing Partner, 1025 North Fillmore St., Ste. 280, Arlington, VA 22201
Fax: 703-248-8814
E-mail: gregschraff@grobit.com
Web site: www.grobit.com

Hensel Eckman YMCA

General Information: Association that provides the best in fitness, child development, and aquatics
Contact: Jerry Duncan, Program Director, 615 Oakhurst Ave., Pulaski, VA 24301
Phone: 540-980-3671
Fax: 540-980-7422
E-mail: pulaski6@i-plus.net
Web site: www.i-plus.net/~pulaski6/

National Wildlife Federation Campus Ecology Program

General Information: Program that supports practical conservation projects on college and university campuses by assisting with project implementation, providing training, and documenting lessons learned nationally and beyond
Contact: Kathy Cacciola, Coordinator, 11100 Wildlife Center Drive, Reston, VA 20190-5362
Phone: 703-438-6318
Fax: 703-438-6468
E-mail: cacciola@nwf.org
Web site: www.nwf.org/campus ecology

Office of Historic Alexandria

General Information: Office involved with the preservation of historic sites, artifacts, records, and the enhancement and preservation of the cultural diversity of Alexandria; provides programs to bring people and business to the city
Contact: Jean Taylor Federico, Director, PO Box 178, City Hall, Alexandria, VA 22313
Phone: 703-838-4554
Fax: 703-838-6451
E-mail: jean.federico@ci.alexandria.va.us
Web site: www.ci.alexandria.va.us/oha

Youth Venture

General Information: National, not-for-profit organization that enables young people (ages 12-20) to create, lead, and launch their own organizations, clubs, or businesses that make a difference in their community
Contact: Lorenley Baez, Program Assistant, 1700 North Moore St., Ste. 2000, Arlington, VA 22209
Phone: 703-527-4126, Ext. 315
Fax: 703-527-8383
E-mail: info@youthventure.org
Web site: www.youthventure.org

West Virginia

Harpers Ferry National Historical Park

General Information: Park whose mission is to preserve and protect the natural and cultural resources of the Harpers Ferry area including natural heritage, transportation, water-powered industry, John Brown's raid, the Civil War, and African-American history for the education of current and future generations
Contact: David Fox, Volunteer Coordinator, PO Box 65, Harpers Ferry, WV 25425
Phone: 304-535-6282
Fax: 304-535-2912
E-mail: david_fox@nps.gov
Web site: www.nps.gov/hafe/home.htm

SUMMER OPPORTUNITIES

Delaware

University of Delaware Summer College
Newark, DE
General Information: Coed residential academic program established in 1983.
Contact: Ms. Elizabeth B. Reynolds, Coordinator, 206 Elliott Hall, Newark, DE 19716-1256
Phone: 302-831-6560
Fax: 302-831-4339
E-mail: summercollege@udel.edu
Web site: www.udel.edu/summer college

District of Columbia

Catholic University Benjamin T. Rome School of Music
Washington, DC
General Information: Coed residential and day arts program.
Contact: Jessica Madrigal, Director of Summer Sessions, 330 Pangborn Hall, 620 Michigan Ave., NE, Washington, DC 20064
Phone: 202-319-5257
Fax: 202-319-6725
E-mail: cua-summers@cua.edu
Web site: summer.cua.edu

Catholic University Capitol Classic Debate Institute
Washington, DC
General Information: Coed residential and day academic program established in 2000.
Contact: Jessica Madrigal, Director of Summer Sessions, 330 Pangborn Hall, 620 Michigan Ave., NE, Washington, DC 20064
Phone: 202-319-5257
Fax: 202-319-6725
E-mail: cua-summers@cua.edu
Web site: summer.cua.edu

Catholic University College Courses for High School Students
Washington, DC
General Information: Coed residential and day academic program.
Contact: Jessica Madrigal, Director of Summer Sessions, 330 Pangborn Hall,

620 Michigan Ave., NE, Washington, DC 20064
Phone: 202-319-5257
Fax: 202-319-6725
E-mail: cua-summers@cua.edu
Web site: summer.cua.edu

Catholic University Communication and Media Studies Workshops
Washington, DC
General Information: Coed residential and day academic and arts program established in 2000.
Contact: Jessica Madrigal, Director of Summer Sessions, 330 Pangborn Hall, 620 Michigan Ave., NE, Washington, DC 20064
Phone: 202-319-5257
Fax: 202-319-6725
E-mail: cua-summers@cua.edu
Web site: summer.cua.edu

Catholic University Experiences in Architecture
Washington, DC
General Information: Coed residential and day academic program.
Contact: Jessica Madrigal, Director of Summer Sessions, 330 Pangborn Hall, 620 Michigan Ave., NE, Washington, DC 20064
Phone: 202-319-5257
E-mail: cua-summers@cua.edu
Web site: summer.cua.edu

Catholic University Eye on Engineering
Washington, DC
General Information: Coed residential academic program.
Contact: Emma Cox, School of Engineering, 102 Pangborn Hall, Washington, DC 20064
Phone: 202-319-516
E-mail: coxe@cua.edu
Web site: summer.cua.edu

Georgetown University College Prep Program
Washington, DC
General Information: Coed residential and day academic program.
Contact: Ms. Emma Harrington, Special Programs Director, School for Summer and Continuing Education,

PO Box 571010, Washington, DC 20057-1010
Phone: 202-687-5719
Fax: 202-687-8954
E-mail: harringe@georgetown.edu
Web site: www.georgetown.edu/ssce/spp/hscp

Georgetown University International Relations Program for High School Students
Washington, DC
General Information: Coed residential and day academic program.
Contact: Ms. Emma Harrington, Special Programs Director, School for Summer and Continuing Education, PO Box 571010, Washington, DC 20057-1010
Phone: 202-687-571
Fax: 202-687-8954
E-mail: harringe@georgetown.edu
Web site: www.georgetown.edu/ssce/spp/hsir

Georgetown University Summer College for High School Juniors
Washington, DC
General Information: Coed residential academic program.
Contact: Ms. Emma Harrington, Special Programs Director, School for Summer and Continuing Education, PO Box 571010, Washington, DC 20057-1010
Phone: 202-687-5719
Fax: 202-687-8954
E-mail: harringe@georgetown.edu
Web site: www.georgetown.edu/ssce/spp/hsj

George Washington University Summer Scholars Program
Washington, DC
General Information: Coed residential academic program.
Contact: Ms. Margaret Myers, Program Assistant, 2100 Foxhall Rd., Mount Vernon Campus, Washington, DC 20007
Phone: 202-242-6802
E-mail: memyers@gwu.edu
Web site: www.gwu.edu/summer/scholars

iD Tech Camps-Georgetown University
Washington, DC
General Information: Coed residential and day academic program established in 1999.
Contact: Client Service Representatives, 1885 Winchester Blvd, Ste. 201, Campbell, CA 95008,
Phone: 888-709-TECH
Fax: 408-871-2227
E-mail: requests@internaldrive.com
Web site: www.internaldrive.com

Junior Statesmen Summer School-Georgetown University
Washington, DC
General Information: Coed residential academic program established in 1981.
Contact: Preeta Nayak, Summer School Director, 60 East 3rd Ave., Ste. 320, San Mateo, CA 94401 **Phone:** 650-347-1600
Fax: 650-347-7200
E-mail: jsa@jsa.org
Web site: www.jsa.org

National Student Leadership Conference: Business and Commerce
Washington, DC
General Information: Coed residential academic program established in 1989.
Contact: Mr. Mike Sims, Executive Director, 111 West Jackson Blvd, 7th Floor, Chicago, IL 60604
Phone: 312-322-9999
Fax: 312-765-0081
E-mail: information@nslcleaders.org
Web site: www.nslcleaders.org

National Student Leadership Conference: International Diplomacy
Washington, DC
General Information: Coed residential academic program established in 1989.
Contact: Mr. Mike Sims, Executive Director, 111 West Jackson Blvd, 7th Floor, Chicago, IL 60604
Phone: 312-322-9999
Fax: 312-765-0081
E-mail: information@nslcleaders.org
Web site: www.nslcleaders.org

National Student Leadership Conference: Law and Advocacy
Washington, DC
General Information: Coed residential academic program established in 1989.
Contact: Mr. Mike Sims, Executive

Director, 111 West Jackson Blvd, 7th Floor, Chicago, IL 60604
Phone: 312-322-9999
Fax: 312-765-0081
E-mail: information@nslcleaders.org
Web site: www.nslcleaders.org

National Student Leadership Conference: Mastering Leadership
Washington, DC
General Information: Coed residential academic program established in 1989.
Contact: Mr. Mike Sims, Executive Director, 111 West Jackson Blvd, 7th Floor, Chicago, IL 60604
Phone: 312-322-9999
Fax: 312-765-0081
E-mail: information@nslcleaders.org
Web site: www.nslcleaders.org

National Student Leadership Conference: Medicine and Health Care
Washington, DC
General Information: Coed residential academic program established in 1989.
Contact: Mr. Mike Sims, Executive Director, 111 West Jackson Blvd, 7th Fl., Chicago, IL 60604
Phone: 312-322-9999
Fax: 312-765-008
E-mail: information@nslcleaders.org
Web site: www.nslcleaders.org

Summer Discovery at Georgetown
Washington, DC
General Information: Coed residential academic program established in 1994.
Contact: The Musiker Family, Director, 1326 Old Northern Blvd, Roslyn Village, NY 11576 **Phone:** 888-878-6637
Fax: 516-625-3438
E-mail: discovery@summerfun.com
Web site: www.summerfun.com

Maryland

The Arts! at Maryland
College Park, MD
General Information: Coed residential and day arts program established in 2004.
Contact: Dr. Christopher Patton, Artistic Director, The Arts! at Maryland, 2103 Reckord Armory, College Park, MD 20742
Phone: 301-405-8174
Fax: 301-314-9572
E-mail: cpatton@umd.edu
Web site: www.summer.umd.edu/arts

Georgetown Prep School Summer English Program
Rockville, MD
General Information: Coed residential and day academic program established in 1974.
Contact: Ms. Rosita Whitman, 10900 Rockville Pike, Rockville, MD 20852
Phone: 301-214-1250
Fax: 301-214-8600
E-mail: rwhitman@gprep.org
Web site: www.gprep.org/esl/index.cfm

Johns Hopkins University Zanvyl Krieger School of Arts and Sciences Summer Programs
Baltimore, MD
General Information: Coed residential and day academic program.
Contact: Jill Kearney, Assistant Director of Academic Services, 3400 North Charles St., Ste. G1/Wyman Park Building, Baltimore, MD 21218
Phone: 800-548-0548
Fax: 410-516-5585
E-mail: summer@jhu.edu
Web site: www.jhu.edu/summer

National Debate Institute - Education Unlimited
College Park, MD
General Information:
Coed residential and day academic program established in 1995.
Contact: Mr. Robert Thomas, Associate Director, 1678 Shattuck Ave., #305, Berkeley, CA 94709
Phone: 510-548-4800
Fax: 510-548-0212
E-mail: ebate@educationunlimited.com
Web site: www.educationunlimited.com

University of Maryland Young Scholars Program
College Park, MD
General Information: Coed residential and day academic program established in 2002.
Contact: Ms. Terrie Heuzd, Program Manager, 2103 Reckord Armory, College Park, MD 20742
Phone: 301-405-8588
E-mail: heuzd@umd.edu
Web site:
www.summer.umd.edu/youngscholars

New Jersey

Appel Farm Summer Arts Camp
Elmer, NJ
General Information: Coed residential arts program established in 1959.
Contact: Mr. Matt Sisson, Director, PO Box 888, Elmer, NJ 08318-0888
Phone: 856-358-2472
Fax: 856-358-6513
E-mail: appelcamp@aol.com
Web site: www.appelfarm.org

Drew Summer Music
Madison, NJ
General Information: Coed residential and day arts program established in 1995.
Contact: Dr. Virginia Schulze-Johnson, Director, Drew University, Madison, NJ 07940
Phone: 973-408-3428
Fax: 973-408-3885
E-mail: vschulze@drew.edu
Web site: www.depts.drew.edu/music/beyond/dsm/dsmindex.htm

ECOES: Exploring Career Options in Engineering and Science
Hoboken, NJ
General Information: Coed residential academic program established in 1978.
Contact: Ms. Rae Talerico, Director, Pre-College Programs, Lore-El Center, Castle Point on Hudson, Hoboken, NJ 07030
Phone: 201-216-5245
Fax: 201-216-5175
E-mail: ataleric@stevens-tech.edu
Web site: www.attila.stevens-tech.edu/lore-el/pre-college/ecoes

The Hun School of Princeton American Culture and Language Institute
Princeton, NJ
General Information: Coed residential and day academic program established in 1994.
Contact: Ms. Dianne Somers, Director, 176 Edgerstoune Rd., Princeton, NJ 08540
Phone: 609-921-7600
Fax: 609-683-4410
E-mail: summer@hunschool.org
Web site: www.hunschool.org

The Hun School of Princeton-Summer Academic Session
Princeton, NJ
General Information: Coed residential and day academic program established in 1990.
Contact: Ms. LeRhonda Greats, Summer Academic Director, 176 Edgerstoune Rd., Princeton, NJ 08540
Phone: 609-921-7600
Fax: 609-683-4410
E-mail: summer@hunschool.org
Web site: www.hunschool.org

The Hun School of Princeton Summer Theatre Classics
Princeton, NJ
General Information: Coed residential and day arts program established in 1995.
Contact: Ms. Julia Ohm, Summer Programs Office, 176 Edgerstoune Rd., Princeton, NJ 08540
Phone: 609-921-7600 ext. 2339
E-mail: summer@hunschool.org
Web site: www.hunschool.org

iD Tech Camps-Princeton University
Princeton, NJ
General Information: Coed residential and day academic program established in 1999.
Contact: Client Service Representatives, 1885 Winchester Blvd, Ste. 201, Campbell, CA 95008
Phone: 888-709-TECH
Fax: 408-871-2227
E-mail: requests@internaldrive.com
Web site: www.internaldrive.com

Junior Statesmen Summer School-Princeton University
Princeton, NJ
General Information: Coed residential academic program established in 1997.
Contact: Preeta Nayak, Summer School Director, 60 East 3rd Ave., Ste. 320, San Mateo, CA 94401
Phone: 650-347-1600
Fax: 650-347-7200
E-mail: jsa@jsa.org
Web site: www.jsa.org

Junior Statesmen Symposium on New Jersey State Politics and Government
Princeton, NJ
General Information: Coed residential academic program established in 1996.

Contact: Preeta Nayak, Program Director, 60 East 3rd Ave., Ste. 320, San Mateo, CA 94401
Phone: 650-347-1600
Fax: 650-347-7200
E-mail: jsa@jsa.org
Web site: www.jsa.org

The New York Film Academy, Princeton University
Princeton, NJ
General Information: Coed residential arts program established in 1992.
Contact: Admissions, 100 East 17th St., New York, NY 10003
Phone: 212-674-4300
Fax: 212-477-1414
E-mail: film@nyfa.com
Web site: www.nyfa.com

Rider University Opportunity for Academically Gifted and Talented High School Students
Lawrenceville, NJ
General Information: Coed residential and day academic program established in 1980.
Contact: Susan Christian, Dean of Enrollment, 2083 Lawrenceville Rd., Lawrenceville, NJ 08648,
Phone: 609-896-5042
Fax: 609-895-6645
Web site: www.rider.edu

The Summer Institute for the Gifted at Drew University
Madison, NJ
General Information: Coed residential academic program established in 1994.
Contact: Dr. Stephen Gessner, Director, River Plaza, 9 West Brd. St., Stamford, CT 06902-3788
Phone: 866-303-4744
Fax: 203-399-5598
E-mail: sig.info@aifs.com
Web site: www.giftedstudy.com

Westminster Choir College Composition Week
Princeton, NJ
General Information: Coed residential arts program.
Contact: Scott R. Hoerl, Director of Continuing Education, 101 Walnut Lane, Princeton, NJ 08540-3899
Phone: 609-924-7416
Fax: 609-921-6187
E-mail: woce@rider.edu
Web site: westminster.rider.edu

Westminster Choir College High School Solo Pianist

Princeton, NJ

General Information: Coed residential arts program established in 2000.
Contact: Scott R. Hoerl, Director of Continuing Education, 101 Walnut Lane, Princeton, NJ 08540-3899
Phone: 609-924-7416 ext. 227
Fax: 609-921-6187
E-mail: woce@rider.edu
Web site: westminster.rider.edu

Westminster Choir College High School Solo Vocal Artist: A Performance Workshop for Singers

Princeton, NJ

General Information: Coed residential arts program established in 1999.
Contact: Scott R. Hoerl, Director of Continuing Education, 101 Walnut Lane, Princeton, NJ 08540-3899
Phone: 609-924-7416
Fax: 609-921-6187
E-mail: woce@rider.edu
Web site: westminster.rider.edu

Westminster Choir College Middle School Piano Camp

Princeton, NJ

General Information: Coed residential arts program established in 2000.
Contact: Scott R. Hoerl, Director of Continuing Education, 101 Walnut Lane, Princeton, NJ 08540-3899
Phone: 609-924-7416
Fax: 609-921-6187
E-mail: woce@rider.edu
Web site: westminster.rider.edu

Westminster Choir College Middle School Vocal Camp

Princeton, NJ

General Information: Coed residential arts program established in 1995.
Contact: Scott R. Hoerl, Director of Continuing Education, 101 Walnut Lane, Princeton, NJ 08540-3899
Phone: 609-924-7416
Fax: 609-921-6187
E-mail: woce@rider.edu
Web site: www.westminster.rider.edu

Westminster Choir College Music Theater Week

Princeton, NJ

General Information: Coed residential arts program established in 1995.
Contact: Scott R. Hoerl, Director of Continuing Education, 101 Walnut Lane,

Princeton, NJ 08540-3899
Phone: 609-924-7416
Fax: 609-921-6187
E-mail: woce@rider.edu
Web site: westminster.rider.edu

Westminster Choir College Organ Week

Princeton, NJ

General Information: Coed residential arts program.
Contact: Scott R. Hoerl, Director of Continuing Education, 101 Walnut Lane, Princeton, NJ 08540-3899
Phone: 609-924-7416
Fax: 609-921-6187
E-mail: woce@rider.edu
Web site: www.westminster.rider.edu

Westminster Choir College Piano Camp

Princeton, NJ

General Information: Coed residential arts program.
Contact: Scott R. Hoerl, Director of Continuing Education, 101 Walnut Lane, Princeton, NJ 08540-3899
Phone: 609-924-7416
Fax: 609-921-6187
E-mail: woce@rider.edu
Web site: www.westminster.rider.edu

Westminster Choir College Vocal Institute

Princeton, NJ

General Information: Coed residential arts program established in 1948.
Contact: Scott R. Hoerl, Director of Continuing Education, 101 Walnut Lane, Princeton, NJ 08540-3899
Phone: 609-924-7416
Fax: 609-921-6187
E-mail: woce@rider.edu
Web site: westminster.rider.edu

Westminster Conservatory of Music-Flute Camp

Princeton, NJ

General Information: Coed residential and day arts program.
Contact: Conservatory Office, Westminster Choir College of Rider University, 101 Walnut Lane, Princeton, NJ 08540-3899
Phone: 609-921-7104
Fax: 609-921-7296
E-mail: wccconserv@rider.edu
Web site: www.rider.edu/westminster/conserv

New York

Acteen August Academy

New York, NY

General Information: Coed residential and day arts program established in 1978.
Contact: Rita Litton, Acteen Director, 35 West 45th St., New York, NY 10036
Phone: 212-391-5915
Fax: 212-768-8918
E-mail: rita@acteen.com
Web site: www.acteen.com

Acteen July Academy

New York, NY

General Information: Coed residential and day arts program established in 1978.
Contact: Rita Litton, Acteen Director, 35 West 45th St., New York, NY 10036
Phone: 212-391-5915
Fax: 212-768-8918
E-mail: rita@acteen.com
Web site: www.acteen.com

Alfred University Summer Institute in Astronomy

Alfred, NY

General Information: Coed residential academic program established in 1998.
Contact: Ms. Melody McLay, Director of Summer Programs, Alumni Hall, Saxon Drive, Alfred, NY 14802-1205
Phone: 607-871-2612
Fax: 607-871-2045
E-mail: summerpro@alfred.edu
Web site: www.alfred.edu/summer/html/astronomy.html

Alfred University Summer Institute in Entrepreneurial Leadership

Alfred, NY

General Information: Coed residential academic program established in 1998.
Contact: Ms. Melody McLay, Director of Summer Programs, Alumni Hall, Saxon Drive, Alfred, NY 14802-1205
Phone: 607-871-2612
Fax: 607-871-2045
E-mail: summerpro@alfred.edu
Web site: www.alfred.edu/summer/html/entrepreneurial.html

Alfred University Summer Institute in Writing
Alfred, NY
General Information: Coed residential academic and arts program established in 2000.
Contact: Ms. Melody McLay, Director of Summer Programs, Alumni Hall, Saxon Drive, Alfred, NY 14802-1205
Phone: 607-871-2612
E-mail: summerpro@alfred.edu
Web site: www.alfred.edu/summer

Barnard's Summer in New York City: A Pre-College Program
New York, NY
General Information: Coed residential and day academic program established in 1985.
Contact: Director of Pre-College Programs, 3009 Brd.way, New York, NY 10027-6598
Phone: 212-854-8866
Fax: 212-854-8867
E-mail: pcp@barnard.edu
Web site: www.barnard.edu/pcp

Bristol Hills Music Camp
Canandaigua, NY
General Information: Coed residential arts program established in 1962.
Contact: Irene Hebert, Registrar, 4304 Hepatica Hill Rd., Manlius, NY 13104
Phone: 315-682-6786
E-mail: rhebert694@earthlink.net
Web site: www.bristolhillsmusiccamp.com

Columbia University Summer Program for High School Students
New York, NY
General Information: Coed residential and day academic program established in 1987.
Contact: Ms. Darlene Giraitis, Director of Secondary School Programs, Columbia University, 2970 Brd.way, Mail Code 4110, New York, NY 10027
Phone: 212-854-3771
Fax: 212-854-5861
E-mail: hsp@columbia.edu
Web site: www.ce.columbia.edu/hs

Cornell University Summer College Programs for High School Students
Ithaca, NY
General Information: Coed residential academic program established in 1962.
Contact: Abby H. Eller, Director, B20 Day Hall, Ithaca, NY 14853-2801

Phone: 607-255-6203
Fax: 607-255-6665
E-mail: summer_college@cornell.edu
Web site: www.summercollege.cornell.edu

Dunnabeck at Kildonan
Amenia, NY
General Information: Coed residential and day academic program established in 1955.
Contact: Ronald A. Wilson, Headmaster, 425 Morse Hill Rd., Amenia, NY 12501
Phone: 845-373-8111
Fax: 845-373-9793
E-mail: bsattler@kildonan.org
Web site: www.kildonan.org

Eastern U.S. Music Camp, Inc.-Colgate University
Hamilton, NY
General Information: Coed residential and day arts program established in 1976.
Contact: Dr. Thomas A. Brown, Director, Dana Arts Center, Hamilton, NY 13346-1398
Phone: 315-228-7041
Fax: 315-228-7557
E-mail: eusmc@hotmail.com
Web site: www.easternusmusiccamp.com

Environmental Studies Summer Youth Institute-Hobart and William Smith Colleges
Geneva, NY
General Information: Coed residential academic program established in 1993.
Contact: Prof. Brooks McKinney, Director, ESSYI, Geneva, NY 14456-3397
Phone: 315-781-4401
Fax: 315-781-4400
E-mail: essyi@hws.edu
Web site: academic.hws.edu/enviro

Gold Coast Film Camp
Brookville, NY
General Information: Coed residential and day arts program established in 2001.
Contact: Aurora Rozak, Administrative Director, 206 Bowery, 2nd Floor, New York, NY 10012
Phone: 212-941-7711
Fax: 212-965-9933
E-mail: aurora@manhattanfilmschool.com
Web site: www.manhattanfilmschool.com

The Gow School Summer Program
South Wales, NY
General Information: Coed residential and day academic program established in 1990.
Contact: Mr. Robert Garcia, Director of Admissions, 2491 Emery Rd., PO Box 85, South Wales, NY 14139
Phone: 716-652-3450
Fax: 716-687-2003
E-mail: summer@gow.org
Web site: www.gow.org

Hartwick College Summer Music Festival & Institute
Oneonta, NY
General Information: Coed residential and day arts program established in 1947.
Contact: Ms. Jungeon Kim, Director, Summer Music Festival, PO Box 4020, Oneonta, NY 13820-9923
Phone: 607-431-4801
Fax: 607-431-4245
E-mail: kimj3@hartwick.edu
Web site: www.hartwickmusicfestival.org

Houghton Academy Summer ESL
Houghton, NY
General Information: Coed residential academic program established in 1995.
Contact: Mr. Ron Bradbury, Director of Admissions, 9790 Thayer St., Houghton, NY 14744
Phone: 716-567-8115
Fax: 716-567-8048
E-mail: admissions@houghtonacademy.org
Web site: www.houghtonacademy.org

iD Tech Camps-Vassar College
Poughkeepsie, NY
General Information: Coed residential and day academic program established in 1999.
Contact: Client Service Representatives, 1885 Winchester Blvd, Ste. 201, Campbell, CA 95008
Phone: 888-709-TECH
Fax: 408-871-2227
E-mail: requests@internaldrive.com
Web site: www.internaldrive.com

Ithaca College Summer College for High School Students: Session I
Ithaca, NY
General Information: Coed residential academic program established in 1997.
Contact: Mr. E. Kimball Milling, Director of Continuing Education and Summer

Sessions, 120 Towers Concourse, Ithaca, NY 14850-7141
Phone: 607-274-314
Fax: 607-274-1263
E-mail: cess@ithaca.edu
Web site: www.ithaca.edu/summer college

Ithaca College Summer College for High School Students: Session II
Ithaca, NY
General Information: Coed residential academic program established in 1998.
Contact: Mr. E. Kimball Milling, Director of Continuing Education and Summer Sessions, 120 Towers Concourse, Ithaca, NY 14850-7141
Phone: 607-274-3143
Fax: 607-274-1263
E-mail: cess@ithaca.edu
Web site: www.ithaca.edu/summer college

Ithaca College Summer College for High School Students: Minicourses
Ithaca, NY
General Information: Coed residential academic program established in 2002.
Contact: Mr. E. Kimball Milling, Director of Continuing Education and Summer Sessions, 120 Towers Concourse, Ithaca, NY 14850-7141
Phone: 607-274-3143
Fax: 607-274-1263
E-mail: cess@ithaca.edu
Web site: www.ithaca.edu/summer college

Ithaca College Summer Piano Institute
Ithaca, NY
General Information: Coed residential arts program established in 2000.
Contact: Mr. E. Kimball Milling, Director of Continuing Education and Summer Sessions, 120 Towers Concourse, Ithaca, NY 14850-7141
Phone: 607-274-3143
Fax: 607-274-1263
E-mail: cess@ithaca.edu
Web site: www.ithaca.edu/cess

Louis Tannen Summer Magic Camp
Central Islip, NY
General Information: Coed residential arts program established in 1974.
Contact: Mr. Tony Spina, Director, 24 West 25th St., 2nd Floor, New York, NY 10010

Phone: 212-929-4500
Fax: 212-929-4565
E-mail: spinamagic@aol.com
Web site: www.tannenmagic.com

Manhattan Film Camp
New York, NY
General Information: Coed residential and day arts program established in 2001.
Contact: Aurora Rozak, Administrative Director, 206 Bowery, 2nd Floor, New York, NY 10012
Phone: 212-941-7711
Fax: 212-965-9933
E-mail: aurora@manhattanfilmschool.com
Web site: www.manhattanfilmschool.com

Maplebrook School's Summer Program
Amenia, NY
General Information: Coed residential and day academic program established in 1945.
Contact: Jennifer L. Scully, Director of Admissions, 5142 Route 22, Amenia, NY 12501
Phone: 845-373-8191
Fax: 845-373-7029
E-mail: mbsecho@aol.com

Parsons Summer Intensive Studies
New York, NY
General Information: Coed residential and day arts program established in 1970.
Contact: Ms. Charlotte Rice, Associate Director for Special Programs, 66 Fifth Ave., New York, NY 10011
Phone: 212-229-8925
Fax: 212-229-5970
E-mail: summer@newschool.edu
Web site: www.parsons.edu/sis

Power Chord Academy
New York City, NY
General Information: Coed residential academic program.
Contact: Mr. Bryan J. Wrzesinski, 7336 Santa Monica Blvd, #107, Los Angeles, CA 90046
Phone: 800-897-6677
Fax: 775-306-7923
E-mail: bryan@powerchordacademy.com
Web site: www.powerchordacademy.com

Pratt Institute Summer Pre-College Program for High School Students
Brooklyn, NY
General Information: Coed residential arts program.
Contact: Johndell Wilson, Program Assistant, 200 Willoughby Ave., 113 Engineering Building, Brooklyn, NY 11205
Phone: 718-636-3453
Fax: 718-399-4410
E-mail: precollege@pratt.edu
Web site: prostudies.pratt.edu

PREFACE Summer Program
Troy, NY
General Information: Coed residential academic program established in 1979.
Contact: Mark D. Smith, Dean of Students, 110 Eighth St., OMSA Troy Building, 4th Floor, Troy, NY 12180-3590
Phone: 518-276-6266
Fax: 518-276-4034
E-mail: smithm@rpi.edu
Web site: www.rpi.edu

Redemption Christian Academy Summer STEER Program
Troy, NY
General Information: Coed residential and day academic program.
Contact: Ms. Laura Holmes, Vice Principal, 192 9th St., Troy, NY 12180
Phone: 518-272-6679
Fax: 518-270-8039
E-mail: info@rcastudents.com
Web site: www.rcastudents.com

Rensselaer Summer Science Enrichment
Troy, NY
General Information: Coed residential and day academic program established in 1994.
Contact: Mark D. Smith, Dean of Students, 110 Eighth St., OMSA Troy Building, 4th Floor, Troy, NY 12180-3590
Phone: 518-276-6266
Fax: 518-276-4034
E-mail: smithm@rpi.edu
Web site: www.rpi.edu

St. John's University's Education Adventure
Jamaica, NY
General Information: Coed residential academic program established in 2003.
Contact: Doug Murphy, Director, 800

Utopia Pkwy, Jamaica, NY 11439
Phone: 800-370-0392
E-mail:
educationadventure@stjohns.edu

Signature Band and Choir Jazz Camp

Ithaca, NY
General Information: Coed residential arts program established in 2002.
Contact: Dr. Richard W. Ford, Executive Director, 138 Fellows Ave., Syracuse, NY 13210
Phone: 315-478-7480
Fax: 315-478-0962
E-mail:
director@signaturemusiccamp.org
Web site:
www.signaturemusiccamp.org

Skidmore College-AP/Art (Acceleration Program in Art)

Saratoga Springs, NY
General Information: Coed residential and day arts program established in 1985.
Contact: Ms. Marianne Needham, Coordinator, 815 North Brd.way, Saratoga Springs, NY 12866
Phone: 518-580-5052
Fax: 518-580-5029
E-mail: mneedham@skidmore.edu
Web site: www.skidmore.edu/summer

Skidmore College-Pre-College Program in the Liberal Arts for High School Students

Saratoga Springs, NY
General Information: Coed residential and day academic program established in 1978.
Contact: Dr. James Chansky, Director of Summer Special Programs, 815 North Brd.way, Saratoga Springs, NY 12866
Phone: 518-580-5590
Fax: 518-580-5548
E-mail: jchansky@skidmore.edu
Web site: www.skidmore.edu/summer

Skidmore College-Pre-College Program in the Liberal Arts for High School Students

Saratoga Springs, NY
General Information: Coed residential and day arts program established in 1978.
Contact: Dr. James Chansky, Director of Summer Special Programs, 815 North Broadway, Saratoga Springs, NY 12866
Phone: 518-580-5590

Fax: 518-580-5548
E-mail: jchansky@skidmore.edu
Web site: www.skidmore.edu/summer

Stony Brook Summer Music Festival

Stony Brook, NY
General Information: Coed residential and day arts program established in 1998.
Contact: Dr. Linda M. Sinanian, Director, Stony Brook Summer Music Festival, Department of Music, Stony Brook, NY 11794-5475
Phone: 631-220-0911
Fax: 631-632-7404
E-mail: lsinanian@notes1.cc.sunysb.edu
Web site: www.stonybrook.edu/music

Stony Brook University-Biotechnology Summer Camp

Stony Brook, NY
General Information: Coed residential academic program established in 1995.
Contact: Judy Nimmo, Department of Biochemistry and Cell Biology, Stony Brook, NY 11794-5215
Phone: 631-632-9750
Fax: 631-632-9791
E-mail: jnimmo@notes.cc.sunysb.edu
Web site: www.stonybrook.edu/ligase

The Summer Institute for the Gifted at Vassar College

Poughkeepsie, NY
General Information: Coed residential academic program established in 1992.
Contact: Dr. Stephen Gessner, Director, River Plaza, 9 West Brd. St., Stamford, CT 06902-3788 **Phone:** 866-303-4744
Fax: 203-399-5598
E-mail: sig.info@aifs.com
Web site: www.giftedstudy.com

"Summer in the City"

New York, NY
General Information: Coed residential and day academic and arts program.
Contact: Admission Office, 39 West 19th St., 12th Floor, New York, NY 10011
Phone: 888-645-0030 ext. 772
Fax: 212-624-0117
E-mail: admission@sft.edu
Web site: www.sft.edu

Summer School at New York Military Academy

Cornwall-on-Hudson, NY
General Information: Coed residential academic program established in 1954.

Contact: Maureen T. Kelly, Director of Admissions, 78 Academy Ave., Cornwall-on-Hudson, NY 12520
Phone: 845-534-3710 ext. 4233
Fax: 845-534-7699
E-mail: admissions@nyma.ouboces.org
Web site: www.nyma.org

Summer Theatre Institute-2004

New York, NY
General Information: Coed residential arts program established in 1989.
Contact: Ms. Allyn Sitjar, Artistic Director, 23 Tomahawk Trail, Sparta, NJ 07871
Phone: 201-415-5329
Fax: 973-729-3654
E-mail: youththeatreallyn@yahoo.com

Syracuse University Summer College

Syracuse, NY
General Information: Coed residential and day academic and arts program established in 1961.
Contact: Ms. Nance L. Hahn, Director, 111 Waverly Ave., Ste. 240, Syracuse, NY 13244-1270
Phone: 315-443-5297
Fax: 315-443-3976
E-mail: sumcoll@syr.edu
Web site: www.syr.edu/summer

Tisch School of the Arts-Summer High School Programs

New York, NY
General Information: Coed residential academic and arts program established in 1985.
Contact: Virginia Gonzales, Assistant Director for Special Programs/Admissions, Tisch School of the Arts, 721 Brd.way, 12th Floor, New York, NY 10003-6807
Phone: 212-998-1575
Fax: 212-995-4578
E-mail: tisch.highschool@nyu.edu
Web site: www.nyu.edu/tisch/specialprograms

Pennsylvania

Carnegie Mellon University Advanced Placement Early Admission

Pittsburgh, PA
General Information: Coed residential and day academic program established in 1974.

Contact: Office of Admission, Pre-College Programs, 5000 Forbes Ave., Pittsburgh, PA 15213-3890 **Phone:** 412-268-2082
Fax: 412-268-7838
E-mail: precollege@andrew.cmu.edu
Web site:
www.cmu.edu/enrollment/pre-college

Carnegie Mellon University Pre-College Program in the Fine Arts
Pittsburgh, PA
General Information: Coed residential and day arts program established in 1955.
Contact: Office of Admission, Pre-College Programs, 5000 Forbes Ave., Pittsburgh, PA 15213-3890
Phone: 412-268-2082
Fax: 412-268-7838
E-mail: precollege@andrew.cmu.edu
Web site:
www.cmu.edu/enrollment/pre-college

Dickinson College Research and Writing Workshop
Carlisle, PA
General Information: Coed residential academic program established in 2002.
Contact: Office of Summer Programs, PO Box 1773, Carlisle, PA 17013
Phone: 717-245-8782
Fax: 717-245-1972
E-mail: summer@dickinson.edu
Web site: www.dickinson.edu/summer

Dickinson Summer College Program
Carlisle, PA
General Information: Coed residential academic program established in 2001.
Contact: Office of Summer Programs, PO Box 1773, Carlisle, PA 17013
Phone: 717-245-8782
Fax: 717-245-1972
E-mail: summer@dickinson.edu
Web site: www.dickinson.edu/summer

iD Tech Camps-Carnegie Mellon
Pittsburgh, PA
General Information: Coed residential and day academic program established in 1999.
Contact: Client Service Representatives, 1885 Winchester Blvd, Ste. 201, Campbell, CA 95008
Phone: 888-709-TECH
Fax: 408-871-2227
E-mail: requests@internaldrive.com
Web site: www.internaldrive.com

iD Tech Camps-Villanova University
Villanova, PA
General Information: Coed residential and day academic program established in 1999.
Contact: Client Service Representatives, 1885 Winchester Blvd, Ste. 201, Campbell, CA 95008
Phone: 888-709-TECH
Fax: 408-871-2227
E-mail: requests@internaldrive.com
Web site: www.internaldrive.com

Julian Krinsky Business School at Haverford College
Haverford, PA
General Information: Coed residential and day academic program established in 1995.
Contact: Julian Krinsky, Owner, PO Box 333, Haverford, PA 19041-0333
Phone: 800-TRY-JKST
E-mail: info@jkcp.com
Web site: www.jkcp.com

Julian Krinsky Business School at Temple University-Summer Business Leadership Academy
Philadelphia, PA
General Information: Coed residential and day academic program established in 2003.
Contact: Mr. Steven Bernstein, PO Box 333, Haverford, PA 19041
Phone: 610-265-9401
E-mail: info@jkcp.com
Web site: www.jkcp.com

Julian Krinsky Business School at Wharton (Leadership in the Business World)
General Information: Coed residential academic program.
Contact: Julian Krinsky, PO Box 333, Haverford, PA 19041-0333
Phone: 800-TRY-JKST
E-mail: info@jkcp.com
Web site: www.jkcp.com

Julian Krinsky Junior Enrichment Camp at Cabrini College
Radnor, PA
General Information: Coed residential and day academic program established in 2003.
Contact: Julian Krinsky, PO Box 333, Haverford, PA 19041-0333
Phone: 800-TRY-JKCP
E-mail: info@jkcp.com
Web site: www.jkcp.com

Julian Krinsky Junior Enrichment Camp at Cabrini College
Radnor, PA
General Information: Coed residential and day arts program established in 2003.
Contact: Julian Krinsky, PO Box 333, Haverford, PA 19041-0333
Phone: 800-TRY-JKCP
E-mail: info@jkcp.com
Web site: www.jkcp.com

Julian Krinsky Senior Enrichment Camp at Haverford College
Haverford, PA
General Information: Coed residential and day academic program established in 1991.
Contact: Julian Krinsky, Owner/Director, PO Box 333, Haverford, PA 19041-0333
Phone: 800-TRY-JKST
Fax: 610-265-3678
E-mail: info@jkcp.com
Web site: www.jkcp.com

Julian Krinsky Senior Enrichment Camp at Haverford College
Haverford, PA
General Information: Coed residential and day arts program established in 1991.
Contact: Julian Krinsky, Owner/Director, PO Box 333, Haverford, PA 19041-0333
Phone: 800-TRY-JKST
Fax: 610-265-3678
E-mail: info@jkcp.com
Web site: www.jkcp.com

Julian Krinsky Yaish Shabbat Summer Camp
Glenside, PA
General Information: Coed residential and day academic and arts program established in 2002.
Contact: Steven Bernstein, Director, PO Box 333, Haverford, PA 19041
Phone: 610-265-9401
Fax: 610-265-3678
E-mail: info@jkcp.com
Web site: www.jkcp.com

Jumonville Creative and Performing Arts Camps
Hopwood, PA
General Information: Coed residential arts program established in 1941.
Contact: Jane Fiedler, Camp Registrar, PO Box 5002, Cranberry Township, PA 16066
Phone: 800-886-3382
Fax: 724-776-1355
E-mail: umcamp@umchurch.org
Web site: www.jumonville.org

Lebanon Valley College Summer Music Camp
Annville, PA
General Information: Coed residential and day arts program established in 1987.
Contact: Dr. Robert H. Hearson, Director, Summer Music Camp, 101 North College Ave., Annville, PA 17003
Phone: 717-867-6289
Fax: 717-867-6390
E-mail: hearson@acad.lvc.edu
Web site: www.lvc.edu/music-camp

Mercersburg Brave New Music Workshop
Mercersburg, PA
General Information: Coed residential and day arts program.
Contact: Rick Hendrickson, Director of Summer and Extended Programs, 300 East Seminary St., Mercersburg, PA 17236
Phone: 717-328-6225
Fax: 717-328-9072
E-mail: summerprograms@mercersburg.edu
Web site: www.mercersburg.edu

Mercersburg ESL Plus Program
Mercersburg, PA
General Information: Coed residential academic program established in 1999.
Contact: Mr. Rick Hendrickson, Director of Summer and Extended Programs, 300 East Seminary St., Mercersburg, PA 17236
Phone: 717-328-6225
Fax: 717-328-9072
E-mail: summerprograms@mercersburg.edu
Web site: www.mercersburg.edu

Mercersburg Onstage! Young Actors Workshop
Mercersburg, PA
General Information: Coed residential and day arts program established in 2001.
Contact: Mr. Rick Hendrickson, Director of Summer and Extended Programs, 300 East Seminary St., Mercersburg, PA 17236
Phone: 717-328-6225
Fax: 717-328-9072
E-mail: summerprograms@mercersburg.edu
Web site: www.mercersburg.edu

Mercersburg The World's A Stage Theatre Workshop
Mercersburg, PA
General Information: Coed residential and day arts program.
Contact: Mr. Rick Hendrickson, Director of Summer and Extended Programs, 300 East Seminary St., Mercersburg, PA 17236
Phone: 717-328-6225
Fax: 717-328-9072
E-mail: summerprograms@mercersburg.edu
Web site: www.mercersburg.edu

National Computer Camps at La Roche College
Pittsburgh, PA
General Information: Coed residential and day academic program established in 1998.
Contact: Dr. Michael Zabinski, President, PO Box 585, Orange, CT 06477
Phone: 203-795-9667
E-mail: info@nccamp.com
Web site: www.nccamp.com

Pathways at Marywood University
Scranton, PA
General Information: Coed residential and day academic program established in 1984.
Contact: Meg Cullen-Brown, Program Director, Pathways, 2300 Adams Ave., Scranton, PA 18509
Phone: 800-724-0399
Fax: 570-961-4776
E-mail: brownm@ac.marywood.edu
Web site: www.marywood.edu

The Performing Arts Institute of Wyoming Seminary
Kingston, PA
General Information: Coed residential and day arts program established in 1998.
Contact: Nancy Sanderson, Director, The Performing Arts Institute of Wyoming Seminary, 201 North Sprague Ave., Kingston, PA 18704
Phone: 570-270-2186
Fax: 570-270-2198
E-mail: onstage@wyomingseminary.org
Web site: www.wyomingseminary.org/pai

Pre-College Summer Institute, The University of the Arts
Philadelphia, PA
General Information: Coed residential and day arts program established in 1981.

Contact: Erin Elman, Director, Pre-College Programs, 320 South Brd. St., Philadelphia, PA 19102
Phone: 215-717-6430
Fax: 215-717-6433
E-mail: precollege@uarts.edu
Web site: www.uarts.edu/precol

Study Tours in the USA-Lock Haven
Lock Haven, PA
General Information: Coed residential academic program established in 1987.
Contact: Veronica Perez, Director of Admissions, 101 East Green St., #14, Pasadena, CA 91105
Phone: 626-795-2912
Fax: 626-795-5564
E-mail: veronica@fls.net
Web site: www.fls.net

Summer Academy for Minority Scholars
Pittsburgh, PA
General Information: Coed residential and day academic program established in 2001.
Contact: Office of Admission, 5000 Forbes Ave., Pittsburgh, PA 15213-3890
Phone: 412-268-2082
Fax: 412-268-7838
E-mail: precollege@andrew.cmu.edu
Web site: www.cmu.edu/summerminorityscholars

The Summer Institute for the Gifted at Bryn Mawr College
Bryn Mawr, PA
General Information: Coed residential academic program established in 1991.
Contact: Dr. Stephen Gessner, Director, River Plaza, 9 West Brd. St., Stamford, CT 06902-3788
Phone: 866-303-4744
Fax: 203-399-5598
E-mail: sig.info@aifs.com
Web site: www.giftedstudy.com

Summer Language Camps for High School Students
Millersville, PA
General Information: Coed residential academic program established in 1981.
Contact: Dr. Celica Milovanovic, Chair, Department of Foreign Languages, Millersville University, Millersville, PA 17551-0302
Phone: 717-872-3526
Fax: 717-871-2482
E-mail: camps@millersville.edu
Web site: www.millersville.edu/~forlang

Summer Study at Penn State

University Park, PA
General Information: Coed residential academic program established in 1991.
Contact: Mr. Bill Cooperman, Executive Director, 900 Walt Whitman Rd., Melville, NY 11747
Phone: 800-666-2556
Fax: 631-424-0567
E-mail: precollegeprograms@ summerstudy.com
Web site: www.summerstudy.com

Susquehanna University Advanced Writers Workshop for High School Students

Selinsgrove, PA
General Information: Coed residential academic program established in 1988.
Contact: Gary Fincke, Workshop Director, Selinsgrove, PA 17870
Phone: 570-372-4164
Fax: 570-372-2774
E-mail: gfincke@susqu.edu
Web site: www.susqu.edu/writers

University of Pennsylvania-Penn Summer Art Studio

Philadelphia, PA
General Information: Coed residential and day arts program established in 2002.
Contact: Ms. Emma Foley, Assistant Director of Summer Sessions, 3440 Market St., Ste. 100, Philadelphia, PA 19104-3335
Phone: 215-746-6900
Fax: 215-573-2053
E-mail: hsprogs@sas.upenn.edu
Web site: www.upenn.edu/summer

University of Pennsylvania-Penn Summer Science Academy

Philadelphia, PA
General Information: Coed residential and day academic program.
Contact: Ms. Emma Foley, Assistant Director of Summer Sessions, 3440 Market St., Ste. 100, Philadelphia, PA 19104-3335
Phone: 215-746-6900
Fax: 215-573-2053
E-mail: hsprogs@sas.upenn.edu
Web site: www.upenn.edu/summer

University of Pennsylvania-Precollege Program

Philadelphia, PA
General Information: Coed residential and day academic program established in 1981.

Contact: Ms. Emma Foley, Assistant Director of Summer Sessions, 3440 Market St., Ste. 100, Philadelphia, PA 19104-3335
Phone: 215-746-6900
Fax: 215-573-2053
E-mail: hsprog@sas.upenn.edu
Web site: www.upenn.edu/summer

Wyoming Seminary-Sem Summer 2004

Kingston, PA
General Information: Coed residential and day academic program established in 1991.
Contact: John R. Eidam, Dean of Admissions/Director of International and Summer Programs, Wyoming Seminary, 201 North Sprague Ave., Kingston, PA 18704
Phone: 570-270-2187
Fax: 570-270-2198
E-mail: semsum@wyomingseminary.org
Web site: www.wyomingseminary.org

Virginia

All Arts and Sciences Camp-George Mason University

Fairfax, VA
General Information: Coed residential and day academic and arts program established in 1991.
Contact: Jeff Bounds, Camp Director, PO Box 26170, Greensboro, NC 27402-6170
Phone: 336-334-5414
Fax: 336-334-4733
E-mail: allarts@uncg.edu
Web site: allarts.uncg.edu

All Arts and Sciences Camp-The College of William and Mary

Williamsburg, VA
General Information: Coed residential and day academic and arts program established in 1991.
Contact: Jeff Bounds, Camp Director, PO Box 26170, Greensboro, NC 27402-6170
Phone: 336-334-5414
Fax: 336-334-4733
E-mail: allarts@uncg.edu
Web site: allarts.uncg.edu

All Arts and Sciences Camp-Virginia Tech

Blacksburg, VA
General Information: Coed residential and day academic and arts program established in 1991.
Contact: Jeff Bounds, Camp Director, PO Box 26170, Greensboro, NC 27402-6170
Phone: 336-334-5414
Fax: 336-334-4733
E-mail: allarts@uncg.edu
Web site: allarts.uncg.edu

4 Star Academics Junior Camp at the University of Virginia

Charlottesville, VA
General Information: Coed residential and day academic program established in 1995.
Contact: Ms. Marietta Naramore, Admissions Director, PO Box 3387, Falls Church, VA 22043-0387
Phone: 800-334-7827
Fax: 703-866-7775
E-mail: info@4starcamps.com
Web site: www.4starcamps.com

4 Star Academics Scholars at the University of Virginia

Charlottesville, VA
General Information: Coed residential and day academic program established in 2002.
Contact: Ms. Marietta Naramore, Admissions Director, PO Box 3387, Falls Church, VA 22043-0387
Phone: 800-334-7827
Fax: 703-866-7775
E-mail: info@4starcamps.com
Web site: www.4starcamps.com

4 Star Academics Senior Camp at the University of Virginia

Charlottesville, VA
General Information: Coed residential and day academic program established in 1995.
Contact: Ms. Marietta Naramore, Admissions Director, PO Box 3387, Falls Church, VA 22043-0387
Phone: 800-334-7827
Fax: 703-866-7775
E-mail: info@4starcamps.com
Web site: www.4starcamps.com

iD Tech Camps-University of Virginia, Charlottesville, VA

Charlottesville, VA
General Information: Coed residential and day academic program established in 1999.

Contact: Client Service Representatives, 1885 Winchester Blvd, Ste. 201, Campbell, CA 95008
Phone: 888-709-TECH
Fax: 408-871-2227
E-mail: requests@internaldrive.com
Web site: www.internaldrive.com

Massanutten Military Academy Summer Cadet Program
Woodstock, VA
General Information: Coed residential and day academic program established in 1899.
Contact: Frank Thomas, Director of Admissions, 614 South Main St., Woodstock, VA 22664
Phone: 877-466-6222 ext. 263
Fax: 540-459-5421
E-mail: admissions@militaryschool.com
Web site: www.militaryschool.com

Oak Hill Academy Summer Program
Mouth of Wilson, VA
General Information: Coed residential and day academic program established in 1878.
Contact: Dr. Michael D. Groves, Director of Admissions, 2635 Oak Hill Rd., Mouth of Wilson, VA 24363
Phone: 276-579-2619
Fax: 276-579-4722
E-mail: info@oak-hill.net
Web site: www.oak-hill.net

Randolph-Macon Academy Summer Programs
Front Royal, VA
General Information: Coed residential and day academic program established in 1966.
Contact: Ms. Tiffani Thompsen, Admissions Counselor, 200 Academy Drive, Front Royal, VA 22630
Phone: 800-272-1172
Fax: 540-636-5419
E-mail: admissions@rma.edu
Web site: www.rma.edu

Sidwell Friends REACH Riverview Enrichment Program
Tappahannock, VA
General Information: Coed residential and day academic program established in 2000.
Contact: Sidwell Friends Summer Programs, 3825 Wisconsin Ave., NW, Washington, DC 20016
Phone: 202-537-8133
Fax: 202-537-2483
E-mail: sidwellsummer@yahoo.com
Web site: www.sidwell.edu/summer

Summer Leadership Education and Training
Woodstock, VA
General Information: Coed residential and day academic program established in 2003.
Contact: Mr. Frank Thomas, Director of Admissions, 614 South Main St., Woodstock, VA 22664
Phone: 540-459-2167 ext. 263
Fax: 540-459-5421
E-mail: admissions@militaryschool.com
Web site: www.militaryschool.com

Woodberry Forest Junior Adventure
Woodberry Forest, VA
General Information: Coed residential and day academic program established in 1998.
Contact: Dr. W. David McRae, Director, Woodberry Forest Summer Experience, Woodberry Forest, VA 22989
Phone: 540-672-6047
Fax: 540-672-9076
E-mail: wfs_summer@woodberry.org
Web site: www.woodberry.org

Woodberry Forest Senior Adventure
Woodberry Forest, VA
General Information: Coed residential and day academic program established in 1922.
Contact: Dr. W. David McRae, Director of Summer Programs, 354 Woodberry Station, Woodberry Forest, VA 22989
Phone: 540-672-6047
Fax: 540-672-9076
E-mail: wfs_summer@woodberry.org
Web site: www.woodberry.org

Buckswood ARC: English Language (ESL) and Activities
General Information: Coed residential academic program established in 1978.
Contact: Ms. Judith Parkinson, Buckswood ARC Summer Programs, Avatar Education Ltd., Westminster House, Bolton Close, Uckfield, East Sussex, TN22 1PH
Phone: 44-1825 760 900
Fax: 44-1825 760 911
E-mail: info@buckswood.com
Web site: www.buckswood.com